COMMUNICATING
EFFECTIVELY

Saundra Hybels
Lock Haven University

Richard L. Weaver, II
Bowling Green State University

RANDOM HOUSE • NEW YORK

First Edition

9876543

Copyright © 1986 by Newbery Award Records, Inc.

All rights reserved under International and Pan-American Copyright Conventions. No part of this book may be reproduced in any form or by any means, electronic or mechanical, including photocopying, without permission in writing from the publisher. All inquiries should be addressed to Newbery Award Records, Inc., 201 East 50th Street, New York, N.Y. 10022. Published in the United States by Newbery Award Records, Inc., a subsidiary of Random House, Inc., New York and simultaneously in Canada by Random House of Canada Limited, Toronto. Distributed by Random House, Inc.

Portions of this book are based on an earlier book by the authors: *Speech/Communication*, Second Edition, published by D. Van Nostrand Company.

Library of Congress Cataloging in Publication Data

Hybels, Saundra.
    Communicating effectively.

    Bibliography.
    Includes index.
    1. Oral communication.   I. Weaver, Richard L.,
1941-   .   II. Title.
P95.H9   1986   001.54′2   85-25799
ISBN 0-394-33931-2

Manufactured in the United States of America

Developmental Editor: Kathleen Domenig; Acquisitions Editor: Roth Wilkofsky; Project Editor: Elaine Romano; Cover and Text Designer: John Lennard; Cover Illustrator: Thom Ricks; Production Manager: Andy Roney

PERMISSIONS ACKNOWLEDGMENTS

Text

14: "Pink Clink," *Time*, November 26, 1979, p. 98. Copyright © 1979 by Time, Inc. All rights reserved. Reprinted by permission from Time.
31, 85: Reprinted by permission of the Putnam Publishing Group from *Speak the Language of Success* by Gloria Hoffman and Pauline Gravier (as told to Jane Phillips). Copyright © 1983 by Pauline Gravier and Gloria Hoffman.
32: "The Investigation," by John Jonik. Copyright © 1984 by John Jonik. Reproduced by permission.
36: From *The Height of Your Life* by Ralph Keyes. Copyright © 1980 by Ralph Keyes. By permission of Little, Brown and Company.
38: From *Growing Up* by Russell Baker. Copyright © 1982 by Russell Baker. Reprinted by permission of Congdon & Weed, Inc., New York.
53: Adapted from L. Barker et al., "An Investigation of Proportional Time Spent in Various Communication Activities by College Students," *Journal of Applied Communication Research* 8 (1980): 101–109. Used by permission of the University of South Florida.
60, 185, 195: From *The Craft of Interviewing*. Copyright © 1976 by John Brady. Used by permission of Writer's Digest Books.

68: From *Brothers and Keepers* by John Wideman. Copyright © 1984 by John Wideman. Reprinted by permission of Holt, Rinehart and Winston, Publishers.
84, 93: Excerpts from *Say It My Way* by Willard R. Espy. Copyright © 1980 by Willard R. Espy. Reprinted by permission of Doubleday & Company, Inc.
98, 148: Excerpted from *Miss Manners Guide to Excruciatingly Correct Behavior* by Judith Martin. Copyright © 1982 by United Feature Syndicate, Inc. Reprinted with the permission of Atheneum Publishers, Inc.
109: Adapted from Daniel Goleman, "Researchers Identify True Clues to Lying," *New York Times*, February 12, 1985. Copyright © 1984/85 by The New York Times Company. Reprinted by permission.
113: Adapted from *Every Night at Five* by Susan Stamberg. Copyright © 1982 by Pantheon Books, a division of Random House, Inc. Reprinted by permission.
121: From *Realities of Teaching: Explorations with Video Tape* by Raymond S. Adams and Bruce J. Biddle. Copyright © 1970 by Holt, Rinehart and Winston, Publishers. Reprinted by permission of CBS College Publishing.
125: Adapted from Sherry Suib Cohen, "The Amazing

351: From *Basic Oral Communication*, Third Edition, by Glenn R. Capp, G. Richard Capp, Jr., and Carol C. Capp. Copyright © 1981, p. 287. Adapted by permission of Prentice-Hall, Inc., Englewood Cliffs, NJ.

352: From *Developing Your Speaking Voice*, Second Edition, by John P. Moncur and Harrison M. Karr. Copyright © 1972 by John P. Moncur and Harrison M. Karr. Reprinted by permission of Harper & Row, Publishers, Inc.

357: From *The Chronicle of Higher Education*, 29 (September 26, 1984): 1. Copyright © 1985 by The Chronicle of Higher Education. Reprinted with permission.

361: From *New York Times*, December 18, 1984, p. 61. Copyright © 1984 by The New York Times Company. Reprinted by permission.

363: From *Iacocca: An Autobiography* by Lee Iacocca with William Novak. Copyright © 1984 by Lee Iacocca. Reprinted by permission of Bantam Books, Inc. All rights reserved.

364: From *How to Talk Your Way to Success*. Copyright © 1983 by Paul J. Micali. Reprinted by permission of the publisher, E. P. Dutton, a division of New American Library.

377–378: Professor Grover Krantz quoted in "The Search for Bigfoot," by Patrick Huyghe, *Science Digest*, September 1984, p. 56. Copyright © 1984 by the Hearst Corporation.

383–389: Kathy Weisensel, "David: And a Whole Lot of Other Neat People," from Linkugel, Allen, and Johannesan, *Contemporary American Speeches*, Second Edition. Copyright © 1969 by Kendall/Hunt Publishing Company, Dubuque, Iowa.

403: Data based on Hierarchy of Needs from *Motivation and Personality*, Second Edition, by Abraham Maslow. Copyright © 1970 by Abraham H. Maslow. Reprinted by permission of Harper & Row, Publishers.

410–417: Used with permission of Kathy Atkinson, Speech student, Fall 1984.

Photos:

2: (Top left) Frank Siteman/The Picture Cube; (top right) Joan Liftin/Archive; (bottom left) Sylvia Plachy/Archive; (bottom right) Fredrik D. Bodin/Stock, Boston. **11:** Mark Godfrey/Archive. **21:** *Interlude*, 1960, by Milton Avery; oil on canvas, Philadelphia Museum of Art: Given by the Woodward Foundation. **28:** International Museum of Photography at George Eastman House. **39:** Sylvia Johnson/Woodfin Camp & Associates. **43:** Joel Gordon. **50:** Joel Gordon. **59:** Paris, Musée d'Orsay—La Bibliothèque Nationale. **71:** Untitled (early figure painting), 1965, by Richard Estes; oil on canvas, 26″ × 34″, Allan Stone Gallery. **78:** Hazel Hankin. **81:** Andrew Brilliant/The Picture Cube. **87:** J. Schweiker/Photo Researchers. **106:** Alan Carey/The Image Works. **117:** Jim Anderson/Woodfin Camp & Associates. **122:** Bettye Lane/Photo Researchers. **132:** Arthur Grace/Stock, Boston. **138:** Hazel Hankin/Stock, Boston. **143:** Hazel Hankin. **152:** Suzanne Szasz/Photo Researchers. **159:** *Jimmy and John*, 1957–1958, by Fairfield Porter; oil on canvas, 36¼″ × 45½″, private collection. **170:** Joan Liftin/Archive. **180:** Sandra Johnson/The Picture Cube. **194:** Owen Franken/Stock, Boston. **202:** Joel Gordon. **212:** Bohdan Hrynewych/Southern Light. **219:** Sybil Shelton/Peter Arnold. **224:** Elizabeth Crews/Stock, Boston. **230:** David Witbeck/The Picture Cube. **235:** L. J. Weinstein/Woodfin Camp & Associates. **244:** Michal Heron/Woodfin Camp & Associates. **252:** Van Bucher/Photo Researchers. **256:** Peter Miller/Photo Researchers. **272:** Joel Gordon. **280:** Owen Franken/Stock, Boston. **288:** Frank Siteman/The Picture Cube. **301:** Carl Bergquist/Shenandoah Photo—Illustrator's Stock Photos. **308:** Jim Anderson/Woodfin Camp & Associates. **315:** Frank Siteman/The Picture Cube. **322:** Will McIntyre/Photo Researchers. **336:** Peter Vandermark/Stock, Boston. **348:** Melissa Shook/The Picture Cube. **359:** Sepp Seitz/Woodfin Camp & Associates. **368:** Richard Wood/The Picture Cube. **371:** Ken Robert Buck/The Picture Cube. **392:** Lionel J. M. Delevingne/Stock, Boston. **398:** Peeter Vilms/Jeroboam. **406:** Michal Heron/Woodfin Camp & Associates.

ACKNOWLEDGMENTS

Almost everyone you know is affected when you write a book, sometimes negatively. So first I would like to acknowledge all those friends and family members who didn't get letters for months on end, put up with last-minute cancellations because there was a deadline, or were willing to listen to ideas in which they probably had no interest. These are the people who are the support system behind any writer.

Specifically, I would like to mention Doug Campbell, my department chairperson, who was willing to let me get by with less than my share of committee work and who was always willing to listen when I was having problems working out an idea. Bob Bravard, the head of the library, provided invaluable assistance on several occasions when a reference was unusually elusive. I am also indebted to Joe Thomas, who figured out how my computer worked when it came with no instruction book. My neighbors Alice deGarmo and Fern Seybold kept my household going when I was in the last year of writing, and Gerry and Art English were there to help sort and duplicate a huge manuscript when I needed them. Even Emma, my cat, helped by keeping me company as she sat on the computer as I worked. To all of them, thank you.

I am most indebted, however, to Kathleen Domenig, the editor of the book. As well as conveying a clear sense of direction and exhibiting endless tact in suggesting changes, she was a constant source of interesting and stimulating ideas. She gave the greatest gift one could give a writer: she believed in the book and in its authors.

SAUNDRA HYBELS

There is no way to thank all those people who have in some way touched my life or contributed to this work, but I would like to acknowledge those who have made major recent contributions or who continue to influence me. My thanks, then go to:

- Gloria Gregor and Mary Lou Willmarth for their support and assistance in getting volumes of material duplicated—time after time.

- All the teaching assistants associated with the basic speech communication course at Bowling Green State University over the past 12 years and who have offered numerous comments and suggestions. With over 400, they are too numerous to mention by name.

- All the undergraduate and special students who haven taken the basic course and who, through their evaluation forms and comments, have helped to make the course and material stronger, more beneficial, and relevant.

- All the members of the Midwest Basic Course Directors' Conference for their interest in, concern for, and love of a basic speech communication course; they have offered guidance and a sense of balance and perspective.

- My many teachers who have helped me formulate my own values, principles, and procedures, and who continue to touch my life in rich and rewarding ways.

- Edgar E. Willis for continuing to share his wisdom and insights.

- My other colleagues in the profession, especially those at Bowling Green: Raymond Tucker, James Wilcox, Donald Enholm, Nelson Ober, Carl Holmberg, and Frank Tutzauer.

It is a joy being part of a close, professional community, and I am grateful for your understanding, support, and affection.

I offer a special thank you to my children—Scott, Jacquelynn, Anthony, and Joanna—for their love and continuing comfort and encouragement; and to Andrea, my wife, who has had to work around my various labors of love and yet provides the equilibrium I need to continue.

Finally, I too want to express thanks and appreciation to Kathleen Domenig, the editor of this book. The warmth, concern, and dedication she has shown have been supportive and encouraging. More important has been her willingness to prod and challenge in a rich and rewarding manner. The experience of writing this book has been exciting, although demanding, because of her care and responsibility. It has been a joy working with such a professional.

DICK WEAVER

We would both like to thank all of those people who participated in the review process. The following individuals reviewed part or all of the manuscript and offered much useful advice: Phil Backlund, Central Washington University; James Benjamin, Southwest Texas State University; Mary Bozik, University of Northern Iowa; Anne Busse, Northern Illinois University; Virginia Chapman, Anderson College; Carol Diekhoff, State Community College; Robert T. Dixon, St. Louis Community College; Jerry Feezel, Kent State University; Donna L. Friess, Cypress College; Larry Galloway, Green River Community College; William Hahn, Illinois Central College; Albert M. Katz, University of Wisconsin—Superior; Larry Kraft, Eastern Washington University; Donald L. Loeffler, Western Carolina University; Michael R. McDonald, Volunteer State Community College; Donald W. Olson, Texas Lutheran College; John E. Preas, Westark Community College; Richard G. Rea, University of Arkansas; Rita Rinner, Bradley University; Patricia Rochelt, Western Wisconsin Technical Institute.

PREFACE

Communicating Effectively is intended for the introductory course in speech communication. Focusing on interpersonal, group, and public communication, the book is designed to build skills in each of these areas.

Features and Pedagogical Devices

We believe that new concepts can best be explained by examples, so we have made extensive use of them throughout the book. To help students identify with the examples, we have drawn them from actual experiences on campus, at work and in the community.

To help students apply what they have read, in every chapter we have included boxed sections called "Try This," where each student can experiment with the concept just discussed. Although the ideas in these boxes can be worked out individually by students, many of them can also serve as a basis for group discussion.

The boxed readings called "Consider This," which are also in every chapter, are made up of high-interest, short readings from current books, magazines, and newspapers. Each reading illustrates a concept that has been discussed in the chapter, and each shows how the concept works in the world in or outside the classroom.

To help students master the words and concepts of speech communication, we have incorporated a number of pedagogical devices. We help students focus on the important ideas in each chapter by beginning with an outline and chapter objectives. So that students can review what they have learned, we end each chapter with a list of vocabulary words that are defined in the chapter and repeated in the Glossary.

Additional readings are also listed at the end of each chapter. These readings provide a variety of scholarly and popular materials that students may use for course projects or to explore topics that interest them. Each is annotated for greater ease of use.

Organization

Communicating Effectively is organized into four parts. Part 1 sets forth the basic principles of communication in five chapters:

- Chapter 1 discusses the need for communication skills, introduces the various elements of communication by explaining a communication model, and focuses on communication as a process and a transaction.

- Chapter 2 covers intrapersonal communication through a discussion of what makes up self-concept and how perception and self-concept are interrelated. This chapter does not use only visual models to explain perception; it shows how perception works in communication and how our perception of others affects our communication.

- Chapter 3 focuses on how the listening process works. Listening habits and attitudes are discussed, with many examples and illustrations. The chapter gives direction on how to listen for information, how to listen critically and reflectively, and how to enhance listening for enjoyment.

- Chapter 4 concentrates on verbal communication. It begins with a discussion of some theories of language and then emphasizes skill building through a discussion of style, language appropriateness, and language choices.

- Chapter 5 talks about nonverbal communication and how pervasive it is in our communication. As well as giving some of the principles of nonverbal communication, the chapter discusses the various kinds, with an emphasis on paralanguage, body movement, space, time, and touch.

Part 2, which focuses on interpersonal communication, as divided into three chapters:

- Chapter 6 is the first of two chapters that focus on the process of interpersonal communication. It begins with a discussion of interpersonal needs and goes on to consider why we are attracted to others and how we talk to each other. The chapter ends with a detailed discussion of self-disclosure.

- Chapter 7 concentrates on relationship stages—how relationships are formed and how they come apart. The chapter suggests criteria for evaluating relationships, gives communication strategies to pursue and avoid, and explains a model for resolving conflict.

- Chapter 8, on interviewing, looks at two kinds of interview experiences: the information interview and the employment interview. The section on the information interview focuses on how a student should prepare and conduct such an interview; the employment interview section concentrates on how students can prepare and conduct themselves while being interviewed.

Part 3 consists of two chapters on small groups and how they work:

- Chapter 9 begins with the characteristics of small groups and then discusses why groups can often solve problems more readily than individuals. It also describes a sequence that groups might use to solve problems.

- Chapter 10 emphasizes leader and participant responsibilities. Beginning with a discussion of leadership styles, it proceeds to a consideration of how a leader should act in a group discussion. The chapter also looks at the positive and negative roles that members can play a group.

Part 4, which contains six chapters, deals with public communication and emphasizes how to research, put together, and deliver a speech:

- Chapter 11 tells how a student should get started on a speech. It focuses on selecting the topic, narrowing it, and choosing a purpose for the speech. The student is given detailed instructions and examples for selecting a general and a specific purpose as well as the central idea. The chapter also has a detailed description of how to go about audience analysis.

- Chapter 12 tells the student how to research a topic using personal experience, interviews, and library research. It explains where to look for supporting materials and gives the various kinds of supporting materials a student might want to use.

- Chapter 13 is about organizing and outlining the speech. Various patterns of organization are discussed as well as why one pattern might work better than another. Separate sections treat speech introductions and conclusions. The chapter concludes with the mechanics of outlining.

- Chapter 14 tells how to deliver a speech using impromptu, manuscript, memory, and extemporaneous methods. It also discusses how the speaker should look and sound, and what kinds of visual aids to use during the speech. This chapter emphasizes the importance of practice and evaluation of delivery.

- Chapter 15 focuses on the informative speech. As well as explaining the goals of the informative speech, it describes some of the more sophisticated ways of developing supporting material.

- Chapter 16 concentrates on the persuasive speech and explains the concepts of speaker credibility and logical and emotional appeals. It also introduces some of the research about persuasive speech organization.

Instructor's Manual

To enhance *Communicating Effectively* we have written an extensive *Instructor's Manual* that contains several suggestions for activities to accompany each chapter. Some of these activities are classic ones that always seem to work well; others are new ones we have developed in our own classes. The manual also has sample course outlines and a variety of questions to accompany each chapter. To augment the public speaking section of the text, the manual includes annotated sample speeches given by students and professional speakers. All of the material in the manual will be printed on large-format 8″ × 11″ paper that is perforated so it can be easily removed and photocopied.

We have enjoyed writing *Communicating Effectively*. We like teaching the basic speech communication course: our combined experience with it totals more than 35 years. We hope our enthusiasm for the subject will capture the reader's attention. Our hope will be realized if students learn from the book and enjoy the study of speech communication and the practice of communication skills. We hope, too, that teachers will find this text to be an interesting and useful tool, adaptable to their own needs.

CONTENTS

PART TWO: INTERPERSONAL COMMUNICATION   131

PART THREE: COMMUNICATING IN GROUPS   211

PART FOUR: COMMUNICATING IN PUBLIC   251

part 1

BASIC PRINCIPLES OF COMMUNICATION

1 THE COMMUNICATION PROCESS

CHAPTER OUTLINE

The Need for Communication Skills

Communication as a Process
A definition of communication
The elements of communication

Communication as a Transaction
The three principles of transactional communication

Types of Communication
Intrapersonal communication
Interpersonal communication
Interviewing
Small group communication
Public communication

Communicating Effectively
Where to begin

CHAPTER OBJECTIVES

After reading this chapter, you should be able to:

1. Explain communication needs and relate them to your life.
2. Define communication and explain what is meant when we talk about communication as a process.
3. Identify and label the various elements involved in any communication situation.
4. Explain why communication is a transaction.
5. Explain how a transactional perspective helps us to understand communication better.
6. Describe the various types of communication.
7. Discuss the ways in which you can improve your own communication skills.

3

Larry is the sales manager of a large car dealership. Every Monday morning he meets with all of his salespersons. They discuss what has sold well and what has sold poorly over the past week, and everyone offers suggestions of how they might do better. Larry doesn't say very much, but he listens attentively to what everyone says and takes detailed notes. The next week he implements several of the suggestions. The work atmosphere is very good; all employees feel a strong sense of identity with their job.

Jackie and Brian are best friends. They first met at the campus radio station and discovered they had the same taste in music. After gaining some experience as disk jockeys, they decided to try out for management positions. Jackie became station manager, and Brian program director. Now they spend most of their free time at the station. They make decisions about the music that will be played, they work out the rules that disk jockeys should follow, and they make commercials together. They work so well together that the station is running smoothly and the students are all happy with its operation.

Kim is the manager at a fast-food restaurant. She notices one day that food is not moving very fast and long lines of customers are waiting at the counters. After the lunch-hour rush is over, Kim holds a meeting with all the employees at the restaurant. Rather than scolding them for being so slow, she asks if they have any ideas about how to speed up the service. Most of them agree that the new drink machine is in the middle of a busy pathway and there is so much congestion that everyone gets held up at that spot. Kim agrees and moves the drink machine to a less busy corner. The move solves the problem.

Pam is a member of a study group in her sociology class. She and the other members of the group got together to study for their first exam, and they all did well. However, one member, Greg, did not contribute anything to the group. Now that group members are ready to study for the second exam, they decide to tell Greg that he cannot be a member of the group without contributing. Pam is appointed as spokesperson, and after she tells him, he immediately apologizes and promises to do additional work in preparation for this exam. Greg follows through with his promise, and the members work together so efficiently that they all do well on their second exam.

Tim is the manager of a men's clothing store and a member of the Downtown Business Association (DBA)—a group devoted to improving the downtown area. Tim feels that the DBA needs more money and should support a fundraising effort. He prepares a proposal that the group sponsor a dance. He also finds a place for the dance and tentatively lines up a band. When he proposes the dance to other members of the DBA, they immediately vote approval and several members agree to help in the planning.

Larry, Jackie, Brian, Kim, Pam, and Tim all have something in common: they achieved success because of their communication skills. Larry was able to listen and respond to the needs of his employees. Brian and Jackie have remained good friends because they can communicate with each other and with the students who are working at the station. Kim succeeded because she is able to talk to her employees in a nonthreatening way in order to solve a problem. Pam helped her study group by conveying the group's feelings to

Greg. Tim's fundraising proposal was approved because he was able to make a well-planned and persuasive presentation.

THE NEED FOR COMMUNICATION SKILLS

We fulfill many different needs through communication, and effective communication can give us considerable pleasure. We have a stimulating conversation with a friend, we participate in a group discussion that leads to solving a problem, we give a good persuasive speech and several members of our audience sign our petition. Sometimes, however, communication doesn't work, and we end up feeling frustrated. We have a fight with a friend and don't know how to resolve it. There are certain subjects our parents refuse to discuss. We suspect that our audience was not exactly stimulated by our report.

Even though we have been communicating since birth, we are not always as effective as we could be. Effective communication seems to be a problem to many people—otherwise there wouldn't be such a barrage of books, articles, and workshops telling us how to communicate.

Edgar H. Schein, in his book *Career Dynamics*, reports the results of a long-term study of MIT graduates. He says that for these graduates, talent, technical training, and graduation from a prestigious school were not enough. To achieve a successful and fulfilling life, effectiveness in communication was one of the, if not *the*, most important skill.[1]

Peter Drucker, who writes about business management, says that an employee's success is directly related to communication:

> Your success as an employee—and I am talking of much more here than getting promoted—will depend on your ability to communicate with people and to present your own thoughts and ideas to them so they will both understand what you are driving at and be persuaded.[2]

All communication depends on understanding others and having them understand us. Much of our communication is intended to influence what people think and feel. We want a friend to stop studying and go shopping; we want our friends to like each other; we want someone to join our church or vote for a particular candidate.

Perhaps our most important need is to maintain and improve our relationships with others. We use communication to discover each other's needs and to share our own needs. Anyone involved in any kind of relationship has to have open and accurate lines of communication. Only then will he or she feel free to voice important thoughts and feelings.

Our need for communication, then, is important to most areas of our lives. To live is to communicate. Working on the premise that increased knowledge helps us do things better, let's begin with a discussion of how communication works.

TRY THIS

Think of an experience you have had with each of the following kinds of communication:

- Gaining information and understanding
- Talking and listening for fun
- Trying to change someone's mind
- Maintaining and improving a relationship
- Trying to make a good impression

COMMUNICATION AS A PROCESS

A Definition of Communication

Communication *is a process in which people share information, ideas, and feelings.* To see how this definition works, let's look at a short exchange between Bob and Carol. The two run into each other in the student union. They have known each other for two years, and although each likes the other, they are not close friends.

Carol: How you doing, Bob? I haven't seen you for a couple of weeks.

Bob: I've been hiding out. I've been working on an oral project for my business management class, and I really want to do a good job. Only an hour to go before I present it.

Carol: You look a little jumpy.

Bob: Yeah. I'm feeling pretty nervous. I've been working on this thing so carefully that I'm afraid I might forget something.

Carol: I'm sure you'll do fine. I still remember that great report you did in economics class last year.

In this example, Carol and Bob have communicated. They have exchanged information (what Bob has been up to) and feelings (how Bob is feeling about his report and how Carol feels about Bob's feelings).

However, Carol and Bob's communication was made up of more than this short exchange. Because communication is a process and is ongoing,[3] it also occurs before and after the time when people actually talk to each other. For example, Bob and Carol communicate with each other on the basis of impressions they *already have*. Because of what Bob knows about Carol, he is willing to reveal his feelings. Their communication will also not end with this conversation. Carol later thinks she was surprised to see Bob looking so nervous. Bob later thinks that by telling Carol how nervous he had been, he was helped to feel calmer. These conclusions that Bob and Carol draw from this communication will probably remain in their minds to influence their next communication.

The Elements of Communication

The communication process is made up of various elements. These elements are: senders and receivers, messages, channels, feedback, and setting.

Senders and Receivers

People get involved in communication because they have ideas and feelings they want to share. This sharing, however, is not a one-way, turn-taking process, where one person sends ideas and the other receives them, and then the process is reversed. In most communication situations, people are senders and receivers at the same time; they are **senders-receivers**. Let's say, for example, that you and your friend are discussing baseball. He is sending a message to you by talking, and you are receiving that message by listening. It is also likely, however, that you are sending him a message at the same time (even if you do not say a single word). You might be communicating disapproval—with a frown or an "I don't believe you" expression on your face. Or you might be conveying approval—by smiling or leaning forward in anticipation. Whatever you do, the two of you are both sending and receiving messages simultaneously, as Figure 1-1 shows.

FIGURE **1-1** **Senders-receivers send and receive messages simultaneously.**

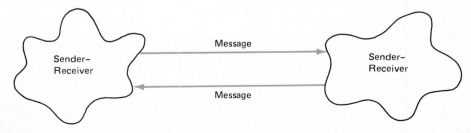

Message

The **message** is made up of the ideas and the feelings that the senders-receivers want to share. In the case of Carol and Bob, Bob's message was what he was doing and feeling while Carol's message was a reaction to what Bob was telling her.

Ideas and feelings can be shared only if they are represented by symbols. **Symbols** are things that stand for something else. All of our communication messages are made up of two kinds of symbols: verbal and nonverbal. Let's begin by looking at verbal symbols.

Every word in our language is a **verbal symbol** that stands for a particular thing or idea. We generally agree that when we use these words we mean the same thing. For example, when we use the word "chair," we all agree it refers to something we sit on. However, that might be the only point on which we agree. If someone gives you $100 and tells you to go to the store and buy a chair, the two of you might have an entirely different idea of what you should buy. You might come back with a lawn chair when the other person intended that you buy a kitchen chair. The message between the two of you was not successful because you didn't have the same meaning for the symbol.

Verbal symbols can be even more complicated when they are abstract rather than concrete (like the chair). **Abstract symbols** stand for ideas rather than objects. When two people use abstractions (such as love, beauty, or justice), they often have different meanings for these words because they have had different experiences with the concept. For example, when John hears the phrase "a wonderful place to live," he immediately thinks of living in the woods far away from any neighbors. To Erin, however, a wonderful place to live is an apartment on Hollywood Boulevard in Los Angeles. Because of our different experiences, there is a greater likelihood of confusion when we use abstract symbols in messages.

Nonverbal symbols are anything we communicate without using words, such as facial expressions, gestures, posture, vocal tones, appearance, and so on. As with verbal symbols, we all attach certain meanings to nonverbal symbols. A yawn means we are bored or tired; a furled brow indicates confusion; not looking someone in the eye may mean we have something to hide.* Like verbal symbols, nonverbal symbols can also be misleading. For example, let's imagine that you have tried several times to talk to the person sitting next to you in class. Each time, she has responded with a short answer and then has turned away from you. You also notice that she hardly ever meets your eyes. You might conclude either that she's a snob or that she doesn't like you. You find out later, from someone else, that she is very shy and would like to talk to you but finds it hard to come up with the right words. She has not intended to send you the message that she doesn't like you—even though that's the nonverbal message you have received.

---

*Sometimes we communicate nonverbally using objects. Sunglasses keep people from looking us in the eye. Our clothing gives out information about our life style.

We cannot control all of our nonverbal behavior, and we often send out information we are not even aware of. For example, a student telling her friend about her encounter with her economics professor said, "I knew he wasn't going to raise my grade when he sat there in his chair with his arms crossed over his chest." Chances are the professor did not even know that he was using a standard nonverbal symbol to indicate resistance. Whether or not we are aware of them, nonverbal symbols are extremely important to messages. Some communication scholars believe that over 90 percent of the messages we send and receive are made up of nonverbal symbols.[4]

Symbols are important to communication: the ideal message in communication is one that is received as it is intended. This can occur, however, only when the senders-receivers have the same meanings for the symbols they use.

Channels

The **channel** is the route traveled by a message as it goes between the senders-receivers (see Figure 1-2). In face-to-face communication, the primary channels are sound and sight: we listen to and look at each other. Other channels might also be used. For example, when Bill goes to see an instructor about a grading error, he uses the channels of four senses to send out information. These

FIGURE 1-2 The channel is the route traveled by a message.

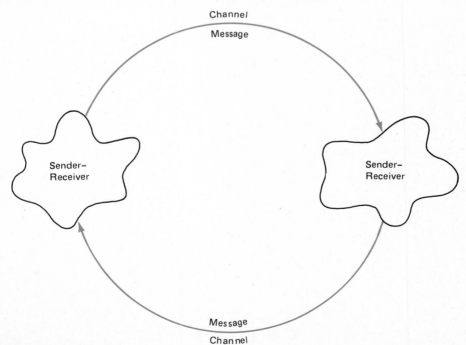

Channel

Message

Sender–
Receiver

Sender–
Receiver

Message

Channel

channels include a firm handshake (touch), pleasant-smelling aftershave (smell), nice clothes (sight), and a respectful voice (sound).

Channels also exist in communication that is not face-to-face, such as writing, telephoning, or sending a cassette recording. In the mass media we are familiar with the channels of radio, television, records, newspapers, and magazines.

Feedback

Feedback is the response of the receivers-senders to each other (see Figure 1-3). You tell me a joke and I smile. That's feedback. You make a comment about the weather and I make another one. More feedback.

Feedback is very important to communication because it lets the participants in the communication see whether ideas and feelings have been shared in the way they intended. If Sally tells John, for example, that she will pick him up at 8 P.M. and he is ready and waiting at that time, he shows by his behavior that the message has been understood. However, let's suppose at another time they agree to meet at the intersection of Brown and Keller Streets at 8 P.M. They both arrive on time but wait at different corners. When they finally discover each other, at 9, they have a big fight and each accuses the

FIGURE 1-3 Feedback is the response of the senders-receivers to each other.

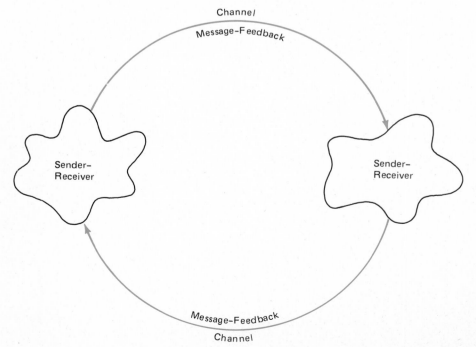

These Kansas legislators are giving a speaker feedback by means of their posture and expressions. But what is their message? Are they interested or bored, enthusiastic or skeptical?

other of being in the wrong place. In this case they thought they had understood the message but come to realize that not enough feedback had occurred. One of them should have asked "*Which* corner of Keller and Brown?"

When the senders-receivers meet in a face-to-face setting, they have the greatest opportunity for feedback. In this kind of setting, they have a chance to see whether the other person understands and is following the message. A teacher working with a child, for example, can readily see by the child's face whether he is confused. She can also see when he is getting bored, by the way he moves around and begins to lose attention. A speaker who is speaking in a large lecture hall, however, is not as aware of the feedback from his audience. Those listeners he can see might look attentive; but he can't see the ones in the back row, who may have gone to sleep. In general, the fewer the people involved in the communication event, the greater the opportunity for feedback.

Noise

Noise is interference that keeps a message from being understood or accurately interpreted. As Figure 1-4 shows, there are two kinds of noise. The first, **physical noise**, keeps the message from being heard. An example might be that your talk with someone is interrupted by a group of people talking loudly in the hallway, a helicopter passing overhead, or a power saw outside the window.

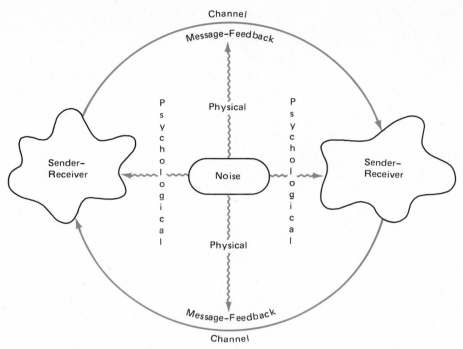

FIGURE 1-4 Two Kinds of Noise: Physical and Psychological

Psychological noise, on the other hand, occurs in the minds of the senders-receivers. This second kind of noise usually occurs when the senders-receivers are distracted by something: a student doesn't hear the lecture because he is thinking about lunch; a wife can't pay attention to what her husband is saying because she is thinking about something that happened in the office. Sometimes psychological noise occurs because the sender-receiver doesn't want to listen to what the other person has to say. For example, a child might look attentive when she is being scolded by a parent, but she is working hard to ignore the scolding. A husband might "switch off" whenever his wife tries to talk about their relationship. Whatever the cause, psychological noise is a mental process that keeps people from accurately sending or receiving symbols.

Setting

The **setting** is where the communication occurs (the surrounding, as Figure 1-5 shows). Settings can be a significant influence on communication. Some settings are formal and lend themselves to formal presentations. An auditorium, for example, is a formal setting that is good for giving speeches and presentations but not very good for conversation between the speaker and his

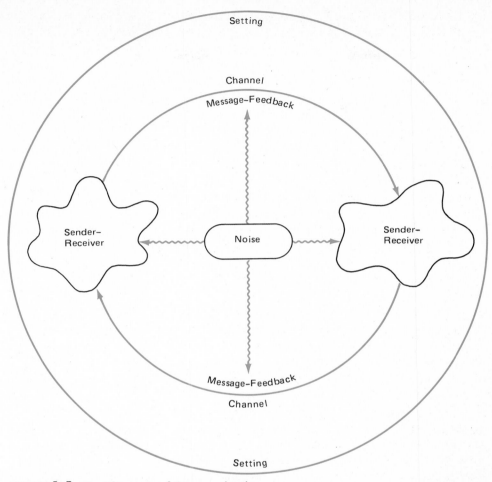

FIGURE 1-5 **The Elements of Communication**

or her audience. If communicators want to converse, they would be better off in a comfortable room where they could sit and face each other.

Setting is made up of several components, which can range from the way a place is lighted to the colors used for decoration. Let's look at lighting. Your local discount store is lighted with fluorescent lights. These lights communicate a message: you are not there to relax, but to do business and move on. On the other hand, if you are going to buy a fur coat in a department store, you are not going to find fluorescent lighting. The lighting will be subdued, and the showroom will probably look more like your living room than like a sales place.

The color of a room might determine how comfortable you feel. For example, our culture recognizes feminine colors (pink, lavender) and mascu-

CONSIDER THIS

According to one study, color may be an important factor in communication settings:

Green is such a calming color that many school walls are painted "educational green" to reduce the restlessness of students. Now educational green may have to yield to an even more soothing tint: "jailhouse pink." According to Alexander Schauss, director of biosocial research at City College in Tacoma, Wash., the sight of the color pink changes the secretion of hormones, thus reducing aggressiveness. A jail commander in San Jose, Calif., who has tested the theory says it works—for a while. Lieut. Paul Becker found that prisoners were less hostile for the first 15 minutes in a cell that had been painted pink. But after 20 minutes, the hostility grew, and after three hours some of the men started to tear the paint off the walls. Conclusion: pink may be best for inmates whose sentences range from 10 to 15 minutes.

Source: Time.

line colors (gray, brown). If men were going to have a meeting in a pink room, they might feel out of place. If the room were decorated with frilly curtains and spindle-legged chairs, they might feel downright uncomfortable.

The arrangement of furniture in a setting can also affect the communication that takes place. For example, a college library we knew was one of the noisiest places on campus. The problem was solved by rearranging the furniture. Instead of sofas and chairs arranged so that students could sit and talk, the library used study desks—thus creating a quiet place to study.

All communication is made up of senders and receivers, messages, channels, feedback, noise, and setting. Every time people communicate, these elements are going to be somewhat different. They are not the only factors that influence communication, however. Communication is also influenced by what we bring to it. That is the subject of our next section.

COMMUNICATION AS A TRANSACTION

So far, our discussion of communication has described the factors involved in communication. Now this discussion is taken one step further as we look specifically at the receivers-senders who are involved in the communication.

A communication transaction involves not only the physical act of communicating but also a psychological one: impressions are being formed in the minds of the people who are communicating.[5] As I communicate with you, for example, what I think and know of you will directly affect my communication with you.

The Three Principles of Transactional Communication

Communication as a transaction—**transactional communication**—involves three important principles. First, people engaged in communication are sending messages continuously and simultaneously. Second, communication events have a past, present, and future. Third, participants in communication play certain roles. Let's consider each of these principles in turn.

Participation Is Continuous and Simultaneous

Even if you are not actually talking in a communication situation, you are actively involved in getting and giving symbols. For example, let's say you stop to ask directions to a particular building on campus. From the directions the person is giving, you are determining how far away the building is and how easy it will be to reach. At the same time you are giving feedback on how well you are receiving and understanding the directions. You may also be making some judgments about how effective the person giving the directions is as a communicator. You are participating continuously and simultaneously. You can see, then, that you are both a sender and a receiver.

All Communications Have a Past, Present, and Future

To understand the importance of past, present, and future in a communication, let's look in on Stewart and Chris, husband and wife, who are engaged in a heated argument. Stewart wants to go south for Thanksgiving; Chris wants to visit relatives instead.

It is impossible to understand this argument without knowing some history and how it affects what is going on now. During the last holiday (*past*), they visited Stewart's parents. Now Chris is trying to get Stewart to be fair and visit her family. Knowing some future implications can also be helpful. Chris knows that for the next holiday (*future*), Stewart has already made plans to go to a professional convention in the South. This will mean two trips south and none to see her relatives in St. Paul. The heated argument (*present*) is occurring because Chris is feeling cheated. The past and future are affecting Chris's ideas and feelings in the present. Stewart, however, seems to be ignoring both past and future.

Even if you have never met someone before, the past still affects your communication with that person—because your response to new people you meet is based on your past experience. You might respond to the physical type (short, tall, fat, thin), to the occupation (accountant, gym teacher), or even to a name (remember how a boy named Eugene always tormented you and you've mistrusted all Eugenes ever since?). Any of these things you call up from your past might influence how you respond to these people—at least at the beginning.

The future also influences communication. If you want a relationship to continue, you will say and do things in the present to make sure it does. ("Thanks for dinner. I always enjoy your cooking.") If you think you will never see a person again, this also might affect your communication. You might be more businesslike, leaving the personal aspects of your life out of the communication.

All Communicators Play Roles

Roles are parts we play or how we behave with others. And those roles are established by society. For example, Carol, the student, is supposed to communicate in a particular way with her instructor, Professor Jones. Because she is in the role of student and he is in the role of teacher, she is expected to show him a certain amount of respect, not call him by his first name, and so on.

Communication changes as roles change. When Carol later talks to her father, they will probably communicate from the roles of parent and child. When she goes to work, she will communicate with her boss in the role of employee.

As Carol plays the role of student, child, and employee, we can make some predictions about how she will communicate, since the society in which we live gives us some idea of what is expected in these roles. ("Don't talk back to your father." "Let your boss know you're energetic.") In other cases the role is not so clear, and it may change according to how the participants define their relationship. Let's say, for example, that Carol meets her boyfriend after work. As she comes out to the parking lot, he says, "Get in the car." This sentence tells us a good deal about their relationship and how they have defined it. If, instead, he gets out of the car, walks to meet her, puts his arm around her shoulder, and says, "Hi, honey," we have a completely different impression of their relationship. How we communicate, then, is based on our roles in relation to one another. That is why no two communications are the same; they change to meet the needs of each particular relationship.

The roles we play—whether established by individual relationships or by the society—are also perceived differently by different people. These different perceptions affect the communication that results. For example, Tom, in his role of youth director, is well organized and maintains tight control over the classes he teaches. The kids who take his classes know they have to behave, or they'll be in big trouble. Therefore they speak to him in a respectful voice and stay quiet when they're supposed to. To other kids, however, Tom's discipline indicates rigidity and inflexibility. These kids don't go by the Youth Center; they choose not to communicate with him at all.

TRY THIS

Think back about the last conversation you had with your best friend. How did your relationship history affect the communication? What roles do you play with each other? Do these roles determine what you can and cannot say to each other?

The Principles in Action

Let's see how the three principles of transactional communication work as we listen to a conversation between Jane and Stacy:

Jane: Hey, Stacy. Can I borrow your sweater?

Stacy   (Steps back, slight frown): Well . . .

Jane   (Steps forward): You know. The brown one with the white ducks.

Stacy   (Folds her arms in front of her): What happened to all those new sweaters you got for your birthday?

We know right away in this scene that Stacy does not want to cooperate, even though she never says so. As Jane speaks, Stacy simultaneously and continuously sends out signals: she frowns, she steps back, she folds her arms in front of her—all nonverbal symbols of resistance. Jane reinforces her verbal symbols by stepping forward—a nonverbal way of showing assertiveness.

This scene between Jane and Stacy would probably take no more than 30 seconds in real life, yet it is filled with symbols—some of which nonparticipants would be unable to detect. For example, let's speculate on the past and future aspects of this communication. How many times has Jane borrowed things from Stacy? How willing has Stacy been to lend them before? What has been their condition upon return? What is Jane and Stacy's relationship? Do they get along? Do they respect each other and each other's property?

We must also look at the roles that Jane and Stacy play. Their roles seem to be equal because they are friends. From their conversation, however, Jane is willing to play the role of borrower but Stacy is not willing to play the role of lender. The roles they play in this transaction will depend on the experience they have had with these roles in the past. If in the past Jane had returned a sweater dirty, this might make Stacy reluctant to continue in the role of lender.

When we look at this conversation between Jane and Stacy, we can see how complicated even a simple conversation can be. Still, we can never really understand what goes on in communication unless we look at it from a transactional perspective. Then we can begin to see the complexity and uniqueness of each communication event. As Heraclitus, the Greek philosopher, once observed, we cannot step into the same river twice because not only are we different but so is the river. The same is true of communication.

TYPES OF COMMUNICATION

As you can see in Figure 1-6, there are different kinds of communication. The figure shows the kinds most often used: intrapersonal, interpersonal, interviews, small group, and public.

Intrapersonal Communication

Intrapersonal communication is the kind of communication that occurs within us. It involves thoughts, feelings, and the way we look at ourselves. Figure 1-7 (p. 20) shows some of the things that make up the self and, hence, intrapersonal communication.

Because intrapersonal communication is centered in the self, you are the only sender-receiver. The message is made up of your thoughts and feelings. The channel is your brain, which processes what you are thinking and feeling. There is feedback in the sense that you talk to yourself, or discard certain ideas and replace them with others.

Even though you are not directly communicating with others in intrapersonal communication, the people and the experiences you have had determine how you "talk" to yourself. For example, if you have had a good day, you are likely to look at yourself in a positive way. If a teacher was disappointed with your work, or if you had a fight with a fellow student, you are likely to focus more on your depression or anger. You can never look at yourself without being influenced by the relationships you have with others.

Interpersonal Communication

Interpersonal communication occurs when we communicate on a one-to-one basis—usually in an informal, unstructured setting. This kind of communication occurs mostly between two people, though it may include more than two.

Interpersonal communication uses all the elements of the communication process. In a conversation between friends, for example, each brings his or her background and experience to the conversation. During the conversation each functions as a sender-receiver. Their messages consist of both verbal and nonverbal symbols. The channels they use the most are sight and sound.

INTRAPERSONAL COMMUNICATION

INTERPERSONAL COMMUNICATION AND INTERVIEWING

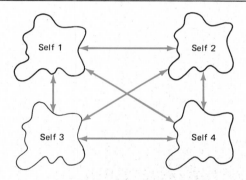

SMALL–GROUP COMMUNICATION

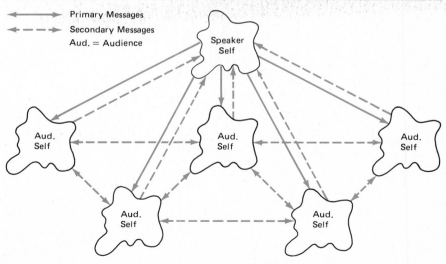

PUBLIC COMMUNICATION

FIGURE 1-6 Kinds of Communication

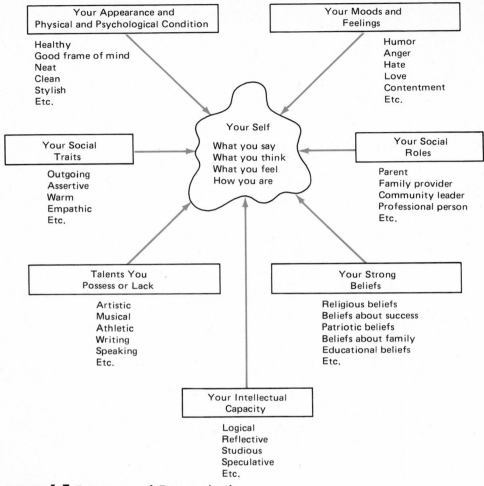

FIGURE 1-7 Intrapersonal Communication

Because interpersonal communication is between two (or a few) people, it offers the greatest opportunity for feedback. Psychological noise is likely to be minimal because each person can see whether the other is distracted. The persons involved in the conversation have many chances to check that the message is being perceived correctly. Interpersonal communication usually takes place in informal and comfortable settings.

Interviewing

An interview is a series of questions and answers usually involving two people—whose primary purpose is to obtain information on a particular sub-

Milton Avery's painting
Interlude *conveys the essence of interpersonal communication: informal, conversational, involving an exchange of both verbal and nonverbal symbols.*

ject. One common type is the *job interview*, in which the employer asks the job candidate questions to determine whether he or she is suitable for the job. Another type is an *information interview* where the interviewer tries to get information about a particular subject.

In interviewing, the verbal roles of the senders-receivers alternate, as one person asks a question and the other responds. Both persons, however, are continuously and simultaneously sending nonverbal messages. Because interviews usually take place face-to-face, a lot of nonverbal information is exchanged. Feedback is very high in an interview; and because the communication is so structured, concentration is high and there is little noise. Both participants respond directly to questions and answers. Since the interview has a specific purpose, the communication setting is usually quite formal.

Small-Group Communication

Small-group communication occurs when a small number of people meet to solve a problem. The group must be small enough so that each member in the group has a chance to interact with all of the other members.

TRY THIS

In each of the communication situations listed below, identify the following: the kind of communication, the participants, the message, the channel, the amount of potential feedback, and the likely setting. What are the possible sources of physical and psychological noise in each situation?

- The local garden club meets to decide what plants to put in the city park.
- You meet with a study group to study for a biology test.
- You go to the student union for coffee with a friend.
- You are writing a story for the student newspaper and interview the president of the college to see whether there will be a tuition increase.
- You think about ways you can improve your relationship with your girlfriend or boyfriend.
- You give a speech in front of your class.
- A senatorial candidate makes a brief stop in your town and speaks on the courthouse steps about his platform. Television cameras are there to cover the event for the local newscast.

Because small groups are made up of several senders-receivers, the communication process is more complicated than in interpersonal communication. With so many more people sending messages, there are more chances for confusion. Messages are also more structured in small groups because the group is meeting together for a specific purpose. Small groups use the same channels as interpersonal communication, however, and there is also a good deal of opportunity for feedback. In view of their problem-solving nature, small groups usually meet in a more formal setting than people involved in interpersonal communication.

Public Communication

In **public communication** the sender-receiver (the speaker) sends a message (the speech) to an audience. The speaker usually delivers a highly structured message, using the same channels as in interpersonal and small-group communication. In public communication, however, the channels are more exaggerated than in interpersonal communication. The voice is louder and the gestures are more expansive because the audience is bigger. The speaker might also use additional visual channels such as slides, flip charts, and so on. Generally the opportunity for verbal feedback in public communication is limited. The audience members may have a chance to ask questions at the end of the speech, but usually they are not free to address the speaker as he or she is talking. However, they can send nonverbal feedback. If they like what the speaker is saying, they may interrupt the speech with applause. If they dislike it, they may move around a lot or simply stop paying attention. In most public communication the setting is formal.

COMMUNICATING EFFECTIVELY

Once you understand the process of communication, you can begin to understand why communication does or doesn't work. In an ideal communication situation the message is perceived in the way it was intended. For example, you ask your roommate to pick up a loaf of bread after school and she does so. The message was perceived as you intended it to be. If she comes back without the bread or the wrong kind of bread, then you have to examine the communication process. If you had wanted her to bring white bread and she brought rye bread, then the verbal symbols in your message were not specific enough. If she forgot the bread altogether, maybe there was a problem with the channel. It wasn't enough to tell her; you also should have written a note. Or maybe psychological noise interfered—she was thinking about her class and didn't really hear the message. Your communication could have broken down in any one of these ways. When messages don't work, then, it is useful to ask these questions: Was there a problem with the message? Was the best channel used? Did psychological noise occur? Knowing the right questions to ask is essential to building skills in communication.

Most of us already have considerable communication skills. We have been sending and receiving verbal and nonverbal signals all our lives. Nevertheless, we have all had times when we have not communicated as effectively as we should. We got a lower grade on a paper than we expected, we unintentionally hurt somebody's feelings, or the instructor did not understand our question when we asked it in class.

Where to Begin

The information and research about communication are so vast that most of us could spend a lifetime studying communication and not learn even a fraction of what there is to know. As a beginning student of communication, here are five questions to ask yourself.

Which Communication Skills Am I Most Likely to Need?

Find out what communication skills are important to you. What do you intend to do in your life? What kind of work do you expect to do? What communication skills are required in this work? Which of these skills do you already have? Which ones need improvement? Which ones do you need to acquire?

Going into politics, for example, would require a broad range of communication skills. Public speaking skills would be the most valuable, as well as the ability to talk to strangers and to make an impression on them. Perhaps you are majoring in social work. Since most social workers work one-to-one with clients, they need both interpersonal and interviewing skills. A career in business requires almost every communication skill. You need interpersonal skills to get along with the people you work with, interviewing skills (especially if you're going to work in personnel), and public speaking skills for making presentations. Although you may use some communication skills more than others, at one time or another you are going to need every one we have discussed in this chapter.

Which Communication Skills Am I Most Lacking In?

Which kinds of communication are most difficult for you? Intrapersonal? Interpersonal? Interviewing? Small-group? Public speaking? Why do you have difficulties in these areas? What problems do you have to overcome before you can perform effectively in these areas?

Probably you would prefer *not* to work in the area that gives you the most trouble. For example, if you are anxious about public speaking, you might feel inclined to avoid any circumstance where you have to give a speech. It will be much more to your advantage, however, if you can conquer this fear by plunging in and practicing the thing that gives you the most trouble. You will find some big rewards in doing so; not only will you learn how to do something, but you will feel much better about yourself.

How Can I Get Communication Practice?

Are there situations, other than class, where you can practice communication skills that will be useful to you? Are there groups and organizations you can join that will help you develop these skills? It's always a good idea to take what you have learned in class and try it out on the world. Using new skills helps to develop and refine them.

Where Can I Get Help?

What people do you know who will help you to develop these skills and give you feedback on how you are doing? Are there people you can ask who will give you support when you try to do something new and scary? Are you willing to ask them to support you? We can usually count on this kind of support from our friends. Most of us have at least one friend who would be willing to listen to one of our speeches and tell us if it works or where we might improve it. Also, don't forget your instructors. Many of them sit there all alone during office hours and would welcome a visit from a student.

What Timetable Should I Set?

Have you set a realistic timetable for improvement? Knowing that it is difficult to learn new skills or break bad habits, are you willing to give yourself that time? Your speech class is going to last for a semester or a quarter. Although you will be making steady improvement in your speeches, you still might be a long way from making a perfect speech at the end of the term. This does not mean, however, that you will never be able to make a perfect speech; it is a matter of needing more time. The same is true of bad habits. Let's say, for example, that you have asked your friends to remind you to stop saying "he don't." You're not going to break the habit in a couple of weeks; look how long you've been saying it that way. Perhaps the most realistic timetable, then, is one where you say, "I'm going to keep working at this until I am effective."

SUMMARY

We engage in communication because it brings us success, gives us pleasure, helps us to change the way others act and behave, and aids us in maintaining and improving relationships.

Communication is a process in which people share ideas and feelings. It is a process because it is ongoing. The elements of communication include senders-receivers, messages, channels, feedback, noise, and setting.

All communication is a transaction. Viewing communication as a transaction focuses on the people who are communicating and the changes that take place in them as they are communicating. It also implies that all participants are involved continuously and simultaneously; that communication events have a past, present, and future; and that the roles the participants play will affect the communication.

Five kinds of communication are discussed in this book. Intrapersonal communication is communication with one's self. Interpersonal communication is informal communication with one or more other persons. Interviewing is a structured question-and-answer type of communication with the specific purpose of obtaining information. Small-group communication occurs when a small group of people get together to solve a problem. Public communication is giving a speech to an audience.

Communication can be improved if you concentrate on several important areas. You need to find out what communication skills are important to you. You need to discover the kinds of communication that are most difficult for you and work to improve them. You need to seek out people who will help you develop these skills and give you support and feedback. Finally, you need to set a realistic timetable for improvement.

VOCABULARY

The following is a list of words you must know to understand the concepts in this chapter. You will find the words defined the first time that each is used in the chapter. All Vocabulary words also appear, with their definitions, in the Glossary at the end of the book.

abstract symbol
channel
communication
feedback
interpersonal communication
interview
intrapersonal communication
message
noise
nonverbal symbol

physical noise
psychological noise
public communication
roles
senders-receivers
setting
small-group communication
symbol
transactional communication
verbal symbol

FURTHER READING

CAMPBELL, KARLYN KOHRS. *The Rhetorical Act*. Belmont, Calif.: Wadsworth, 1982. Although this is primarily a book on public communication, we have included it here because it takes a traditional, humanistic approach to public speaking (rhetoric) drawn from the classics. The author's opening chapters on the rhetorical perspective and the rhetorical act provide a clear orientation to this perspective.

HOWELL, WILLIAM S. *The Empathic Communicator*. Belmont, Calif.: Wadsworth, 1982. Howell's perspective is that communication is an ever-changing, often unpredictable joint venture. We include this book because of his emphasis on empathy, sending and receiving, and messages. Howell explores competence in spontaneous interactions.

LITTLEJOHN, STEPHEN W. *Theories of Human Communication*, 2nd ed. Belmont, Calif.: Wadsworth, 1983. Littlejohn offers a comprehensive examination of major communication theories. His discussion of the strengths and weaknesses of theories is useful; however, the book is designed for the more serious student of communication.

NAISBITT, JOHN. *Megatrends: Ten New Directions Transforming Our Lives*. New York: Warner, 1984. This author provides numerous insights into the kinds of changes occurring in communication. In addition, he demonstrates how these changes will directly affect our lives.

QUBEIN, NIDO R. *Get the Best from Yourself*. Englewood Cliffs, N.J.: Prentice-Hall, 1983. This self-improvement book is for those who need the motivation, the personal incentive, to fulfill themselves. Qubein offers readers a rich source of ideas and inspiration. His is an enjoyable, practical, easy-to-read book full of suggestions for improving skills.

STEWART, JOHN, ED. *Bridges Not Walls: A Book About Interpersonal Communication*, 4th ed. New York: Random House, 1986. This is an anthology of readings. We have included it because the first major chapter contains readings that explain and develop the transactional approach to communication. Stewart offers a broad, interesting approach to interpersonal communication through a variety of well-known authors.

TOMPKINS, PHILLIP K. *Communication as Action: An Introduction to Rhetoric and Communication.* Belmont, Calif.: Wadsworth, 1982. Tompkins challenges the reader to define what it is to be human and how to function effectively in a society that is the sum total of human communicative acts. He discusses interpersonal, group, and organizational communication. This is a textbook for the serious student.

2 SELF AND COMMUNICATION

CHAPTER OUTLINE

Our Perceptions of the World
Perception and Self-Concept
The Development of Perception and Self-Concept
    Our bodies
    What other people tell us
    Our past experiences

Our Perceptions of Others
    The perceptual process
    When perceptions don't match
Checking Out Your Perceptions
Improving Your Self-Concept
    The need for psychological safety
    How to improve your self-esteem

CHAPTER OBJECTIVES

After reading this chapter, you should be able to:

1. Explain why perception differs from one person to another.
2. Describe how perception and self-concept are related.
3. Explain how each of the following influences perception: our bodies, what people tell us, and past experience.
4. Outline the six steps in the perceptual process and give an example that shows how each step works.
5. Describe some of the ways you can improve your own self-esteem.

Lewis Hines, The Ellis Island Madonna.

Ms. Banning was teaching a college class for the first time. A few weeks after the semester started, she asked her five seminar students to write a research paper on the subject of First Amendment rights and the student press. When they asked how long the paper should be, she replied, "whatever length you need to cover the subject adequately." When the papers were turned in, they ranged in length from seven to twenty-nine pages.

Why were the words "whatever length you need to cover the subject adequately" perceived in such different ways? How could one student interpret this remark as seven pages while another perceived it as twenty-nine pages? To discover the answer to these questions, let's take a look at how the students were thinking as they worked on this assignment.

- Barb (18 pages): Barb dropped out of school to get married and raise a family. Now that her children have grown up, she has decided to return to college and get her degree. She is anxious about being a student and wants to do as well as possible in this class. She feels that a paper somewhere in the vicinity of 15 to 20 pages will do the job well without seeming excessive.

- Bob (7 pages): Bob is taking this class but is also working full-time. Just about the time Ms. Banning made this assignment, Bob got promoted and was given much more responsibility. Although he would like to do well in class, he has decided his job is more important and that he will try to get away with minimum work.

- Roger (29 pages): Roger believes that all instructors are impressed by length in research papers. When he writes his paper he throws in everything he can think of—even if some of it is not very relevant. In his college career, Roger has never written a paper under 25 pages.

- Carol (12 pages): Carol is the most active participant in the seminar. She and Ms. Banning often go for coffee after the seminar and she knows that Ms. Banning likes her and is impressed by her. Carol feels she doesn't have to prove anything; she can write 12 carefully reasoned and researched pages.

- Matt (21 pages): Matt decides that since the seminar has only five students, Ms. Banning is going to have a lot of time to read and grade the papers carefully. Therefore he had better do a paper that looks substantial.

These five students have all had the same experience. The difference among them is that they interpret "adequate length" in terms of their **perceptions**—how they see the world. For example, Barb feels a need to prove herself with her paper. Bob sees the paper as taking him away from his job. Roger believes the only good research papers are long ones. Carol is confident of her relationship with the instructor so she doesn't worry about the length of the paper. Matt knows the paper will be under careful scrutiny, so he wants to do

CONSIDER THIS

There is a story of three men, each of whom saw the Grand Canyon from the viewpoint of their different occupations.

> The archaeologist looked at it and said, "What a wonder of science."
> The clergyman said, "One of the glories of God."
> The cowboy said, "That's a heck of a place to lose a cow."

Source: Adapted from Gloria Hoffman and Pauline Graivier, as told to Jane Phillips, *Speak the Language of Success.*

the job thoroughly. Ms. Banning has yet another perception; she believes students should write on a subject until it is covered and then stop.

Like the students and Ms. Banning, we often have experiences that are similar to those of others but perceive these experiences in different ways. However, we also share many of our perceptions with others. Most of us, for example, agree on what color something is, whether something smells bad, or even whether someone has been rude. If we did not share some of these perceptions, we couldn't live together in the world, because each of us would be perceiving everything in a different way. For example, if your friend wants a yellow sweater for his birthday, you and he have to agree on what color yellow is before you can buy one and he can be satisfied with what you've bought.

OUR PERCEPTIONS OF THE WORLD

Although people's fundamental perceptions are the same, variations on these fundamentals will arise with differing individual knowledge and experience. For example, if two students—one from Kansas and the other from Colorado—are talking about the height of the mountains of central Pennsylvania, the Kansas student, who has never before seen mountains, might feel the Pennsylvania mountains are very high, whereas the Colorado student, who grew up with a view of the Rockies from his window, might regard the Pennsylvania mountains as mere foothills. This difference could occur even though they agree on the definition of a mountain as a very high hill. Thus although their fundamental perception of "mountain" is the same, what they perceive as a high mountain depends on their experience.

Perceptions change with knowledge and experience. If the Kansas student were to go to Colorado, her perception of what constitutes a high mountain

CONSIDER THIS

The Investigation

would probably change. If she were to go to Nepal and view the Himalayas, her perception would probably change again. In another example, a teen-ager might think his parents are too strict because they give him so many "must" and "should" messages. "You must be in by midnight." "You should study harder." Yet when that teen-ager grows up, becomes a parent, and has teen-agers of his own, he finds himself giving "must" and "should" messages to his own kids. His perception has changed because of his experience.

If you were to compare your perception of the world with that of other people, you would discover that no one sees the world in *exactly* the same way you do. You might share an opinion about Professor Warren with the person who sits next to you in class; however, you might not share the same perception of the conflict in the Middle East, of whether violent cartoons are harmful to children, of whether string beans taste better than carrots, and so on.

The way in which you view the world is greatly influenced by the way you view yourself. This view of yourself—your **self-concept**—is so closely tied to perception that the relationship between the two is our next consideration.

PERCEPTION AND SELF-CONCEPT

While perception is the way you see yourself, others, and the world around you, your self-concept is made up of the conclusions you draw about yourself. Perception and self-concept are so closely related that it is often difficult to separate them.[1] How you look at the world depends on what you think of yourself; what you think of yourself will influence how you look at the world. For example, Jane and Bob, who have majored in the same subject, sit around one day and talk about jobs in their field. Jane, who has a lot of self-confidence, says, "I looked in the newspaper last night and there are all kinds of jobs I can do." Bob, who doesn't feel nearly so confident, says, "I have just the opposite experience. Every time I look at the paper, I never find anything. It depresses me so much, I've stopped looking." Because Jane's self-concept is one of confidence, her perception of the job market is optimistic. Bob's self-concept, however, is much more negative, so he perceives the world as a more threatening place.

Not only your perceptions but what you choose to notice or ignore will be influenced by your self-concept. For example, Kathleen notices the announcement of a beauty pageant in the newspaper and decides to enter. Her self-concept tells her that she is pretty enough to enter a pageant and because of this, she notices the announcement. Later Kathleen runs into her friend Judy and says, "Have you heard about the beauty pageant? I'm going to enter it. You should too." Judy, who does not have a self-concept of "pretty" or "possible beauty contest candidate," says, "You must be crazy, Kathleen. There's no way I would have a chance in a beauty contest." Since Judy perceives herself this way, she chooses to ignore information about the pageant.

Both self-concept and perception are subjective—they are influenced more by feeling than by thought. For example, think of the last time someone took a picture of you or you heard your voice on a tape recording. You may have reacted with the exclamation, "That isn't me!" Yet both the tape recording and the photograph are objective portrayals of you. Your reaction has been subjective because your perceptions of how you look and how you sound are different from this objective evidence.

When we see how unique and subjective self-concept and perception are, it seems reasonable to ask, "Why are we all so different?" Where does perception come from? How does self-concept develop? That is the subject of our next section.

THE DEVELOPMENT OF PERCEPTION AND SELF-CONCEPT

Perception and self-concept develop from three areas: the body we are born into, what people tell us about ourselves, and our past experiences.

Our Bodies

Every individual is born into a unique body, and to some extent the body one has influences one's perception of the world. Most people have five senses, but those senses are not necessarily equal in all people. For example, most people can see well enough to get through life, but there are ways in which some see differently from others. Why, otherwise, can some children hit a ball better than others? Why do some children learn to read very quickly while other children struggle? Clearly what is seen and how it is interpreted by the brain can differ greatly among people. The same is true of the other senses. In hearing, some people have perfect pitch while others can never stay in tune. Although tastes can be acquired, people also seem to be born with a taste for certain things. Even babies have their preferences among kinds of baby foods.

The way your body is functioning can affect your perception. Hormones can influence emotional cycles. Health can be a factor, as can such states as tiredness or hunger. When you are feeling good, you are more likely to want to interact with other people. When you are tired or hungry, you are more likely to be irritable.

Physical size can influence perception too. Tall people see tops of heads; short people see bottoms of chins. Where you decide to live, the chairs you choose for your house, the kind of car you drive, the person you choose to marry or date—all might be chosen because of your physical size.

What Other People Tell Us

Body Image

Although one is born with certain physical characteristics, how one *feels* about them is learned. A man who is five feet tall could live a perfectly happy life if he did not have to contend with society's message that this is much too short for a man. Because of this message, he is probably going to have some negative feelings about himself. Our society also says thin women are more attractive than fat women and that fair-skinned people are better looking than dark-skinned people. Society sets a standard as well on what is normal or subnormal intelligence. These standards, in turn, are communicated to us by those who take care of us (parents, baby-sitters), by institutions we are part of (school, church), and by the mass media (particularly the movies and television). Whether a person measures up to these societal standards of physical attractiveness and mental alertness has a good deal to do with determining his or her self-concept.

As well as giving its people messages about their bodies, every society also teaches what is expected of them. This process, called **social conditioning**, starts in earliest childhood. And much of it takes the form of teaching people to play various roles.

Roles

Remember the story of Tarzan? Although Tarzan was a human, he believed he was an ape because he was brought up by the apes and had no human experience. Tarzan's story reminds us that we are not born with an identity— it is given to us by someone else. Our parents, or the first people who take care of us, tell us through their words and actions that we are good or bad, stupid or intelligent, lovable or unlovable.

Many of these messages are given to us in terms of the roles we are to play in life. A role, as Chapter 1 noted, is how a person behaves in a particular situation. A role does not mean phony behavior—it merely means that people in different situations act in different ways. In class, for example, you play the role of student. When you relate to your children, you play the role of parent. When you talk to your boss, you play the role of employee.

Every role we play requires certain communication behavior—behavior that has been determined by our society. If you are being interviewed for a job, you are expected to ask some questions and show interest in the job. If you don't do this, you will lessen your chances of getting the job. In your role as a speech student, you are expected to speak up in class and give your speeches on the day they are due. If you violate any of the expectations of this role, you will probably be in trouble and be punished with a low grade.

When Ralph Keyes was writing a book about how height affects one's life, he kept a file of clippings from newspapers and magazines that described public figures on the basis of their size. Here are some of his choice items.

Tall

... tall, handsome, athletic ...

—*San Francisco Examiner* on then vice-presidential candidate Sargent Shriver

... a tall stalk of black-haired loveliness ...

—*Parade* on former Alabama first lady Cornelia Wallace

... a big, likeable bear of a man ...

—*Newsweek* on former New York Yankee pitcher Floyd Bevens

... tall, handsome and polished ...

—DAVID BRODER in *The Atlantic* on Texas politician John Connally

Mr. Gann is a tall, soft-spoken, polite man who prefers to play golf or visit his four children and 11 grandchildren ...

—*New York Times* on California Proposition 13 cosponsor Paul Gann

With his tall, powerful build, mane of blond hair and rugged features, the 29-year-old Godunov cuts an overwhelming figure onstage.

—*Newsweek* on dancer Aleksandr Godunov

... a handsome, imposing man who stands over six feet four inches tall ...

—*Current Biography* on Australian Prime Minister Malcolm Fraser

He is a tall, dark, handsome brute, 6 feet 5 inches in height with Hollywood looks and bearing.

—*New York Times* on Boston Red Sox pitcher Mike Torrez

Small

... small, pallid, inexorably bland ...

—*Newsweek* on U.S. Budget Director James McIntyre

... a short, slightly chunky woman who wears white socks and loafers ...

—*Esquire* on umpire Bernice Gera

... a small, balding troll of a man ...

—*Time* on drag racer Bill Jenkins

... a tiny dandy who dangles his toes from his swivel chair ...

—DAVID BRODER in *The Atlantic* on Texas politician John Tower

Mr. Jarvis, short and stocky, is an abrasive, cocky campaigner with a booming voice who likes to relax by smoking cigars ...

—*New York Times* on California Proposition 13 cosponsor Howard Jarvis

With his short stature, hook nose, beady eyes, unkempt hair, he looks like a loser ...

—*Parade* on screen actor Dustin Hoffman

... tiny (4'11"), unimposing and charismatic as a bowl of rice ...

—*People* on Chinese Vice-Premier Deng Xiaoping (Teng Hsiao-ping)

... he is small and squat, a slug of a man, with large reptilian eyes blinking out from behind horn-rimmed glasses.

—*Philadelphia Inquirer* on author Theodore White

Source: Ralph Keyes, *The Height of Your Life.*

Roles and perceptions are closely related. We make judgments of people based on whether we perceive them as playing their roles properly. For instance, Alice says that Betty is a good mother because she always listens to her children. Tom, however, does not agree. He thinks Betty is a bad mother because she works full time. Both Alice and Tom have a precise idea of what the role of "good mother" entails, and they evaluate others on the basis of this perception. Judgments based on the perception of how roles should be played are very common. Every teacher has an idea of the role of a "good student." All bosses know what they expect from a "hard worker." And every parent has an idea of how a "good child" should behave. If we can fit in with others' perceptions of these roles, then we will be judged favorably.

Scripts

As well as being told how we should play our roles, we are also given lines to speak. These lines are often so specific that some people refer to them as **scripts**.[2]

Some scripts are given to us by our parents, and they contain directions that are just as explicit as any script intended for the stage. We are given our lines ("Say thank you to the nice lady"), our gestures ("Don't point!"), and our characterizations ("You're a good boy"). The scripts tell us how to play future scenes ("Everyone in our family has gone to college") and what is expected of us ("I will be so happy when you make us grandparents").

People outside our family also contribute to our scripts. Teachers, coaches, ministers, friends, even the media—all tell us what they expect from us, how we should look, how we should behave, and how we should say our lines.

Self-Fulfilling Prophecies

Part of our self-concept develops because of **self-fulfilling prophecies**.[3] These are predictions that come true because we (and others) predict them. For example, Professor Farley says to Kevin, "I'm sure you are going to be a very good student." This statement makes Kevin want to be a good student, so he works hard to live up to Professor Farley's prophesy. Similarly, negative prophecies can have a negative impact. If someone tells a child that he will "never amount to much," there is a good chance the child will do just that.

Most children get their self-fulfilling prophecies from others. If these prophecies have been largely positive ("You're a good looking kid"; "I know you'll do well on your test"; "If you practice, you will be really good"), the child will grow up with a positive self-concept. The opposite is also true: a child who has been subjected to many negative prophecies is unlikely to view himself or herself in a very positive way.

CONSIDER THIS

In his autobiography, Russell Baker writes about how he and his sister, Doris, learned their roles and scripts from their mother:

> She began telling me I was "the man of the family," and insisting that I play the role. She took me to a Newark department store and bought me a suit with knickers, a herringbone pattern that must have represented a large fortune on her meager resources. But a suit and necktie and a white shirt wasn't enough; she also insisted on buying me a hat, a junior-scale model of the gray fedora Uncle Allen wore.
>
> "You're the man of the family now," she said. "You have to dress like a gentleman. . . ."
>
> On the journey to church she instructed me in how a proper man must walk with a woman. "A gentleman always walks on the outside," she explained, maneuvering me to the curb edge on the sidewalk. If in childish excitement I dashed ahead of her and ran through a door she called me back for another lesson in manhood: "The man always opens the door for a woman and holds it so she can go first."
>
> In her urgency to hasten me into manhood my mother did not neglect Doris, but I was unaware that Doris was not expected to take up the heavy burdens someday that I was. It was enough for my mother to enroll Doris in dancing classes. Dancing was an asset for a girl. Eventually it might help her find the husband a woman needed for survival. Doris was taught the arts of housekeeping: washing dishes, setting the table, making beds, dusting.

Source: Russell Baker, *Growing Up*.

Our Past Experiences

Our self-confidence and many of our perceptions come from our past experiences. On a very simple level, a child who says a bad word in front of his parents learns very quickly that some language is inappropriate. If his experience is very negative—his parents spank him, for example—he might be careful before he uses any other new words in their presence. He reasons that if he was spanked because he used this word, other words might lead to similar punishment.

Through our experience we decide what we will risk and what we will stay away from. Picture the junior high student going to her first dance. She has a new dress and has spent several hours getting ready. She is excited about what will happen at the dance, and she can't wait to get there. Once she is

---

CONSIDER THIS

Children Learn What They Live

If a child lives with criticism
he learns to condemn.
If a child lives with hostility
he learns to fight.
If a child lives with ridicule
he learns to be shy.
If a child lives with shame
he learns to feel guilty.
If a child lives with tolerance
he learns to be patient.
If a child lives with encouragement
he learns confidence.

If a child lives with praise
he learns to appreciate.
If a child lives with fairness
he learns justice.
If a child lives with security
he learns to have faith.
If a child lives with approval
he learns to like himself.
If a child lives with acceptance and friendship
he learns to find love in the world.

—Dorothy Law Nolte

Whether we choose to risk encounters with our peers depends on our previous experience. Rejection can lead to shyness and withdrawal.

there, however, no one asks her to dance and hardly anyone even talks to her. When her girlfriend asks her to go to the next dance, she refuses. After her experience she is not willing to take another risk.

But our perceptions do not always remain the same: they might change greatly from the time when we are children to when we grow into adults. To a child a carnival seems like a wonderful place—full of bright lights and exciting things to do. The child tells her mother that when she grows up, she is going to go to every carnival she can. When she is grown, however, her perception changes: now the carnival seems tawdry and tacky.

Our past experiences can be both good and bad. Whatever they are, they influence our perception of life and the world around us. What we do, say, think, and believe will, in many cases, be influenced by our past.

OUR PERCEPTIONS OF OTHERS

The Perceptual Process

Picture this scene. Dan and Jean sit next to each other in class. They have several interests in common, including an interest in each other. Each would like to see the other outside of class, but neither has made a move in that direction. Now they find themselves in the student center at the same time. Dan sees Jean sitting alone at a table, so he joins her. As they talk casually about the weather and the assignments they have for their class, completely different thoughts are going through their heads. Dan is thinking: "I really would like to ask her out to the movies. I wonder if she would go with me. I'd feel pretty bad if she turned me down." Jean's thinking is taking a similar line. She thinks: "He really is a nice guy. I'd like to get to know him better, but he is so shy. I think he likes me, but I'm really not sure."

Although Dan and Jean's conversation and thoughts seem to be somewhat ordinary, they are going through a very complicated perceptual process. On one level, what Dan is saying and thinking reflects how he feels about himself. ("In this situation, I am feeling somewhat insecure.") On another level, it reflects how he feels about Jean. ("I like her and I would like to know her better.") On yet a third level, they are influenced by how he thinks Jean sees him. ("I think she likes me but I'm not sure.") Jean is going through a similar perceptual process. Her thoughts and what she says are influenced by how she sees herself, how she perceives Dan, and how she thinks Dan perceives her.

Like Dan and Jean, whenever we have a conversation with another person, we go through the same six-step perceptual process:

1. How I see myself

2. How I see you

3. How I think you see me

4. How you see yourself

5. How you see me

6. How you think I see you[4]

These six perceptual levels are useful in explaining why we communicate better with some people than with others. If your perception of me is basically the same as my perception of myself, we have a better chance of communicating. However, if your perception of me is greatly different from my perception of myself, we are probably not going to communicate very effectively.

When Perceptions Don't Match

Let's look at these levels in a practical example. Jay Brown, a student, is taking a class from Professor Black. How do they perceive themselves and each other?

SELF-PERCEPTION

Jay Brown: Sees himself as a good student. Studies two or three hours a night. Has a 3.1 grade average.

Professor Black: Sees himself as a hard-working professor. Prides himself on preparing material students can understand.

HOW THEY SEE EACH OTHER

Jay Brown: Sees Professor Black as a hard teacher. Believes Black is rigid and unsympathetic to students.

Professor Black: Because he saw Jay Brown falling asleep in class one day, he assumes Jay is lazy and unmotivated.

HOW HE THINKS THE OTHER SEES HIM

Jay Brown: I don't think he likes me very much. Whenever I try to ask a question in class, he seems to ignore me.

Professor Black: If this student sleeps in my class, he must think I'm pretty boring.

Sometimes we aren't able to check out our perceptions of others. If Jay manages to pass the class, he makes it a point never to take another class from Professor Black. Let's assume, however, that Jay has failed an exam and has to talk to Professor Black. Based on their perceptions of themselves and each other, their conversation might go something like this:

Jay: I am having a lot of trouble in your class. The material is hard and I can't seem to do very well on your exams.

Professor: The material is hard. You're probably not studying enough. You can't just skim the book and hope to do well on the exams.

Jay: I study for this class every day. I probably could understand the book better if the lectures were clearer.

Professor: You can always ask questions in class.

Jay: I am so confused I don't even know what questions to ask.

Professor: Well, all I can say is that you should study more.

Jay and Professor Black have reached a dead end. Each entered into the communication with negative perceptions of the other, and these perceptions were reinforced during the communication. Each gave the other a negative message (Jay that the lectures are not clear; Professor Black that Jay doesn't study hard enough).

But if something had happened in their conversation to change their perceptions of each other? Let's go back to where Jay says: "I am so confused I don't even know what questions to ask." Professor Black changes his reply to: "You might understand more if you could manage to stay awake in class." Now Jay has some information of how he is perceived by Professor Black. Jay thinks for a minute and says, "Oh, I remember. Remember that day when we had the big rain? The basement of our house flooded, and I was moving furniture out of there all night. You're right. I did fall asleep in class. I'm sorry."

Professor Black now has new information about Jay, and he decides to accept it as legitimate information. As his perception of Jay (as a lazy student) begins to change, he tries harder to help Jay with his problems in the class. He asks Jay if he has his lecture notes with him, and Jay hands him the notes. Professor Black is impressed with their thoroughness, but he realizes that Jay is writing down too much information and has a problem distinguishing major points from minor ones. He spends some time explaining to Jay how to take better notes. Jay is so quick to respond and understand that Professor Black's perception of him becomes more and more positive and he begins to see Jay in the way Jay sees himself. The result of the conversation is that both of them leave it feeling better about themselves and each other. A couple of months later, when someone asks Jay if she should take a class from Professor Black, Jay responds: "He's a good teacher. I really learned a lot from him."

We get along better with people when they see us in much the same way as we see ourselves. Thus our image of our friends is similar to how they see themselves, and they are likely to see us as we see ourselves. In each case, both parties largely approve of what they see.[5]

In marriage as in friendship, similar attitudes and values contribute to close ties.

CHECKING OUT YOUR PERCEPTIONS

When we have problems communicating with or liking other people, much of the problem is likely to be perceptual. We see them differently from how they see themselves; we think they see us in an unfavorable way. If their perceptual view of the world is much different from ours, we will probably have trouble finding common ground for a relationship.

Sometimes it doesn't matter how we perceive others and how they perceive us because our lives do not connect enough for it to make any difference. It doesn't matter, for example, if the local supermarket manager regards you as a spendthrift—the only time you see him is when you do your grocery shopping. In other cases, when getting along with someone is important to our happiness or livelihood, it is worthwhile to check out our perceptions.

A good deal of miscommunication can occur because people do not understand messages in the way they were intended. When a misunderstanding occurs, you will learn a lot if you check out your message with the other person. There are lots of ways in which messages can go astray.

Often it's a matter of people using language incorrectly or imprecisely. For example, if someone tells you a movie was "awesome," it is not very clear what that person means. If a student tells you that Professor Nelson is "hard," that person's meaning of "hard" might be different from your own. If you want to understand what these people are saying, it would be a good idea to ask for clarification.

Sometimes people seem to be sending us negative messages about ourselves. Let's say that you have a class where you often raise your hand but your teacher seldom calls on you. When this happens you are probably going to think the teacher doesn't like you or doesn't like the answers you give. Before you jump to this conclusion, however, it might be a good idea to ask the teacher something like this: "Do you think I am in trouble with this class? I often raise my hand but you don't call on me." The teacher might explain that because you are out of her direct eye range, she hasn't even noticed you. Not only has this answer relieved your anxiety about the class, but the problem is easily solved—you just have to change your seat. In another case if you are not getting along with someone but you can't put your finger on what is wrong, it would probably be useful to say something like this: "We don't seem to be communicating very well. Have I said something that offended you?"

Sometimes it helps to check out our perceptions with other people. For example, Jane and Mary are talking about their boss and Jane says, "I like working for her, but she doesn't explain things very well." Mary replies, "You're right about that. She explained this computer program to me three times, and I still didn't understand it. When I asked you about it, you were able to explain it in five minutes." After finding that someone else shares her perceptions, Jane no longer feels that she is always to blame when she doesn't understand something. However, you might get a different perception when you compare notes. For example, when Gerry complains that Ted often hurt her feelings, Bob replies, "I know. A lot of people feel that way. But it's only Ted's way of joking. He would be upset if he thought he made you feel bad." Gerry has discovered that her perception of Ted might have been wrong, and she now has a new and more favorable perception of him.

IMPROVING YOUR SELF-CONCEPT

The most difficult thing any human being can do is to change his or her sense of self-worth for the better. In fact, many of us do not want to change at all. What we have is a known factor; the unknown seems filled with dangers.

The Need for Psychological Safety

For most people, **psychological safety**—the approval and support that we get from people we love, admire, and respect—is an important need. Our safety needs prompt us to seek out people who approve of us while avoiding people and situations we see as potentially hostile and threatening. For example, many people feel great anxiety when they are going to give a speech. Although they feel safe talking to friends and colleagues, the thought of facing an audience is very threatening because there is no assurance of getting the psychological support they need. A person's need for safety may determine an entire life style. If you go to a restaurant, do you try something new on the menu, or do you stick with meat and potatoes? Do you make an attempt to meet new people with new ideas, or do you prefer to stay with old friends?

Most human beings will live a more fulfilling life if they have a chance to grow. A child continues to try to walk even though she falls many times. Her need to grow is greater than her need to feel safe. If we were afraid of growth, we would never travel to new places or meet new people; in fact we would probably never leave our homes.

Abraham Maslow was a psychologist who emphasized self-fulfillment. He realized that the needs for safety and growth pull us in opposite directions (as shown in Figure 2-1).[6] In Maslow's view, people who feel emotionally safe and secure are willing to take greater **psychological risks**. For example, a person who feels sure of herself is more likely to go after a better job or complain to her boss about the problems on the present job. Although doing either of these things might involve risk, they are worth doing because they lead to personal growth. In this case, she might get a better job or improve her working conditions. Even if she is not successful, she might learn something from the experience and know better how to go about it the next time.

People who do not feel safe, however, are afraid of taking any kind of risk. For example, many people who have become unemployed are unwilling to take the risk of going to a new community to look for something else. The old community is familiar and safe; they are afraid to risk a place they are not familiar with. These people, because of their needs of safety, are unable to attain the personal growth that a new community and a new job might bring.

Growth and risk taking are essential ingredients of improved self-esteem. People who have problems with self-esteem are usually stuck in some kind of rut. They stick with the familiar: the same people and the same places. They never have a chance to improve their self-esteem because they never put themselves into new situations. On the other hand, people who try new things and are successful, even moderately successful, feel better about themselves.

How to Improve Your Self-Esteem

Self-esteem, the value you put on yourself, is a matter of taking risks. How do you go about doing this without getting yourself in serious trouble? Here are some suggestions that might help you.

FIGURE **2-1** **The needs for psychological safety and personal growth pull us in opposite directions.**

Safety ⟩——————————⟨ Person ⟩——————————⟨ Growth

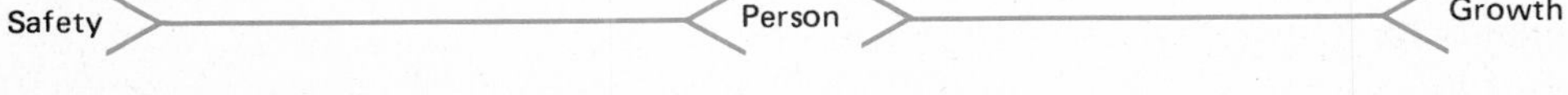

Decide What You Want to Change About Yourself

Pick one area in which you would like to improve yourself and, hence, your self-esteem. See if you can figure out why you have had problems in this area. Were you given a script saying you were inadequate? Are you living out a self-fulfilling prophecy?

Consider Your Circumstances

Are you living in circumstances that are holding you back? Do the people around you support you in risk taking? Sometimes the people we live with try to hold us back—even though they might not be conscious they are doing so. Tutors who teach adults how to read often discover that a student's spouse is working against him or her. One husband said, for example, "Why do you need to read the newspaper? I'll tell you what's important."

Sometimes we are locked into roles that are uncomfortable for us. Many women feel trapped when their children are small; some people hate their jobs; some students hate school. Are you in a role that you have chosen for yourself, or has someone else chosen it for you? Has someone else defined how you should play this role? Can you play this role in a way that it will be more comfortable for you? Can you change the role so it fits better with your self-concept?

If we are playing roles that don't work for us, we must find a way to change them or to drop them if we are going to feel better about ourselves. When we are in relationships and situations that hold us back, we sometimes have to make difficult choices. If we want something badly enough, we might have to break off the relationship. This is a situation where we might have to take a big risk and move away from psychological safety.

Set Reasonable Goals

Too often, people decide they are going to change their behavior overnight. Students who have done poorly in their grades will often announce that this semester they are going to get all A's. This is an unreasonable goal.

If you are going to try to change your behavior, see if you can break the problem down into pieces you can handle. Let's say that you are shy but you would like to speak up in class more because you often know the answers. Why not set a goal to speak up once a week in one class? That is probably a goal you can manage. Once you feel comfortable with that, you might increase it to two or even three times a week. If you keep increasing the times, you will probably find yourself overcoming some of your shyness.

Pick People Who Will Support You

Whenever we are going to try to bring about a change in ourselves, it is very useful to surround ourselves with people who will support us. These are people who understand how difficult it is to change and who understand our

TRY THIS

Among the following examples, choose one that applies to you:

- You leave everything until the last minute. You stay up all night because you have to read the textbook for a test or have to write a term paper. You really don't enjoy your leisure time because you're always feeling guilty about work you haven't done.
- You are out of shape and you don't like to exercise, but you really think you should—especially when you see your friends jogging or going for a workout at the gym.
- You have a bad habit you want to break. You have had this habit for a long time and have always thought you should do something about it.

   Now, let's assume you would feel better about yourself if you could change your behavior in one of these examples. See if you can answer the following questions:

1. Why do you have this behavior? Is it part of a script you were given when you were young? Does it have anything to do with any of the roles you play?
2. If you were going to change this behavior, would any of your friends or family be upset? Do they influence this behavior in any way?
3. What would be a reasonable goal to set in changing this behavior? Can you really try to pursue this goal—week after week and month after month? If you don't think you can, do you think you should set a more modest goal?
4. What people do you know who might be able to support you in this goal? Are you willing to tell them what you want to do? What people might have a negative influence? Is there a way you can deal with them while trying to reach your goal?
5. If you can accomplish your goal, how will you feel about yourself? Will reaching this goal improve your self-concept?

need to do so. Let's take the example of speaking up in class. If you are very apprehensive about doing this, you might consider discussing the problem with an instructor you like and trust. Tell him that you are occasionally going to try to say something, and ask for his support. Also tell a couple of your friends in your class what you are going to try to do. Just having other people know what you are trying to do is often good moral support.

   When we want to change, it's important to pick our supporters carefully. It is also important that we tell them what we want to do and give them some direction on how they can help us. All of us find it easier to make changes in our lives when we get support from others. Asking others for support is also a way of reaching out and letting people know they are important to us.

SUMMARY

Each of us perceives events, people, and things somewhat differently from others. How we perceive the world depends on our knowledge and on our experience.

The self-concept each of us has is made up of conclusions we draw about the way we act and think. It determines how we look at the world and those around us. Self-concept will determine what we notice and what we ignore. Both self-concept and perception are subjective.

The development of perception and self-concept is determined by several factors. First is the body each of us is born with. Second is what others tell us about ourself. This is done in the form of roles, scripts, and self-fulfilling prophecies. A role is how we behave in a particular situation; a script is the lines we say when we play the role; and self-fulfilling prophecies are predictions that come true because we (and others) predict them.

Our perception of others, and theirs of us, is a six-step perceptual process that involves (1) how I see myself, (2) how I see you, (3) how I think you see me, (4) how you see yourself, (5) how you see me, and (6) how you think I see you. Part of understanding communication is understanding how each of these steps work.

A self-concept can be improved, but it involves taking risks rather than seeking safe territory. If you want to make changes in your life, the following steps are useful: decide what you want to change about yourself; consider your circumstances; set reasonable goals; pick people who will support you.

VOCABULARY

The following is a list of words you must know to understand the concepts in this chapter. You will find the words defined the first time that each is used in the chapter. All Vocabulary words also appear, with their definitions, in the Glossary at the end of the book.

perceptions	self-concept
psychological risk	self-esteem
psychological safety	self-fulfilling prophecies
scripts	social conditioning

FURTHER READING

CARR, JACQUELYN B. *Communicating with Myself: A Journal*. Dubuque, Iowa: Brown, 1984. The value of this book is in the wealth of exploratory ways that Carr offers readers for becoming better acquainted with aspects of themselves that are often hidden from consciousness. Carr includes chapters on perception and the self-concept as well as other aspects of communication.

CENTI, PAUL J. *Up with the Positive, Out with the Negative: How to Like the Person You Are*. Englewood Cliffs, N.J.: Prentice-Hall, 1981. Centi offers a practical guide to understanding and breaking the patterns of negative thinking and behavior that stem from a poor self-concept. More than half of his chapters treat the self-concept directly.

DOLAN, EDWARD F., JR. *Be Your Own Man: A Step-by-Step Guide to Thinking and Acting Independently.* Englewood Cliffs, N.J.: Prentice-Hall, 1984. This book is addressed exclusively to men and the problems they share in the area of independence. However, women are likely to find general points that will be helpful in their lives, too. This is a practical, personal book.

GALLOWAY, DALE E. *Dare to Discipline Yourself.* Old Tappan, N.J.: Revell, 1984. Galloway helps us gain control of our life—our health and energy, anger, moods, habits, and finances. Using clear explanations and colorful examples, Galloway shows us how to gain self-control.

HAMACHEK, DON E. *Encounters with the Self*, 2nd ed. New York: Holt, Rinehart and Winston, 1978. This is a book about self-concept—how it grows, changes, and expresses itself in behavior. Hamachek's assumption is that the better we know ourselves, the more able we will be to forget ourselves. It is a readable aid in facilitating self-awareness.

HARRIS, THOMAS A. *I'm OK, You're OK: A Practical Guide to Transactional Analysis.* New York: Harper & Row, 1969. Harris applies the P-A-C system (parent, adult, and child), or transactional analysis, to marriage and child-rearing concerns, mental retardation, violence, student revolt, racial prejudice, creativity, adolescence, religion, and international problems, including war. Harris confronts readers with the fact that they are responsible for what happens in the future, no matter what has happened in the past. The book is very readable and enjoyable.

JAMES, MURIEL, AND DOROTHY JONGEWARD. *Born to Win: Transactional Analysis with Gestalt Experiments.* Reading, Mass.: Addison-Wesley, 1971. The authors provide a rational method for analyzing and understanding behavior. Their insights and examples help readers discover and foster awareness, self-responsibility, and genuineness. This readable book is full of interesting, useful examples.

LAING, R. D., H. PHILLIPSON, AND A. R. LEE. *Interpersonal Perception: A Theory and a Method of Research.* New York: Harper & Row, 1966. The authors focus on the experiences, perceptions, and actions of two human beings as they meet and become acquainted. Although intended for the advanced, serious student, the book is rewarding for anyone interested in a technique for studying two-person human relations.

PARKER, ROLLAND S. *Self-Image Psycho-Dynamics: Rewriting Your Life Script.* Englewood Cliffs, N.J.: Prentice-Hall, 1983. Parker's thesis is that by knowing yourself better, particularly those qualities that make you unique, you will become more effective. He offers readers specific ways for clarifying and modifying their self-image. The book is full of quizzes, questionnaires, and examples.

VISCOTT, DAVID. *Risking.* New York: Pocket Books, 1977. Viscott's thesis is that if your life is going to get better, you'll have to take risks. This book is a guide to help you understand exactly what happens whenever you take a risk. Viscott includes steps for successful risk taking, ways to deal with troublesome feelings, and procedures for managing potentially risk-filled situations. The book contains much useful and practical material.

3 LISTENING

CHAPTER OUTLINE

Why Listen?

The Process of Listening
 Predictions and assessment
 Receiving messages
 Attending
 Assigning meaning
 Remembering

Attitudes Toward Listening
 Poor listening habits
 Active listening

Listening for Information
 Identifying the main idea
 Identifying supporting material
 Forming a mental outline
 Predicting what will come next

 Relating points to your experience
 Looking for similarities and differences
 Questioning and paraphrasing

Critical Listening
 Determining the speaker's motives
 Challenging and questioning ideas
 Distinguishing fact from opinion
 Recognizing our own biases
 Assessing the message

Reflective Listening
 Listening for feelings
 Negative listening responses
 The reflective listening response

Listening for Enjoyment

CHAPTER OBJECTIVES

After reading this chapter, you should be able to:

1. Explain why listening is important.
2. Identify and explain the various parts of the listening process.
3. List the benefits of active listening.
4. Understand the meaning of listening for information and how to improve your skills in listening for information.
5. Understand the meaning of critical listening and how to improve your skills in critical listening.
6. Understand the meaning of reflective listening and how to improve your skills in reflective listening.
7. Understand the meaning of listening for enjoyment and how to improve your skills in listening for enjoyment.

WHY LISTEN?

If you were to keep a log of how much time you spend listening, you would probably be surprised to discover that in a typical day it is your main communication activity. On a school day you probably get up in the morning to the sound of your clock radio. As you are getting dressed, you listen for the temperature so you know how to dress. You have a conversation with your roommate, in which you play the role of both speaker and listener. If you eat breakfast, you have the same dual roles with the people at your table. In class, about 90 percent of your time is spent listening to the instructor. If you stop to discuss a grade on a paper with an instructor, you probably end up listening more than talking.

After classes are over, you talk to your friends—some face-to-face and some on the telephone. You turn on your stereo as you settle down to study, and some of your attention is given to the music. If you turn on the television, you listen with even more attention. Finally, you go to bed—again listening to your radio.

In the day just described, you were surrounded by messages demanding your attention. If you had listened to every one of them, you would be so overwhelmed you would not be able to function. In fast-moving American society, we all suffer from message overload—exposure to more messages than we can process. The average American, for example, is exposed to 900,000 advertising messages each year, and most of these messages are designed to be listened to. If we listened carefully to even one-tenth of these messages, we would not have time to do anything else. The mass media also offer us all kinds of diverting and entertaining messages. In the average American household, the television set is on over six hours a day; the radio, between two and three hours a day. In addition, the average student probably has enough records or cassettes to listen to them for an entire day without ever repeating a single one.

If you are relaxing in the student union, there are many sounds to be heard: the clatter of dishes, noise from the video games, bits and pieces of various conversations. Sitting in class, in addition to the instructor's voice, you hear a lawnmower outside the classroom window, faculty members having a conversation outside the door, and two students whispering right behind you.

You may also be experiencing psychological noise as you try to listen. In your 11 o'clock class you are thinking about lunch. In your afternoon class you are thinking about what you are going to do in the evening. You are wondering if you got any mail today, and you are thinking about how well you played in that last baseball game. Will your parents send you more money if you ask? Should you go to the fraternity party—even if you have a big test tomorrow?

With all these distractions, it's not surprising that many of us are poor listeners. Yet most of us would not admit to being poor listeners, we would only admit to "mislistening" from time to time. How, then, can we tell if we have a serious problem in listening?

One way to get at the question of how well you listen is to ask yourself the following questions about your listening behavior: Have you done any class assignment incorrectly while the rest of the class did it correctly? Have you asked an instructor to reexplain an assignment he or she gave to the class? Did anyone tell you where to find something and you couldn't find it? Have you been lost because you didn't follow directions someone gave you? Have your classmates laughed at you when you asked a question that had just been answered? Have you missed an appointment because you got there at the wrong time? Has anyone accused you of not listening? Have you said to anyone, "I don't want to talk about it (when you really meant "I don't want to listen to your point of view")?

If you answer yes to one or more of these questions, you are a person who is not listening as well as you could. The next question, then, is what can you do about it?

Listening is a skill that can be learned. Although listening is often taught in the elementary grades, it is unfortunately ignored as students go on to higher grades. Figure 3-1 shows the percentage of time we devote to the four communication skills: listening, speaking, reading, and writing. Although we spend the greatest amount of time in listening, it is the skill that is taught the least.[1]

Listening, like any skill, has to be practiced. Because we listen every day we think we know how to do it. Yet, like any skill, we can learn to do it better. We can continue to improve our listening skills throughout our lives.[2] In fact, when researchers polled 450 graduates of business programs as to what kind

FIGURE 3-1 Percentage of Time Devoted to Various Communication Skills

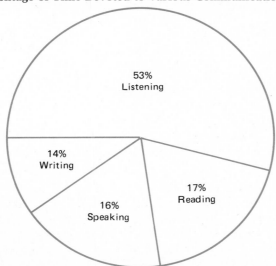

CONSIDER THIS

"While the right to talk may be the beginning of freedom, the necessity of listening is what makes the right important."

—Walter Lippman

TRY THIS

Stop what you are doing right now. Listen carefully for three minutes. While you are listening, list all the sounds you can hear. Whether they are as small as the ticking of a clock or the whirring of a blow dryer down the hall or as large as an airplane flying overhead or construction work somewhere nearby, list them all. Birds singing, people talking, a radio playing, dogs barking, someone yelling— these are all possible sounds of our immediate environment. And these are all messages to which we could listen. Have you ever thought of them as messages? No wonder you are sometimes distracted from your work!

of communication skills they needed on the job, they responded that listening was the most important skill for success in one's job. When they were asked what communication skill they wished they had been taught in college, listening ranked number one.[3]

THE PROCESS OF LISTENING

Predictions and Assessment

When we speak of listening as a process, we mean it is ongoing, that is, not confined to the actual time when we are engaged in it. Before we go into a listening situation, we make **predictions** about what will occur. Before going to a class where we don't like the subject, for example, we might predict that the class will be boring but that we will have to pay attention and take careful notes in order to pass the test. Our listening behavior, then, is based on our predictions.

When we leave the class, we engage in **assessment**—an evaluation of what occurred. We might have a sense of satisfaction because we paid attention and took careful notes. On the other hand, we might feel upset because we didn't pay attention and will do badly on the test that is coming up. In the latter case, after assessing the situation, we might vow to do better and listen more carefully the next time.

The listener predicts what will happen *before* the listening event takes place and assesses what has happened *after* the event. What happens *during* the listening event? As you can see in Figure 3-2, actual listening has four stages: receiving messages, attending to them, assigning meaning to them, and remembering them. In an ideal listening situation, all of these stages will be completed. If listening is ineffective, however, the process might break down at any stage. Let us look at each of these stages.

FIGURE **3-2 The Listening Process   At any step in the process, information may be lost. For example, our auditory system can handle only a certain number of stimuli; we can attend to only a portion of what we hear; we can assign just so many meanings; and there is a limit to how much we can remember.**

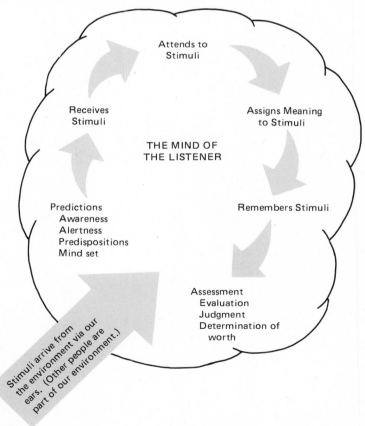

CONSIDER THIS

"Hearing is one of the body's five senses. But listening is an art."

—Frank Tyger

Receiving Messages

In any one day, all of us receive far more messages than we need or can process. Some of these messages we mentioned earlier: commercials, someone shouting in the hallway, a lawnmower's drone, an instructor's lecture, a conversation with a friend. We *hear* many of these messages but we do not *listen* to all of them.

Hearing is done with the ears; **listening**, however, involves responding intellectually and emotionally. We hear sounds—such as words and the way they are spoken—but when we listen, we respond to far more. It is as if hearing is a mechanical process involving the various parts of the ear, whereas listening is a more composite perceptual process involving our total response to others, with spoken words being just a part of what we respond to.

Thus receiving messages does not involve hearing alone. Messages come in all forms and from a variety of sources. When we listen, we filter out the irrelevant ones—which brings us to the next step in the listening process, that of attending to what we consider important or interesting.

Attending

We are able to focus our perception on a particular stimulus. A mother, for example, may hear several noisy things occurring around the house. The garbage men are picking up the trash, the radio is on, and she is rattling pots and pans in the kitchen. When she hears the baby cry, however, she focuses her perception on that one event and blocks out all other noise.

The ability to focus perception—called **selective attention**—is quite extraordinary. For generations parents have told their children that they can't possibly concentrate on studying with the television set or stereo blaring away in the background. If you like to study that way, too, you will think that these parents are wrong—and research will support you. In one study, listeners were seated in the middle of four loudspeakers, all with different messages, and were told to pay attention to the message coming from only one particular speaker. In all cases, listeners were able to show an almost perfect performance in recalling the message from that speaker.[4]

Although we are able to focus our attention in very specific ways, our attention span is very short. Generally people can give full attention to a message for no more than 20 seconds.[5] Something in the message reminds us of something else, or we don't like the message and let our minds wander in a completely different direction. Fortunately we are quickly able to refocus our attention on the message, but every listener and speaker should be aware of just how elusive attention is.

Several other factors may determine how much attention we give to messages. First, we must be receptive to the speaker. We all experience occasions when we don't have time to listen. There are also occasions when we didn't want to listen. Children often do not want to listen to their parents; teachers often do not want to listen to their students. Without a receptive attitude to the speaker, however, no attention will take place and, hence, no listening.

Another factor affecting attention is mental alertness. There are days when we are too tired or too preoccupied to listen carefully to other people. When we are tired, it is especially difficult to focus our attention. Under these circumstances, we choose to listen only to messages that are easy and do not challenge us. Or we might be so preoccupied that we are unable to listen. For example, you might not hear a thing if you were trying to remember if you left your car lights on.

Psychological state affects attention. How open are we to messages we don't want to hear? Every teacher has had the experience of students who do not want to listen to criticism of their work—it is too threatening to their sense of self-esteem. All of us tune out messages that are threatening to us by refusing to give these messages our attention.

Assigning Meaning

When we decide to attend to a message, our next step is to *assign it meaning*. This involves assimilating the message—making it part of our knowledge and experience. To assign meaning we must decide what in the message is relevant and how it relates to what we already know. Basically, then, the process of assigning meaning is one of selecting material and trying to relate it to our experience. In assigning meaning we also evaluate. We weigh what the speaker has said against the personal beliefs we hold, we question the speaker's motives, we wonder what has been omitted, and we challenge the validity of the ideas.

Remembering

The final step in the listening process is *remembering*. Again, remembering is a selective process of determining what is important and what is not. As students, few of you would record the whole of an instructor's lecture. Instead you take notes that help you remember the important points. Tests also help you remember important information. Research studies have shown that students remember more when they know they will be graded on the material.[6]

For effective listening to take place, all of these stages must be passed through. It is easy, however, to give the appearance of listening without listening at all. Many people master the art of looking attentive and interested without hearing a word that is being said. And as a student, you probably know that it is possible to take notes without understanding what the instructor is talking about.

The extent to which you complete the steps involved in the listening process will depend on who and what you are listening to as well as how important the information is to you. You are not an effective listener in every situation, and because you are listening so much, you probably could not be. You have to make judgments about worth and about costs and rewards—how much it will cost you in time and effort to listen effectively, and what the benefits are likely to be.

ATTITUDES TOWARD LISTENING

Many people go into a listening situation and think they are listening, but instead they are doing something that is causing interference with the listening process. Many of us are less-than-perfect listeners. Poor listeners often have bad listening habits.

Poor Listening Habits

The Lazy Listener

Some people believe that listening involves no work. Their attitude is, "I don't have to do anything. I can just sit back and listen." These listeners are often found in a classroom. They hear what the instructor says and may even take pages and pages of notes. At exam time, however, they do poorly because they haven't tried to *understand* what was said.

The Take-Turns Listener

Some people don't really want to listen, but they know it is expected of them so they appear to be listening. In reality, they are paying no attention at all. They are only interested when it's their turn to talk.

The Insecure Listener

Some people are so insecure that when they are talking to someone, they are worried about what they will say next. Because they're concentrating on their own anxiety, they usually don't hear what the other person is saying.

The Self-Centered Listener

Some people listen only for messages about themselves. When they hear such a message, they perk up and listen. If the subject is about someone or something else, they lose interest.

The Competitive Listener

Some people regard listening as a competition. If you tell them that you own a 20-pound cat, they will tell you about someone who owns a 25-pound cat. If you tell them you're going to Spain, they will tell you that you really should go to Spain *and* Portugal to make the trip worthwhile.

Active Listening

The way to break all bad listening habits is to become a good **active listener**. You are an active listener when you make a mental outline of important points and think up questions or challenges to the points that have been made. Even though you might not say anything, you are mentally involved with the person who is talking.

People who are active listeners receive greater rewards. As students they get better grades than **passive listeners**, who record but do not evaluate what

Paul Nader's classic photo from the Art of Living a Hundred Years *shows (at left) a very active 100-year-old man—active too at listening. His posture indicates that he is an aggressive listener.*

CONSIDER THIS

In an experiment conducted by F. E. Abel at Stanford University, two matched groups of students listened to a seven-minute taped interview regarding an off-shore oil leak. One group took extensive notes; the other group took none whatsoever. Each had 40 minutes in which to write a story after listening to the interview. It was found that the group taking no notes omitted some 26 percent of the "units of meaning" from their stories (as compared with 21 percent in the other group), but they also made only about one-third as many errors as did the notetakers. Thus, notetaking should not be so profuse as to interfere with the simple act of listening attentively—the interviewer's first function.

Source: John Brady, *The Craft of Interviewing.*

they hear. In fact, one of the authors of this text had an experience that illustrates this point very well. She was teaching a class where she lectured on a good deal of material that was completely unfamiliar to students. She noticed, with some annoyance, that one student in the class did not take a single note—he didn't even bring anything to class to take notes with. She also noticed, however, that the student was listening carefully. He often asked questions to help him clarify and interpret the material. When the time came for examinations, it was clear this student was an active listener—on all exams he had the highest score in the class. Although most students would consider it very risky to give up note taking in class, this illustration demonstrates that careful listening has a definite advantage over slavishly recording everything the instructor says.

Because active listeners focus on the subject, they are not so easily distracted. All of us can think much faster than we hear. The difference between thinking and hearing might be as much as 400 words a minute.[7] If we use this time gap to distract ourselves, we can easily lose track of what is being said. Our other option is to use this time to think about what is being said and to listen actively to the speaker.

Active listening also helps to avoid boredom. We are more likely to be bored if we are observing rather than participating in an event. Active listening is a way of involving yourself, and once you are involved, you are likely to get interested. If you use active listening techniques when you listen to a lecture, you might be surprised to find how quickly the time passes.

Active listening, then, involves active participation on the part of the listener. An active listener, however, does not listen in the same way in every listening experience. There are four basic listening experiences you can have, and they all involve different listening skills. These experiences are listening

TRY THIS

Have you ever thought that a class might be giving you difficulty because you are not listening properly? Test this out by selecting your hardest class and keeping a listening log for one week. Throughout the class period, note times of active and passive listening. List each time when you stopped listening actively and what you were thinking about at that time.

At the end of the week, answer the following questions:

- What was the average length of your attention span?
- What was the most common reason for your distraction?
- Did keeping the log make you aware of your listening behavior and therefore more attentive as the week went on?
- Did the differences between active and passive listening become clear?

for information, listening critically, listening reflectively, and listening for enjoyment. Let's consider each of these.

LISTENING FOR INFORMATION

Any college student will find that most of the time in classes is spent in listening and this listening is primarily for information. Listening to the instructor talk about the reasons for the Civil War, the economic structure of the broadcast industry, or the definition of a paranoid are all examples of listening for information.

The business world also requires people to listen for information. The secretary listening as her boss tells her to type a letter, the customer listening as the salesperson tells her what is stocked in the warehouse, a shipping clerk listening as she is told to ship 100 boxes to Omaha—all are examples of listening for information. In business, listening can be seen in dollars-and-cents terms. The Sperry Corporation has pointed out that if each of the 100 million U.S. workers made a $10 listening error, the total cost would be $1 billion![8]

Even when it is critical to listen well, some people don't do it. Researchers who tested jurors on how well they understood crucial instructions about the law discovered that only 40 percent correctly applied the rules for circumstantial evidence.[9] Not listening carefully to the rules of circumstantial evidence could result in an unjust life sentence or even death for the accused.

Identifying the Main Idea

What, then, should be our approach to listening for information? If we are listening to a speech or to a lecture, our first approach should be to listen for and identify the **main idea**—the central main thought that runs through the passage. Then we are listening for **supporting points**—the materials that reinforce the main point. It is important that we identify the main idea because all of the other points will relate to it. Identifying the main idea also aids memory. If we remember the main idea, then the supporting points will follow. If we remember only the latter, we will have unrelated points that make no sense; and because they make no sense, we will more easily forget them.

In recent years, trivia has become popular on college campuses. When listening to a speech or lecture, however, it is important not to be distracted by trivia—especially at the expense of forgetting the main idea. Let's suppose, for example, you are listening to a lecture about Louis XIV and the women in his life. One piece of trivia you might hear is that Louis' wife, Maria Theresa, clapped her hands before her ladies-in-waiting whenever Louis spent a night with her. This is such an odd and amusing piece of trivia that you will find no difficulty remembering it. The question you must ask, however, is what does this example say about Louis' relationship to his wife? Does it mean that he so seldom spent a night with her that she had to applaud whenever it happened? Does it mean he didn't like his wife and spent time with her out of a sense of duty? Does it mean that he was spending time elsewhere? With other women? Most important, what does it mean in relation to the speaker's subject?

Identifying Supporting Material

Once you have identified the main point of the lecture or the speech, your next step is to look for the material that supports the main idea. The purpose of supporting points is to build evidence for the main point. Supporting points often consist of illustrations and examples that make the main idea clearer to the listener. Let's suppose that a speaker is explaining why the legislature has passed a law requiring that children be strapped into car seats. Her main idea would be that children who are not strapped into these seats have a much greater chance of being killed or seriously injured if the car is involved in an accident. One supporting point she might give is actual figures about children killed in accidents who were not strapped into car seats. Another supporting point might be the number of strapped in children who were able to survive accidents. By way of illustration, she might describe an accident where a child was actually killed.

Forming a Mental Outline

When you are listening to a speech, your job is to form a mental outline. You identify the main idea and then you listen for the supporting points. The idea and its supporting points are the ones to remember. The illustrations are examples that function to help you remember the supporting points better. In the overall organization of the speech, however, the examples are merely trivia. If you remember only the details of how the child was killed and do not remember *why* the child was killed, you were not listening well.

Predicting What Will Come Next

Earlier we discussed the role of prediction in the listening process. When we are listening for information, it helps us to focus our attention by predicting what is coming next. Once we hear the speaker's main point in the above example, we might logically predict that she is going to give us figures about children involved in accidents. Prediction might seem difficult, but we do it all the time. The next time you are listening to a joke, notice how much predicting you are doing—it will continue right up to the punch line.

Relating Points to Your Experience

Another useful way to listen is to try to *relate the points to your own experience.* When a speaker makes the point that professional football is getting too violent, you might try to remember any particularly violent games you have seen. Good listeners are those who attempt to relate material to their own experience. When you try to do this, you are engaged in active listening.

Looking for Similarities and Differences

Your understanding of a subject is often aided if you can discover the *similarities and differences* in relation to what you already know. Sometimes the similarities and differences are obvious. When you hear that 95 percent of marriages in India are arranged by parents, this is an obvious difference from the American custom. A more subtle difference begins to emerge when you examine the role that parents play in marriage in both countries. You might ask, for example, why Indians of marriageable age permit their parents to arrange their marriages. And this question might lead you to ask whether parents and children relate differently in Indian society than they do in American society.

TRY THIS

Listen to an informative speech. Write down the main idea of the speech. Then identify the supporting ideas as well. If possible, check your assessment against that of the speaker. Is the speaker's assessment of his or her main idea different from your own? If so, why? Try to figure out why your perception is different from the speaker's. Did you listen carefully enough? Did the speaker present his or her main idea clearly? How could it have been made clearer?

Questioning and Paraphrasing

Questioning is an important aid to active listening. Questions might be ones that you ask yourself. If you cannot answer them, then it is important that you ask them of the speaker. Even if you have answers to your questions, you might want to ask them anyway so you can check out your perceptions with those of the speaker. Another useful method for ensuring that your information is correct is *paraphrasing*—simply restating in your own words what the other person has said.

We also listen for information in interpersonal and small-group settings. Many of the methods for active listening outlined above are appropriate for such setting, too; however, relating points to your experience, looking for similarities, and especially questioning and paraphrasing would probably be the most applicable.

CRITICAL LISTENING

Critical listening requires all of the ingredients of informative listening. The listener still should identify the main idea and the supporting points. But in **critical listening**, the listener also should evaluate and challenge what has been heard. These challenges might take place in the listener's mind or they might be expressed directly to the speaker.

Ideally, all communication should be listened to critically. When we are receiving new information, however, it is sometimes difficult to evaluate it critically because we do not know very much about the subject—and possibly about the speaker either.

The area of persuasion offers the greatest opportunity to use critical listening skills. Products are advertised every day with the promise that they will bring romance, adventure, or success into our lives. It takes no genius to be critical of those sorts of messages! But commercials are not the only persuasive messages that we are subjected to. A candidate wants our vote, we are asked to sign a petition for a freeze on nuclear weapons, a friend tries to persuade us to stop studying and go shopping. All of these messages require evaluation and critical thinking.

Determining the Speaker's Motives

When we use critical listening, our first job is to *question the communicator's motives*. With commercials, it's easy. Someone wants to sell a product. With political candidates the motive is more complex. Obviously they want to be elected to office. So then the question is, Why? Are they after money? Power? Do they want to bring about social change? Do they want to keep things the way they are?

A petition for a freeze on nuclear weapons is even more complex and requires more in-depth questions. It also requires the questioner to have some background on the subject. What, for example, is a freeze? How would a freeze affect defense strategies? Does the petition call for a freeze on all nuclear weapons or just some of them?

Even when a friend tries to persuade us to stop studying and go shopping, we must address a number of questions. What are his or her motives? What are the effects likely to be? When we are involved in persuasive situations, questioning the persuader's motives is a normal, proper response. In public speaking situations we often check the speakers' motives by examining their backgrounds. Some give lengthy introductions that are designed to establish their **credibility**, or believability. Not every speaker has to be an expert; it is enough if he or she has done the proper amount of homework needed to give a credible speech.

Challenging and Questioning Ideas

Critical listening also involves *challenging ideas* and *questioning* the validity of ideas. Where did the speaker get her information? Did it come from a source that is generally regarded as credible? Is the speaker quoting the information accurately or is she taking it out of context? Does she identify her sources of information so they can be checked later by her audience?

In persuasive situations, speakers sometimes omit information that does not support their cause. If you have information contrary to what a speaker presents, keep it in mind so you can ask questions later. You can assess whether information has been omitted by asking questions about the speaker's sources. In a political speech, for example, is all of the supporting material from one particular party or viewpoint—say liberal or conservative? Does this mean that important information may have been omitted?

Distinguishing Fact from Opinion

Part of challenging ideas and questioning their validity is the ability to *distinguish fact from opinion*. A fact is something that can be verified. Everyone who applies the same test should be able to get the same information. Today's temperature is a fact. If we put several thermometers in the same place, they should all show the same temperature. A fact is always true, whereas an opinion is someone's belief. Because people sometimes present opinions as facts, it is important that you, as the listener, make the distinction. The statement "Women should stay home and take care of children" is an opinion—regardless of how authoritative the speaker may sound.

Although all facts are equal, some opinions are more reliable than others. We are more likely to trust the opinions of speakers who have been right before, who have a high degree of authority or credibility, or whose opinions have been (or are) supported by others.

Recognizing Our Own Biases

Sometimes there are messages we don't want to hear because they contradict our own attitudes and beliefs. If you're a Democrat, you don't go to Republican rallies; if you're a religious liberal, you don't go to revival meetings. If, for some reason, you were forced to go to either of these, you would probably tune out most of what you heard.

In some cases, we might not even be aware that we are blocking out messages. Earlier we mentioned that although jurors had heard instructions about the rules of circumstantial evidence, only 40 percent correctly followed these instructions. The authors concluded that this misunderstanding of the law was not merely a matter of poor listening. They believed that jurors were likely to misinterpret the law when they didn't believe in it. Their interpretation was compatible with the view they held of the law.[10] This tendency to interpret information in the light of our beliefs can lead to distorting the information we hear. As listeners, we have to be aware of our own values and attitudes—especially when we hear information we might resist or disagree with.

Assessing the Message

Earlier in this chapter, we discussed listening as an ongoing process that includes *assessment* of the communication. This assessment can take place while the event is taking place and can continue long after the event is over. Assessment is basically a critical process; it is chewing over what you have heard before you swallow it. An idea that may seem acceptable when we first hear it may not be so palatable when we have had time to think about it. For

TRY THIS

For one day, keep a log in which you record other people's motives. For *every* persuasive message you receive, fill in the following information:

- *Communicator*
- *Topic*
- *Motive*

After the day is over, examine your results. Who gave you the greatest number of persuasive messages? What was the most often cited motive of the communicators? What does this tell you about the persuasive messages to which you are most often exposed? That is, what conclusions can you draw—from this limited survey—about the persuasion that goes on in your life? Do these conclusions offer any surprises?

important ideas, it is important to reflect on them before they become part of us and of our thinking. We must learn to *suspend judgment*—delay taking a position—until all the facts and other evidence are in, we have had a chance to test the facts in the marketplace of ideas, or they have been chewed over sufficiently for digestion.

REFLECTIVE LISTENING

When we are involved in interpersonal communication, talking to one other person or to a group of friends, we can use our skills in listening for information. We ask, for example, what is the cheapest way to get to California? Should we buy new tires or retreads? Or what did the instructor say in class today? We also listen critically to friends. We favor the idea of a consolidated school; our friend favors the neighborhood school. As we discuss school systems, we challenge and question the validity of each other's ideas.

One day, however, we see that a friend is very upset. He knows what he's upset about—he is failing a class—and he is looking for a good listener. Now your skills in informative and critical listening are not going to be very helpful. In this situation it is not listening for main points or criticizing ideas that is called for but *listening for feelings*. This kind of listening is called reflective or empathic listening.

CONSIDER THIS

"Hear twice before you speak once."
—Scottish saying

CONSIDER THIS

In the following passage, a well-known author, John Wideman, writes about the problems of listening to his brother—a brother who had often been in trouble with the law and who had spent much of his life in prison.

The hardest habit to break, since it was a habit of a lifetime, would be listening to myself listening to him. That habit would destroy any chance of seeing my brother on his terms; and seeing him in his terms, learning his terms, seemed the whole point of learning his story. However numerous and comforting the similarities, we were different. The world had seized on the difference, allowed me room to thrive, while he'd been forced into a cage. Why did it work that way? What was the nature of the difference? Why did it haunt me? Temporarily at least, to answer these questions, I had to root my fiction-writing self out of our exchanges. I had to teach myself to listen. Start fresh, clear the pipes, resist too facile an identification, tame the urge to take off with Robby's story and make it my own.

I understood that, but could I break the habit? And even if I did learn to listen, wouldn't there be a point at which I'd have to take over the telling? Wasn't there something fundamental in my writing, in my capacity to function, that depended on flight, on escape? Wasn't another person's skin a hiding place, a place to work out anxiety, to face threats too intimidating to handle in any other fashion? Wasn't writing about people a way of exploiting them?

Source: John Wideman, *Brothers and Keepers.*

Listening for Feelings

We are often asked or expected to listen for feelings, and we often want to share our feelings with others. We are all upset or happy at one time or another, and if we share these feelings with someone else, it permits us to reveal ourselves. Sharing our feelings also helps us to cope with them. Often when we talk our feelings over with other people, we can gain control of them or deal with them better. Sharing feelings, then, helps us to feel better; our joy is greater and our distress is lessened whenever sharing takes place.

But many of us do not do a very good job of listening for feelings. Because it is one of the most common forms of listening, we assume we can all do it. You will probably be surprised to learn, however, that you might not be listening as effectively as you could be. Let's look at some of the responses you might make that hamper your effectiveness as a listener.

Negative Listening Responses

In order to look at negative listening responses, let's assume that your best friend has been feeling depressed for the last few days. You ask her what is wrong and she responds that she is having a terrible time at her job because her boss is picking on her so much. Here are some possible ways you could respond—responses that we all use, but none of them very helpful.

Denying Feelings

If you respond "You shouldn't feel that way—everyone knows how hard it is to get along with him," you are focusing on the personality of the boss rather than on what your friend is feeling. When our feelings are very intense, we want them recognized. We don't want them pushed aside while other, less important items are dealt with.

Evaluating

If you respond, "Why don't you just stop trying? There are other jobs" or "He really doesn't appreciate all the work you do," you are making an evaluative response—one that passes judgment on and offers an opinion of either your friend or of the boss. Often an evaluative response is a way of trying to dispose of another's problems. The listener does not take the time to listen to the problem; he or she just makes some generalizations that are designed to make the problem go away.

Being Philosophical

The philosophical response is so broad and sweeping that it does nothing to solve the problem. In this kind of response, you might say, "All bosses are hard to get along with; it's the nature of the boss-employee relationship." Like an evaluative response, this response ignores the problem and the feelings of the person with the problem.

Giving Advice

"Go out and get a new job. Your boss will never get any better." This is concrete and specific advice. When people have problems, however, it is better to let *them* find the solutions to their problems. Your job is not to give advice but to listen in such a way that your friend can find her own solution.

Defending the Other Person

Sometimes we think it might be helpful to present the other person's viewpoint: "Well you have to understand his side. He has a lot of employees to supervise." But your friend with the problem doesn't want to hear any defense of the boss. If you defend him, she might wonder where your loyalties lie.

Expressing Pity

Sometimes we are tempted to give total sympathy: "I really feel sorry for you. It must be terrible to work for a person who treats you so badly." But with a response like this, your friend is going to feel even worse.

Questioning

Sometimes our response to a friend's problem is to ask a series of questions: "What did you do to make him disapprove of you?" "Is there anything you can do to make the situation better?" Question asking can be a valuable interpersonal skill but not when emotions are very high. Once the *feeling* has lost some of its intensity, questions might be useful to help to solve the problem.

All of these responses are weak because they do not deal with the problem of feelings. They all, in one way or another, lead the person with the problem away from her feelings. How, then, can we respond in such a way that we focus on feelings?

The Reflective Listening Response

The best way to listen for feelings is through **reflective listening**—where you try to understand what the person is feeling *from his or her point of view* and reflect these feelings back. As the listener, your job is to put aside your own feelings and enter into the feelings of the person who is speaking. In order to do this you need to recognize what feelings are involved, let the person tell you what has happened, and then encourage him or her to find the solution to the problem.

In this painting by Richard Estes, a woman seems to be engaged in reflective listening. In good relationships the partners listen for feelings below the surface and offer support and encouragement in response.

Identify the Emotion(s)

First, and this is often the most difficult part, you need to "hear" what the person is really saying. If, for example, your roommate comes home and bursts through the door saying, "I would really like to kill Joe!" he is obviously not saying that he literally wants to kill Joe. When we are listening reflectively, we first need to identify what the speaker is feeling. In this case, it would be reasonable to assume he is feeling anger, and we respond with "Boy, you really sound mad." With this kind of response, it is almost certain your roommate will tell you what has happened.

Listen to the Story

The second part of a reflective response is to listen to what the person has to say. As the whole story comes out, there is no need to respond with anything very specific. This is the point where the person just wants to be listened to. You can show your interest by paying attention and looking sympathetic.

Let's go back to your roommate and his problem with Joe. What did Joe do to make him so mad? You discover that Joe borrowed your roommate's favorite shirt—the one he got from his girlfriend for his birthday. While Joe was wearing the shirt, he stopped to pick some blueberries and got blueberry stains all over it.

After your roommate has told you the whole story, he is not quite so mad, but he is still pretty upset. As you listen, you discover other feelings in addition to anger. Because the shirt is a gift from your roommate's girlfriend, he may be feeling guilt that he betrayed her by lending it to Joe. He may also be feeling upset because he is going to have to tell his girlfriend what happened to it. Usually people do not feel just one emotion—they have a whole series of them.

If you can let your roommate talk through the entire problem, without making judgments but giving him sympathy, it is likely that the full range of the problem may be revealed. One way to reach this point is through *paraphrasing*—restating the other person's thoughts or feelings in your own words. If your roommate says, "My girlfriend is really going to be mad when she finds out," an appropriate paraphrased response might be, "You sound worried about your girlfriend's reaction." This response not only helps to identify the feeling, it is also a way to find out whether you have been hearing accurately and it shows you are paying attention. A paraphrased response is a way of providing a mirror for the other's remarks.

Let the Person Work Out the Problem

Sometimes just listening for people's feelings and letting them explain what is upsetting them largely solves the problem. We often hear someone say, "I feel better just because I've talked to you." People sometimes just want to ventilate their feelings, and once they have done so, they feel better.

But sometimes mere listening is not enough; your friend has a problem, and he or she wants some help in solving it. In such a situation the best solution is usually to trust in the other person and in his or her ability to work out the problem. This does not mean, however, that you ignore the problem. Reflective listening includes helping the other person find a way to solve the problem.

The last step in reflective listening, then, is to give the person a chance to work out his or her problem. In the case of the roommate, you don't want to say, "You should make Joe buy a new shirt." Let your roommate decide what he wants to do. If the emotion in the situation has died down, it might be appropriate to ask some very broad and general questions, such as, "What are you going to do now?" It might also be possible to ask some questions that might lead to a solution the other person has not thought of: "Do you think the dry cleaners might be able to get the stains out?" "Has Joe offered to do anything about the shirt?"

The important thing to remember at this stage is that you do not have to solve the other person's problem. If you are going to try to solve every problem that someone brings you, you are putting a heavy burden on yourself. Think

TRY THIS

Identify the emotions you are hearing in the following statements. Then check your answers in section A. Now think of a reflective response you would make to each statement. Check your answer with section B. (Your answer doesn't have to be exactly like the answers given but it should reflect the general sense.)

1. "Boy, am I upset. I read the assignment before I went to class, but when Mr. Parker asked me three question, I didn't know the answer to any of them."
2. "I thought I had saved enough money to go to Florida over spring break. Now I have to pay to have my car fixed and I won't be able to go."
3. "I really would like to go to the fraternity party tonight, but I don't know if I want to go alone."
4. "I'm never going to lend my sweaters to Carol again. She always stretches them."
5. "I'll never go to the cafeteria again. Today I slipped and fell, and my tray of food went all over the place."

Section A

1. embarrassment, humiliation
2. disappointment
3. anxiety, insecurity
4. resentment, anger
5. humiliation, embarrassment

Section B

1. "You must have felt embarrassed."
2. "It must be a real disappointment to you to not be able to go."
3. "You sound like you feel insecure about going alone."
4. "You must feel resentment when they come back stretched."
5. "You must have felt humiliated."

of the person with the problem as *owning* that problem. This attitude also will help the other person to grow in his or her ability to deal with problems. If parents, for example, tried to solve all of their children's problems, the children would not be able to live independent lives.

If you are the kind of person who feels burdened because everyone comes to you with problems, you are probably taking on more responsibility than is required. Rather than focusing on solutions, try focusing on feelings and listening reflectively. You will be surprised at how well this system works.[11]

Reflective listening can be very useful in many situations, but there are times when it might not work very well because you, as the listener, are feeling too much stress and conflict. If you are really angry with someone, it is very difficult to use reflective listening because you are not interested in the other person's feelings; you are interested in your own. But if you are not under stress and are able to listen to another person without feeling threatened in any way, reflective listening can work very well.

The important thing to remember is that when strong emotions are involved, people often just need a sounding board. To be there and to utter an occasional "Oh," "Mmm," or "I see" is often enough. Much comfort is derived from just being listened to.

LISTENING FOR ENJOYMENT

Few of us have any problem when we listen for enjoyment. We turn on the television or stereo, lean back, and relax. The information is easy to listen to because we have chosen it. If we like what we hear, we don't even have much problem remembering it. We can often recite, with perfect fidelity, song lyrics from a record or a dialogue we heard in a movie.

As college students, however, your instructors often ask you to enjoy information that is complex and difficult to listen to. When your English teacher puts on a record of a famous actor reading from *Hamlet*, he hopes that you will both understand and enjoy it. Your theater instructor does not stick to uncomplicated Broadway plays and musical comedies; she also wants you to enjoy George Bernard Shaw and Eugene O'Neill. As a student, you too are probably interested in increasing your ability to listen with enjoyment to more complex information.

When we want to listen to something for enjoyment but it is too complex to understand, we can try listening in the same way we listened critically for information and listened for feelings. A course in music appreciation is a good example of a place to employ all these skills. Since most of us enjoy music, it is not unreasonable to assume that we will enjoy some of the music we hear in such a class. In addition to enjoying the music, however, we will also be asked to use other listening skills. Our informational skills might be tested: Can you identify the theme? What is the rhythm of the piece? What does *allegretto* mean? Our critical skills might be tested if we are asked to listen for the way two different composers treat the same theme or to indicate whether we agree with the way the musician interprets the piece. Since music involves feelings, we are asked to listen for the mood of the piece: Is it solemn or light? How does it make the listener feel? By requiring listening skills other than those needed for enjoyment, the music instructor is hoping to increase your enjoyment of music—because the more one knows about music, the more one is able to appreciate and enjoy more complex forms of it.

TRY THIS

Go to a play or a movie, or watch a television drama, with the idea of reviewing it. Concentrate on answering some or all of these questions:

- *Informative*: What was the play, movie, or drama about? Who were the principal actors? What roles did they play? What were the sets and costumes like?
- *Critical*: Did the actors play their parts in a way that was believable? Were the sets and costumes appropriate for the period? Did the drama hold your attention?
- *Emotional*: Did you identify with any of the characters and what they were feeling? Did you respond emotionally to this drama? What emotions did you feel?
- *Enjoyment*: Did you enjoy the drama? Did others enjoy it too? How do you know? Did your reasons for enjoying it come from any of your answers to the above questions?

Listening for enjoyment, then, can be a more sophisticated process than merely sitting back and letting the sounds wash over us. Complex material, even when we enjoy it, involves greater listening skill. In music, for example, if we had not worked on these skills, we would all still be listening to "Twinkle, Twinkle, Little Star."

The same skills can be applied when we listen to a play. Listen for information: What is the play about? What is the plot? Listen critically: Do the scenes flow into each other? Are the characters believable? Listen reflectively: What is the character feeling? How does she relate to the other characters?

Listening is often more enjoyable if we can relate what we are hearing to our own experience. Someone who plays to violin can enjoy a violin concerto because he knows what to look for and is aware of the discipline and practice that it takes to play such a piece. Watching a play, we can sometimes think, "I have felt that way too."

You will find it worthwhile working to enjoy more complex information. Remember, however, that listening for enjoyment can require skills just as complex as those needed in any other listening situations.[12] The only difference is in the rewards. What could be better than listening to enjoy yourself?

SUMMARY

All of us are surrounded by hundreds of messages every day. Because we are surrounded by so much information, it is often difficult to listen, and many of us become poor listeners.

Listening is a skill, and like any other skill it must be learned and practiced. It is also a process. We make predictions about messages before we hear them, we listen to them, and then we assess what we have heard. How well we listen is determined by the attention we give to a message. We are able to tune out unwanted messages through the process of selective listening. Once we hear a message, we must assign meaning to it by selecting and organizing the material we have heard. Our final step in listening is to select out what we need to remember.

In order to be good listeners we must become actively involved in the process of listening. As active listeners we evaluate and criticize the material as we listen to it. When one listens actively, one is less likely to be distracted or bored.

There are four kinds of listening: listening for information, critical listening, reflective listening, and listening for enjoyment. Listening for information involves listening for facts. In this kind of listening it is important to identify the main point and distinguish it from the supporting points. Critical listening involves evaluating the material one hears. To listen critically, one listens for the motives of the speaker and mentally challenges the speaker's ideas and information. Critical listening is especially effective when one is listening to persuasive messages.

Reflective listening is listening for feelings. This kind of listening is most often done in interpersonal communications, and it often has the purpose of helping the speaker to cope with his or her feelings and problems. Listening for enjoyment is most often listening that we choose to do. We can learn to enjoy complex material by using all of the other listening skills.

VOCABULARY

The following is a list of words you must know to understand the concepts in this chapter. You will find the words defined the first time that each is used in the chapter. All Vocabulary words also appear, with their definitions, in the Glossary at the end of the book.

active listener	passive listener
assessment	prediction
credibility	reflective listening
critical listening	selective attention
listening	supporting points
main idea	

FURTHER READING

BANVILLE, THOMAS G. *How to Listen— How to Be Heard*. Chicago: Nelson-Hall, 1978. Banville describes "schizophrenic" listening. He explains how feelings and emotions are part of total listening, and he offers specific techniques to improve your ability to listen actively.

BISHOP, NAN, SARAH HAMILTON, AND CLARE BOWMAN. *Nan, Sarah, and Clare.* New York: Avon, 1980. Three best friends in college go their separate ways. Later they reestablish ties through letters to each other. The letters show some of the distinctions between merely hearing and listening.

BURLY-ALLEN, MADELYN. *Listening: The Forgotten Skill.* New York: Wiley, 1982. The author provides exercises and techniques designed to improve the way we listen to others. She examines listening, why we listen as we do, various barriers, how to listen to ourselves, making listening work for us, and, finally, how to get others to listen to us.

EDWARDS, CHRISTOPHER. *Crazy for God.* Englewood Cliffs, N.J.: Prentice-Hall, 1979. This is the best of the books about what it is like to be swept into a religious cult—in this case, the Moonies. The author dramatically shows what it means when you are encouraged *not* to listen.

EPSTEIN, HELEN. *Children of the Holocaust.* New York: Bantam, 1980. Epstein discusses people who have survived Nazi concentration camps and later told their children about their experiences. The book makes the point that listening to parents' experiences can make a strong impression on children—an impression that is not always positive.

FABER, ADELE, AND ELAINE MAZLISH. *How to Talk So Kids Will Listen and How to Listen So Kids Will Talk.* New York: Rawson, Wade, 1980. Although this book is directed to parents who want to improve communication with their children, it explains reflective listening so well that everyone can learn and benefit from it.

HAYDEN, TOREY L. *One Child.* New York: Putnam, 1980. Hayden, a teacher who works with disturbed children, describes how she broke down the barriers to teach a child whom others considered hopeless. Much of her strategy in reaching the child involved careful listening.

LEAR, MARTHA. *Heartsounds.* New York: Simon & Schuster, 1979. Lear writes about her husband's life-threatening heart attack and what it is like to communicate with health professionals. She discovers that doctors are among the poorest listeners.

RICHARDSON, JERRY, AND JOEL MARGULIS. *The Magic of Rapport: How You Can Gain Personal Power in Any Situation.* San Francisco: Harbor, 1981. Although this book is on communication, the focus is dealing successfully with others through a method called neurolinguistic programming. One of the essential skills in this method is effective listening.

WOLVIN, ANDREW D., AND CAROLYN GWYNN COAKLEY. *Listening.* Dubuque, Iowa: 1982. This complete textbook on listening examines the need for, process of, and types of listening. The authors look at appreciative, discriminative, comprehensive, therapeutic, and critical listening. This is a useful, well-documented resource.

4 VERBAL COMMUNICATION

CHAPTER OUTLINE

How Words Work
People Determine Meanings
The Language Environment
    People, purposes, and rules
    Rituals
    Appropriate language
    Specialization
Style: Your Role and Your Verbal Image
    Role and language style
    Dialect
    Speaking and writing
Working on Your Communication

What do you want to say?
How do you want to say it?
To whom are you talking?
Metatalk
Language Choices
    Clarity
    Energy
    Vividness
Improving Your Verbal Style
    Increasing your vocabulary
    Adapting your oral language
    Breaking bad habits

CHAPTER OBJECTIVES

After reading this chapter, you should be able to:

1. Explain how thought processes and language are linked.
2. Explain what is expected of a speaker in a particular language environment.
3. Give examples of the ritual use of language.
4. Explain the function of role in a language environment.
5. Define style.
6. Describe how role and style are interrelated.
7. Distinguish between instrumental and expressive language.
8. Explain the advantages and disadvantages of dialect.
9. Describe the ways in which speaking and writing differ.
10. Define and give examples of metatalk.
11. Describe some of the ways to make your verbal style clearer, more energetic, and more vivid.

Think, for a moment, about the last time you communicated something in words to another person. Was it just a minute ago, when you told a friend you had to study? Was it at dinner, when you asked someone to pass the salt? Was it after your last class, when you asked someone what the reading assignment was? Whatever the situation, the importance of verbal communication is obvious. If we were to go through a whole day without speaking, most of us would feel frustrated. Travelers in a country where they do not know the language feel not only frustrated but exhausted from the effort of trying to communicate without a common means of verbal communication.

Even when we are not talking out loud, we use language. It would be difficult to think something through without using the symbolism of language. Our dreams and daydreams, indiscernible to observers, consist of images that depend on language.

Ideally, language is used to achieve mutual understanding and communication with others. Sometimes, however, language is manipulated by its users. Naming a real estate development "Woodland Heights" implies that the land has woods and hills. If it has neither, language is being used to create an impression rather than to reflect reality. And language can be used in such subtle ways that even when it is accurate, it can still distort meaning. McDonald's, for example, calls one of its hamburgers the "Quarter Pounder"—language designed to make a mere four ounces sound like an ample portion.

It is important to remember that even though we use language in most communication situations, what we mean to say is conveyed by more than the words themselves. We usually add all sorts of nonverbal communication to our words, and the two become so interrelated that it is difficult to tell where one begins and the other leaves off.

This chapter is largely concerned with the language behavior of speakers and listeners; to divorce words from how they are spoken and how they are heard is to look at them in isolation—and words are never isolated in oral communication. It is impossible, for this reason, to discuss language behavior without discussing the people who are using the language. This applies equally to the speaker and listener. If you speak perfect French to someone who does not understand the language, you will not be understood, no matter how clear your words are. Successful communication depends on the completion of the transaction, and much of the emphasis in this chapter is on the two ends of the communication chain: the speaker and the listener.

Part of the communicator's effectiveness in conveying thoughts and emotions is derived from his or her language.

An understanding of language will help you to express what you really want to say, honestly, clearly, and straightforwardly. When messages are misunderstood or when a communication has no effect on the listener, it may be the language of the speaker that is at fault. And no matter how skillful it may be in other ways, any communication that is not understood cannot be successful.

HOW WORDS WORK

When you use a word orally, you are vocally representing something—whether that thing is a physical object such as your biology textbook or an abstract concept such as peace. The word is, as Chapter 1 noted, a symbol; it stands for the object or concept that it names. This is what distinguishes a word from a random sound. The sounds that are represented in our language by the letters *c a t* constitute a word because we have agreed that these sounds will stand for a particular domestic animal. The sounds represented by the letters *z a t* do not make up a word in our language because these sounds do not stand for anything.

A word that stands for a concrete and emotionally neutral thing—such as the word "mailbox"—can usually be interpreted with good fidelity because most people respond primarily to its **denotative meaning**—that is, the dictionary definition.

Other words stand for abstract concepts about which people may have strong feelings. Words such as "freedom" and "love" are easily misunderstood because they carry a lot of **connotative meaning**—the feelings or associations we have about a word. For example, when we hear the word "love," we don't just think about the word; we associate it with a person, an experience we have had. Figure 4-1 shows how some words are concrete while others are abstract.

Denotative language is the first type of language we learn. Our parents teach us how letters and their sounds relate to the people and things we experience.

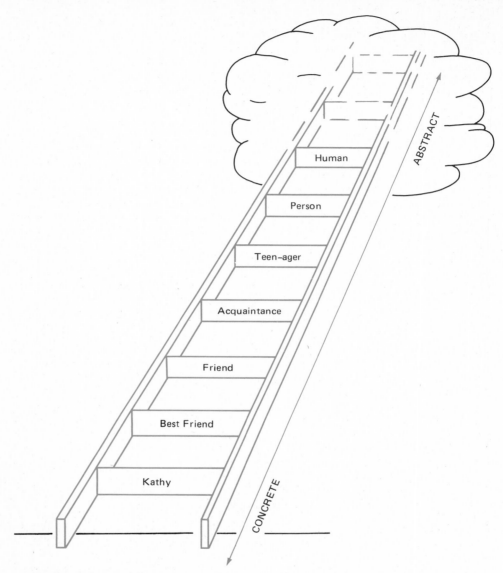

FIGURE 4-1 **A Ladder of Abstraction**

When you study a language, whether it is your native tongue or a foreign one, you must learn what the words stand for in that language; that is, you have to know both their denotative and their connotative meanings. Another thing you need to know is how to put the words together to make the clauses and sentences that express relationships among the words. This is the grammar of a language.

When you say that another person understands your language, you mean that he or she knows what your words stand for and how the words are put together to express ideas and relationships. You and that person both interpret the verbal sound that is being made in approximately the same way. Each of you has learned the connection between the sound and what it represents, and each of you can use the sound intelligibly.

Notice, however, that your idea of an object or a concept is never exactly the same as another person's, because each individual has had different experiences. Your notion of what "cat" means comes from all the cats you have ever known, read about, seen on television, heard others talk about, and so on. This composite cat is unique to you, but you can use the sound of the word to refer to cats in general because cats have certain qualities on which we all agree.

A theory of language developed by Edward Sapir and Benjamin L. Whorf suggests that language helps us to determine how we see and think about the world. They believe that language restricts the thoughts of people who use it and that the limits of one's language become the limits of one's world. For example, speakers of the Eskimo language are able to label seven types of snow, and this ability says something about the world they live in. Snow dominates their lives and at times becomes a matter of life and death. English speakers, however, cannot distinguish among the different kinds of snow. Thus, according to this hypothesis the English speakers' "world of snow" is more restricted and narrowed. We cannot even think about the different kinds of snow because the labels or names do not exist. Naming, then, is essential to thinking.[1]

PEOPLE DETERMINE MEANINGS

For the listener to understand what the speaker intends, the speaker should have something definite in mind. The more general the idea or impression the communicator wishes to convey, the more likely that catchall words or words that are hazy, vague, or ambiguous will be used. Understanding is the core of meaning, and understanding is a two-way process; that is, the speaker is responsible for presenting the idea clearly, and the listener is responsible for trying to understand it accurately. Meanings are determined by people, not by words.

Sometimes, for meaning to occur, we have to use a very specialized vocabulary before we can talk about a subject. A medical student who calls each of the various bones in the leg the "leg bone" is in trouble; the language is not specific enough. People who buy home computers find they must learn a new language if they want to understand the instruction manual or talk to other computer users. Most important, however, is that this language must be learned even to *think* about the subject.

CONSIDER THIS

Language is always based on experience. The national experience of baseball has offered many colorful expressions to our language. Few Americans are likely to misunderstand these expressions.

- He was born with two strikes against him.
- He couldn't get to first-base with that girl.
- He sure threw me a curve that time.
- I'll take a rain-check on it.
- He went to bat for me.
- I liked him right off the bat.
- He was way out in left field on that one.
- He's a foul ball.
- I think you're way off base on that.
- It was a smash hit.
- Let's take a seventh-inning stretch.
- I hope to touch all the bases on this report.
- Could you pinch-hit for me?
- He doesn't even know who's on first.
- I just call 'em as I see 'em.
- He's only a bush-leaguer.
- Major league all the way.
- We'll hit 'em where they ain't.
- He has a lot on the ball.
- He really dropped the ball that time.
- We'll rally in the ninth.
- No game's over until the last man's out.

Source: Adapted from Willard R. Espy, *Say It My Way*.

Another example of different language use often occurs in communication between parents and children. The world of adults is different from the world of children or adolescents. A parent might wish, for example, that his or her child were popular. But "popular" to a teen-ager means being able to stay out late and use the family car—possibly unacceptable conditions to the parent.

CONSIDER THIS

An American visitor to England was driving through London with his English friend, and the friend observed that the windscreen needed cleaning.

"You mean the windshield," the American corrected.

"Well, over here we call it a windscreen," the Englishman said.

"Then you are wrong," the American said, "because we Americans invented the automobile and we call it a windshield."

"That's quite true," the Englishman countered, "but just remember who invented the *language*."

Source: Gloria Hoffman and Pauline Graivier, as told to Jane Phillips, *Speak the Language of Success.*

Because the experiences of the teen-ager and parent are so different, their values and vocabulary also differ.

New meanings are continually created by all of us as we change our ideas, our feelings, and our activities. As we think, read, travel, make friends with others, and experience life, the associations and connections that words have for us are changed.

THE LANGUAGE ENVIRONMENT

All language takes place within a particular environment. A minister speaks in the environment of a church, two friends have a conversation in the student center, an instructor gives a lecture in a classroom. Language that is appropriate to one environment might appear meaningless or foolish in another. The language you use in a dormitory, for example, might be completely inappropriate in a classroom.

People, Purposes, and Rules

According to Neil Postman, a writer about language, the **language environment** is made up of four elements: people, their purpose, the rules of communication by which they achieve their purpose, and the actual talk being used in the situation.[2] To illustrate these elements, let's take the simple example of John and Mary seeing each other on the street. Their main purpose in communicating is to greet each other.

Mary: "Hi. How are you?"

John: "Fine. How are you?"

Mary: "Good."

The rules for this sort of conversation are well known to all of us, since we often participate in it ourselves. If John had failed to follow the rules, however, and had stopped to talk for five minutes about how miserable he felt, Mary would probably have felt annoyed, because John would have gone beyond the limits of that sort of conversation.

The kind of conversation Mary and John had illustrates language as a ritual. **Ritual language** takes place when we are in an environment where a conventionalized response is expected of us.[3] Greetings are a ritual; we briefly respond to each other—usually only half-listening to what the other person has said—and then go about our business.

Rituals

The rituals we use are determined by the language environment. If we are at a funeral, we are expected to respond in conventional, ritualized ways to the family of the person who has died: "He was a wonderful man and I will miss him"; "She had a rich and full life"; "It's a blessing he is no longer suffering." At a wedding we wish the couple happiness and tell the bride that she looks beautiful.

Every society's language rituals are determined by the cultural values of that society. In rural East Africa, it would be rude to pass someone you know well with a brief "Hello." You are expected to stop and inquire about the person, his home, his livestock, and his health. At an East African wedding, it would be appropriate to tell the couple that you hope they will have many sons; in American society, such a response would be considered highly inappropriate.

We learn ritualized language when we are very young, and we learn it from our parents or other adults around us. Research indicates that young children often do not make the conventional response of "Hi," "Goodbye," or "Thanks" unless they are prompted by their parents. In a study of 22 children who ranged in age from 2 to 5, only 27 percent of them responded to "Hi," 25 percent to "Goodbye," and 7 percent to "Thanks." After being prompted by their parents, 44 percent said "Hi," 86 percent said "Thanks," and 84 percent said "Goodbye." The researchers concluded that children do not use politeness rituals spontaneously; they use them on the insistence of adults.[4]

As children grow older, they begin to assimilate and use ritual language. Anyone who has handed out candy on Halloween can tell you that although

In our everyday encounters we engage in highly formalized ritual language. What would the dialog in this ritual of ordering in a restaurant sound like?

the younger children may have to be prompted, this is no longer necessary with the older children; they will offer their thanks spontaneously.

Appropriate Language

Through social conditioning, then, children learn appropriate language. They also learn, often dramatically, not to use inappropriate language. Do you remember the first time you used an obscene or a blasphemous word in your home? If the reaction to your word was typical, you were probably severely reprimanded or even spanked by one of your parents. You were probably surprised by the vehemence of the reaction to the word because you didn't know exactly what the word meant. You learned something from that experience, however. You learned never to use *that* word with *them* ever again!

By the time we enter college, we have a good idea of the appropriate language for a particular language environment. We have been thoroughly socialized as to what is appropriate and inappropriate in language choices. Whether we *want* to use the words that are prescribed for us is largely irrelevant. The language environment dictates the language that is *expected* of us. If we violate these expectations, we run the risk of having people respond to us negatively.

TRY THIS

For one day, listen to your friends and classmates talk. Write down all the words and expressions they use with each other that are typical of the way they speak. After you have made your list, decide what words and expressions would not be appropriate for teachers or parents. What does your list tell you about the language environment?

Specialization

Language environments can often be very specialized. A doctor who tells a patient that he or she has a hematoma is likely to be met with a blank stare. The patient would have understood if the doctor had used the word "bruise"— a layperson's term for hematoma. Many other areas, especially those of work, have specialized vocabularies. Computer scientists, cooks, and teachers all use a language that is special to their particular environment.

Even where a highly specialized language is used, there may be variations in the language used within a language environment. For example, a person using a home computer will use a somewhat different language to talk about his or her computer than a computer programmer who works on a large mainframe computer.

Sometimes people create a special language when they feel they don't have as much power as the people around them. Quite often this is a language that those in power do not understand, and it is deliberately used to keep information from them. Students, especially those in high school and college, are one example of special language groups. They use slang or a special meaning to exclude outsiders or members of the adult establishment. American blacks are another example. Often they use words in a way that deliberately misleads members of the white population. Not only is the special language used by the group to hide information from outsiders, but it is used to create a sense of group identity and kinship among its users, and it is important for forging a group identity. Among blacks, there is strong pressure to use "black English" when talking to other blacks.

When a group has created a special language, we usually cannot step into that group and use its language unless we have some legitimate claim to membership. How we speak in a language environment depends on the role we are playing. Students, for example, might be using their own variations of the language, but if a teacher joins the group, the language and the language environment will change because the roles have changed. A similar change occurs when an adult joins a group of children.

Whenever we shift roles, we are also shifting our language environment. Let's say that, in a single day, you talk to friends in the dorm, you go to class, and you talk to your mother on the telephone. Your role will have shifted three times: from peer–peer, to student–instructor, to child–parent. Each circumstance has entailed a different language environment, and you have probably changed your talk accordingly—often without even realizing it.

The important thing to remember about language environment is to choose language that is appropriate to the particular environment. The language used in one environment usually does not work in another. When we think about the environment, we need to ask ourselves whom we are going to be talking with and in what context our language is going to occur. If we don't adapt to the environment, our language will not work, and we will lose the chance for effective communication.

STYLE: YOUR ROLE AND YOUR VERBAL IMAGE

The words you use are determined by all your past experiences, by everything in your individual history. You learn words in order to express thoughts, and thought and language develop together. The way you think and the way you talk are unique; they form a distinctive pattern. In a sense, you *are* what you say because language is the chief means of conveying your thoughts. Neither language nor thought can be viewed in isolation. They are related and constantly growing. Together, they determine your verbal style.

Style is the result of the way we select and arrange words and sentences. People choose different words to express their thoughts, and every individual has his or her own verbal style. Styles not only vary among different people; each person also uses different styles to suit different situations. In the pulpit, a minister often has a scholarly and formal style. At a church dinner, however, his or her style is likely to be informal and casual. When an actress meets her fans, she might speak in a style similar to her best-known role—even though this is not her natural style among friends.

Sometimes style can negate a communicator's other good qualities. We all know someone who remembers all the jokes he has ever heard and then retells them so badly that we feel embarrassed. Style, because of its power and influence, is as important to the acceptance of ideas as all the other aspects of communication. Even if we have the proper information, the right occasion, and a listener interested in our message, what we have to say may be lost if our style is inappropriate.

Impressions of personality are often related to verbal style. When you characterize a person as formal and aloof, your impression is due in part to the way that person talks. Since your style partially determines whether others accept or reject you as a person, it also influences how others receive your messages. Style is so important that it can influence people's opinion of you, win their friendship, lose their respect, or sway them.

Role and Language Style

Like language environment, verbal style is very much connected with role. Professionals, for example, are expected to speak grammatically correct English—both in private and in professional life. A college student is also expected to use correct grammar. Yet if he takes a factory job during summer vacation, using correct grammar might get him into trouble with his fellow workers, for his verbal style could identify him as a "college kid."

Should we always speak in the style that is expected of us? Could our adaptation to others' expectations cause us psychological harm? To answer these questions, it might be illuminating to look at two different examples of groups that historically have not been very powerful in our society: blacks and women.

At one time, many linguists believed that the mass media, particularly radio and television, would lead to standardized speech throughout the country. Among blacks, however, this has not been the case. A recent study shows that black dialect is moving further and further away from standard English. The linguists who conducted the study believe that this has happened because blacks are becoming increasingly segregated from whites—particularly in urban areas. They point out that black children often do not meet a white person until they enter school. This segregation has led to a black dialect with unique sentence structures and idioms that are not found in standard English.[5]

Blacks are not the only group to have developed a language that differs from the dominant language. In recent years there have been numerous studies of the different language styles used by men and women. Although much of the discussion about gender-related language differences is still speculative, there seems to be evidence that men and women do speak in different ways—especially when they are playing traditional gender roles. Much of female language reflects the submissive role.

Some people who have studied male and female language have labeled male language as instrumental and female language as expressive. **Instrumental language** is the language of orders and getting things done, and it is used largely by men—since they are most often the ones who are in a position to give orders, especially in their jobs.

Expressive language is the language of description and feelings. Robin Lakoff has described some of the aspects of women's language. She claims that certain words are used only by females. Females, for example, make use of the "empty" adjectives ("cute," "nice," "divine," "fascinating"). Women are also likely to turn a declarative sentence into a question. ("It's a nice day, isn't it?" or "We'll have dinner at 6?") Other characteristics of female speech include modifiers and hedges ("sort of," "I guess," "kind of"). All these are examples of the language of submission: a woman does not like to commit herself to a position until she is certain that the position is acceptable to the listener, who is often a male.

Finally, women often make an effort to "speak like a lady," which results in language that is hypercorrect and polite.[6] It is considered unusual for women to use strong slang or profanity. Sometimes men will apologize for using profanity in the presence of women.

Where does this "gender-appropriate" use of language come from? As girls grow up, they are given many instructions about what language is or is not appropriate for their gender ("Nice girls don't say that"). They are also told that it is important that they listen—especially to boys they are interested in. Women are expected to talk less than men. In fact, in our culture, women who talk too much are the butt of many jokes and derogatory remarks.[7]

One encouraging aspect of "gender-appropriate" speech is that women are not locked into it. Once a female plays a role equal to that of a male, her language becomes more similar to male speech. Faye Crosby and Linda Nyquist discovered, for example, that when women are in a position of authority, they use basically the same speech as their male counterparts.[8] Their study indicates that language strongly reflects the role we play in society, and as our role changes, so does our language.

To go back to the original question of whether we should speak in the style that is expected of us, the answer must be a qualified no. If oppressed groups use language that reflects oppression, these groups are not going to be able to change their status. Like the chicken/egg argument, it is difficult to establish whether language determines role or role determines language. It seems likely, however, that when a group changes its language, public perception of that group will change too.

On the other hand, there are times when it is desirable to adapt one's language to the expectations of one's listeners. When we give a speech in class or write a paper, we aim for a style that is grammatical and literate; but among friends, our style can be more casual. Those who are skillful in their use of language are able to change their style to suit the situation.

Dialect

Americans speak a variety of dialects. We are all familiar with the differences in speech between Southerners and those who live in the North. When we travel, we are often surprised to discover that people use different words for the same thing. A large sandwich, for example, may be called a hoagy, a grinder, a submarine, a hero, or a Dagwood. The name depends on where you live.

A **dialect** is the habitual language of a community. It is distinguished by a unique grammatical structure, certain ways of pronouncing words, even by characteristic figures of speech. The community members who use the dialect may be identified by region or by such diverse factors as education, social class, or cultural background. In many cases, dialect may change as people move to new regions and are influenced by new experiences. A Northerner who has moved to Mississippi might decide, for example, to substitute the colorful expression "Say what?" for the more formal expression "I beg your pardon?" A woman living in the Pennsylvania Dutch area might begin to say she is going to "red up" her house—meaning she is going to clean it.

Linguists refer to dialect as a nonstandard form of language. As well as using unique words, a dialect often also uses nonstandard grammar. Linguists generally try to avoid such questions as whether dialect is a correct form of speech or whether one dialect is superior or preferable to another. The debate over dialect is often heard in the schools, however—especially when a dialect uses a nonstandard grammar.

One way to decide on the desirability of a dialect is to talk to members of the group that uses it. Does the group consider the dialect to be desirable? In one study, Mexican-Americans were asked to evaluate speakers of standard English and standard Spanish against speakers of nonstandard Tex-Mex (Texas Spanish) or of accented English. The researchers found that how the dialects were rated depended on how group members defined themselves. Participants who labeled themselves as Latin or American were less tolerant of nonstandard forms. Persons who called themselves Mexicano or Mexican-American gave higher ratings to accented English than they did to Tex-Mex. Those who called themselves Chicanos, the group having the strongest ethnic identity, had a favorable response to both nonstandard forms.[9] It would appear, then, that persons with a Mexican-American background rate nonstandard dialects more highly if they have a strong sense of ethnic identity or if they see ethnic identity as a political issue.

A similar study, this time of black Americans, examined the attitudes of black Americans to the black dialect. In this study, 85 percent of the black Americans surveyed found standard black English—English with some black variations—to be acceptable. When asked about nonstandard black English, they responded that it was acceptable in many contexts and depended on the topic, the situation, and the person spoken to.[10] The strong sense of ethnic identity among blacks might explain the willingness to accept black dialect.

Ethnic groups may favor the use of dialect within the ethnic group; but what happens when people from these groups move into a society that considers **standard English** (use of conventional grammar, words, and expressions) to be the only acceptable way to speak? Is there a danger that a dialect (**nonstandard English**) might be considered ''inferior''? Robert Hopper attempted to study whether use of black dialect affects a person's ability to get a job. He discovered that when black speakers used standard English, they seemed to get the job more frequently than any other applicants—white or black.[11]

A related study was conducted in Canada. English-Canadian participants were asked to rank a person speaking with a French-Canadian accent as opposed to a person speaking with an English-Canadian accent. In this case, even though the material spoken was the same for both groups, the English-Canadian speakers were judged more competent and trustworthy than those who spoke with a French-Canadian accent. Speaker competence and trustworthiness, then, was judged on the basis of ethnic origin rather than speech content.[12]

Although there is no clear-cut answer as to where and when it is appropriate to use a dialect, it is possible to make some generalizations from these studies. A dialect is appropriate in a group with a strong ethnic identity but it may be inappropriate when standard English is the language spoken. But

CONSIDER THIS

Dialect consists of many colorful expressions. Traveling across this country, you might hear these expressions:

Some Pennsylvania Dutch Terms:

Aint' she will? . . . Make the window shut. . . . I want out. . . . It wonders me where he went. . . . It's going to give a storm. . . . You're coming, ain't? . . . I mind of the time. . . . Nice crop, say not? . . . Throw the cow over the fence some hay. . . . He looked over the top out. . . . Leave it stay lay. . . . He don't know what for. . . .

Tidewater:

We has plenty time. . . . Ah might could help you. . . . Gotta study on it first. . . . Didn't nobody go. . . . Ain't got no call bawling me out. . . . Don't know but what I'll take some. . . . I got a right smart (a great deal) of work. . . . That was powerful good. . . . It's nigh onto sundown. . . . I'm fixin' to go out. . . . I'm going to law him in court. . . . It was worth a sight more than I paid. . . . I'm plum beat out. . . . He's all-fired lazy. . . . Pay her no mind. . . .

Mountain:

It was just a small, puny, little old thing. . . . I disremember which was worser. . . . I'd be right proud to go. . . . He had a power of cash money. . . . We-uns ate a heap of chickens. . . . I don't know as I ever confidenced him. . . . Hit's acomin' on to rain. . . . I knowed in reason hit were his'n. . . . Hain't never heared no such thing. . . . Whyn't yu much me 'stead of faultin' me? . . . That 'ere buck deer'll meat us for a spell. . . .

Louisiana-French:

You been try make me mad. . . . What you do now? . . . I don't got but five cents, me. . . . He's the bestest child. . . . He all time drink, my uncle. . . . I don't got fine clothes. . . . I go three times. . . . I used to couldn't smoke. . . .

Cajun:

That man, he know the true. . . . I don't see those girl. . . . I don't going go. . . . For why you ask me? . . . Us, we ride two hour. . . .

Source: Willard R. Espy, *Say It My Way.*

linguists agree that some dialects have more prestige than others and that prestige is determined by the people who speak the dialect. Thus if you want to be accepted by and identified with people who use a dialect or who use a standard English different from your own, you might have to adapt to their

TRY THIS

Do a quick study of a dialect which you have heard. List the various words and phrases that most obviously distinguish this dialect. Is the dialect one which you speak? If so, does it emanate from the community in which you grew up? What are the strengths and weaknesses of the dialect? Do nonusers view the dialect positively? Why or why not? Is the dialect important to you? Why or why not?

way of speaking. Many Americans have discovered that it is not difficult to speak two "languages": a dialect and standard English. By so doing, it is possible to keep one's ethnic roots as well as function in a world where expectations are different.

Speaking and Writing

The English language includes many more words than most of us will ever use. The largest English-language dictionary contains about half a million words, but most of us will use only about 2 percent of them in our everyday reading, writing, and speaking.

We use a more limited vocabulary in speaking than we do in writing. Speech is intended to be understood as soon as the listener hears it. (Only with recording is there an opportunity to go back and hear it again.) We can, however, ask questions, respond to feedback from our listeners, and rephrase our message if we are not being understood. Speech also has ways of adding meaning that a writer does not have. The speaker can emphasize certain words, make dramatic pauses, slow down or speed up. A speech that might look dull on paper may have been very exciting to listen to because the speaker used his or her voice effectively.

The writer has time to go over words, phrase sentences, and check grammatical construction. Because of this increased time and the possibility that the reader will reread the material, the writer can deal with more difficult concepts. If a speaker is going to deal with highly complex ideas, he or she needs to allow opportunities for feedback—that is, for questions from the audience.

Perhaps the most important difference between speaking and writing is that the speaker's audience consists of people who are listening and reacting to the message *as it occurs.* In contrast, writers have no direct relationship with their audience—most writers don't even know who their readers are.

Words work best in oral communication if they are kept relatively simple and are chosen with a firm idea of who the listeners will be. Listener energy should be expended on trying to understand the ideas rather than on trying to understand the words or the language construction. Although you should not insult the intelligence of your listener by using language that is oversimplified, you should use language that is immediately understandable.

WORKING ON YOUR COMMUNICATION

When we set out to communicate verbally we are more likely to be successful if we use words and ideas that have the same meaning to us as they do to the person with whom we are communicating. Unfortunately, although we think we are being clear, the other person often does not perceive what we think we have communicated. Communication can break down at various stages. Let's look at some of the places where this might happen.

What Do You Want to Say?

In 1938 Orson Welles wrote a radio play about Martians invading the United States called *War of the Worlds*. We can assume that in writing this play, Welles had the intent of entertaining his audience. Although Welles's intent was clear to him, at least 1 million people misunderstood his intent and believed the play was real—they believed that Martians really had landed and that their lives were in peril. By the time the misunderstanding was cleared up, many people had already reacted to the play by leaving their homes and trying to find a place of safety.

Although this is an extreme example of intent going astray, most of us have had times when people responded to us in a way different from what we intended. You intend to tell your roommate to buy a loaf of whole wheat bread; she brings white bread instead. You intend to make a joke and end up insulting someone. When we are involved in one-to-one communication, we often have a chance to clear up misunderstandings. We see that the other person looks confused or annoyed, or the verbal response we get indicates that we have not communicated something as precisely as we intended, and we have a chance to clarify what we have said.

When we are talking to an audience, however, it is not so easy to clear up misunderstandings. In a public speaking or mass communication setting, we don't have a chance to respond to feedback—or at least we usually can't do it until the communication is over. Therefore, when we are going to communicate to a large audience, we have to engage in much more thought and preparation than in an interpersonal setting.

The first thing we must consider then is, What exactly do we want to say? Students who are new to public speaking often do not think out this step clearly enough. Let's say that you are going to give a speech about satellites. Do you want to describe what a satellite is? What it does? Do you want to

CONSIDER THIS

The difference between the right word and the almost-right word is the difference between lightning and the lightning bug.

—Mark Twain

persuade your audience to have a certain view of satellites? Answers to these questions will help to bring into focus your intent in giving the speech.

How Do You Want to Say It?

Once we have decided on our intent, we must choose the language we are going to use. A speech on satellites might entail the use of a highly specialized vocabulary that our audience does not know. To what extent do we have to define and explain our terms? If we have highly technical information to impart, how can we modify the language so our audience will understand our concepts on the basis of their own experience?

If descriptive and informative language has to be carefully chosen, we run into an even greater problem when we are dealing with abstractions. In speaking about justice, for example, we have to consider our language very carefully. "Justice" is not only an abstract word but an emotional one, and it might have as many different meanings as there are members in the audience. One person might think about a low grade she felt she didn't deserve; another might think of prison reform; still another might think about the backlog of cases in the courts. It would therefore be a mistake to think that people know what you are talking about when you use this word. When we use the language of abstraction and emotion, we must be careful to define our language from our *point of view* as it relates to the subject we are talking about.

To Whom Are You Talking?

When you seek a specific response from a listener, your words have to have meaning within the person's experience. If you were talking about snow to a student who had lived all of his life in Puerto Rico, for example, he would have little idea of what it means to live with snow—even though he might understand the concept intellectually. By the same token, a professor lecturing to a beginning psychology class would probably assume that students do not

TRY THIS

Sometime in the next 24 hours listen for someone using metatalk—talk that has more than one level of meaning. What is this person saying at each level of meaning? Do you have any idea why this person is using metatalk?

know the words "affective" and "cognitive" and therefore would define them as she lectured. Some knowledge of the listener's (or audience's) interests, experiences, and expectations will help the speaker to choose the words and arrange the ideas in the way that will be most effective.

Metatalk

Even interpersonal communication is not without its problems. Although we get immediate feedback and can rephrase our talk, we are faced with the problem that words and phrases do not always mean what they appear to mean. If someone says, for example, "My teacher told me to take a walk," it could mean that the teacher wanted her to go out and get some fresh air or that the teacher wanted to get rid of her.

In this kind of talk—called **metatalk**—the meaning lies behind the words and it exists on three levels: what the speaker is saying, what the speaker intends to say, and what the listener thinks the speaker is saying.[13] If the meaning is not the same on all three levels, then confusion results. If your mother says, "After all, I'm only your mother, . . ." what message is she really communicating to you? Although the phrase "only your mother" appears to be a put down, what she may really be saying is, "It's important that you listen to me (or do what I want you to do) because I am your mother." When you hear her say this, you might think either "I'd better take her seriously" or "She's trying to manipulate me with her 'mother line' again."

Language is filled with metatalk, and we have to listen for this kind of talk and understand its meaning if we are going to have accurate communication. We also should be aware of sometimes using metatalk ourselves. For example, it is not unusual for a student speaker to begin his or her speech by giving some indication that the speech will not be very good: "I just finished this speech this morning," "I couldn't find any research on this topic," or "You'll have to excuse me because I am feeling sick." If we say anything of this sort, we may be engaging in metatalk; what we may really be saying is, "I am feeling extremely nervous and anxious about giving this speech."

CONSIDER THIS

Metatalk

Judith Martin, who writes about manners, points out some of the meanings behind metatalk:

- *How do you do? How are you?* Both of these mean *Hello.* The correct question, when you want to know how someone's digestion or divorce is getting along, is *Tell me, how have you really been?*
- *Call me.* This can mean *Don't bother me now—let's discuss it on office time,* or *I would accept if you asked me out* or *I can't discuss this here* or *Don't go so fast.*
- *I'll call you.* This has opposite meanings, and you have to judge by the delivery. One is *Let's start something* and the other is *Don't call me.*
- *Let's have lunch.* Among social acquaintances, this means *If you ever have nothing to do on a day I have nothing to do, let's get together.* Among business acquaintances, it means *If you have something useful to say to me I'll listen.*
- *Let's have dinner.* Among social acquaintances, it means *Let's advance this friendship.* Among business acquaintances, it means *Let's turn this into a friendship.*
- *Please stop by some time and see me.* Said to someone who lives in the same area, it means *Call me if you'd like to visit me.* Genuine dropping in disappeared with the telephone, so if you want to encourage that, you have to say *I'm always home in the mornings. Don't bother to call; just drop by.*
- *Please come and stay with me.* Said to someone from another area, this means *I would consider extending an invitation at your convenience if it coincides with my convenience.*
- *We must get together.* Watch out here, because there are several similar expressions. This one means *I like you but I'm too busy now to take on more friendship.*
- *We really must see more of each other.* One of the tricky ones, this actually means *I can't make the time to see you.*
- *We must do this more often.* Another variation. This one is really *This was surprisingly enjoyable, but it's still going to happen infrequently.*
- *Yours truly, Yours sincerely.* The first is business, the second distant social. Both mean *Well I guess that's all I've got to say so I'll close now.*

Is all that clear? Oh, one last thing. People who say *I only say what I really mean,* really mean *I am about to insult you.*

Source: Judith Martin, *Miss Manners' Guide to Excruciatingly Correct Behavior.*

LANGUAGE CHOICES

Although we are often told that we should use clear and precise language, most of us wouldn't know how to go about it. Command of the language requires years of practice and study. Since it is impossible to lay down strict rules that govern the choice of language for all occasions and for all circumstances, the discussion here is limited to three important aspects of language choice: clarity, energy, and vividness.

Clarity

Sometimes when our meaning is unclear, it is because our sentence structure is faulty. Our ideas may be clear to us, but we are not expressing them very well. The restaurant manager who posted the sign, "If you don't like our waitresses, you should see our manager," did not express his message clearly. We could be excused for thinking that the sign meant that the manager was worse than the waitresses; what it meant to say was that restaurant patrons should complain to the manager if they were dissatisfied with the waitresses.

In oral communication, we often have a chance to straighten out the confusion caused by poor sentence structure. If our listeners look baffled or ask a question, we can try again. There are other times, however, when the need to speak as clearly and precisely as possible is more urgent. If we are saying something of special importance or if we are in a formal speaking situation, clarity is essential, since the opportunity to make our point clear probably will not arise.

Some language is so specialized that it is inappropriate to use it outside the field where it has come into use. "Input" and "output," for example, are computer terms that do not work very well in describing human relations or activities. "I would like your ideas for this project" is much better than "I would like to have your input." Although specialized words and phrases can be effective in their appropriate settings, we do not need them—nor should we use them—in everyday communication.

Also to be avoided is the pseudopsychological jargon that is so widespread in our society. In a novel satirizing this kind of language, the author described her main character in this way:

> She had decided to play the whole scene off the wall, to just go with the flow. Everybody knew, in these days of heightened consciousness, that the rational mind was a screw up; the really authentic thing to do was to act on your impulses.[14]

Other phrases occurring in the same novel include "heavy trip," "get your act together," "dump on you," "schizzed out," and "freak out," among others.

The problem with this kind of jargon is that it gives the listener or reader very little idea of what is really going on. What does it mean to "freak out"? Is it to go insane? To start screaming? To be frightened? If you don't know precisely what the expression means, how do you respond? Another problem is that jargon can become boring. If everyone were to use the expression "heavy trip" to describe a bad experience, all the different words and expressions in our language that describe these experiences would fall into disuse.

One of the delights of language is that it has so many subtleties and shades of meaning. Choosing jargon to express all our ideas is like eating Big Macs for dinner every night. Language is a marvelous banquet providing us with a vast array of choices for anything and everything we want to say.

Energy

When there is energy in a communication, listeners experience a feeling of excitement, urgency, and forcefulness. Energy, or the lack of it, can be communicated both verbally and nonverbally. Although a lack of energy is obvious in such nonverbal cues as slouching or speaking slowly, most of us are not as aware of how language itself can convey a lack of energy.

A sense of urgency is communicated mainly by verbs—the action words of the language. "Judy slapped him" and "The children jumped up and down" are both sentences that have energy and excitement. Adjectives and adverbs slow the language down, as in "The outraged Judy slapped him soundly." Another way to add energy to language is to put sentences in the active rather than in the passive voice. "The boy hit the ball" is more energetic than "The ball was hit by the boy."

Many of us slow down our speech by using complicated words when simple ones would be more vivid. The weather forecaster who says "There is a 10 percent chance of rain" sounds much livelier than the one who says "The probability of precipitation is 10 percent." "Fire" is a more active word than "conflagration." The verb "left" has more action than the verb "departed."

Language also has more energy when the speaker avoids tired, worn-out phrases. "Blushing bride," "Mother Earth," "busy as bees" are all examples of clichés—phrases that have been used so much they have lost their impact.

Energetic language is active and direct. It expresses ideas in the simplest, liveliest, most forceful way possible. Energetic language is one way of telling your listener, "Hey look. This is important. Listen to me!"

Vividness

Think back on some of the ghost stories you heard when you were a child. The best were the ones that filled you with terror—the ones laced with blood-curdling shrieks, mournful moans, mysterious howling. They were usually set in dark places, with only an occasional ghostly light or a streak of lightning. If any smells were mentioned, they were sure to be dank and musty.

A ghost story is usually told by the person who had the experience. Any narrative told from the point of view of "I was there" or "It happened to me" is particularly vivid. By recreating the experience for your listeners, you can often make them feel what you felt. Thus the quality of vividness in communication is a result of the recreation of a personal experience.

Vividness also comes from unique forms of speech. Some people would say that a person who talks too much "chatters like a magpie," a phrase that has become a cliché. To one Southern speaker, however, this person "makes a lot of chin music." When we say that language is vivid, we often mean that someone has found a new way of saying old things. Children often charm us with the uniqueness of their language because they are too young to know all the clichés and overused expressions. One of the best places to look for vivid language is among poets and song writers. Although more words have been written about love than any other subject, many song writers have given us new expressions and therefore new ways of looking at the experience. Their unique perspectives make an old idea sound original and exciting.

IMPROVING YOUR VERBAL STYLE

Your verbal style says a good deal about you. If you make a favorable impression, do well in a job interview, or make a good grade in a class, some of your success has come about because of your verbal style. Thus it is to your advantage to pay attention to the way you talk and to question whether you can improve.

Three ways to improve your verbal style are by increasing your vocabulary, by adapting your speech to the language environment, and by making a determined effort to break bad verbal habits. You can become actively involved in one or all of them during the course of daily interactions.

Increasing Your Vocabulary

Since you hear thousands of words every day, you can benefit from this continuous access to other people's vocabularies. By becoming more conscious of the words used by the television or radio advertiser and how skillfully and subtly he tries to sell his product, or of the politician and how she presents her ideas, or of the teacher and how she teaches a lesson, you can take advantage of a resource that is readily available.

When you hear a new word, try to understand it in its *context*—that is, from the words or actions that precede or follow and that are directly connected with it. Although you may not always be able to stop another person to ask what he or she means by a certain word, it is sometimes helpful to do so if possible. People sometimes use words incorrectly, of course, and contexts can be deceiving or misleading. When you hear a word that is unknown to you or when you hear a word in an unfamiliar context, check its meaning. You can also develop sensitivity to the meanings of words by paying attention to people's feelings as they are revealed in verbal expression and in nonverbal cues. This will help you to become more aware of the emotional content in the messages of others.

Another way to build your vocabulary is by reading and by looking up and remembering the meaning of any new words you encounter. When you are reading, just as when you are listening to your friends talk, try to be aware of new words—then find opportunities to fit those words into your own conversation. A word that is not actually used will not be remembered for long.

When you increase your vocabulary, you increase your chances of getting your intended meaning across to your listener. The more words you have at your command, the more precise you will be. This does not mean that you should search for big words; on the contrary, familiar words are often the best. But by increasing your vocabulary, you will enrich your conversation.

In addition to building your vocabulary, note how the words you read and hear are used in combination. It is the combination of words that makes style effective or ineffective. Thus you should not examine just the individual trees—the words—but the way the trees combine to make up the forest—the sentences, phrases, and the ideas themselves. Thoughts are expressed in groups of words—seldom as words alone.

Adapting Your Oral Language

As you talk to people, become conscious of them as particular people for whom you need to adapt your message. Note the language environment in which your conversation is taking place, and make the adaptations that are necessary. Also, be aware of the topic you are discussing, since it too can influence your choice of words. Be conscious of what you are saying. This added consciousness will increase your sensitivity to other people as well as your awareness of language choice and use.

Sometimes people confuse personal authenticity with inflexible language usage, and they equate undisciplined speech with spontaneity. "Telling it like it is" becomes an excuse for allowing the first words that come into your head to spill out in a torrent. Such language choices reflect a kind of self-centered indulgence that says to your listener, "Never mind who you are; listen to me." Adapting your language to the individual with whom you are talking can result in more satisfying exchange.

Breaking Bad Habits

Although we are sometimes told that we are making language mistakes such as using poor grammar or misusing or mispronouncing certain words, it is difficult for us to correct ourselves because we are so accustomed to talking this way. If we live in a language environment where these mistakes are constantly being made, it is even more difficult, because the errors are reinforced by hearing them so often. The only way to correct such mistakes is to have someone point them out to you—someone with whom you spend a lot of time. In using this method, it is advisable to tackle only one wrong usage at a time. Once you get that one cleared up, then you can begin to work on the next one. All habits are hard to break, and when you are trying to break one, you need all the help you can get.

SUMMARY

We all use language to communicate. Language is tied into our thought processes, and without language, we would not be able to think. Ideally, language is used to achieve understanding; but sometimes it is used to deceive and to manipulate.

Language occurs in a language environment, and to be successful it must be appropriate to that environment. The language that we should use in a particular environment is often determined by the role we are playing in that environment. Since language choices are role-related, if we do not modify our language to fit to our role, we may speak in ways that are inappropriate to the occasion.

A word is a symbol; it stands for the object or concept it names. In order for us to understand each other, we must agree on what the particular word-symbols stand for.

Language is directly linked to our perception of reality and to our thought processes. Our perceptions and our thought processes begin in earliest childhood. Our experiences determine how we use language.

Style, the way we express ourselves, is an important aspect of language. The style that is expected of us is often determined by the role we play. Language styles may differ from one group to another, and we must be aware of different styles if we are to communicate effectively.

Speaking and writing differ, in that oral communication is more spontaneous, personal, and immediate than written communication. Our speaking vocabularies are smaller than either our reading or writing vocabularies; spoken discourse is most effective when it is simple and direct.

It is impossible to lay down strict rules for making good language choices. But language that is clear, energetic, and vivid will be most effective. You can improve your use of language by making a conscious effort to become more aware of these qualities.

VOCABULARY

The following is a list of words you must know to understand the concepts of this chapter. You will find the words defined the first time that each is used in the chapter. All Vocabulary words also appear, with their definitions, in the Glossary at the end of the book.

connotative meaning
denotative meaning
dialect
expressive language
instrumental language
language environment

metatalk
nonstandard English
ritual language
standard English
style

FURTHER READING

BANDLER, RICHARD, AND JOHN GRINDER. *Frogs into Princes: Neuro Linguistic Programming*. Moab, Utah: Real People Press, 1979. This very readable, practical, and entertaining book presents some interesting and challenging therapeutic techniques that provide a way of looking at human behavior and communication. The authors look at verbal and nonverbal signals as ways of discovering that we know much more than we think we do. The approach is a sophisticated one for beginners.

BERGER, CHARLES R., AND JAMES J. BRADAC. *Language and Social Knowledge: Uncertainty in Interpersonal Relations*. London: Edward Arnold, 1982. The authors focus on the role that language plays in the processes of developing and maintaining relationships with others. The basic proposition of this book is that individuals prefer to avoid uncertainty in social interactions. The authors outline linguistic strategies that can be used to reduce uncertainty. This is primarily a theoretical work designed for the discriminating reader.

ENGEL, S. MORRIS. *The Language Trap: Or How to Defend Yourself Against the Tyranny of Words*. Englewood Cliffs, N.J.: Prentice-Hall, 1984. Engel discusses the language traps of distorted meaning—logical short-circuits, emotion-laden irrelevancies, disguised ambiguities, specious appeals to authority or principle, and other linguistic devices that lead us to believe things that are unproven or false. This book is a manual of verbal self-defense, answering the questions: How do fallacies work? How can you spot them? How can you combat them?

JAKSA, JAMES A., AND ERNEST L. STECH. *Voices from Silence—The Trappists Speak*. Toronto: Griffin House, 1980. The absence of speech is the subject of this book. It looks at the Trappist monks, a religious order dedicated to silence, and tells what happens when the monks are given permission to speak again. The authors emphasize the importance of speech if interpersonal relationships are going to exist.

KILPATRICK, JAMES J. *The Writer's Art*. New York: Andrews, McMeel & Parker, 1984. This is a finely crafted, witty guide to writing well. Intended for laymen and professionals alike, it highlights techniques and examples of good writing and includes more than 200 personal judgment calls on word usage that are often controversial as well as funny. The book is very useful, interesting, and readable.

MILLER, CASEY, AND KATE SWIFT. *Words and Women*. Garden City, N.Y.: Anchor Books, 1977. This book is a survey of the way that gender bias is built into the English language. The authors conclude with a section of practical suggestions on how to avoid this bias in writing and speaking.

NEWMAN, EDWIN. *Strictly Speaking.* New York: Warner Books, 1975; *A Civil Tongue.* Indianapolis: Bobbs-Merrill, 1976. Both of these books are intended for people who have some sophistication in using language. Written by a television newscaster, the books offer many examples of the misuse of language in contemporary American life.

PEARSON, JUDY CORNELIA. *Gender and Communication.* Dubuque, Iowa: Brown, 1985. Pearson divides her text into four parts: Considerations, Components, Codes, and Contexts. She includes both theory and practice. This very complete, well-researched textbook offers excellent material.

ROTHWELL, J. DAN. *Telling It Like It Isn't: Language Misuse & Malpractice/ What We Can Do About It.* Englewood Cliffs, N.J.: Prentice-Hall, 1982. Rothwell encourages us to become more effective communicators by understanding how language misuse and malpractice encourage and promote violence, racism, sexism, dehumanization, false attributions of mental illness, language censorship, and political, social, and international upheaval.

SAFIRE, WILLIAM. *William Safire on Language.* New York: Avon Books, 1980. Safire comments on more than 250 of the items, arranged in alphabetical order, on which readers have attacked him in his column on the American language for the *New York Times Magazine.* Included in the collection are many of the letters he received from readers. His is a witty, humorous, and erudite approach to language usage.

STRUNK, WILLIAM, JR., AND E. B. WHITE. *The Elements of Style,* 3rd ed. New York: Macmillan, 1979. Although it was designed for the writer, speakers take note: for the brevity, clarity, and truth it contains, this little book is worth considering. It treats the fundamentals—the rules of usage and the principles of composition most commonly violated. It will make you more conscious of the words you use.

ZINSSER, WILLIAM. *On Writing Well: An Informal Guide to Writing Nonfiction,* 2nd ed. New York: Harper & Row, 1980. Zinsser has good advice for speakers, too! His readable, personal book will help all those who want to gain control of their material.

5 NONVERBAL COMMUNICATION

CHAPTER OUTLINE

The Importance of Nonverbal Communication

  The use of nonverbal communication
  Verbal and nonverbal differences
  The functions of nonverbal communication

The Principles of Nonverbal Communication

  Nonverbal communication is culturally determined
  Nonverbal messages may conflict with verbal messages
  Nonverbal messages are largely unconscious

  Nonverbal channels are important in communicating feelings and attitudes

Types of Nonverbal Communication

  Paralanguage
  Body movement
  Body type
  Attractiveness
  Body Adornment
  Space and Distance
  Touch
  Time

Changing and Improving Your Nonverbal Communication

CHAPTER OBJECTIVES

After reading this chapter, you should be able to:

1. Enumerate the differences between verbal and nonverbal communication.
2. List the various functions of nonverbal communication.
3. Explain the basic principles that govern nonverbal communication.
4. Describe the various types of nonverbal communication.
5. Be more sensitive to your own use of nonverbal cues.

1:41 P.M.:   Barbara Johnson sits at her desk staring blankly into space. Evita passes her desk, looks at her, hesitates briefly; Barbara shakes her head, as if to say "This isn't the time," and Evita moves on. Barbara is still contemplating her lunchtime conversation with friends.

1:43 P.M.:   Sam passes her desk, touches her on the shoulder, and says, "Good luck." (Sam was one of those at lunch with Barbara.)

1:45 P.M.:   Barbara pounds on her desk with both fists, gets up, and walks briskly toward the president's office.

1:47 P.M.:   The president's secretary is on the phone but waves Barbara into the inner office. The president, Ms. Davis, looks at Barbara and says, "I see something is *really* troubling you." She waves Barbara to a seat but Barbara shakes her head, refusing.

1:48 P.M.:   Barbara looks briefly at Ms. Davis, paces back and forth, shakes her head, takes a deep breath, and says, "Ms. Davis, I just don't know how to say this . . ." Ms. Davis watches her and waits for her to go on.

1:49 P.M.:   Then, in a slow and determined manner, Barbara says, "Ms. Davis, I've worked for you for two years; you know the stories I write are good, and you know that my assignments have gotten bigger and bigger. I really think I deserve a raise." (On this last sentence, she pounds her right fist into her left palm.)

1:50 P.M.:   Davis looks directly at Barbara, raises a cup of coffee to her lips, takes a long, slow drink, then turns in her chair toward the window. Then she says, "Tell you what, Barbara. You kind of caught me off guard. Let me think about it and I'll get back to you before the end of the afternoon. O.K.?" She extends her hand to Barbara.

1:51 P.M.:   Barbara tentatively shakes her extended hand. "Thank you, Ms. Davis. You've always been honest and straightforward with me. I'll talk to you later then."

These ten minutes in the life of Barbara Johnson give us a good idea of the importance of nonverbal communication. Some of the nonverbal elements were obvious: the pounding on the desk, the brisk walk, being waved into the office, and the handshake. In this particular scene, much more was communicated by nonverbal means than through the use of language.

THE IMPORTANCE OF NONVERBAL COMMUNICATION

Albert Mehrabian, a contemporary writer on nonverbal communication, has determined from his research that as much as 93 percent of communication is nonverbal.[1] **Nonverbal communication** is any information we communicate without using words. Thus the way a person uses voice, body movement (for example, eye contact, facial expression, gesture, and posture), clothing and body appearance, space, touch, and time is an essential part of every message that he or she sends.

CONSIDER THIS

Can You Tell When Someone Is Lying to You?

Most of us believe that there are certain indicators that people are lying to us: refusal to make eye contact, hesitation before answering questions, and a general nervousness are some of the ways we believe liars behave. We also believe that some people are better at detecting liars than others.

None of these beliefs is true according to recent research on lying. College students are as good at detecting liars as are police detectives or customs inspectors—although all of these people do little better than chance.

Are there any signs that show people are lying? Dr. Paul Ekman, a psychologist, says, "Most liars can fool most of the people most of the time." There are a few very subtle signs, however, that might point to a liar. Ekman has discovered that most people who are lying are trying to cover up distress, fear, or anxiety.

People who are feeling distressed, for example, lift just the inner part of the eyebrows. Ekman says, "Fewer than 15 percent of the people can control this movement at will." When people are afraid, they will raise their eyebrows and pull them together. "Not a single person we've tested can produce this movement deliberately," according to Ekman. Finally, angry people often narrow and tighten the red margin of the lips.

If you want to try to detect the people who are lying to you, it is going to be hard work. In a study at the University of Virginia, subjects were asked to keep diaries of their lies. The average person admitted to two a day!

Source: Adapted from Daniel Goleman, "Researchers Identify True Clues to Lying," *New York Times.*

The Use of Nonverbal Communication

Communicators exert little or no control over such nonverbal cues as sex, race, body size, age, region of origin, social status, and to a certain degree, emotional state. Whether control is exerted or not, all these elements are part of any face-to-face communication situation, although we are not always aware of them. We often send and receive nonverbal cues unconsciously.

Most nonverbal communication involves several related messages. For example, a particular posture is not in itself proof that a person is sad or depressed. A number of other elements would affect our reading of the person's state of mind—downcast eyes, an absence of gestures, and a lack of vitality in general. As we get to know people better, we become more familiar with their mannerisms and the way they express themselves nonverbally. Some of the cues we observe in close friends are different from those we observe in strangers. With experience, we become more aware of cues, and nonverbal communication becomes even more complex. How do you show someone else you are frustrated, angry, lonely, or indifferent? How does your best friend express these same emotions? How about your mother and father? When you make comparisons, you will discover that people express the same emotion in a variety of nonverbal ways.

Verbal and Nonverbal Differences

Verbal and nonverbal communication differ in five ways: continuity, channel, the extent to which they can be controlled, their structure, and how they are acquired. Let us consider each of these differences in turn.

Continuity

Verbal communication begins and ends with words, whereas nonverbal communication is continuous. Imagine the waiting room of a doctor's office. Several people are waiting to see the doctor, and although some of them might occasionally talk to each other, they are all engaged in continuous nonverbal communication. Several people are looking at magazines—and occasionally at their watches. One person sits for a few minutes, then gets out of his chair and paces a few steps before he sits again. Another person, probably a mother, keeps checking the child who is resting quietly in her arms. All of these people, then, are continuously sending out nonverbal messages about how they are feeling in this situation.

Channel

Verbal communication requires a single channel, words, whereas nonverbal communication uses several channels. In the doctor's office, as we watch the mother with her sick child, she is communicating her state of mind through several channels: her posture is tense, her facial expression is worried, and her gestures are such as to comfort and reassure the child.

Control

Whereas verbal communication is under our control because we can choose our words, nonverbal communication is under our control only part of the time. It is under our control, for example, when we decide what to wear when we get up in the morning. The nonverbal cues that are not under our control are those that are habitual and unconscious. Some instructors jiggle coins in their pockets when they lecture. Others pace back and forth across the room. Most of us are not even aware of these nonverbal cues unless they are pointed out to us.

Structure

Verbal communication is structured. It follows formal rules of grammar. Because so much of nonverbal communication occurs unconsciously, however, there is no planned sequence. If you are sitting and talking to someone, you don't plan when you will cross your legs, get up out of your chair, or look at the other person. These nonverbal actions will occur depending on what is happening during the conversation. The only rules that govern nonverbal communication are those that determine whether the behavior is appropriate or permissible. A child, for example, learns that to stare at people or to point at them is rude behavior.

Acquisition

Many of the formal rules for verbal communication are taught in a structured, formal environment such as a school. We learn that words such as "ain't" or grammatical constructions such as "he don't" are not acceptable forms of English. We also learn what style is appropriate to particular situations—that formal English is required for essays whereas informal English is more suitable for speech. In contrast, much of nonverbal communication is not formally taught; we pick it up through imitating others. Young children commonly imitate the nonverbal communication of their parents, siblings, or peers.

The Functions of Nonverbal Communication

Nonverbal cues *complement* a verbal message when they add to its meaning. When you meet someone for the first time you might say, "I am really glad to meet you. I've heard a lot about you." If you say this with a warm smile and shake his or her hand, you are complementing your verbal message.

Nonverbal cues also *regulate* verbal communication. If you are talking to your boss or one of your teachers, how does she tell you that it's time for the conversation to end? She might get up out of her chair, or she might look pointedly at the clock on the wall—two ways to indicate the conversation is over.

Nonverbal messages can also *substitute* for, or be used in place of, verbal messages. The secretary waves you into the boss's office without telling you to go in. We raise a hand in greeting instead of saying hello, or we give someone a hug—a wordless way of saying we like that person.

Often nonverbal messages *accent* what we are saying. The politician pounds the lectern to make sure everyone realizes his or her message is important. A mother tells a child he is a bad boy and swats him on the rear end to emphasize the point. Whenever people are communicating something they consider important, they are likely to accent it with a nonverbal message.

THE PRINCIPLES OF NONVERBAL COMMUNICATION

Four fundamental principles underlie the workings of nonverbal communication. The first is that the nonverbal communication we use is largely that used by other persons in our culture. Second, verbal and nonverbal messages may be in conflict with each other. Third, much of nonverbal communication operates at a subconscious level—we are not even aware of it. Fourth, our nonverbal communication shows our feelings and attitudes.

Nonverbal Communication Is Culturally Determined

Much of our nonverbal behavior is learned in childhood, passed on to us by our parents and others with whom we associate. Through the process of growing up in a particular society, we adopt the traits and mannerisms of our cultural group. Americans, for example, teach their children to look other people right in the eye. This behavior, however, is not taught to all cultural groups. An African child who looked directly at an adult would be considered disrespectful.

As well as belonging to a broad cultural group such as a nation, we also belong to cultural subgroups. Hispanic, Chinese, and black children might grow up with a broad American cultural conditioning, but they also belong to subgroups that have nonverbal behaviors of their own. American blacks, for example, have a variety of handshakes they use only with each other. Other groups, formed because their members have something in common other than ethnic or national identity (fraternal organizations such as the Moose or the Elks are examples), might have specific ways of dressing or of gesturing that enable members to identify and communicate with one another.

Nonverbal Messages May Conflict with Verbal Messages

Nonverbal communication is so deeply rooted, so unconscious, that we often say something verbally and then directly contradict it with a nonverbal message. Take the professor who says, ''I want to help you as much as I can. Feel free to stop by my office any time.'' Yet whenever you stop by during his office hours, he is not there. The one time he is there, he keeps sneaking looks at his watch and leafing through the papers on his desk while he is talking to you. This instructor gave you a **mixed message**. His words said one thing but his actions sent a completely different message.

In the case of mixed messages, the nonverbal communication is often more reliable than the verbal. We learn to manipulate words, but it is difficult for us to manipulate our nonverbal communication. Your instructor probably was not even aware that he was giving you the nonverbal message that he didn't have time to talk to you. The message, however, was coming through loud and clear.

CONSIDER THIS

Researchers at the University of Pennsylvania took photographs of six people, and made twelve composites of the left and right sides of faces. The left side showed much more emotion. Happiness, surprise, anger, fear, disgust, and sadness all show up more intensely on the left side of the face. The hemispheres of the brain create the differences. People tend to look at the right side of faces, which is the wrong side for perceiving intense emotions.

Source: Adapted from Susan Stamberg, *Every Night at Five.*

Nonverbal Messages Are Largely Unconscious

Your mother calls you to see how you are doing. Right after the "Hello" and "I'm fine," she says, "What's wrong?" She has sized up your emotional state on the basis of vocal tone alone. Did you know tone of voice could be so revealing?

Do you realize that when you don't like people you tend not to stand as close to them as you do to those you like? Do you know that your facial expression often reveals whether you like something—no matter what your words express? Do you know that your body position (as well as where you place your arms and legs) can reveal your feelings toward those you are seated next to? Do you know that you try to prevent people from moving into territory that you consider "yours"? Do you know that head and eye movements are central to beginning and ending conversations with others?[2]

When we consider all these nonverbal behaviors, it is hardly surprising that we are unaware of much of our nonverbal communication. Research has shown, however, that outgoing, aggressive people are more aware of nonverbal cues than are shy and passive people.[3]

Nonverbal Channels Are Important in Communicating Feelings and Attitudes

The various nonverbal channels communicate our feelings and emotions to others. The feelings and emotions others can detect in our faces include happiness, sadness, surprise, fear, anger, disgust/contempt, and interest.[4] Research has also shown that most people can accurately identify emotions expressed by the voice.[5] If the emotion in the face and voice is combined with similar body movements, nonverbal communication becomes a powerful means for expressing emotion. You may have heard stories of legendary actors who could bring their audiences to tears while merely reciting the alphabet. These were actors who understood how to use nonverbal communication.

TRY THIS

The next time you are watching your favorite soap opera or television program, turn down the volume for five minutes and see how much of the story you can follow with only nonverbal cues to guide you. Then turn the volume back up to see how accurate you have been.

TYPES OF NONVERBAL COMMUNICATION

Paralanguage

Paralanguage is the way we say something. There is a clear distinction between a person's use of words (verbal communication) and a person's use of voice (nonverbal communication). Paralanguage includes such characteristics as rate (speed of speaking), pitch (highness or lowness of tone), volume (loudness), and quality (pleasing or unpleasing sound). When any or all of these factors are added to the words, they can modify the meaning. Albert Mehrabian estimates that 39 percent of the meaning in communication is affected by vocal cues—not the words that are spoken but the way in which they are said.[6]

Rate

The **rate** (speed) at which one speaks can have an effect on the way a message is received.[7] A very rapid rate can dull the senses just as a very slow rate can. Varying the rate is important. Speakers will hold the attention of listeners best if the rate of speaking changes with the nature of the ideas, the mood, and the kind of feedback the speaker is receiving. A good example of rate change is the television evangelist. Notice how he will start slowly and then, as the emotional intensity increases, he will also increase his rate. Rate often indicates emotional meaning. Anger, stress, and fear are associated with faster rates of speech, whereas grief or depression are associated with slower rates.

Pitch

Pitch refers to the highness or lowness of the voice. Pitch can determine whether a voice sounds pleasant or unpleasant. High-pitched voices are not considered as pleasant as low-pitched ones. High-pitched voices often sound shrill and grating to the ear. But a pitch that is too low can also cause problems. Lower pitches are more difficult to hear, and people who have low-pitched

TRY THIS

Read the following sentence aloud, each time emphasizing a different word in the sentence:

I saw her in the room yesterday.

How many different meanings can you get by emphasizing different words? Could you get more variations by reading the sentence each time as a question rather than as a statement?

voices may be perceived as insecure or shy because they don't seem to speak up. Pitch can be changed, but it requires working with someone who has had professional training in voice work.

Volume

The meaning of a message can be affected also by its **volume**—how loudly we speak. A loud voice is fine if used for the appropriate purpose and in moderation. The same is true of a soft voice. Notice how effective parents and teachers change their volume when dealing with children. A change in volume is particularly good for gaining attention.

Vocal Fillers

Vocal fillers—the sounds and words that we use to fill out our sentences or to cover up when we are searching for words—may be actual words ("you know," "O.K.," "well") or meaningless sounds ("uh," "er," "um"). In either case, they are a nonverbal way of indicating that we are temporarily stuck and are searching for the right word. We all use vocal fillers; they become a problem only when they become excessive or if they are distracting to listeners.

Quality

The overall sound of the voice, its **quality**, is useful for conveying different feelings. We can probably all agree on what are unpleasant voices: perpetual whining, constant yelling. Pleasant voices generally are quite low in pitch, have a lot of variety, and are soft. Creating a pleasant voice is not easy. Students who see and hear themselves on videotape are almost always more unhappy with how they sound than with how they look. Voices can be changed, with hard work and professional help.

Body Movement

Body movement, also called **kinesics**, is responsible for a lot of our nonverbal communication. Paul Ekman and W. C. Friesen, researchers on nonverbal communication, divide body movement into five categories: emblems, illustrators, regulators, displays of feeling, and adaptors.[8]

Emblems

Emblems are body movements that have a direct translation into words. The extended thumb of the hitchhiker is an emblem that means "I want a ride." Making a circle with the thumb and index finger can be translated into "O.K." These emblems are known by most of the people in our society, and they are used to send a specific message. Emblems often cannot be carried from one culture to another. If you shake your head back and forth in southern India, for example, it means yes!

Emblems are often used when words are inappropriate. It would be impractical for a hitchhiker to stand on the side of the road shouting for a ride. Sometimes we use emblems when we don't feel like talking. Also, subgroups in a society often use emblems that members of the group understand but whose meanings are intentionally kept from outsiders—the special handshake of blacks is an example.

Illustrators

Illustrators accent, emphasize, or reinforce words. If someone asks how big your suitcase is, you will probably describe it with words and illustrate those words by indicating the dimensions with your hands. If someone is giving you directions, she will probably point down the road and gesture left and right at the appropriate points. Illustrators can help to make communication more exact. If someone tells you he has just caught a fish, you will have an idea of how big the fish is by how far apart he holds his hands. He could tell you the size in inches, but somehow you will get an even better idea if he uses his hands as an illustrator. But not all illustrators are gestures. If an instructor underlines something she has written on the blackboard, she is telling you that this point is particularly important. A car salesman emphasizes that a car is well built by slamming the door so you can hear how solid it sounds.

Regulators

Regulators control the back-and-forth nature of speaking and listening. They include the head nods, hand gestures, shifts in posture, and other body movements that signal the beginning and end of interactions. At a very simple level, a teacher uses a regulator when she points to the person she wants to speak next. On a more subtle level, someone might turn slightly away when you are

TRY THIS

What emblems might accompany or substitute for the following words or phrases?

- Yes.
- I don't care.
- Maybe.
- Stop.
- Shame on you.

talking—perhaps indicating "I don't like what I'm hearing" or "I don't want to continue this conversation."

Displays of Feelings

Displays of feelings show, through our faces and our body movements, how intensely we are feeling. If a student walks into a professor's office and the professor says, "I can see you are really feeling upset," he or she is responding

In this wedding reception line, it is not just the words but the gestures and facial expressions that combine to convey the emotional content to the observer.

to nonverbal cues the student is giving about his feelings. The student might have come in tearfully or with a body posture indicating "We really are going to fight this out"—a variety of body movements could have shown that the student was feeling upset.

Adaptors

Adaptors are nonverbal ways we have of adapting to the communication situation. We use such a wide variety of adaptors and they are so specific to our own needs and the communication situation that they are difficult to classify or even describe. Let's look, however, at how they work in some specific communication situations.

You have rented your first apartment and your mother has come to visit. While she is there, she spends a good deal of time moving objects and furniture around. By moving things around, she is using adaptors. What does her non-verbal behavior mean? On a simple level, she might be telling you that you are not very tidy. On a more complicated level, she might be telling you that you are still her child and that she, your mother, is still in charge.

People often use adaptors when they are nervous or uncomfortable in a situation. We might play with jewelry, drum on the table, move around a lot in our seats. Each of these behaviors is an adaptor—a way of helping us to cope with the situation. We all use adaptors, but we are generally not aware of them unless someone points them out.

Body Type

Our body type communicates a message. However we may perceive ourselves, others tend to judge us by our body type. Ernst Kretschmer, a professor of psychiatry and neurology, made the first known effort to classify *body types* as early as 1925.[9] Those with skinny, bony, narrow bodies are *ectomorphs*. *Mesomorphs* have athletic, hard, firm, muscular bodies. *Endomorphs* have oval-shaped bodies with heavy, large abdomens. In the 1940s, William Sheldon related body type and temperament.[10] His work has been updated by research-ers W. Wells and B. Siegel.[11] They asked subjects to make judgments about silhouettes of each of these body types. Ectomorphs (thin people) were rated as more ambitious, younger, more suspicious of others, more tense and nervous, more inclined to be difficult, more pessimistic, and quieter. Mesomorphs (athletic people) were seen as stronger, more adventurous, more mature, more self-reliant, younger, and taller. Endomorphs (fat people) were considered to be more old-fashioned, lazier, weaker, more talkative, older, more warm-hearted and sympathetic, more good-natured and agreeable, more dependent on others, and more trusting.

Attractiveness

People who are perceived as attractive get a more positive response from others than people who are not perceived as attractive. In our society, greatly influenced by what we see on the television screen, attractiveness consists in being thin, tall (especially if you're a man), and having a lot of hair.

Not surprisingly, attractive people have an easier time in life. Researchers have discovered that women perceived as attractive have more dates, receive higher grades in college, persuade males with greater ease, and receive lighter court sentences.[12] Men or women rated as attractive are also perceived as being more sensitive, kind, strong, sociable, and interesting.[13] In business, attractiveness pays off in several ways, including finding jobs and obtaining higher starting salaries.[14]

Body Adornment

We are also sending messages by how we adorn our body. Although most of our adornment is in the form of clothing, adornment also involves make-up, jewelry, and hairstyle.

When we enter a job interview, for example, we are giving out a good deal of information about ourselves by the way we dress and adorn ourselves. The interviewer might notice whether our clothing fits the company image of how employees should be dressed. A former military officer might pay particular attention to how well our shoes are polished. Other people might be sensitive to make-up or jewelry. If we are dressed appropriately for the job we are interviewing for, we have a better chance of being hired. If we are inappropriately dressed, the interviewer may pay little attention to our qualifications—even if they are very good.

Most of us like to feel that we are not generally influenced by what another person wears; we prefer to think we judge a person by what he or she is. But a survey by one poll-taking organization, Roper, suggests otherwise.[15] The results of the survey showed that when meeting someone of the opposite sex, women first notice clothes, then eyes, followed by body build. Men first notice body build, then face, followed by dress.

This order is somewhat changed when meeting someone of the same sex. Women notice, in the following order, clothes, hair, face, smile, and figure. Men also notice clothing first, followed by face, smile, and body build. In the area of the body build, men usually notice height.

Unlike much of nonverbal communication, clothing and adornment are things over which we have some control; we use them to create a particular image of ourselves. Since they are sending messages about us, we need to be aware of what is appropriate and what will do us the most good.

TRY THIS

The next time you come to class, wear something that is completely different from what you normally wear.

Notice the reactions and comments from your classmates. What reactions did you get? What comments did you receive?

Do you think clothes are important to the perceptions you receive from others? What is the message *your* clothes reveal about you?

Space and Distance

The study of space and distance, called **proxemics**, concerns the way we use the space around us as well as the distance we stand or sit from others. The minute you enter a classroom, you are faced with a decision that relates to how you use space. You have to decide where to sit. You may choose to sit in the back because you do not want to be noticed, because you feel it is a "safer" distance from the teacher, because you do not want people behind you staring at you, or because it will give you an opportunity to see other students' reactions and thus give you confidence. On the other hand, you might select a front-row seat because you have a lot of confidence or because you want to be noticed.

What is interesting about your choice of seating is that you might be sending your instructor a message. When he sees you sitting in the back row in the far corner, he might decide you are not very interested in the subject and are looking for a place to go to sleep. If you are there in the front row, he might conclude that you are an unusually bright and attentive student and he should give you special attention. You could also be sending your classmates a message. They might interpret the front-seat choice as a way of trying to win points with the instructor. If you are more toward the back of the room, you are one of them—since that's where most students decide to sit—yet that's where least interaction with the instructor is likely to take place (see Figure 5-1).

We make judgments about how others are thinking and reacting to us by the way they use space. It was Edward T. Hall, author of *The Silent Language* and *The Hidden Dimension*, two popular books on nonverbal communication, who labeled the study of space and distance proxemics.[16] From his observations and interviews, Hall has discovered that people use four distance zones when they are communicating with others: intimate distance, personal distance, social distance, and public distance.[17]

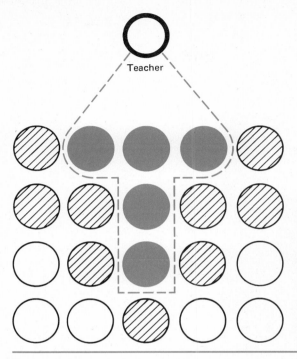

FIGURE 5-1 In a traditional classroom arrangement, those students occupying the colored seats will account for a large proportion of the total interaction that occurs between teacher and students. Those in the striped seats will interact some; those in the white seats will interact very infrequently. The area enclosed in dotted lines has been called the "action zone."

Intimate Distance

In *intimate distance*, people are in direct contact with each other or are no more than 18 inches apart. Look at a mother with her baby. She picks him up, caresses him, kisses him on the cheek, puts him on her lap. All of her senses are alert when she is this close to the baby. She can touch him, smell him, and hear every little gurgle he makes. We also maintain an intimate distance in love relationships and with close friends. Intimate distance exists whenever we feel free to touch the other person.

When our intimate distance is violated by people who have no right to be there, we feel apprehensive. If we are on a crowded bus, subway, or elevator, and people are pressed against us—they are in our intimate distance. We react by ignoring these people and by not making eye contact. In this way we can protect our intimate distance—psychologically if not physically.

Personal Distance

In *personal distance* people stay anywhere from 18 inches to 4 feet from each other. This is the distance we keep most often when we are in casual and personal conversations. It is close enough to see the other person's reactions but far enough away not to encroach on his or her intimate distance. If we

Freedom to touch is a sign of intimate distance.

move closer than 18 inches, he or she will probably back away. If we move farther away than 4 feet, it will be difficult to carry on a conversation without having the feeling that it can be overheard by others.

Social Distance

When we do not know people very well, we are most likely to maintain a *social distance* from them—that is, a distance of 4 to 12 feet. Impersonal business, social gatherings, and interviews are examples of situations where we use social distance.

Whenever we use social distance, business becomes more formal. Have you ever noticed the size of the desks in the offices of important people? They are large enough to keep visitors at the proper social distance. In a large office with many workers, the desks will be this distance apart. This distance makes it possible for each worker to concentrate on his or her work and to use the telephone without affecting others in the office. Sometimes people will move in and out from social distance to personal distance. Two co-workers might, for example, have desks that are several feet apart. When they want to discuss something more privately, they will move into each other's personal distance.

Public Distance

Public distance—a distance of more than 12 feet—is typically used for public speaking. At this distance, people usually speak more loudly and use more exaggerated gestures. Communication at this distance is more formal and permits few opportunities for people to be involved with each other. Figure 5-2 shows the dimensions of the four distance zones.

Space/Distance as an Indicator of Intimacy

When we observe the distances that people maintain between themselves and others, we can tell which people have close relationships and which people have more formal relationships. If you enter the college president's office and she remains behind her desk, you can assume that your conversation is going to be formal. If she invites you to the corner where there are easy chairs and you sit side by side, she has set up a much more intimate situation, and consequently, the conversation is going to be more informal.

As we get to know people better, we are permitted into their more personal space. Remember when you were in junior high and went with a boy or a girl to the movies for the first time? When your hands met in the popcorn box, you were exploring the possibilities of moving from a personal to an intimate distance. The opposite can also happen. A married couple experiences a lot of intimate distance. If there are problems in the marriage, however, the couple's communication will be conducted mostly at a personal distance. If they start to negotiate a divorce, they will probably carry out most of their negotiations at a social distance.

FIGURE 5-2 **The Four Distance Zones**

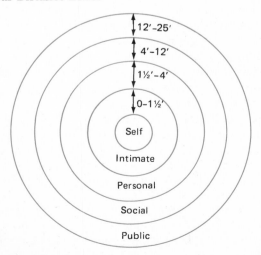

TRY THIS

Imagine having a conversation with each of the following people. How much space do you think would be between you in each case?

- Queen Elizabeth
- A U.S. senator
- A state legislator
- John Travolta
- The president of your college
- Your favorite instructor
- A good friend of yours
- Your brother or sister

Space/Distance as an Indicator of Status

Besides degrees of intimacy, degrees of status are communicated through the use of space. Executives, presidents of colleges, and high government officials all have large offices with expansive windows and elaborate furnishings, whereas their secretaries and support staff are in smaller spaces—spaces that are often used by many people. In a household children have the least amount of space. Even if they have their own room, that space is often controlled by adults. It is planned and decorated by an adult, and the adult sets the rules for how the space will be used. Adults also punish children by depriving them of space. Commands such as "Go to your room" or "Stay out of my room" limit children's access to space within the household.

Touch

The closer we stand to each other, the more we increase the likelihood of our touching. We are all familiar with the use of touch in intimate situations. We kiss babies, hold hands with loved ones, and hug family members.

When and where we touch each other is governed by a strict set of societal rules. Richard Heslin has described five different categories of touch behavior.[18] The first is *functional-professional touch*, in which you are touched for a specific reason, as in a physical examination. This kind of touch is impersonal and businesslike. *Social-polite touch* is used to acknowledge someone else. The handshake is the most common form. Although the two people move into an intimate distance to shake hands, after the handshake is over, they move away from each other. In close relationships people use the *friendship-warmth touch*. This kind of touch involves hugs and casual kisses between friends. In more intense relationships the *love-intimacy touch* is common. Parents stroke their children; boyfriends, girlfriends, and spouses kiss each other. The final touch Heslin describes is *sexual-arousal touch*—touch used as an expression of physical attraction.

CONSIDER THIS

The Value of Touch

Touch is one of the most important ways we have of communicating. In various studies researchers have found that:

- When volunteers went to a hospital to touch and stroke very sick babies regularly, the babies began to gain weight, became alert, and thrived.
- When mothers gave their children a good deal of cuddling and touching within 12 hours of their birth, the children later showed greater language development, higher reading readiness scores, and higher IQs than children who did not receive this physical contact.
- When library clerks touched the hands of some book borrowers, the borrowers whose hands had been touched were later found to have higher positive feelings about themselves and about the library than did borrowers who were not touched.
- When a researcher left a dime behind in a public telephone booth and, when the next person entered the booth, asked if it was there, the answer was almost always no. However, if the researcher gently touched the person on the arm for a few seconds and asked the question, she almost always got the dime back.

Although touch is clearly beneficial, Americans have unfortunately been culturally conditioned not to touch other people. Sidney Jourard, a psychologist, observing touching behavior in coffee shops around the world, kept count of how often people touched each other. In Puerto Rico, there were 180 touches an hour; in France, there were 110. In American, however, there were only 2.

Source: Adapted from Sherry Suib Cohen, "The Amazing Power of Touch," *Ladies Home Journal.*

As in distance, the kind of touch that is used communicates information about the relationship. The more intense the relationship, the more frequent and more intimate the touch. Often we can tell how much others are involved and the quality of their relationship by how much they touch each other. For example, nurses know that if a mother does not frequently touch her child, this is an indication that something is wrong in the relationship.

Time

People seem to be divided into those who are always on time and those who are always late. Have you ever noticed in a class that certain people always come late whereas others are always in their seats when the class begins?

From the viewpoint of an instructor, the person who is always late may be communicating considerable negative information: he is really not interested in this class, he doesn't respect an instructor, and so on. By the same token, students might resent an instructor who is always late. They might think he doesn't plan well enough or that he doesn't respect the class.

At one time or another we all use time for psychological effect. If you have a date with someone you don't know very well, you probably will not arrive too early because this might make you appear too eager. If you dent the family car, you wait for the right time to tell your parents about it. Our control of time, then, is an important form of nonverbal communication.

Often time is connected with status: the higher our status the more control we have over our time. A child has little control over time. His higher-status mother interrupts his play to have him eat dinner or makes him go to bed far earlier than he wants to. Professionals in our society often make others wait for them. How long do you wait in the doctor's office before you can see him or her? Students have little say in how their time is spent. If they want a particular class and it is only offered at 8:00 A.M., they have little choice but to take it then. They also have no choice as to when papers are due or when they have to take examinations. If we want to discover who has the most status in our society, we might do well by watching who waits for whom.

CHANGING AND IMPROVING YOUR NONVERBAL COMMUNICATION

Because our nonverbal behavior is so tied in with our social and cultural conditioning, it is not very easy to change it. Fortunately, most of us don't need to make any drastic changes. We should mostly be concerned with nonverbal communication that distracts from what we want to say or that contradicts our verbal messages. If we find that people regularly misunderstand us, we might do well to ask whether this might be due to nonverbal cues people are picking up—remembering that as much as 93 percent of what we are communicating may be nonverbal.

If we want to change our nonverbal behavior, it is important to pay attention to feedback we get from others. "Why have I been misunderstood?" "Why do people see me as unfriendly, rigid, unhappy . . . ?" For example, if a number of people tell you that when they first met you they thought you were a snob, it might be a good idea to ask if they know what you did to make them feel that way. Once you have this feedback, you will be able to figure out more precisely what you have been doing, with the goal of changing your behavior.

If you realize you have distracting mannerisms (playing with your hair, saying "you know" too much), it might be useful to have friends and family members remind you when you are doing these things so you can break the habit.

Probably the single most important tool for discovering negative nonverbal behavior is videotape. Most people who see themselves on tape know immediately what their bad habits are. If you have access to a videotape recorder, take advantage of it. Have someone tape you giving a speech or in conversation with another person. You will be amazed at what you can learn about yourself. If you have a chance to tape your voice, don't spend all your time reacting to it emotionally; see if you can figure out what there is about your voice you don't like and might be able to change.

Observe people in the roles they play. How do bosses act? How much of their communication is nonverbal? What nonverbal elements are desirable? Undesirable? When you get to be a boss, which of these behaviors would you want to imitate? Which people *don't* you want to be like? Is it their nonverbal behavior that is turning you off? Do you do any of these same things? Can you stop doing them?

Time and space are two nonverbal areas over which you can take some control. What does your room, apartment, or house look like? What will people think of you when they see your space? How about time? Are you sensitive to other people's time, or do you make them wait for you? How do you think they feel about you when they have to wait?

Our greatest problem with nonverbal communication is that we don't think about it enough. When we realize how important a part of our total communication it is, we are more likely to realize that we should all pay careful attention to it.

SUMMARY

As much as 93 percent of the impact of a message can depend on its nonverbal elements. Verbal communication and nonverbal communication often reinforce each other, but there are clear differences as well. Verbal communication begins when a word is uttered, requires a single channel, is under your control, is structured, and is formally learned. Nonverbal communication is continuous, is multichanneled, is mostly habitual and unconscious, is largely unstructured, and is learned informally.

Nonverbal communication serves important functions. With respect to the verbal message, it can complement it, regulate it, substitute for it, or accent it. In addition, basic principles tell us that most nonverbal communication is culturally determined, may conflict with verbal messages, is sent subtly, perhaps even unconsciously, and communicates feelings and attitudes.

There are several types of nonverbal communication. They include: paralanguage, body movement, clothing and body appearance, space/distance, touch, and the use of time.

Much of nonverbal communication is difficult to change. But through feedback from others it is possible to modify some of our nonverbal behavior— particularly that which is distracting to others. Videotape and audiotape recorders are valuable tools for discovering the nonverbal cues we are sending to others.

VOCABULARY

The following is a list of words you must know to understand the concepts in this chapter. You will find the words defined the first time that each is used in the chapter. All Vocabulary words also appear, with their definitions, in the Glossary at the end of the book.

adaptors
body movement (kinesics)
displays of feeling
emblems
illustrators
mixed message
nonverbal communication
paralanguage

pitch
proxemics
quality (of speech)
rate (of speech)
regulators
vocal fillers
volume (of vocal sound)

FURTHER READING

DAVIS, FLORA. *Inside Intuition.* New York: New American Library, 1973. This is a good introductory book about intuition and the role it plays in nonverbal communication. It is well written and interesting.

ELLISON, RALPH. *Invisible Man.* New York: Vintage Books, 1972. This now classic novel is about a man who, because of his race, seems invisible to those around him. The book illustrates brilliantly how a person's self-concept is defined on the basis of how people react to his or her physical appearance.

HALL, EDWARD T. *The Hidden Dimension.* Garden City, N.Y.: Anchor Books, 1969. In this paperback book the author deals with spatial experience as it is dictated by culture. The "hidden dimension" is people's use of space, and the author is very convincing in presenting the idea that virtually everything a person is and does is associated with the experience of space. This is an immensely interesting and exciting book full of examples and illustrations that develop the concepts of social and personal space and how they are perceived.

————. *The Silent Language.* New York: Fawcett, 1959. This paperback book examines the cultural component of nonverbal communication, especially how American behavior differs from that of people in other cultures. The author is an anthropologist and uses numerous examples and anecdotes to examine the world of nonverbal communication. The book will stimulate you to make your own observations and analysis of the nonverbal behavior of others.

HARRISON, RANDALL P. *Beyond Words: An Introduction to Nonverbal Communication.* Englewood Cliffs, N.J.: Prentice-Hall, 1974. The author provides a broad, lively, thought-provoking guide to the nonverbal domain based on research, teaching, and his background as a cartoonist.

KEY, WILSON BRYAN. *Subliminal Seduction.* New York: New American Library, 1972; *Media Sexploitation.* Englewood Cliffs, N.J.: Prentice-Hall, 1976; *The Clam-Plate Orgy: And Other Subliminal Techniques for Manipulating Your Behavior.* New York: New American Library, 1980. This author's thesis, which is somewhat overstated, is that advertisers are attempting to influence us with messages that appeal to our subconscious. Of particular interest in these books is the idea that subconscious messages are another form of nonverbal communication.

JACKSON, CAROLE. *Color Me Beautiful.* New York: Ballantine Books, 1980; *Color for Men.* New York: Ballantine Books, 1984. Jackson offers simple principles for understanding the color of our skin, hair, and eyes, and thus which shades of color in clothes complement our natural coloring. When we highlight our features, we project a positive image, according to Jackson.

KNAPP, MARK L. *Essentials of Nonverbal Communication.* New York: Holt, Rinehart & Winston, 1980. Although brief, this book is comprehensive and well written. The research base is large. For an extended version, see Knapp's *Nonverbal Communication in Human Interaction,* 2nd ed. New York: Holt, Rinehart & Winston, 1978. It is more thorough.

MALANDRO, LORETTA A., AND LARRY BARKER. *Nonverbal Communication.* New York: Random House, 1983.
The authors provide examples, applications, research findings, a historical perspective, contemporary information, and complete reference lists. This textbook is enjoyable to read. It is also intellectually and emotionally challenging.

MARSHALL, EVAN. *Eye Language: Understanding the Eloquent Eye.* New York: New Trend Publishers, 1983. This is a surprisingly thorough examination of eye language. Chapters explore the eye language of love and lies, staring, cutoffs, "the evil eye," physiognomy, pupillometry, iridology, and eye adornment. The book is interesting, readable, and full of contemporary examples.

MEHRABIAN, ALBERT. *Silent Messages: Implicit Communication of Emotions and Attitudes,* 2nd ed. Belmont, Calif.: Wadsworth, 1981. This experimentally based textbook is by far the most intellectually challenging of any mentioned in this list. More than 400 references are cited.

MOLLOY, JOHN T. *Dress for Success.* New York: Warner Books, 1975. This book reinforces the importance of clothes as a significant nonverbal element. The spotlight is on the dress of business executives, but Molloy clearly indicates that the clothes one wears evoke conditioned responses from others. See also Molloy, *The Woman's Dress for Success Book.* Chicago: Follett, 1977.

part 2

INTERPERSONAL COMMUNICATION

6 INTERPERSONAL RELATIONSHIPS

CHAPTER OUTLINE

Interpersonal Needs
    Personal discovery
    Inclusion
    Affection
    Control

Attraction to Others
    Physical attractions
    Similarities
    Differences
    Proximity
    Who likes whom?

Talking to Each Other

    Roles, relationships, and communication
    Beginning conversations
    The value of small talk
    The value of gossip

Self-Disclosure: Important Talk
    The importance of self-disclosure
    The process of self-disclosure
    The risks of self-disclosure
    How should we go about self-disclosure?

CHAPTER OBJECTIVES

After reading this chapter, you should be able to:

1. Define interpersonal communication.
2. Identify and explain interpersonal needs.
3. Explain why people are attracted to each other.
4. Explain how roles influence interpersonal communication.
5. Give some ways of beginning a conversation.
6. Explain the uses of small talk and gossip.
7. Define self-disclosure and tell why it is important.
8. Explain the four panes of the Johari Window.

Mike spent the whole morning at work discussing blueprints with his boss. At lunchtime he went out with several people in his office. After lunch he spent most of the afternoon on the telephone talking to various contractors. When work was over, he stopped off and had a cup of coffee with a friend before he caught the bus home. Arriving home, he called his girlfriend and they made arrangements to eat dinner out and see a movie. When Mike returned from his date, he made a couple of calls—one to his sister and one to a friend.

During the course of his day, Mike has had a lot of communication with various people. This was *interpersonal communication*—communication where we talk to people on a one-to-one basis, usually in an informal setting. In Mike's case, he talked to his boss, his friends at lunch, the contractors, his girlfriend, his sister, and his friend. All of these conversations took place in the course of a single day. Yet Mike's extensive use of interpersonal communication is not unusual. If we were to keep track of our own conversations, we might find that we had as many as Mike, for interpersonal is the kind of communication we use most often. It occurs whenever we are in a relationship with another person or persons. Talking to a friend, arguing with a spouse, scolding a child, negotiating a business deal—all are situations where we use interpersonal communication.

Interpersonal communication is important to all of us. When a fire destroyed a telephone switching system in New York City and over 90,000 households were left without a telephone for 23 days, the people who were without phones said that they most missed the opportunity to make calls to friends and family. Over two-thirds felt isolated and uneasy without the telephone and felt "more in control of things" when service was restored. Most of the sample also said that there were no other forms of communication that could substitute for the immediacy of the telephone.[1]

In this study, it was not the loss of the telephone that mattered; the real loss was the ability to maintain relationships with friends and family. The loss of the telephone became a loss of interpersonal communication.

INTERPERSONAL NEEDS

There is probably no other behavior that is as important to us as our interpersonal communication. We use it for personal discovery, to discover the world outside us, to establish relationships, and to change attitudes and behaviors. We use it to fulfill all of the social needs that allow us to survive.

Personal Discovery

Interpersonal communication helps us discover who we are. If we were to live in complete isolation, we would have no sense of self. For example, if a child were born and his parents took care of his physical needs but completely ignored his emotional needs, the child would grow up to be emotionally disturbed. Our self-concept depends on our relationships and how those in our relationships respond to us. When we are small children, our parents label us as "good" or "bad." Our teachers say "You are not living up to your potential." Our friends tell us that they like us because we have certain qualities that appeal to them. All of these reactions to us add up to how we see ourselves. If the reactions are positive, then we are likely to have a positive sense of self.

John Powell, author of *Why Am I Afraid to Tell You Who I Am?*, describes how our communication in our relationships determines who we are:

> *I have to be free and able to say my thoughts to you, to tell you about my judgments and values, to expose to you my fears and frustrations, to admit to you my failures and shames, to share my triumphs, before I can really be sure what it is that I am and can become. I must be able to tell you who I am before I can know who I am.*[2]

Inclusion

The need for **inclusion**—involvement with others—is one of the most powerful human needs.[3] Do you have childhood memories of being chosen last on the team, or of all the other kids going off without you? Remember how terrible you felt because you weren't included?

Ralph Keyes, in a book he has written about the high-school experience, describes the feeling of being excluded.[4] He says that in the world of high school, students divide other students into innies and outies. The innies are the ones who control the school and are usually the athletes, cheerleaders, and beauty queens. The outies are those who do not fit into this inner circle. The experience of not being included as an innie is so powerful that many people feel pain about this experience years after high school—even when they have achieved great success in the world. The pain of not being included is just as great for an adult as it is for a child. Adults, however, are better able to avoid situations where they might be excluded.

Affection

Affection, the feeling of warm, emotional attachment to other people, is another important interpersonal need.[5] Whether it is expressed nonverbally (hugging, pats on the back) or verbally ("I'm really glad you called me today"), affection is important to human happiness.

Affection is a one-to-one emotion. Unlike inclusion, which usually occurs in situations where several people are present, affection is a matter of singling out a particular person. People vary in their ability to express affection.

CONSIDER THIS

A relationship based on mutual independence has a better future than one based on mutual dependency. Many dependent people have what the psychoanalytic writer Helmuth Kaiser calls *the illusion of fusion*: the belief that you can become one with another. The illusion that you can fuse with another into one organism hinders intimacy because it feeds dependency. The illusion of fusion causes you to search frantically for perfect understanding from the perfect person. However, you're doomed to be frustrated for the rest of your life because you can never become one with another. No matter how close you become with another and no matter what you think, you always remain a separate individual.

Source: Geary Emery, *Own Your Own Life: How the New Cognitive Therapy Can Make You Feel Wonderful.*

Control

If we are going to have a good relationship with another person it is important that we have some control.[6] In an interpersonal sense, **control** means having options and choices in life rather than always being manipulated by others and submitting to people and circumstances.

Control is exercised in various forms. It might have to do with simple decision making: deciding which movie to see, which restaurant to eat in. It can also be more broad-ranging: how to raise the children, where one is going to live, how money is going to be spent. Control can also be used to dictate emotional responses: "I hate it when you cry"; "I am willing to discuss this but only if you act in a more rational manner."

ATTRACTION TO OTHERS

In the course of a week, most of us have hundreds of casual encounters with other people. With most of the people we meet, we conduct our business and go on our way. Most of us, for example, will not remember the waitress who served us the last time we ate out or the bank teller who cashed our check. These people recede into a kind of human landscape. Occasionally, however, we have an encounter where we think, "I would like to get to know that person better." Out of all the people we meet, how do we pick out some we want to know better? What ingredients make up our attraction to others?

Physical Attraction

Often, we are attracted to others because of the way they look. We like the way someone looks and want to get to know the person better. In some cases physical attraction may be sexual attraction. In most cases, however, it goes beyond that. Sometimes we are attracted to people because of the way they dress. They choose a style of clothing that is our own style or is a style we would like to imitate. They have a certain "look" that we like very much.[7]

Since physical attraction is superficial, it usually recedes into the background as we get to know the person. Physical attraction, then, is a reason for getting to know somebody; it is seldom the basis for a relationship.

Similarities

Often we are attracted to people because we like what they say. We are attracted to people because they seem knowledgeable about subjects we also find interesting and important. Even more important, we are attracted to people because they share our beliefs and values. Although we like to believe that opposites attract, when it comes to a strongly felt belief, we look for people who believe as we do. For example, it would be difficult for a Palestinian and an Israeli to be close friends—their politics are too far apart. Although a born-again Christian and an Orthodox Jew might share similar ideas, they would be so far apart in religious beliefs that they probably would not seek each other out.

An advantage of sharing similar beliefs and values with another person is that you can make accurate predictions about each other. For example, Bob doesn't have to consult Alice when he plans the evening. He knows her well enough to know that she will enjoy the Mexican restaurant and a cops-and-robbers movie. On the other hand, Stacy does not even bother to ask Marie to play Scrabble with her. She knows that Stacy doesn't like word games of any sort.

Differences

Although two people who have very different beliefs are unlikely to form a strong and lasting relationship, people with different personality characteristics might well be attracted to each other. For example, a person who doesn't like making decisions might be attracted to a strong decision maker. Because these qualities complement each other, they might help to strengthen the relationship. In a traditional marriage, complementary differences can be a source of attraction; in looking for a spouse, the woman looks for a breadwinner and the man looks for a homemaker.

Proximity

Often we get to know and like people because of **proximity**—we live or work close to them. Even when people might not otherwise have been attracted to each other, they may begin to know and like each other because they are together so much. This often happens when people work together. After sharing an office or standing next to each other on the assembly line, they begin to share on a day-to-day basis what is happening in their lives. This leads to their becoming friends.

Sometimes people who are attracted to each other form a strong friendship but lose touch with each other when they no longer have proximity. Typically, friends who move to different cities vow to stay in touch. However, if they can't afford telephone calls or if they aren't letter writers, it's not unusual for contact to drop to a yearly Christmas card. Proximity, then, is important not just for starting up relationships but for keeping them going.

Who Likes Whom?

When sizing up others, their reaction to us is also important. It isn't clear whether we like others *because* they like us or whether the knowledge that others like us strengthens our attraction to them. We might be attracted to people because we think they like us.[8]

Some of our closest relationships are formed at work because we are in such close proximity with our coworkers on a daily basis.

TRY THIS

Think about a person you met whom you thought might make a good friend. Analyze your attraction to this person by answering the following questions:

1. Was there anything you noticed about this person that was physically attractive?
   a. Did you notice his or her clothing?
   b. Did you notice anything about his or her nonverbal communication?

2. Did this person say something that interested you?
   a. Was it about a subject you were interested in?
   b. Was it about something you also believed in?

3. Was this person in close physical proximity?
   a. Could you see him or her every day?
   b. At least once a week?

4. Did this person give signs that he or she liked you?

5. Did you notice desirable qualities in this person that you would like to have yourself?

TALKING TO EACH OTHER

Roles, Relationships, and Communication

All relationships are governed by the roles that the participants in the relationships expect each other to play. Sometimes these roles are tightly defined; other times the participants have more flexibility in defining them. A conservative boss, for example, might expect her employees never to engage in personal conversations during working hours and to receive and make no personal telephone calls. In this case, the roles of boss and worker are traditionally defined. In another office, the boss might not interpret the roles so rigidly. He might like to be on a first-name basis with the people who work for him, and he might not care about personal conversations and phone calls as long as the work gets done.

Often the roles we know best are those that are the most traditionally defined. Examples of such roles are those that apply to family relationships (wife-husband, parent-child) or those that apply in an institutional setting (teacher-student, nurse-doctor). Even though the people who work in these

TRY THIS

Last night you intended to stay home and finish a paper that is due today. A friend talked you into going to a party instead. You had such a good time you completely forgot about the paper. How are you going to explain to each of the following people that your paper is not finished?

- To your teacher?
- To your mother?
- To your best friend?

How is your communication different with each of these people? How is this difference in communication influenced by the role you play with each of them?

roles might want more flexibility than is provided by the traditional definitions, there is often social pressure to conform to traditional roles and, thus, traditional behavior. A working mother, for example, is often told she should stay home and take care of her children. That is her traditionally defined role. Nurses who try to become midwives often face opposition from doctors. According to the latter, delivering babies is a doctor's work.

As roles get further away from the nuclear family or the institutions of society, they are not so tightly defined. Often at the beginning of a peer relationship, we can choose the roles we are going to play. Friends, for example, often decide on the role they will play within the friendship. Once the relationship is established and functioning, however, the role expectations become fixed and friends expect each other to react in certain ways.

Our roles and relationships determine how we communicate. Depending on the role we play, certain communication is expected of us. Teachers and parents expect children to speak in a respectful manner. A boss expects employees to follow orders without talking back. Friends and spouses expect the other person in the relationship to disclose what he or she is thinking and feeling. We can see, then, that much of our success in playing a role will depend on how we meet others' communication expectations.

Beginning Conversations

Much of the basis for establishing a relationship rests on reducing uncertainty.[9] For example, a new social situation might make you feel uneasy. You may wonder whether you are dressed right, whether you will be able to begin a conversation, whether you will find people you like and people who like you. The uncertainty you are feeling will probably be shared by other people in the room. How do you go about reducing it?

In new social situations the best way to get started in conversations with others is by asking questions. Questions are the best way to discover a common ground with others. Sometimes we ask questions to find out information. But we also ask them in certain situations just to fill time or to be sociable. People who are setting out on a long plane or bus journey often ask their seatmates questions just to make the time pass better.

In social situations when we want to present ourselves favorably, we show our friendliness by asking questions. People usually like answering questions about themselves. Since most of us are interested in ourselves, it is very flattering when someone else shares this interest. Asking questions is the best way to express interest.

In beginning a conversation with a stranger, certain conventions must be observed in question asking. The main rule is that questions should be more general than personal. "Where do you live?"; "How do you like that instructor?"; "What kind of work do you do?" are all examples of general questions. The purpose in asking these questions is both to find out about the other person and to discover whether you have anything in common. Once you discover common ground, then you are ready to begin a conversation. Focusing your questions on the situation you both are in is probably the best foundation from which to begin. "Do you think this is going to be a good party?" or "Do you know how long this flight will take?" are examples of situational questions.

One other point should be mentioned about questions. It does no good to ask them if you aren't paying attention to the answers. Have you ever had a conversation with someone who was giving you only half attention while looking over your shoulder to see who else was around? Or have you had someone ask you the same question twice in the space of ten minutes? Both of these persons are telling you that they are really just passing the time until something better comes along. It's probably better to ask no questions at all than to communicate this kind of attitude.

The Value of Small Talk

Perhaps the most important value of **small talk**—social talk with others about unimportant information—is that it allows us to maintain contact with a lot of people without making a deep commitment. We are often in situations where it would be uncomfortable to stand around without talking. Therefore there are all sorts of conventions in small talk. Again, we can talk about the situation we find ourselves in. That failing, we can talk about the weather. If we know the people a little, we can ask about their children, their garden, or their cats. None of this information we are asking for is very important or very personal—it just indicates to the others that you are trying to be sociable or that you want to show you have some interest.

Small talk not only helps us maintain contact but is useful for laying a foundation for future contact. It is a way to test the water without getting all wet! As with questions, we can be alert for potential common interests through small talk and see if we might like to get to know a person better.

Because small talk is socially sanctioned, it is a safe procedure. It provides us with a channel to establish who we are with others. It also permits us to find out more about ourselves through the eyes of others. Although personal information is superficial in small talk, the image we give to others can be found reflected in the way others react to us.

The Value of Gossip

When people first meet, they often try to find common ground by engaging in low-level gossip. If you find that a person whom you have just met knows your good friend Diane, it might be a natural response to tell a good story about Diane—something the other person hadn't known. This story, then, would be a form of gossip.

Gossip is behind-the-scene talk of a personal or intimate nature. Unlike small talk, gossip has never been socially sanctioned by everyone. Some people feel it should be discouraged because it is an invasion of another person's privacy. Others, however, are beginning to look at gossip in a new light and feel it has a valuable function in society.

According to Sam Keen, a writer about psychological topics, gossip is gaining a better reputation.[10] He sees gossip as a communication network that keeps us informed about healthy and unhealthy relationships ("Did you know that Amy and Kevin have broken up?").

Gossip, says Keen, allows us to share confidences with others and to share ideas, experiences, and stories. Sometimes we can test our own values with gossip. When, through our gossip, we condemn a couple that is going through a divorce, we affirm our own value of the importance of marriage and of working out problems within the marriage.

Keen also believes that gossip is a valuable way of finding out information that might protect us. We tell someone that the store from which we bought a stereo cheated us. This is a warning to others not to go to that store. Gossip can also help us to reveal hypocrisy ("That professor is always talking about getting work in on time, but have you ever noticed that he always returns papers late?").

It's important, of course, to distinguish between harmless and harmful gossip. Harmless gossip generally is about changes in others' lives: Sally is moving to Colorado; Hank has a new job; Lynn is having an operation. Harmful gossip is more aimed at character assassination—information that can cause harm to someone. Examples might be that Hank got fired from his old job because he drank too much or that you heard (but never saw) that Mr. Brown at the meat market puts his thumb on the scale when he weighs the meat for customers.

Gossip is part of the human experience, and the ability to gossip and to enjoy it is often a basis of attraction between people. People who like the same kind of gossip tend to see the world and the people in it in basically the same way.

SELF-DISCLOSURE: IMPORTANT TALK

Much of interpersonal communication is made up of small talk. We talk to our classmates about a party, we discuss the weather with a stranger, or we talk about a ballgame we saw on TV with a friend. Although this kind of talk is important to keep society functioning, if we used only small talk we would probably end up feeling frustrated. The problem with small talk is that it's not important enough. It doesn't touch on the central issue of who we are and what we need and want from life.

The Importance of Self-Disclosure

If we are going to communicate who we are to other people we are going to have to engage in **self-disclosure**—a process in which one person tells another

People who confide in one another are really engaged in self-disclosure. They trust that they will not be put down or misunderstood by the one they confide in and will gain a sympathetic response.

person something he or she would not tell just anyone. To see how this works, let's look at the case of Robin and Jeff.

Robin and Jeff have been married for a year. They think they understand each other pretty well, but during the course of the past week, Robin has been very irritable and has been snapping at Jeff whenever he talks to her. Jeff thinks to himself: "Have I done something to upset her? I don't think so, but she certainly seems to be mad at me." Finally, after days of misery, Jeff says to Robin, "This has been a terrible week. Is there any way you can tell me what's bothering you?" After some gentle prodding, Robin tells Jeff that a guy at work has been harassing her. She didn't want to tell him about it because she thought it would upset him.

When Jeff hears what has been bothering Robin, his first feeling is one of relief. His perception of her behavior had been that she was mad at him. Now that he knows she is not, they can deal with the real problem. Robin is also relieved. She has not told anyone what has been happening at work, and it is such a relief to talk about it that the problem doesn't seem nearly so overwhelming.

When Robin and Jeff were not talking about what was bothering Robin, there was a good deal of misperception taking place. Jeff was thinking Robin was mad at him. Robin believed that she could not tell her problem to Jeff. Their misperceptions of the crisis continued until they were able to sit down and talk to each other.

From this experience, Robin and Jeff realized that if you don't tell another person what you are thinking and feeling, the other person is likely to assume things that are not true. Resulting communication can be defensive, even hostile. As Robin and Jeff found out, it's important to tell people—especially ones you are close to—what is going on in your head.

The process of communicating one's self to another person, telling another who you are and what you are feeling, is all part of self-disclosure. Through this disclosure we can check out our perceptions, our thoughts, and our feelings.

Most of us will disclose things about ourselves to people we trust. Generally, we trust those people whom we predict will react to us in the way we want them to. They are not likely to tell us that we are bad or that we have done a wrong thing. For example, if you were to confess to a friend that you once flunked out of school, you would tell him this because you would expect him to react sympathetically. You can predict his reaction because you know him well and have experienced his reactions to you and to other situations. Self-disclosure, then, occurs when we discover people who believe the way we do and who react to situations and events the way we would. These are the people we trust enough to talk about ourselves.[11]

The Process of Self-Disclosure

We all make choices about what to disclose and what to keep to ourselves. One way to look at how this process operates in communication is by using a model developed by Joseph Luft and Harry Ingham. By combining their first names, they labeled their device the **Johari Window** (see Figure 6-1).[12]

The "free to self and others" area—or *open pane*—involves information about ourselves that we are willing to communicate as well as information we are unable to hide. A group of students, for example, meets for the first time in a classroom and, following the instructor's suggestion, introduce themselves. Most of them will stick to bare essentials: their name, where they come from, and their major. When people do not know one another very well, the "free to self and others" area is smaller than when they become better acquainted.

The area labeled "blind to self, seen by others"—or *blind pane*—is a kind of accidental disclosure area; there are certain things we do not know about ourselves that others know about us. For example, we may see that the man who must always have the latest model of an expensive car is really trying to hide his feelings of inadequacy and insecurity. Advertisers like to play on our blind pane. They suggest, for instance, that you do not know you have bad breath but everyone else knows.

The *hidden pane*—or self hidden from others—is a deliberate nondisclosure area; there are certain things you know about yourself that you do not want known, so you deliberately conceal them from others. Most people hide things that might evoke disapproval from those they love and admire: "I was a teen-age shoplifter"; "I don't know how to read very well." Others keep certain areas hidden from one person but open to another: a young woman tells her best friend, but not her mother, that her grades are low because she seldom studies.

FIGURE **6-1** The Johari Window

	KNOWN TO SELF	UNKNOWN TO SELF
KNOWN TO OTHERS (Disclosure areas)	Open Pane (Free to self and others)	Blind Pane (Blind to self, seen by others)
UNKNOWN TO OTHERS (Nondisclosure areas)	Hidden Pane (Open to self, hidden from others)	Unknown Pane (Unknown to self and others)

CONSIDER THIS

"Everybody's friend is nobody's," warned Schopenhauer, and I remain wary of men and women who slide too easily into personal confidences, who assume intimacies before they have been willing to serve a probationary period of tactful reserve. Each of us has a core that is not to be invaded without express or tacit permission; nor is this permission to be lightly granted, and then just as abruptly withdrawn.

Source: Sydney Harris, "Strictly Personal," *Toledo Blade.*

The *unknown pane* is a nondisclosure area; it provides no possibility of disclosure because it is not known to the self or to others. This pane represents all the parts of us that are not yet revealed. We might think, for example, that we are very brave, but we really don't know how we will react when we are faced with personal danger. The unknown area is most likely to be revealed when someone undergoes psychological counseling.

The disclosure and nondisclosure areas vary from one relationship to another; they also change all the time in the same relationship. Figure 6-2 shows how the Johari Window might look in a close relationship. In such a relationship, the open pane becomes much larger because a person is likely to disclose more. When disclosure increases, people not only reveal more infor-

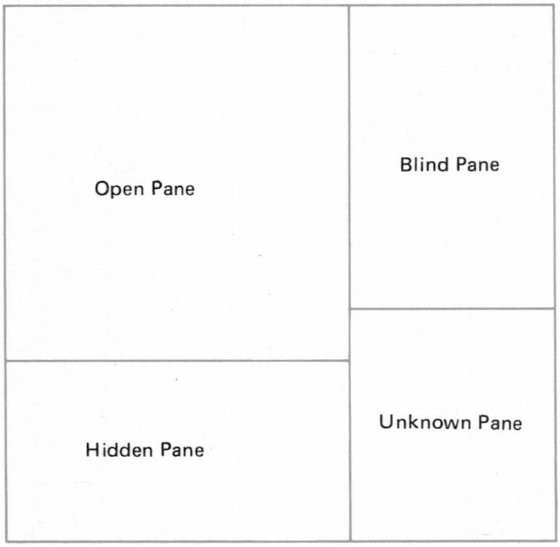

Open Pane	Blind Pane
	Unknown Pane
Hidden Pane	

FIGURE **6-2 This is what the Johari Window might look like after a relationship has had a chance to develop. With more development, the open pane is likely to grow even larger.**

mation about themselves but are also likely to discover things about themselves that they had not known before. If you apply the Johari Window to each of your relationships, you will find that the sizes of the four panes are different in each relationship. In other words, you are likely to be more self-disclosing in some relationships than you are in others.

The Risks of Self-Disclosure

Although we may believe that self-disclosure is very important if we are going to sustain relationships, there are also risks involved.[13] There is the risk of the self-knowledge that disclosure might bring. We may suspect certain things about ourselves but prefer that they remain in the hidden area.

Also, many people fear that if they tell something about themselves, it could be held against them. If someone has been fired from a job, he might not want to tell this to anyone in case it causes people to feel differently about him. In other cases, self-disclosure might threaten a relationship. For example, someone might not want to tell another about her struggle with alcoholism. Perhaps the greatest fear in disclosure is of negative feedback; we are afraid disclosure might mean that the other person will no longer love, accept, or want us.

Sometimes we resist hearing self-disclosure from others because it is so boring and repetitive. Let's say that a good friend is in a relationship that seems very destructive. The friend doesn't want to *do* anything about the relationship—he or she just wants to talk about it. Most of us find this kind of self-disclosure very tedious after a while.

How Should We Go About Self-Disclosure?

Disclosure should occur only in relationships that are important to you.[14] People who do not know you very well are likely to feel uncomfortable if you tell them too much about yourself too soon. Wait until you have some signs that this relationship has a possibility of developing. For example, if someone seeks you out by inviting you to parties or for coffee, this is a sign that he or she wants the relationship to develop.

For disclosure to work, both parties must do it. If one person does all the disclosing and the other party just sits back and listens, this is not a very healthy environment for disclosure to work.

Remember that disclosure is taking a risk. You will never know how another person will respond to your openness until you give it a try. To avoid getting hurt, try testing the water with your toe before you plunge in. One way of doing this is to talk about a subject in general terms and see how the other person reacts before you talk about your own experience with it.

Finally, examine your own motives for self-disclosure. Why do you want the other person to know this information? Will it really enhance the relation-

CONSIDER THIS

Miss Manners advises that you stay away from these topics unless you are among good friends:

Age: "That was an awfully nice young man you brought over the other night, but tell me, isn't he a little young?"

Birth Control: "Isn't this your third? Did you plan it that way?"

Children: "Shouldn't he be talking by now?"

Divorce: "And we thought you were the ideal couple. What went wrong?"

Energy: "Don't you think you keep this house too hot?"

Food: "I'm surprised to see you eating that. Didn't you tell me you were on a diet?"

Good Works: "Our development officer has figured out what a person of your income level can afford to give. Would you like to hear what it is?"

Health: "You didn't tell us what that test was you went into the hospital for. But let me just ask this: Was it benign?"

I: "I think you ought to . . ."

Source: Judith Martin, *Miss Manners' Guide to Excruciatingly Correct Behavior.*

ship or can it do it harm? All of us have some secrets that we should probably keep to ourselves. Sharing them may cause injury or make the other person lose trust in us. Although some secrets are a burden to keep, it may serve the interest of the relationship to do so.

SUMMARY

Interpersonal communication is one-to-one communication and it is the kind of communication we use most frequently. Interpersonal communication helps us to find out about ourselves and others. Without relationships, we would have no sense of self.

Our psychological needs in interpersonal communication are for inclusion, control, and affection. Inclusion is the need for involvement with others. Affection is the feeling of warm emotional attachments to others, and control is the ability to have some say over our environment.

All relationships begin with attraction. Although attraction might vary greatly in different relationships, we are most attracted to people with whom we have similarities and frequent contact.

Relationships with others are governed by the roles we are expected to play. Roles that reflect the structure of society are more rigidly defined than roles we have with friends. Much of the communication we have in relationships depends on the role we are playing.

We get to know each other by asking questions of each other. These questions help us to discover a common ground with others. Questions are often made up of small talk and gossip.

Self-disclosure is the process of communicating one's self to another person, telling another who we are and what we are feeling. If close relationships are going to exist, self-disclosure must take place. Self-disclosure can be understood through the Johari Window, which has four panes: open, blind, hidden, and unknown. As relationships develop and disclosure increases, the open pane gets larger.

VOCABULARY

The following is a list of words you must know to understand the concepts in this chapter. You will find the words defined the first time that each is used in the chapter. All Vocabulary words also appear, with their definitions, in the Glossary at the end of the book.

affection	Johari Window
control	proximity
gossip	self-disclosure
inclusion	small talk

FURTHER READING

BLOCK, JOEL D. *Friendship: How to Give It, How to Get It.* New York: Collier Books, 1980. Block says that we are the architects of our own friendships. His book describes what is happening to friendship relationships today, and he depicts how various kinds of people deal with the desire to be closer to other human beings. His chapter on the key ingredients that make friendships work is especially strong.

BUSCAGLIA, LEO. *Loving Each Other: The Challenge of Human Relationships.* Thorofare, N.J.: Slack, 1984. In this personal book, Buscaglia discusses loving each other through communication, as well as in honesty, forgiveness, joy, and intimacy. Written in the style of his lectures, it is a book about love, tenderness, compassion, caring, sharing, and relating.

CUSHMAN, DONALD P., AND DUDLEY D. CAHN, JR. *Communication in Interpersonal Relationships.* Albany: State University of New York Press, 1985. The authors discuss the communication principles, processes, skills, and patterns that increase the probability of developing emotional relationships. They also look at those that erode or prevent such relationships. This is a sophisticated book using research evidence to support four perspectives: social rules, self-concepts, reciprocity in self-concept support, and organizations and the cultural system.

GALVIN, KATHLEEN, AND BERNARD J. BROMMEL. *Family Communication: Cohesion and Change.* Glenview, Ill.: Scott, Foresman, 1982. The authors examine the family from a communication perspective. They offer an overview of the current scholarship that relates to long-term relationships such as those found in marriage and families. An excellent bibliography is also included. This is a strong, scholarly work.

GIVENS, DAVID B. *Love Signals: How to Attract a Mate.* New York: Pinnacle Books, 1983. Written by a research anthropologist, this book is a nonverbal treasure chest of mating rituals. Well written, enjoyable, and easy to read, the book contains short quizzes at the end of each chapter that highlight the chapter's research.

GOTTMAN, JOHN, CLIFF NOTARIUS, JONNI GONSO, AND HOWARD MARKMAN. *A Couple's Guide to Communication.* Champaign, Ill.: Research Press, 1976. How do married couples function in problem-solving situations? This is a skills book designed to help improve communication. Numerous exercises and examples are offered.

HAMACHEK, DON E. *Encounters with Others: Interpersonal Relationships and You.* New York: Holt, Rinehart and Winston, 1982. Hamachek discusses perception, attraction, and influence. The final two chapters of this textbook treat the development of healthy interpersonal relationships and the psychology and art of good communication skills. This is a well-researched, well-written textbook.

KNAPP, MARK L. *Interpersonal Communication and Human Relationships.* Boston: Allyn and Bacon, 1984. This textbook is about the way people communicate in relationships that are developing and deteriorating. Knapp answers the question of how communication behavior affects our relationships.

PHILLIPS, GERALD M., AND JULIA T. WOOD. *Communication and Human Relationships: The Study of Interpersonal Communication.* New York: Macmillan, 1983. The authors take a unique perspective on communication, rely on case histories of ordinary people, and focus on gender roles as a primary issue in contemporary relationships. They believe that by mastering both theory and practice, readers will increase their chances for a rewarding relationship.

PRATHER, HUGH. *Notes on Love and Courage.* Garden City, N.Y.: Doubleday, 1977. In this touching diary account, Prather looks at love, courage, gentleness, and honesty. He also speaks about problems of friendship and growth. This is a very personal book, but it has deep roots in human experience and emotion.

RAPHAEL, SALLY JESSY, AND M. J. ABADIE. *Finding Love: Practical Advice for Men and Women.* New York: Arbor House, 1984. This book offers a delightful, personal approach and is full of chatty advice, suggestions, steps, checklists, questionnaires, and skills. It is enjoyable, full of energy and fun.

SWETS, PAUL W. *The Art of Talking So That People Will Listen: Getting Through to Family, Friends, and Business Associates.* Englewood Cliffs, N.J.: Prentice-Hall, 1983. Swets offers practical, proven strategies for mastering the art of effective, interpersonal, persuasive communication. He helps readers enhance their personal relationships through better communication.

7 EVALUATING AND IMPROVING RELATIONSHIPS

CHAPTER OUTLINE

The Stages of a Relationship
    Coming together
    Coming apart
Essential Ingredients of Good Relationships
    Commitment
    Dialog
Evaluating Your Relationships
    Change and adaptation
    Costs and rewards
    Roles and expectations

Communication Strategies to Pursue
    Reflective listening
    Reevaluating when roles change
Communication Strategies to Avoid
    Avoidance
    Aggression
    Defensive communication
Interpersonal Conflict and Its Resolution
    Adhering to rules
    Conflict resolution
Relationships That Work

CHAPTER OBJECTIVES

After reading this chapter, you should be able to:

1. Explain the stages of a relationship in coming together and coming apart.
2. Explain why commitment and dialog are important in relationships.
3. Evaluate one of your own relationships in terms of its costs and rewards.
4. Describe some of the roles you are playing and question whether they are satisfying for you.
5. Explain reflective listening and "I" versus "you" messages.
6. Define avoidance and aggression, and give examples of each.
7. Explain the six kinds of defensive communication and how to counter each with supportive behavior.
8. Define legislative and remedial rules.
9. Outline the steps of conflict resolution.

Bill and Rich are both sophomores at the university. They are enrolled in the same political science class, and the class being small, all the members have gotten to know each other. As the class discusses various issues, Bill discovers that Rich says many of the things that Bill is also thinking. Rich has also noticed Bill. One day as he is walking to the parking lot, he sees Bill getting into his car—a car that Rich admires.

Toward the end of the semester, Rich goes to the student union to get a cup of coffee. He notices that Bill is sitting alone, and so he sits with him. They begin by talking about their one shared experience, their political science class. Then their talk branches out into other areas. They like the same pro football team and have the same opinion of the coach. They also discover they share a fascination with cars, and Bill tells how he bought his car as an old wreck and fixed it up. Finally it's time to go. Rich decides that he likes Bill and invites him to come along to a party that night.

Bill and Rich have had an experience that probably occurs in various forms on campuses all over the country. People get together who don't know each other very well. They talk to see if they have any common interests, and on the basis of what they discover, they decide whether to begin a relationship.

THE STAGES OF A RELATIONSHIP

As happened with Rich and Bill, every relationship begins with superficial communication; then, if the people like each other, they take steps to develop the relationship. Rich and Bill have entered into the first stages of a relationship. How does their relationship develop? Mark L. Knapp describes the ten relationship stages—five of them have to do with coming together, and five of them with coming apart.[1] Let's look at these steps and see how they apply to the two classmates.

Coming Together

All relationships, unless they remain at the casual, small-talk level, go through growth. As relationships grow, communication becomes unique to that particular relationship. How does this growth take place—or fail to take place?

Stage One: Initiating

When the classmates started talking together, they began the *initiating stage*. As they conversed, they were probably assessing each other in various areas—such as clothes, physical attractiveness, and beliefs and attitudes. From all of these observations each began to make judgments about the other: "He seems like a nice guy."

In this instance, the two people were interested enough in each other to begin a conversation. Two other people might have decided not to begin the initiating stage at all. On the basis of preliminary impressions, we often decide the other person isn't interesting enough or doesn't look interested enough in us to pursue the relationship any further.

Stage Two: Experimenting

In the *experimenting stage* the persons involved make a conscious effort to seek out common interests and experiences. Even at this early stage, the level of the relationship is already being established. There is already a degree of involvement. The other person has responded and has indicated that he or she is interested in continuing to talk.

Since the classmates found some common interests, they both decide that they want to talk even more. They start going for coffee after class. They tell each other about their families and their friends. They meet once in a while outside of class—to look at cars or to go to movies together. Again, their conversation is mostly small talk—designed to uncover topics of mutual interest or concern and to help them decide whether they want to know each other better. At this stage of the relationship, everything is generally pleasant, relaxed, and uncritical. Many relationships stay at this particular stage—the participants enjoy the level of the relationship but show no desire to pursue it further.

Stage Three: Intensifying

Now the classmates have discovered that they like each other quite a lot. They spend more time with each other. This is the *intensifying stage* of their relationship. They borrow each other's clothes and spend a lot of their free time together. Not only do they enjoy each other's company, they begin some personal disclosure. They tell each other private things about their families and friends. And they begin to share their frustrations, imperfections, and prejudices.

Other things also happen in the relationship. They call each other by nicknames, they develop a "shorthand" way of speaking, they have jokes that no other person can understand. Their conversations begin to reveal shared assumptions and expectations. Trust becomes important. They believe that if they tell the other a secret, it will not be told to third parties. They start to make expressions of commitment: "I'm really glad we're friends." They also start some gentle challenges of each other: "Is that the way you *really* feel, or are you just saying that?" In short, they are on the way to becoming good friends.

Openness has its risks in the intensifying stage. Self-disclosure makes the relationship strong, but it also makes the participants more vulnerable to each other.

Stage Four: Integrating

The classmate-friends have now reached the *integrating stage*—the point in their relationship where their individual personalities are beginning to merge. People expect to see them together. If they see just one of them, they ask about the other.

The friendship has taken on a specialness. They do most things together. They go to the same parties and have a lot of the same friends. They no longer ask if they can play each other's records—they assume it is all right. Each of them is able to predict and explain the behavior of the other.

The integrating stage is reached only when people develop deep and important relationships. Those who reach this stage are usually best friends, spouses, or parents and children.

Stage Five: Bonding

The last coming-together stage of a relationship is the *bonding stage*. In this stage the participants in the relationship make some sort of formal commitment that announces their relationship to those around them. For a couple, an announcement of their engagement or marriage would be an example of bonding. In other cases, as between friends, the bonding agreement might be less formal. Whatever form it takes, the bonding makes it more difficult for either party to break out of the relationship. Therefore it should be a step that is taken when the participants in the relationship have some sort of long-term commitment to their relationship.

How do the two classmates enter into a bonding relationship? As we have seen, their relationship has developed into a very strong friendship. Now, because of their commitment to each other, they have decided they want to live together and so they take steps to rent an apartment. Their bonding involves not only living together but signing a lease. Even though their bonding might not continue for a lifetime, as we assume that of marriage partners might, their lease is a formal, binding contract that commits them to a year together.

Advancing From Stage One to Stage Five

The five coming-together stages build on each other. Whether a relationship will move from one stage to the next depends on both partners. If one partner wants to move to the next stage, it will not be possible unless the other agrees. Because most of us have only limited time and energy for intense relationships, we are willing to let most of our relationships remain at the second or third stages. These first three stages permit us to become involved in friendships and to carry out normal social activity. The fourth and fifth stages, integrating and bonding, demand much more energy and commitment—they are reserved for very special relationships.

TRY THIS

Look at an important relationship in your life that is or was with someone other than an immediate family member. (If you choose a more recent relationship, you will have a better chance of remembering the beginning stages of the relationship.) As you look at this relationship, see if you can discover the stage it is in.

1. *Initiating*: Where did you meet this person? What attracted you to him or her? Do you remember how you started a conversation with this person? What made you think you might be interested in finding out more about him or her?

2. *Experimenting*: How did you get to know this person better? What things did you do and talk about together? What made you think he or she might become more than a casual acquaintance?

3. *Intensifying*: How did you know that you could trust this person? Who was the first to use self-disclosure? How much self-disclosure has occurred by each partner in this relationship?

4. *Integrating*: Do you spend large amounts of time together? Do you have private names, a private language, and private jokes? If people see one of you, do they expect to see the other? Are you happier together than you are apart?

5. *Bonding*: Have you entered into any kind of bonding agreement that shows your commitment? What kinds of public commitments have you made?

Another point should be made about these stages. If a person is in a new relationship, he or she should not try to progress too quickly beyond stages one or two. In all relationships it is important that one partner be sensitive to the feedback from the other. It is this feedback that will determine whether it is time to advance to another stage. Since stage three is the first where there is self-disclosure, moving from stage two to stage three is particularly sensitive. If one person self-discloses too quickly, the other might feel so uncomfortable that he or she will be unwilling to go on to a new stage in the relationship.

Coming Apart

For a relationship to continue, both partners must grow and change together. If they cannot do this in ways that are satisfying to both of them, then the relationships will come apart. Although it is more satisfying to look at relationships coming together, we all know that relationships also fail. Relationships that are failing can also be described in five stages—stages that are the reverse process of coming together.

Stage One: Differentiating

The new semester has started, and our friends, who have signed a one-year lease, are living together. The first month or so goes well enough but in the second month problems begin to emerge. One roommate sees the new apartment as a way of entertaining everyone he knows, and all sorts of people are starting to drop in at all hours of the day. The place is never cleaned up, and all the dishes are dirty. The other roommate has bought a very large dog, and the apartment is beginning to seem very crowded.

This is the *differentiating stage*—the roommates are beginning to focus on how different they are, and much of their conversation is about their differences rather than about their similarities. Also the conversations are beginning to take on a quarrelsome tone: "I did the dishes last week. It's your turn to do them now." "Do your friends have to stay till all hours of the night? I can never get any studying done." "You should start paying more for groceries. That dog eats as much as I do."

The differences you recognized and tolerated before become focal points for discussion and argument. "Why does Fred come over here so much? Doesn't he have a home of his own?" "Did you realize you are snoring even louder than you used to?"

The most visible signs of differentiating is conflict. But differentiating can take place without conflict. It could happen that nothing specific is bothering the roommates but that they are discovering, as they mature and find new interests, that they have less and less to talk about. One, for example, might have become really interested in his subject area and have settled down to study and learn as much as possible. The other, however, might be basically interested in having a good time and unable to understand someone who wants to study so much.

Stage Two: Circumscribing

As a relationship begins to fall apart, less and less information is exchanged. Since points of conflict exist in the relationship, it seems safer to stay away from them as conversational topics to avoid a full-scale fight. Thus this is called the *circumscribing stage*.

Conversation becomes superficial. "Your mail is on your bed." "Did I get any telephone calls?" "Do you want some popcorn?" The number of interactions is decreased, the depth of the subjects discussed is reduced, and the duration of each conversation is shortened. Because communication is constricted, the relationship is constricted.

Most people who find themselves in this stage will try discussing the relationship itself and what is going wrong. At this point, the negative turn in the relationship might be resolved. In the case of the roommates, for example, one could decide to get rid of the dog and the other could take on more responsibility for doing dishes and not inviting so many friends over. In other cases, discussion about the relationship might reveal even greater differences between the partners. In such cases, discussion about the relationship leads to even more conflict, so discussion is limited to "safe" topics.

Persons who are in this stage of a relationship often will cover up their relationship problems. Although they might reveal problems to very close friends, in social situations they give the appearance of being committed to each other. They create a social or public face—in essence, a mask.

Stage Three: Stagnating

The *stagnating stage* is a time of inactivity in a relationship. The relationship has no chance to grow, and when the partners communicate, it is like strangers talking. The subject of the relationship itself is now off-limits. Other subjects are carefully chosen, and little of substance is discussed. When a relationship is stagnating, partners feel frustration at their inability to communicate. The attitude becomes: "Why talk? We'll just fight and things will get even worse."

How long this stage lasts depends on many things. How much pain are the partners suffering? Are they receiving rewards from other relationships?

Fairfield Porter's painting Jimmy and John *shows a relationship under strain. Little or no communication is going on, and the relationship may be stagnating.*

Some partners at this stage live with the hope that their relationship can be revived. Others are planning ways to get out of the relationship.

Stage Four: Avoiding

The *avoiding stage* involves physical separation. Partners avoid face-to-face interaction. They are not interested in seeing each other, in building any kind of relationship, or in establishing any communication channels.

This stage is usually characterized by unfriendliness, hostility, and antagonism. Sometimes the cues are subtle. "Please don't talk long, I have an appointment." They can also be direct and forceful: "Don't call me anymore" or "I'm sorry, I just don't want to see you."

In relationships where physical separation is impossible, the partners may act as if the other person does not exist. Each one carries on his or her work in a separate room and avoids any kind of interaction. In the case of our roommates, each may plan to be sleeping or out of the apartment when the other is there.

Stage Five: Terminating

In the *terminating stage*, the partners find a way to bring the relationship to an end. The persons in the relationship are preparing themselves for life without the other. Differences are emphasized, and communication is difficult and awkward.

In an article called "The Rhetoric of Goodbye," Knapp and his colleagues describe three distinct types of characteristic statements that occur in terminating relationships. First, there are the summary statements: "Well, we certainly have tried to make a go of it" or "This isn't the end for either of us; we'll have to go on living." Second are statements that signal the likelihood of decreased access: "It might be better if we didn't see each other quite so often." Finally, there are messages that predict what the future relationship (if any) will be like: "I don't ever want to see you again," or "Just because we aren't going to live together doesn't mean we can't be friends."

It should be pointed out that some relationships cannot be entirely terminated. There are cases where the partners have to have some contact—even though the relationship has come to a psychological end. If our roommates cannot get out of their lease, they might have to find a way to live together until the lease runs out. Marriage partners who have children cannot entirely terminate their relationship if the children are going to see both parents. In this kind of situation, the parents might terminate their relationship with each other as marriage partners but decide to continue in some kind of relationship as parents to the children. In this case, it would not be unusual for them to set down a list of rules that will govern the relationship.

TRY THIS

Look at a relationship of yours that has come apart. Did it go through each of the coming-apart stages?

1. *Differentiating*: When did you and your partner find that you had more differences than similarities? What were these differences? How did they affect the relationship?

2. *Circumscribing*: At which point did you start limiting self-disclosure? When did you realize that there were areas of conversation you should stay away from? When did you start resorting to "safe" topics?

3. *Stagnating*: Was there a point when you began seeing the other person as a stranger? Did you feel frustration in trying to communicate with this person? What caused you this frustration?

4. *Avoiding*: How did you avoid this person? How did he or she avoid you? Did your avoidance involve physical separation?

5. *Terminating*: How did you end your relationship? Did you make any summary statements? Statements signaling possible decreased access? Predictions about future contacts?

ESSENTIAL INGREDIENTS OF GOOD RELATIONSHIPS

Commitment

All relationships need **commitment**—a strong desire by both parties for the relationship to continue, and a willingness on the part of both parties to take responsibility for the problems that occur in the relationship. It is not enough to want to continue the relationship; both partners have to agree to make changes or compromises. Marriages break up when the partners no longer have a commitment to the marriage or to each other. A partner who wants to stay married but is not willing to commit time and energy to solving problems is dealing a death blow to the marriage.

Relationships such as friendship also require commitment.[2] Friends have certain expectations of each other, and if these expectations are not fulfilled, then the friends must work out their problems together for the relationship to continue. If you look at the good relationships around you, you will discover that the people in those relationships are committed to each other. They may disagree from time to time, but their commitment is the foundation of the relationship.

CONSIDER THIS

A mutual relationship, where there is real mutuality, is like a very clear mirror in which we see ourselves revealed in a deeper way. Consequently, when we go back into that relationship, we can go deeper into ourselves and it is a deeper relationship and it is a clearer mirror and we can see further into ourselves. And it is a spiral that takes us deeper into us ourselves and our relationships. But there is absolutely nothing other than illumination that is added to us by the other person. There doesn't need to be. And it is only, in my experience, in the mutual relationship that this happens.

Source: Jess Lair, *I Ain't Well—But I Sure Am Better.*

Dialog

Partners in good relationships also have ongoing conversations, or dialogs, about the relationship itself. They might search together for ways of reducing conflict; they might discuss expectations they have of each other—or discuss anything else that might affect the relationship. What is important is that the partners agree to discuss the relationship periodically.

Discussing points of conflict is particularly important if the relationship is going to continue. Most of us, however, are conditioned from early childhood to stay away from conflict. We got messages such as "Hold your tongue"; "Don't talk back to your mother"; "I don't ever want to hear you talk that way again." As adults, we have to recondition ourselves to discuss areas of conflict; withdrawing from it or avoiding it is too harmful to relationships.

For partners to continue the relationship, they must find ways of communicating that will be mutually beneficial. Earlier, in the chapter about listening, we talked about the importance of reflective listening—listening for emotions and acknowledging the feelings of one's partner. Often conflict can be reduced when people engage in reflective listening.

EVALUATING YOUR RELATIONSHIPS

Change and Adaptation

Ideally, when a relationship faces conflict, partners are able to change and adapt. For example, when Jane and Tom had an argument about household

CONSIDER THIS

For communication to have meaning it must have a life. It must transcend "you and me" and become "us." If I truly communicate, I see in you a life that is not me and partake of it. And you see and partake of me. In a small way we then grow out of our old selves and become something new. To have this kind of sharing I cannot enter a conversation clutching myself. I must enter it with loose boundaries. I must give myself to the *relationship*, and be willing to be what grows out of it.

Source: Hugh Prather, *Notes to Myself: My Struggle to Become a Person.*

TRY THIS

Take a look at the best relationship you have. (It can be with a friend, a boyfriend, or a girlfriend.)

1. *Commitment*: How would you describe the commitment in this relationship? Is it based on trust, loyalty, faithfulness? Do both partners in the relationship feel the commitment equally? How do they demonstrate it to each other?

2. *Dialog*: How much time do you spend talking about the relationship? Is some of the talk directed toward how the relationship could be better? Is some of it directed toward solving problems? Are both partners willing to talk about the relationship? Do both partners initiate dialog?

After answering these questions, what weaknesses and strengths have you found in your relationship? Are there any changes you would like to make?

responsibilities, Jane pointed out that she was doing less at home because she had a part-time job. Tom agreed to help her with housework every Saturday morning and to take over all responsibilities for laundry. When Larry complained that Mariann was working so hard at her job that he never saw her, she agreed to stop working on weekends.

Not everyone can change as these two couples did. Much of our behavior is programmed into us from earliest childhood, and even if we want to change, we might not be able to. Think back on how many New Year's resolutions you have kept!

When one of the partners is unwilling or unable to change, the other must decide whether to adapt to and accept the other partner's behavior. This adaptation is most likely to come about if the person believes that it is worth adapting to the problem to continue the relationship. A frequent complaint of wives, for example, is that their husbands are never willing to go anywhere. Although this may be a serious complaint, it is usually not serious enough to end the relationship. The wife might adapt to this situation by going out with a friend or taking a vacation with her.

Costs and Rewards

In a relationship, the **costs and rewards** need to be weighed against each other. Sometimes people are in relationships that are not entirely satisfying, but the rewards for staying in the relationship are greater than the costs of getting out. Let's say, for example, that you are working with someone who irritates you by talking too much and by always being late. Although you have discussed this and the person promises to reform, you don't see much of a change in his behavior. On the other hand, this person is willing to lend a sympathetic ear to your problems and is always available to go to lunch. In this case you might ask: Are the rewards of this relationship greater than the costs? Would I rather go to lunch by myself than go with someone who will talk my ear off?

People often stay unhappily married because the costs of getting out are too great. A middle-aged woman who has never worked, for example, might stay in a marriage because she has no way of supporting herself and because even if her husband paid her alimony it would reduce her style of living— something she is not willing to accept. Other partners stay together for the sake of the children, because it is too much of a problem to divide property— any number of reasons.

If you are in a relationship that is not very satisfying, you will have to ask yourself questions about the costs and rewards of staying in it. Often the best way to do this is to make a list: on one side list the rewards, on the other the costs. This list is not one that should be made when you are feeling angry or very upset—your feelings may unbalance the list.

Once you have listed costs and rewards, take some time to evaluate the results. Again, do not make a hasty judgment. Often, you will find additional costs and rewards occurring to you, so give your list time to develop.

Once you have evaluated your list, you are ready to make a decision about the relationship. If the rewards are ones you are not willing to give up, then it is obvious you will want to stay in the relationship. If the costs are greater than the rewards, then your only choices are to terminate the relationship— or try to improve it.

Roles and Expectations

In most successful relationships, the partners know what is expected of them. It seems likely that partners who play **traditional roles**—roles that do not

TRY THIS

Are you in a relationship with someone where you are playing a role that is no longer comfortable for you? (Example: You want your parents to treat you more like an adult; or you want your boss to give you more responsibility on the job.) If you are in an uncomfortable role, ask yourself these questions:

1. What circumstances made me play this particular role? Did I ever feel comfortable with it?
2. What is making me feel uncomfortable now?
3. What changes would I like to bring about? (Try to fantasize what this role would be like if it were changed.)
4. How can I communicate the changes I would like in this role? Are there any changes I could suggest that would be an advantage to the other person?

change from one generation to another—have fewer problems in their relationships than partners who play nontraditional roles. For example, one research study found that married couples who had traditional values about their marriage (the husband as wage earner and the wife as homemaker) were more in agreement, likelier to stay together, and happier in their relationship than couples who had more nontraditional roles.[3]

Friends who are in conflict might also do well to look at their role expectations. Let's say that whenever a boy asks her out, Mary cancels her date with Beth. Beth feels hurt and angry because she believes that this behavior implies she is not as important to Mary as the boy. Mary believes that male-female relationships are more important than female-female ones. Unless the two girls can decide on the roles they will play in regard to each other, their friendship is in jeopardy. To take another example, if a husband expects his wife to cook dinner every night and she does not have the same expectation, then it is time to redefine their roles and expectations. Besides defining their roles, both people in a relationship have to reach mutual agreement on them. Finally, the roles and expectations that people have in a relationship must be satisfying to both parties.

COMMUNICATION STRATEGIES TO PURSUE

Once people have a commitment to a relationship, they can usually improve their communication within it. The aim of this section is to give some direction on how to improve the communication within a relationship. Better communication leads to better relationships.

Reflective Listening

Chapter 3 discussed the subject of *reflective listening* in some detail. Because this kind of listening is so important to relationships, it might be worthwhile to review the main points here.

Reflective listening is listening for feelings from the other person's point of view. In this kind of listening, you put aside your own feelings and try to *hear* what the other person is saying. If your partner says, for example, "Everyone is picking on me today," you would as a reflective listener be sympathetic to your partner and indicate, both verbally and nonverbally, that you are ready to listen to what is bothering him or her.

The most important thing about reflective listening is that you don't try to evaluate the other person's feelings. If you respond to "Everyone is picking on me" with "You're really paranoid today," communication is likely to end. A more appropriate response might be, "You really sound upset. What happened?" This response sets the stage for the other person to talk about what is bothering him or her. In reflective listening, the most important thing to remember is that people often just need a sounding board. Everyone feels happier in a relationship when the other partner is a sympathetic listener.

Rebecca Cline and Bonnie Johnson have done some valuable research that shows the importance of making careful language choices when dealing with conflict. They found that people react negatively when the conversation is filled with "you" messages[4] ("You didn't empty the garbage"; "You always foul up the checkbook"; "You never change the oil in the car").

Cline and Johnson found that this kind of "you" talk made the other party feel defensive. When people used "I" messages, however ("I am afraid we will need a new car if we don't change the oil more often"), they were likely to receive a much less defensive response. The reason for this is that an "I" message focuses on the feelings of the person with the problem rather than the behavior of the other person. Here are some typical "I" messages: "When I am left alone at a party, I feel very shy and embarrassed"; "I can't concentrate when the room is such a mess"; "I feel uncomfortable when we have the only yard in the neighborhood where the grass isn't cut."

Reevaluating When Roles Change

Sometimes relationships have to be reevaluated when the roles in the relationship change. Let's say, for example, that a very young woman marries a man who is a few years older. In this marriage it is likely that she will depend on him to make decisions, to reassure her that she can do things, and so forth. Once she has had a chance to finish her schooling and to work at a job, it is likely that her self-confidence will improve and her dependence on her hus-

TRY THIS

Change the following "you" messages to "I" messages:

- "You never help to clean up the house."
- "You always look embarrassed when I cry."
- "You always start everything at the last minute. Why don't you try starting something on time?"
- "You don't look very good in that shirt. The stripes make you look fat."
- "If you don't retype the paper, your grade will be lower."

band in certain areas will begin to decrease. In this situation the husband might feel that he is no longer needed and the relationship might be threatened. In order to help this relationship, it is going to be necessary to discuss the roles that the partners have been playing with a view to changing them. How can this be done?

When we have been in a role for a long time, we develop habitual ways of behaving as well as assumptions about how our partner will behave. The young wife, for example, lets her husband pay the bills, advise her on her clothes, and make decisions about what social occasions they should attend. If, in her new independence, she announces she wants to change these things, it will come as a shock to her husband.

The best chance for this relationship would be a renegotiation of roles. The wife might tell her husband that she is feeling more secure and would like to make her own choices in what she will wear. Since this is not an unreasonable request, it is likely her husband will agree. The husband might also be interested in renegotiating his own role. He has never gone away for a weekend to hunting camp since he has been married. Whenever he suggested it, his wife said she would feel frightened to stay in the house alone. Since his wife is feeling more secure and independent, he now has a chance to renegotiate his role.

It is much easier to make changes in roles when such changes are seen as being in the best interest of both partners. If one person sees the change as a loss, it will be very difficult for him or her to agree to the change. The ease with which role changes are made depends also on the flexibility of the relationship. When relationships and roles are rigidly defined, change is very difficult. In many cases, the inability to change one's role will lead to the end of the relationship.

COMMUNICATION STRATEGIES TO AVOID

Avoidance

Many people who are in relationships that have problems try to avoid any discussion of the problem. Some people use silence; others change the subject if the other partner tries to begin a discussion. People who avoid discussing relationships are often trying to avoid any kind of conflict. The dilemma of **avoidance**—refusing to deal with conflict or painful issues—is that unless the problem is discussed it probably will not go away.

If avoidance is a problem in a relationship, it might be useful to try the strategies for reflective listening and conflict resolution discussed below. Sometimes people refuse to engage in discussion because nothing is ever resolved or they believe that their partner will not give them a fair hearing. In such cases, discussion can often begin by calling in a third party to listen to both sides. Ideally, this should be a person who is able to listen objectively and not take sides. In the case of roommate conflict, a dorm counselor might be helpful. Partners in marriage often seek out marriage counselors.

Aggression

Aggression is a physical or verbal show of force. Some people resort to physical aggression when they are unhappy in a relationship. Unless the partners can get professional help, these relationships are usually doomed. Other people resort to verbal aggression, such as name calling or saying hurtful things. This is a very dangerous strategy because it is difficult to go back to a good relationship after your partner has said hurtful things to you. People who are tempted to use verbal aggression should be aware that such actions may destroy a relationship.

Perhaps an even more subtle act, and one we are often not aware of committing, is indirect aggression. **Indirect aggression** occurs when people refuse to do anything or they do something in such an inept way that it is hardly worth doing. A secretary who hates making coffee for her boss might show indirect aggression by making it so poorly that it is almost undrinkable. A husband who is coerced into doing the laundry might put all the colored clothes in with the white ones and end up ruining the load. A student who is forced by his parents to go to college may get even by flunking all of his classes.

Why does indirect aggression occur? In all of the above cases, it could occur because people are forced into doing something they don't want to do and are unable to discuss it with the person who is asking them to do it. Indirect aggression, then, is an avoidance technique. Often indirect aggression is not a *deliberate* act. The secretary may not set out to ruin the coffee and the student may not intend to flunk out of school. In these cases, their unconscious selves may be sending a message they are not aware of.

When a partner in a relationship commits an act of indirect aggression, it is often useful for the other to bring it to his or her attention. This should be done very carefully, however, or it is likely to result in more aggression or a defensive response on the part of the partner.

Defensive Communication

Defensive communication occurs when one partner tries to defend himself or herself against the remarks or behavior of the other. If a teacher tells a student, "This is the worst paper I have ever read," the student is likely to think (if not say), "And you are the worst teacher I have ever had." Obviously, this communication is not off to a good start.

How can we avoid defensive communication? Jack Gibb, who spent eight years studying groups and how they communicate, came up with six categories of defensive communication and supportive strategies to counter each of them.[5] Let's look at them.

Evaluation Versus Description

Evaluative statements involve a judgment. If the judgment is a negative one, the person you are speaking to is likely to react defensively. If you tell your roommate, "It is very inconsiderate of you to play your stereo so loud when I am trying to sleep," he is likely to respond, "It's inconsiderate of you to snore every night when I am trying to sleep." Obviously such statements do not lead to solving the problem. On the other hand, a descriptive statement is much more likely to receive a favorable response. If you tell your roommate, "I had trouble sleeping last night because the stereo was on," he is much more likely to do something about the problem. Since you have merely described the problem, the message is not nearly so threatening.

Control Versus Problem Solving

People are also likely to respond to you negatively if they perceive you are trying to control them. Let's say, for example, you are working in a group on a class project. If the group begins by your taking charge and telling everyone what to do, it is likely that the other group members will resent you. A better solution is to engage in *problem solving*, where all members of the group have an opportunity to give their ideas. The same approach applies to relationships. If conflict arises and you decide what should be done ("I'll take the car and you take the bicycle"), your partner is not likely to respond very positively. It is better for you to discuss your transportation problems together.

When family problems arise, sometimes the only way to resolve them is to gather family members together to discuss them. Members are more likely to accept a solution they have had a say in.

Strategy Versus Spontaneity

Often strategy is little more than manipulation. Rather than coming out and asking people to do something, you try to manipulate them into doing it by using such strategies as making them feel guilty or ashamed. A statement that begins with "If you love me, you will . . ." is always a manipulative statement. A better approach is to express your honest feelings spontaneously: "I am feeling overwhelmed with all the housework I have to do. Will you help me out today?"

Neutrality Versus Empathy

How many times have you asked someone, "Where shall we go to eat?" or "What movie should we see?" or "What do you want to do tonight?" and had the person respond, "I don't care"? This kind of neutral response indicates a lack of interest, and it is likely to make you feel defensive enough to respond, "Why do I always have to come up with the ideas?" or "If you don't care enough to make a suggestion, then we'll stay home."

On other occasions, we want and expect family members and friends to take our side. If you receive a low grade on the paper and are still feeling very bad about it, you don't want your friend to say, "Maybe the teacher was right.

Let's look at both sides." When feelings are high, no one wants a neutral, objective response. That can be saved for a later time. What is really needed in such a situation is for the other person to show **empathy**—the ability to recognize and identify with your feelings. An empathic response to a poor grade on a paper might be, "You must feel bad. You really worked on that paper."

Superiority Versus Equality

None of us likes people who act superior to us. Superiority may be communicated in a variety of ways. People who always take charge of situations seem to imply that they are the only ones who are qualified to do so. Others feel superior because of their role: "I am the boss and you are the employee, and don't you forget it." It's not uncommon for parents to give their children a statement of superiority: "I am your father and I will set the rules." Even if we have a position that is superior to someone else's, people will react less defensively if we do not communicate this superiority. An attitude of equality—"Let's work out this problem together"—will produce much less defensive behavior.

Certainty Versus Provisionalism

There are certain people who believe they are always right. Another label for these people is dogmatic. We have all met these people—they need no further description here. It is important that we don't confuse people who are confident and secure with people who are always right. Confident and secure people may hold strong opinions; they are likely, however, to make many more provisional statements—statements that permit another point of view to be expressed. For example, someone might say, "I feel strongly on this subject but I would be interested in hearing what you have to say." People who are willing to take a more provisional approach are also able to change their own position if a more reasonable position is presented.

Table 7-1 shows all of the Gibb categories of defensive and supportive behavior.

TABLE 7-1

CATEGORIES OF DEFENSIVE AND SUPPORTIVE BEHAVIOR

Defensive Climate	Supportive Climate
1. Evaluation	1. Description
2. Control	2. Problem solving
3. Strategy	3. Spontaneity
4. Neutrality	4. Empathy
5. Superiority	5. Equality
6. Certainty	6. Provisionalism

Avoiding Defensive Communication: A Practical Example

Although we have discussed each of the six categories separately, in most communication several of them will appear simultaneously. You can see how this works in the following dialogs.

A DEFENSIVE DIALOG

Dad: You got in two hours late last night. You had better explain yourself, young man. (superiority, control)

Son: I had trouble with the car.

Dad: That's no reason. (certainty, evaluation) You should have called. (evaluation)

Son: I tried but . . .

Dad: I set the rules in this house and you follow them. (superiority, control, certainty) If you're that late again, don't bother to come home. (superiority, control, strategy)

Son: (Gives a sigh and remains silent)

This dialog has left the son feeling defensive, angry, and unable to say anything. Dad doesn't sound as though he feels too good himself. Let's take a look at how the dialog might have gone if Dad had talked in a more supportive way.

A SUPPORTIVE DIALOG

Dad: You got in two hours late last night. What happened? (description, equality)

Son: I had trouble with the car.

Dad: Weren't you near a phone? (still no evaluation)

Son: I tried to call for ten minutes but the line was busy. I had also called for a tow truck, and I was afraid I would miss it if I waited any longer.

Dad: Whenever you are late I really worry about you. (spontaneity) Wasn't there *any* way of letting me know what happened? (problem solving)

Son: Yeah. Tom was with me. I should have had him stay by the phone until he got through. I'm sorry, Dad.

Dad: O. K. As long as you remember the next time. . . .

In this conversation, neither father nor son is left feeling defensive or resentful. Although the role of father is superior to that of son, this father tries hard to not use his position of superior power. The result is a more equal conversation, which leads, in turn, to a stronger relationship between the two.

TRY THIS

1. Change the following statement from an evaluative to a descriptive response: "You really annoy me when you invite your friends over here at all hours of the night."

2. Change this statement from a control to a problem-solving response: "Tonight we will eat at Joe's and then go to see a movie."

3. Change this statement from a manipulative to a spontaneous response. "If you really loved me, you would help me clean the house and do the dishes."

4. Change this statement from a neutral to an empathic response: "I know your boss irritates you, but you must remember that he has very great responsibilities."

5. Change this statement from a superior to an equal response: "Since I earn all the money in this household, I should decide how to spend it."

6. Change this statement from a certain to a provisional response. "The Democrats are always right, and no one is going to persuade me they are not."

INTERPERSONAL CONFLICT AND ITS RESOLUTION

From time to time, all of us face conflict in our interpersonal communication. Sometimes conflict can destroy a relationship; other times, if the participants can work it out, the relationship can become stronger.[6]

Adhering to Rules

When we are communicating without difficulty and our relationships are pleasant and rewarding, we don't pay much attention to rules. When conflict arises, however, we are likely to resort to some set of rules on how communication should proceed. Take a student government meeting. If everyone is in basic agreement, the leader will probably not even count hands when a vote is taken. On a controversial issue, however, where there is a good deal of strong feeling on both sides of the issue, someone will inevitably suggest that everyone start following *Robert's Rules of Order*.

Two communication researchers, G. H. Morris and Robert Hopper, have observed that rules become very important when there are problems. They describe the rules that are used as rules of remediation and rules of legislation.[7]

Remediation rules are rules that already exist but that people have to be reminded of. A student who is late with a paper is reminded by the instructor that it says on the syllabus that the paper was due April 19. This remediation rule helps to resolve the conflict—although not very happily for the student.

Legislative rules are new rules that are created to avoid future problems. A different instructor, for example, does not put the due date for the paper on the syllabus, but announces it in class. The student who is late with the paper insists that the instructor does not remember the date correctly. The instructor then agrees to take the paper but says that from now on, he will put the date on the syllabus.

Who gets to set the rules is determined by the roles of the participants. If roles are equal, as between friends, the rules can be agreed on between them. If the roles are superior-inferior—as between teacher and student or parent and child—the superior-role person is likely to be the rule setter.

Often, in informal interpersonal relationships such as between roommates and friends, there are no apparent rules, and when the parties are in conflict, they must work out their problems. Here it is useful to apply the strategy of conflict resolution.

Conflict Resolution

When two people are in conflict and have decided that nothing will be served by avoidance or aggression, the option left open to them is **conflict resolution**—negotiation to find a solution to the conflict.[8] As one writer has pointed out, conflict exists because the individuals involved do not have compatible goals. Negotiation involves each one having to sacrifice or modify some of his or her goals in order to achieve the greater goal—survival of the relationship.[9]

Deborah Weider-Hatfield has suggested a very useful model for resolving conflict.[10] In this model, each individual looks at the conflict *intra*personally. Then the partners get together *inter*personally to work out the problem.

In the first stage, *intrapersonal evaluation*, each person analyzes the problem by himself or herself. This analysis is accomplished through a series of questions: How do I feel about this problem? How can I describe the other person's behavior? What are the facts?

In determining the facts, it is important not to confuse facts with inferences. If you have an untidy roommate, for example, a fact might be that he doesn't pick up his clothes. An inference would be that he is trying to irritate you by not hanging them up. Throughout this intrapersonal process it is important to *describe*—not judge—the other person's behavior.

In the next stage, the parties in the conflict get together to work out an *interpersonal definition of the problem*. It is important that both parties believe there is a problem and be able to define what it is. Partners in conflict often do not see the problem in the same light; in fact one person might not even believe there is a problem. Therefore, in this stage, it is important that each person listen carefully. To aid in listening, it is useful for one person to

CONSIDER THIS

Also common to the arguing stage are "metacommunication sequences," which are comments not related to the issue under discussion: "You're shouting at me; you don't need to do that" is an example. Dissatisfied couples tend to get stuck in these sequences: "I'm *not* shouting, you're being much too sensitive."

"Too sensitive, huh? What would you know about being sensitive?" And so on.

Partners who are happier with each other get out of these sequences quickly: "You're right, I was shouting. I'm sorry." That breaks the chain right away, and they are free to go back to the matter at hand.

Source: Anthony Brandt, "Avoiding Couple Karate: Lessons in the Marital Arts," *Psychology Today.*

paraphrase what was said, to check the accuracy of what he or she has heard. The same is true for feelings. Because feelings are very intense in a conflict, it is important for each partner to express his or her own feelings and also to make sure he or she is listening accurately, to express the feelings of the other. Then it is useful for each person to describe the other person's behavior. Finally, both partners should agree on the facts that are present in the problem.

Next the partners should *discuss shared goals.* Again, focusing on the problem, the individuals should ask, "What are my needs and desires?" and "What are your needs and desires?" Then they should work to see whether their needs and goals overlap. Let's look, for example, at the tidy and untidy roommates. The tidy roommate needs to have things picked up and the dishes washed. The untidy roommate hates doing housework and doesn't care if the household is in disorder. Thus their needs and goals in housework are incompatible. On the other hand, they like each other and like sharing an apartment. Each is also concerned that the other partner be happy. In this case, then, they have found some goals in common.

At the fourth stage, the partners must come up with *possible resolutions* to the problem. Here it is useful to come up with as large a list as possible. Then each individual can eliminate resolutions he or she considers impossible to live with. The partners then move on to *weighing goals against resolutions.* To see how this works, let's look again at the roommates. Since they want to live together and they want the other person to be happy, their task is to choose a resolution or resolutions that will help to reach this goal. Some compromises are inevitable at this stage. In this particular situation, the tidy roommate might agree to stop nagging, and the untidy roommate might agree to pick up everything and put it away at least once a week. These particular resolutions may not be entirely satisfactory to either partner, but they are a compromise that they hope both can live with.

Since all resolutions are easier to make than to keep, the last stage of the process is to *evaluate the resolution after some time has passed.* Does the resolution work? Does it need to be changed? Should it be discussed again at a later stage? As we mentioned earlier, it is not easy to change human behavior. When partners work to resolve conflict, even when they come up with good resolutions, there is likely to be some backsliding. It therefore makes good sense to give partners a chance to live up to their resolutions. Letting time pass before they are held accountable helps achieve this goal.

Although these guidelines for resolving conflict can be useful in many situations, it must be pointed out that not all conflict can be resolved. If partners cannot find any goals that they share or if they cannot agree on resolutions that will enable them to keep their goals, then the conflict will probably not be resolved.

Also, although this model looks good on paper, it is much like the chair you see advertised in the local discount store; the sign says, "A child can put it together in ten minutes," but when you get it home you find there are 25 nuts and bolts and 14 separate pieces, and after 2 hours' work you have something that only vaguely resembles a chair. In the same way, this model looks simple on paper but it will not always be easy to work with. Human beings are so complex in their communication behavior and there are so many ambiguities and subtleties in meaning that it takes careful thought and analysis through each stage of the process. When both partners are committed to a relationship, however, there is a good chance that conflict can be worked out using this or a similar process.

RELATIONSHIPS THAT WORK

It would be misleading to end this chapter on a negative note, with relationships troubled by defensive communication and conflict. The world is certainly filled with good relationships; we just don't think very much about them because they are working.

What is a relationship that works? It is one where there is intimacy and self-disclosure.[11] When you save up the good things that have happened to you to tell to your partner, that is a good relationship. It is a relationship where you can share the good and the bad things you feel. It is a partnership where you can solve problems and feel happy that you have solved them. Most important, a relationship is the psychological space where you and your partner/friend are closest to being your truest selves.[12] It can happen with a marriage partner, with best friends, or with a parent or child. For us to be happy, it is important that it happen with someone.

SUMMARY

Important relationships go through five stages: initiating, experimenting, intensifying, integrating, and bonding. Relationships that remain superficial might go through only the first or second stage.

Relationships that come apart also go through five stages: differentiating, circumscribing, stagnating, avoiding, and terminating. When a relationship is ending, the partners will often make statements that summarize the relationship and comments that indicate whether the relationship will continue in any form. If it is necessary for a relationship to continue in some form, the partners might decide on a list of rules to govern it.

Good relationships need commitment and dialog. Commitment is a desire by both partners to continue the relationship and to take responsibility for problems that occur in it. Dialog occurs when the parties in the relationship have ongoing conversations about the relationship itself. An important part of dialog is to discuss conflict when it arises.

When there is conflict in a relationship, it helps if partners are able to change or adapt in a way to reduce conflict. If this is not possible, the partners must consider the costs and rewards of staying in the relationship. If the rewards outweigh the costs, partners might decide to continue with the relationship—even though it is not entirely satisfying.

There are communication strategies one can follow to improve a relationship. One of the most useful is reflective listening. In this kind of listening, you concentrate on listening for feelings and avoid evaluating what the other person is saying. Another strategy is to discuss roles and role expectations with one's partner—especially if the partners are not happy with the roles they are playing.

A relationship may also be harmed by certain communication strategies: avoidance—withdrawing or avoiding conflict; aggression—whether physical, verbal, or indirect; and defensive communication. Strategies for avoiding defensive communication include describing rather than evaluating, problem solving with a partner rather than trying to control him or her, being spontaneous rather than manipulative, using empathy rather than remaining neutral, aiming for equality rather than superiority, and being provisional rather than certain.

Using a model of conflict resolution can help reduce conflict in a relationship. The steps involve evaluating the conflict intrapersonally, defining the nature of the conflict with your partner, discussing the goals you and your partner share, deciding on possible resolutions to the problem, weighing goals against resolutions, deciding on a resolution that will reach the goal, and evaluating the resolution after some time has passed. In some conflicts, remedial and legislative rules are helpful.

VOCABULARY

The following is a list of words you must know to understand the concepts in this chapter. You will find the words defined the first time that each is used in the chapter. All Vocabulary words also appear, with their definitions, in the Glossary at the end of the book.

aggression	commitment
avoidance	conflict resolution

costs and rewards
defensive communication
empathy
evaluative statement

indirect aggression
legislative rules
remediation rules
traditional roles

FURTHER READING

BESSELL, HAROLD. *The Love Test*. New York: Warner Books, 1984. This book is intended to help readers better understand what makes a fulfilling romantic relationship and to avoid the common pitfalls that bring misery to so many. There are excellent chapters on "Love in Trouble" and "Love in Double Trouble."

BRIDGES, WILLIAM. *Transitions: Making Sense of Life's Changes*. Reading, Mass.: Addison-Wesley, 1980. Bridges divides his book into "The Need for Change" and "The Transition Process." This is a readable, useful book on how to handle change. He helps us identify and cope with the critical changes in our lives with suggestions and advice for improving skills.

FISHER, BRUCE. *Rebuilding: When Your Relationship Ends*. San Luis Obispo, Calif.: Impact Publishers, 1981. This excellent and insightful book treats denial, loneliness, guilt and rejection, grief, anger, letting go, self-concept, friendships, leftovers, love, trust, sexuality, responsibility, singleness, and freedom.

FOREMAN, NANCY. *Bound for Success*. New York: Simon & Schuster, 1985. Foreman was a divorced mother with little experience and no independent income. Here she shares her strategies for rebuilding her life. This is an inspiring book full of advice and practical suggestions.

GOLDSTEIN, ARNOLD P., AND ALAN ROSENBAUM. *Aggress-Less: How to Turn Anger and Aggression into Positive Action*. Englewood Cliffs, N.J.: Prentice-Hall, 1982. This is a book about aggression reducers and aggression alternatives. With specific procedures the authors show readers how to relax, exert control, and calm down. They offer skills designed to keep our own and others' aggression in check.

NAIFEH, STEVEN, AND GREGORY WHITE SMITH. *Why Can't Men Open Up?* New York: Warner Books, 1984. This book is full of practical advice and experiences that reveal ways to create intimacy in relationships. There is also an excellent bibliography at the back of the book.

PHILLIPS, DEBORA. *How to Fall Out of Love*. New York: Warner Books, 1978. This book is designed to help people overcome the pain of loving others who do not or cannot love them back. It is an interesting and useful book on how to recover from the loss of a lover, end a dead-end affair, or free oneself from a love that hurts.

RAY, SONDRA. *Loving Relationships: The Secrets of a Great Relationship*. Berkeley, Calif.: Celestial Arts, 1980. Ray focuses on attracting ideal males, creating strong relationships, preventing arguments, handling jealousy, and extending relationships. This book is easy to read, full of short chapters and numerous examples.

8 *THE INTERVIEW*

CHAPTER OUTLINE

The Information Interview
    Preparing for the interview
    Conducting the interview
    Analyzing the interview
The Employment Interview

    Preparing for the interview
    Your rights as an interviewee
    Being interviewed
    Assessing the interview

CHAPTER OBJECTIVES

After reading this chapter, you should be able to:

1. List some ways that interviews are used in everyday life.
2. Define interview.
3. Describe the advantages in getting information through an interview.
4. Describe the difference between primary and follow-up questions, between neutral and leading questions, and between closed and open-ended questions.
5. Describe what you should do when you conduct an interview.
6. List the information you should have if you are going to an employment interview.
7. Describe how you should conduct yourself if you are being interviewed for a job.

A member of the city council is trying to discover the feelings of her constituents on a topic of local significance. She knows a vote on the issue is coming up, and she needs guidance. In her door-to-door survey, she asks people how they feel about their neighborhood being rezoned to a commercial area. To those who answer they are in favor of the move, she adds a follow-up question: What kinds of businesses should be permitted in this neighborhood?

A student researching a term paper on a recent court decision about federal aid to colleges and universities goes to the athletic director to ask her if the decision will affect the sports programs on campus. After talking to her, he also goes to the dean to ask whether the decision will have an impact on any of the academic programs.

A student looking for a summer job stops by a local fast-food restaurant and asks the manager if he is looking for any summer help. The manager says he will have a few jobs available and asks the student about her past job experience. After they have talked for a few minutes, the manager says he will know what is available by the end of the week and that the student should stop by and see him then.

All of these examples involve an interview. Like the people in the examples, we all spend time in conducting interviews or in being interviewed—although we might not always label what we are doing an interview.

An **interview** is a series of questions and answers, usually involving two people, which has the purpose of getting and understanding information about a particular subject or topic. Thus, when you ask a professor about a low grade you received on a paper, you are engaged in interviewing. You go in with a purpose—to find out why you received a low grade—and your conversation with the professor involves a series of questions and answers. Again, if you go to pick up your car, which has been in the garage being repaired, you are likely to be involved in an interview with the mechanic who fixed it. You might ask what was wrong with it, what parts had to be replaced, how long the repair is likely to last, and whether you should even keep the car.

What makes an interview different from interpersonal communication is that it is task-oriented—it has the goal of finding out specific information. You interview someone for information you need to put together a speech or you go into a job interview with the goal of presenting yourself so well that the interviewer will want to hire you.

Interviews commonly occur in a setting that is appropriate for an interview. Let's say that you met a car salesman at a party and you casually mentioned you were looking for a new car. You would probably be annoyed if he asked you 20 questions about the kind of car you were looking for and then described all the cars on his lot. Since the interpersonal setting of a party is not very suitable for an interview, it would be more appropriate if he were to give you his business card and suggest you come by his office at a later time. An interview, then, is a highly structured form of interpersonal communication that takes place in a setting appropriate for an interview.

The interviews we are most likely to be involved in are information interviews and job interviews.[1] Let's begin by looking at the first.

THE INFORMATION INTERVIEW

An information interview is a useful tool when you are collecting information for a speech, a group discussion, or a paper. The information interview can be used to supplement the more traditional ways of research—such as getting information from books and periodicals. It also has the advantage of getting kinds of information that are different from what is available in these more traditional sources.

Information interviews help us to get the most up-to-date information. Reporters, for example, make extensive use of the information interview. They interview the mayor of the town about her plans for increasing taxes. They talk to the governor about his plans for reelection. On a college campus, an interview is the most effective way of getting timely information from members of the college community. A student interviews the vice-president for administration as to whether tuition will increase next year; another interviews a department head about the new requirements for a major.

Interviews are also very effective in getting personal reactions to events. You might read about the damage a tornado has caused in a small town, but the interview can give you a chance to discuss someone's experience with the tornado. Personal experience adds another dimension to your information; it tells you what it feels like to be in that situation.

One of the greatest advantages of the information interview is that it allows an opportunity for feedback and follow-up. If you don't understand something, the person being interviewed can explain it to you. An interview also permits you to explore interesting areas of information that surface during the interview—information you may not have been aware of prior to the interview. For example, if you are interviewing a member of the administration about a tuition increase, he might mention that electricity costs have gone up this year. You can explore this area: Have they gone up because the utility company has raised its rates or because of greater electricity use on campus?

The information interview is the most personal way of getting information. You can react with the person being interviewed; you can observe nonverbal behavior; you can ask for clarification. The interview gives you a way of learning and of sharing information in a human setting.

Preparing for the Interview

Choosing the Person to Interview

Once you have chosen the subject you want to research, how do you decide who you should interview? Basically, this depends on the kind of information you are looking for. For a class project, most interviews will focus either on *policy information* (data on how an organization should be run) or *factual information* (data dealing with who, what, where, when, and the like).

Policy Information Every organization has people who make policy and others who carry it out. In the public schools, for example, the school board makes the policy and the principals carry it out within their own individual schools. Therefore, if the budget for music has been cut and you want to know why, you should interview a member of the school board. If, however, you want to know the impact this cut has had on individual schools, then you should interview the principal. By the same token, if you want to know why food stamps have been reduced, it would be more useful to interview someone in the state welfare office than in the local one.

In colleges and universities, policy making is usually divided into two areas: administrative and academic. The administrative area involves setting policies on when tuition has to be paid, allocation of parking spaces, food services, law enforcement, and so on. The academic area involves setting policy on such matters as curriculum, faculty, scheduling classes—anything that might influence teaching and learning. If you want to find out why the parking spaces are so limited for students, you should interview someone in the administrative area. If you wonder why so few courses are scheduled for summer school, you should talk to someone in the academic area.

Factual Information When you are gathering material for a speech or term paper, quite often the information you need is of a factual nature. For example, you might want to know how China is controlling its population or how well women are doing at getting jobs in advertising. In such cases, you should look for the best-informed person on the subject. One of the best places to look is among the faculty on your own campus. Everyone on the faculty is an expert on some subject. If you want to do research on population control in China, for example, you might start with the sociology or political science faculty. If you do not know which instructors specialize in which areas of expertise, ask the department head.

People who work in the community are also valuable sources of information. City council members and county commissioners can tell you about the workings of local government. And don't forget city employees. The tax assessor can tell you how taxes are calculated and collected. His or her office will also have information on who owns what property. Police officials and lawyers are valuable sources of information on how the legal system works. The welfare office and the children's services offices can often provide insight into social problems in the community. Researching a medical subject? Why not talk to some of the local doctors? You will be surprised how many experts are available once you look around you.

Gathering Background Information

Anyone who is planning to conduct an interview should know something about the person being interviewed. Typical information you should have beforehand includes the proper spelling of the person's name and his or her

CONSIDER THIS

Better to be *over*-prepared than to be caught without enough advance preparations for an interview. Associated Press correspondent Eugene Lyons once had an interview with Joseph Stalin, which he was told would last two minutes. "At the end of two minutes I found that Stalin was in no hurry," recalls Lyons, "and there I was without a program of interrogation. I remained in Stalin's office nearly two hours and forever after would reproach myself for having failed in the excitement of the thing to ask significant questions."

Source: John Brady, *The Craft of Interviewing.*

title. If the person is well known, you might be able to discover some biographical information before the interview. *Books in Print*, for example, lists all the titles and names of authors of books recently published in the United States. *Who's Who in America* contains biographical information about prominent Americans. Don't forget to check out the specialized editions such as *Who's Who in the South, Who's Who in American Women*, and so on. If you are going to talk to someone who works for the college or university, the public relations office is likely to have some biographical information about this person.

You should also have background information on the topic of your interview. The purpose of an interview is not to give you a crash course on a particular topic; it is to give you information that is not commonly known or a new insight on an old topic. Let's say you are preparing a speech on the impact of satellites on the broadcast industry and you decide to interview the manager of the local radio station. Before you go into the interview, you should have some idea about what a satellite is and what it can do. Then, when you talk to the station manager, you can concentrate on the impact of satellites on the broadcast business. This kind of information can be found through library research.

As well as having background information, you should decide on the angle you want to take in your interview. The *angle* is the information on which you want to concentrate. If, for example, you decided to interview someone on the position of women in the Middle East, your topic would be so broad that it would be impossible to get any useful information. Women are treated very differently in Saudi Arabia than they are in Jordan. Would it be better to concentrate on just one country? Also, might you narrow down the topic even more by concentrating on one aspect of women's lives such as education, politics, or homemaking? Once you have an angle for the interview, it will be much easier to get information you can use.

Preparing for an interview gives you an advantage. If the people you are interviewing see that you have taken the time to prepare, they are much more likely to treat you as a person with whom they are willing to spend their time. If you start out with such questions as "How do you spell your name?" or "I don't know much about this topic—do you have any ideas for questions?" you are not going to inspire much confidence in your skills as an interviewer! On the other hand, if you show that you know something about the interviewee and about the topic, you are likely to find much more willingness to discuss the topic seriously.

Preparing Questions

Primary Questions Everyone should go into an interview with a prepared set of questions. These questions should be listed in the order you plan to ask them. **Primary questions** are those designed to cover the subject comprehensively, and they should be based on your background research. Let's say you are interviewing a sociology professor on the topic of population control in China. Some of your primary questions might be:

- Why does China need to control its population?

- What is the policy for population control?

- Who sets the policy for population control?

- How does the Chinese government explain the need for population control to the people?

- How is China able to implement its population policy?

Follow-Up Questions Although everyone should go into an interview with primary questions, these will not be the only questions you will ask. As you listen to the answers to your questions, other questions will come to mind— questions that will arise out of the answers given by your interviewee. These are called **follow-up questions**, and they are useful when you want to go into a subject in greater depth. They also enable you to pursue an area that might be new to you or to clarify something you don't understand. You learn that China's policy for population control is "one family, one child." Some of your follow-up questions might be:

- How do families feel when they are told they can have only one child?

- What happens if the family's only child dies or is physically or mentally handicapped?

- If everyone has only one child, in future generations there will be no aunts, uncles, or first cousins. What impact will this have on Chinese society?

TRY THIS

See if you can come up with follow-up questions to the following answers from an interviewee:

- The people I hate most are drunken drivers. Ever since our family suffered such a tragic loss, I have been determined to devote my efforts to getting them off the roads.
- One of the most effective Soviet propaganda tools is disinformation.
- People who live in tornado-prone areas should take some basic safety precautions.
- I believe that children should be more firmly disciplined. There are entirely too many unruly children in today's world.
- Hundreds of chemicals exist that are dangerous to human beings. Everyone should at least be aware of the ones that are found in every household.
- Even though our student body has not decreased, circulation of library books has decreased 25 percent this year.

As you can see, follow-up questions require the interviewer to listen carefully and to think about the answers. Often, the answers to follow-up questions lead into such interesting areas that interviewers concentrate on the follow-up questions and forget about their primary questions altogether.

Open-Ended Questions All of the above questions about China's population policy are **open-ended questions**—ones that permit the person being interviewed to expand on his or her answer. Open-ended questions lead to explanations, elaboration, and reflection. Most in-depth questions are open-ended.

Closed Questions Questions worded in such a way that they restrict the answer are **closed questions**. A question that can be answered with a yes or a no is a closed question. ("Do you plan to stay in this job?" "Are you going to graduate school?") Other closed questions require only a short answer. ("Do you work better on rainy or sunny days?" "What city would you most like to live in?")

Closed questions have some advantages. They are designed to get a lot of information quickly, and they are good for eliciting facts. Closed questions can be useful when the subject of your interview is too talkative. If he or she gives answers that are so long you don't have a chance to ask the rest of your questions, you have lost control of the interview. By interjecting a series of short, closed questions, you can regain control. If, for example, you are interviewing someone about energy costs and she begins to talk at great length about diminishing fossil fuels, you might ask: "What is the cheapest fuel?" "What is the difference between passive and active solar collectors?" "What kind of insulation should you have in the attic if you live in the Northeast or Midwest?" When you prepare your primary questions, they should be a mixture of closed and open-ended questions.

Neutral Questions Versus Leading Questions Questions that do not show how the interviewer feels about the subject are **neutral questions**. Say you are a reporter interviewing the mayor about a tax increase. A neutral question might be: "Many people think this tax increase will create a hardship for people who live in the city. What do you think?"

Leading questions are those that lead the interviewee in a particular direction. If you were to ask the dean, "When is the college going to stop exploiting women?" you would be implying that the college *is* exploiting women. A more neutral way of phrasing this question would be, "Do you think men and women have equal opportunities at this college?" or, if you want to get more specific, "Men's sports get twice as much money as women's sports. Why is that?"

Leading questions often show the bias of the interviewer, and if there is a negative bias, it might arouse hostility in the person being interviewed. Sometimes, however, leading questions can be used effectively. If you were interviewing a member of the Ku Klux Klan, it might be appropriate to ask whether the Klan will ever change its racist policies. Sometimes, interviewers will use a leading question to get a strong emotional reaction from the person being interviewed. When Oriana Fallaci, a famous Italian interviewer, interviewed Prime Minister Indira Gandhi of India, her first question was: "Mrs. Gandhi, I have so many questions to ask you, both personal and political. The personal ones, however, I'll leave for later—once I've understood why many people are afraid of you and call you cold, indeed icy, hard. . . ."[2] (Mrs. Gandhi was so eager to reply that Fallaci never had a chance to finish her question.)

With leading questions, it's important to know when to ask them. Since some questions can lead to hostility, especially when feelings are high, the inexperienced interviewer should leave them for the end of the interview and concentrate on neutral questions at the beginning. You should also remember that leading questions can result in explosive replies, so don't ask them if you are not prepared for the answers they might evoke.

Here are some examples of leading questions (LQ) rephrased as neutral questions (NQ):

LQ: Why doesn't the college give equal funding to men's and women's sports?

NQ: Does the college give equal funding to men's and women's sports?

TRY THIS

Here Alex Haley, the author of *Roots*, is interviewing Miles Davis, a well-known jazz trumpet player. Haley phrases his questions in such a way as to get a strong reaction from Davis. Assume that you do not know Davis so well and are not nearly as brave. Can you try to deal with the same material but phrase the questions in a more neutral manner so they do not sound so offensive?

- Linked with your musical renown is your reputation for bad temper and rudeness to your audiences. Would you comment?
- What types of people do you find especially irritating?
- You feel that complaints about you are because of your race?
- In your field, music, don't some Negro jazzmen discriminate against white musicians?
- Do you find that being the head of your band adds to your problems?
- Would it please you if the image of you changed, that people quit regarding you as a tough guy?
- Have you always been so sensitive about being a Negro?

Source: G. Barry Golson, *The Playboy Interview*.

LQ: Why are you so afraid of being interviewed?

NQ: Some people have noticed that you seem to be apprehensive about being interviewed. Is that true?

LQ: Why do you run student government like a tyrant?

NQ: Some people have called you a tyrant in the way you run student government. Do you think this is true?

LQ: Why don't you ever get anything done on time?

NQ: Do you have problems meeting deadlines?

Questions can be worded in many different ways. A good interview will have a variety of different kinds of questions. Not only will these questions get at different kinds of information, they will also be more interesting to the person being interviewed.

SAMPLE INFORMATION INTERVIEW

In this interview, notice that the interviewer is seeking the most up-to-date information available. The interview format allows for follow-up questions. The information interview is the most personal way of getting information.

This interview was conducted by a student who was gathering material for a speech on alcohol abuse on college campuses and decided the best place to go for information was to the director of the campus alcohol misuse program. (ER is interviewer, EE is interviewee.)

ER: Do you feel that alcohol misuse is a problem on college campuses?

ER opens with a primary question. This question sets the stage for the whole interview because it confirms that a problem exists. It is an open-ended question.

EE: Yes, alcohol misuse is a problem. It's probably due to the fact that drinking is such a common activity in college and alcohol is easily available. Students are away from home, they're feeling a little lost, and they're working to get good grades. All of this creates stress. Drinking to get drunk helps eliminate the stress for awhile.

ER: Why do students choose alcohol?

ER proceeds with a follow-up question. Notice that this question would be inappropriate if the answer to the first one was negative. This is another open-ended question.

EE: It's easy to get. The make-up of alcohol produces a false state of euphoria, even though it is a depressant. Students like the fun feeling they get while they are drinking. Alcohol is socially acceptable. It's seen at family gatherings and other social events.

ER: What percentage of college students drink?

ER asks a question to gain specific, statistical information. This is a closed question because it restricts EE's answer.

EE: According to a 1982 survey conducted by *The Chronicle of Higher Education*, 75 percent of students drink, whether it is experimentally, socially, or frequently.

ER: Do you think the kind of institution (private, public, religious) makes a difference in the percentage of students who drink?

ER's fourth question is a primary open-ended question.

EE: No, I don't think it does. Private and public schools have similar statistics. The only difference I could see is in a very strict religious school where the drinking taboos are greater. No survey has been done recently to compare alcohol use at a religious school as opposed to private and public.

ER: Is there a difference between residential and commuter schools?

Notice that ER is listening to EE's answers. EE spoke of the comparison between religious schools and private and public schools, so ER asks about differences between residential and commuter schools.

EE: Although I don't have any specific information to show this, it seems that students at a commuter college keep the same drinking habits they had in high school. This is usually because they're living at home and they have many of the same friends. The major change comes when a student becomes a resident at a college.

ER: Do you think that smaller campuses are more prone to alcohol abuse?

Another follow-up question attempts to clarify the difference between colleges of different sizes.

EE: No. Size has no relation to drinking problems. At a small, rural school, students drink because there aren't many other activities. At larger schools, students who are out supporting their football teams do so by having tailgate parties.

ER: Is there a specific year in college when students drink more alcohol?

This is a primary, closed question.

EE: Yes. I would have to say that during the freshman year, students generally drink more alcohol, probably due to the experimental aspect.

Notice how specific EE's answer is to a closed question.

ER: What's the definition of "social drinking"?

This is a primary question. It is also a closed question because it restricts EE's answer.

EE: Social drinking is defined as drinking in a social situation, usually in moderation, and as a secondary reason rather than the main reason.

ER: How many students drink "socially"?

This is a follow-up, closed question.

EE: According to *The Chronicle's* survey, 52.1 percent of the students drink socially.

ER: How many students have a serious drinking problem?

This is another closed question. Again it restricts EE's answer. It has elements of being both a primary and a follow-up question. First, it introduces the issue of serious drinking; second, it follows up on ER's earlier question about social drinking.

EE: A serious drinking problem is defined as drinking to the point of intoxication. Sixteen percent of the college students have a serious drinking problem. About 5.6 percent of these students receive treatment for alcohol abuse while they are still in college.

ER: How many of these students can be diagnosed as alcoholics?

This is a follow-up, closed question.

EE: Some follow-up studies have been done after college which determine that probably half of the 16 percent will be diagnosed as alcoholics and have the problem the rest of their lives.

ER: What kind of help is available to students with problems?

This is another follow-up, closed question. Notice how much specific information these questions evoke from EE.

EE: About 68.5 percent of college campuses offer some sort of program to counsel students who have alcohol-related problems. These programs include Alcoholics Anonymous (AA), Al-Anon, and alcohol-education coursework.

ER: Should college campuses have AA chapters?

This question again is partly follow-up, partly primary. It relates to the previous answer, but it introduces the issue of campus responsibility.

EE: Often, it's not necessary to have AA chapters on campus because there are local chapters in town. Students may feel more comfortable attending a group in town rather than on campus because of the stigma attached to being labeled an alcoholic.

ER: Should the college play a role in educating students about alcohol abuse?

This is another primary, open question. Once again, it raises a new issue, and it lets EE say all she wants to on the issue.

EE: Yes. Every person should know the effects of alcohol on the body so he or she can make an educated decision about whether to drink.

ER: Should school administrations make an attempt to control student drinking?

The final question is once again a primary one. It is also open, because it allows EE to expand her answer in any direction she chooses.

EE: In keeping with the law, it would be helpful if the institution put restrictions on students under the legal drinking age. Otherwise students have a right to drink. The best bet is to provide them with as much information as possible so they can make a responsible decision.

Source: Kim Wilkinson did this interview while she was a student at Lock Haven University. Carol Rinaldi, the interviewee, is assistant dean of students and coordinator of the Campus Alcohol Misuse Prevention Service at Lock Haven University.

Tape or Notes?

Before you conduct an interview, you should decide whether you want to tape it. The main advantage of tape is that it allows you to record the interview without taking notes. If you are not tied to note taking, you are able to concentrate on listening and you can pay more attention to the nonverbal cues you receive from the person you are interviewing. Tape also permits you to get precise quotations. This is particularly useful if the subject is controversial and you would like to get exact quotations. If you are looking only for background information, however, exact quotations might not be your goal. Note taking also has some advantages. You don't have to worry about equipment, and it is easier to go through notes to find what you want than it is to go through a tape cassette.

Taping interviews also has disadvantages. Some people do not like to be taped. Albert Schweitzer, a missionary in Africa, once told a reporter he couldn't stand "those infernal taping machines." In other cases, if the subject is very controversial, a subject might not want to be pinned down to his or her exact words. A city council member who calls the mayor "a fool" would probably prefer not to have those words on tape. Sometimes tape recorders make people feel self-conscious, and some of the spontaneous nature of an

This young interviewer apparently feels that his subjects will be more at ease and freer in their responses if he takes notes rather than tapes the conversation. Note taking may also save him time later, when he writes up the information he has gathered.

interview can be lost if the interview is being taped. Another disadvantage of tape is that if you have a very long interview, you will find it time consuming to listen to the tape and pick out the main points. In such a case, note taking might be more efficient.

   If you decide to tape an interview, you should follow these basic procedures:

1. When you are setting up the appointment for the interview, ask whether you may tape the interview.

2. Before you go into the interview, make sure you know how to use the tape recorder.

3. Most cassette recorders have a built-in microphone. Some of these work quite well but others will also pick up a lot of background noise. If you are going to be in a noisy place, take along a microphone that plugs into the tape recorder.

4. Each cassette shows its length in time. Make sure you have adequate cassettes for your interview. Cassettes have two sides. If you have a 60-minute cassette, for example, you will have to turn it over after 30 minutes.

CONSIDER THIS

Many pros apparently feel that use of the tape recorder is strictly high school journalism. Of 234 reporters once polled on the two-headed beast, some 75 percent were agin' it. One reporter found the recorder "makes me less attentive to picking out the important details of an interview. Unless notes are taken, the whole interview has to be replayed—at least twice. A colossal waste of time and a lazy approach to news." Others complained that when the subject was into The Good Stuff, "in the middle of a sentence the tape runs out and has to be flipped over." The final indignity: "I see no circumstances in which a reporter should use a tape recorder. If a verbatim report is wanted, send a secretary."

Source: John Brady, *The Craft of Interviewing*.

5. Try to use a recorder with a counter. When you begin the interview, set the recorder at 000. Later, when you listen to the tape, you can jot down the times where each important segment occurred.

6. If you use a microphone, try to prop it up somewhere between you and the respondent. If you have to handle it, it can become very obtrusive. Never let the interviewee take the microphone out of your hand. If you do, you lose control of the interview.

7. Let the person you are interviewing know how you are going to use the tape. He or she might react differently if you are going to use it for background information as opposed to airing the interview on the campus radio station.

If you decide to take notes instead of recording, it is useful to devise your own form of shorthand. After the interview is over, you should immediately write out your notes in greater detail. More than one interviewer has discovered that he or she has no idea of what some of the notes mean two or three days later. Looking at your notes immediately after the interview will also help you to fill in the gaps while the interview is still fresh in your mind.

Conducting the Interview

Whenever you conduct an interview, the most important thing you can do is to convey the impression that you feel confident and know what you are talking about. Most people will feel flattered if you let them know you have been researching the subject of the interview and have taken the time to find out something about them.

People who are not accustomed to being interviewed might be feeling insecure, so it is also important to make them feel at ease. You can best do this by thanking them for agreeing to the interview and expressing your interest in the subject you will be talking about. If you are taping the interview, try to put the recorder in an unobtrusive place so it will not make the interviewee feel self-conscious.

Once you begin asking questions and listening to answers, don't be afraid to ask for clarification. Sometimes interviewers are afraid of appearing ignorant and don't do this. If the person you are interviewing, for example, mentions a Supreme Court case you have never heard of, you should immediately stop and ask for clarification.

As interviewer, it is important that you keep control of the interview. When you are talking to people in their own area of expertise, quite often they will digress or tell you more than you want to know. If you have scheduled a half-hour interview and after the first ten minutes you are still on your first question, you are losing control of the interview, and if you lose control of the interview, you won't be able to ask all the questions you want to ask. If this happens, the only thing you can do is interrupt. This can be done with such statements as, "This is really very interesting and I would like to talk more about it, but I want to ask you a few more questions."

Although we have stressed the importance of going into the interview with prepared questions, the interview will occasionally take a completely different and more interesting direction. Let's say that you are interviewing the principal of the school about bus safety for children. During the course of the interview, she reveals that two of the drivers are on probation for driving violations. You should immediately follow up on this information: "What are the violations?"; "What is meant by probation?"; "Who made the decision to put them on probation?" One of the advantages of getting information by interview is that it can always take a more interesting and provocative direction. If you stick rigidly to your prepared questions, you can miss a good opportunity.

When you are interviewing, you should watch for nonverbal cues. If the issue is sensitive and you are trying to find out something, is your respondent giving you any cues that he or she is dodging your questions? Is he or she avoiding eye contact? Tapping a pen nervously on the desk? Nonverbal cues can often tell you where to follow up on a subject or steer away from it.

If you are interviewing someone who is on a tight schedule, don't run beyond the time you have scheduled. If you need more time, ask for it at the interviewee's convenience or call back on the telephone to pick up on the loose ends. Occasionally, when you listen to your tape or read your notes, you will discover something you missed or something that needs clarifying. The telephone is a good way to get this information after the interview is over.

Once the interview is completed, the interviewee should be thanked. If it was a good interview, don't be afraid to say so. Even people who are frequently interviewed are pleased to hear they have been helpful. Also, let the person know how you plan to use the interview.

Analyzing the Interview

When the interview is over, you should spend some time thinking about how well you did. Your success can be measured by how the interviewee responded to you and whether you got the information you wanted.

You can tell if your questions were well worded by the way the person answered them. If he or she never quite dealt with the point you were making, the problem may have been with the questions. If he or she asked for clarification, that is another indication your questions weren't very clear.

Looking at your notes will tell you whether you were listening carefully. Do you have notes that are confusing? Are there gaps in them? Your notes will also tell you whether you covered the subject thoroughly enough. Sometimes, after the interview is over, interviewers think of all sorts of questions they should have asked.

Finally, did you conduct the interview in a professional manner? Did you arrange the questions in a logical order beforehand? Had you researched the topic of your interview? Did you know how to run the equipment? The main measure of your professionalism is whether your interviewee took you and your questions seriously.

THE EMPLOYMENT INTERVIEW

Let's assume you have just graduated from college and are looking for your first full-time job. You have taken several communication courses, you have a particular flair for writing, and you decide that you would like to work in advertising. You hear from a friend that a copywriting job is available in the local advertising agency, and you decide to apply. You call the agency, and the manager there decides to interview you next week. You are about to set out for your first important job interview. How do you prepare?

In most jobs, particularly entry-level ones, many people will apply. The main problem the applicant has to face is to distinguish himself or herself from all the other applicants. In many ways the job interview is the most difficult of interviews because it depends on making an impression in a very short time. You can help to make this impression a favorable one by taking some time to prepare for the interview.

Preparing for the Interview

In preparing for an employment interview, you should find out about the company and what it does. Let's look, for example, at the advertising agency.

Are you aware of any of the work it has done? Have you seen its ads or heard its commercials? What are its major accounts? How big is the agency? These are some of the things you might find out before you go to the interview. The interviewer is going to be more impressed by an applicant who can talk about one of the company's ad campaigns than by an applicant who is unfamiliar with any of its work.

Many companies are public—meaning that the public can buy shares in the company—in which case the company is required to issue an annual shareholders' report. This report can provide valuable information about the company—particularly about its profits and losses. If the company is a local one, it has probably been the subject of articles in the local newspaper. The Chamber of Commerce or the Better Business Bureau can also give you information about local businesses. If the company is national, it may have been written about in magazines and in the *Wall Street Journal*. Most businesses are also covered by trade publications—magazines that concentrate on a particular line of business. In advertising, for example, the trade publication is called *Advertising Age* and it is likely to be available in your college library. Such magazines concentrate on trends, and they are an excellent way of finding out what important things are happening in a particular line of business. Professional groups—doctors, lawyers, and teachers—also have specialized magazines which discuss important issues in that profession.

In addition to finding out information about the company, you should prepare information about yourself. Some companies get all their information about a job seeker from the interview and an application form. Others, however, will expect you to have a resume—a summary of your accomplishments. Your college career center or placement office will have information on how to prepare a resume. If you have not already given your resume to the company, you should take it along to the interview.

Interview Questions

Most employment interviews are predictable in that they follow a certain line of questioning. Here are some kinds of questions you are likely to be asked in a job interview. Before you go to the interview you should think about how you would answer them.

Job Expectations The interviewer will want to find out if what you are looking for in a job is compatible with the job the company has to offer. To this end, you will be asked what you want in a job, what kind of job you are looking for, and whether you would be content in this particular job. The best way to prepare for these kinds of questions is to study the job description carefully and see whether your qualifications and expectations match the job description. Sometimes people go into a job interview thinking they can redefine the job to meet their own needs. For example, if you wanted a job as a copywriter at an advertising agency but the agency only had a secretarial job, taking the job might help to get your foot in the door, but it would be unrealistic to think that you are immediately going to be able to write copy. You should also be realistic about how quickly you can advance. If you start as a clerk, you will probably have a long wait before you can become a manager. The job interview is a good time to find out if your expectations are realistic.

Academic Background The interviewer will want to know whether you have had enough education to do the job. To find this out, he or she will ask you questions about the schools you attended, the degrees you have, and the grades you got. This is a good time to mention extracurricular activities that might be pertinent to the job. If you are a social work major, for example, and spent time teaching jail inmates to read and write, this is part of your education too.

Knowledge of the Organization All interviewers will be impressed if you know something about the organization where you want a job. They assume that if you are interested enough in the job, you will have taken the trouble to find out something about the employer. Sometimes you will be asked a direct question: "Why do you want to work for this company?" An answer might be, "I know several people who work here, and they like the company very much" or "I am impressed by your management-training program." Even if you are asked no direct questions, you should be prepared to ask some questions yourself about the company or organization. An example might be, "Do you have a training program for new employees?" or "I know that you have some excellent computer hardware. Do you have any plans to get into software?"

Work Experience The interviewer will want to know about other jobs you have had and whether anything in your past work experience might relate to the present job. Even though your past work experience might not be directly related to the job at hand, you should not necessarily assume it is irrelevant. Let's say that you are applying for a job as manager of a local store and your only job experience has been taking junior-high students on canoe trips every summer. Although this summer job might not be directly relevant, it would certainly show you are a responsible person—a characteristic an employer will be looking for in a manager. You should also consider whether any volunteer experience you have had might be relevant to the job. Someone who has served as chairperson for the annual heart fund drive, for example, has a good deal of administrative and management experience that might be useful in many jobs.

Career Goals Most interviewers will be interested in knowing your short- and long-term goals in relation to the job. Short-term goals concern what you want to do in the next year or two. Long-term goals are directed to a lifetime plan. Typical questions about long-term goals might be, "Where do you see yourself ten years from now?" "What kind of career do you want with a company?" Interviewers ask these kinds of questions to discover whether you are thinking about your future, to gauge your ambition, and to see whether you will fit into the company's long-term goals. If you are interviewing for a management

CONSIDER THIS

"The first thing I look for is a sense of personal worth," says J. Paul Sticht, chairman of R. J. Reynolds Industries. "It's a subjective quality and hard to define, but I generally know when I see it." What Sticht goes on to define is a job seeker who is confident of his own abilities and purpose, a man who is not afraid to be judged with, or compared to, his contemporaries.

Talking about his own experiences in this area, Aristotle Onassis announced, "I have no friends and no enemies—only competitors." A rather cold-blooded admission perhaps, but this single-minded sense of purpose will serve you well during the short time you spend being interviewed.

Source: Theodore T. Pettus, *One on One: Win the Interview, Win the Job.*

trainee position in a bank, for example, the interviewer will try to find out whether you can foresee a long-term career with the bank and whether the bank is justified in putting you in its training program.

Strengths and Weaknesses Most interviewers will want to find out whether hiring you will enhance the organization. To this end you might be asked directly, "What do you see as your greatest strength?" or "What is your greatest weakness?" Before you go into an interview, you should think about both of these points in relation to the job being offered. Even if you are not asked directly about your strengths, you should be prepared to sell yourself on your good points during the interview. If on your last job you reorganized a department and improved its efficiency by 50 percent, now is the time to mention it. You should be cautious when replying to questions about weaknesses. You don't want your answers to ruin the possibility of getting a job. The best approach to a weakness is to admit you have it but are working hard to overcome it. For example, "I am not a very fast computer programmer but I am very good on detail and I expect I will pick up more speed as I get more experience" or "I am not always as well organized as I could be, but I am getting better at setting priorities."

The above kinds of questions will probably make up the bulk of the interview. Since these questions are so often asked, you should think about how you will answer them. The most important thing to remember is that every interview is different; even if the questions are the same, the answers might be different. Your success will depend on how well you can answer in relation to the job being offered.

Your Rights as an Interviewee

You should also know that as a job seeker, you have some rights that are protected by state and federal law. The general principle behind these laws is that employers should ask only questions that are directly relevant to the job. If questions about race, religion, sex, national origin, and age have nothing to do with the job, it is illegal to ask them. The following categories of questions are generally illegal:

- Age
- Religious affiliation
- Whether one is a citizen
- Weight and height
- Marital status
- Whether one has children
- Club memberships and affiliations
- With whom one is living[3]

Interviewers are not always aware of the laws and will sometimes ask illegal questions. You must be careful, however, not to take a too aggressive stance in answering them, since you could lose your chance for the job. If you don't mind the question, go ahead and answer it. If you don't want to answer the question, you should respond, for example, "Does your question about my marital status have anything to do with the job?" or "Do you have height or weight requirements on this job?" If this does not seem to discourage the interviewer, your only alternative might be to say, "I'm sorry but this is an illegal question and I would prefer not to answer it."

If you feel you have been denied a job because of your race, religion, sex, national origin, or age, you have four options. You can make a complaint to the federal office of the Equal Employment Opportunity Commission (EEOC). This complaint should be made within 180 days of the interview. But the EEOC has a large backlog of cases, and it might take years before the complaint is settled. You can also file a complaint with your state office. Since states have different names for these offices you should look in a state directory under "discrimination," "job discrimination," or "human rights." Your third option is to sue the employer. If you take this route, you will probably have to hire a lawyer and pay the expense out of your own pocket. Your last option is to join together with people who have been in a similar situation and file a case together. If you know, for example, that a particular company has not hired women or Hispanics or blacks, you can join with other people who have not been hired and sue the company. Often, joining with other people in this situation will be more effective than trying to do it by yourself.

CONSIDER THIS

Compared to the successful applicants, the unsuccessful applicants used less of the time available to them. Although each interview was scheduled to last 30 minutes, the unsuccessful interviews averaged only 25 minutes of the allotted time. By contrast, interviews of the successful applicants averaged 29.5 minutes. In addition to securing more interview time, the successful applicants spoke a greater percentage of the available period than their unsuccessful counterparts. Only 37% of the words in unsuccessful interviews were spoken by the applicants, while successful applicants talked 55% of the total time. The latter also controlled the interviews to a greater extent, having initiated 56% of their comments whereas the unsuccessful applicants initiated only 36%. Thus, the successful interviewees behaved as active participants in the interviews; the unsuccessful interviewees behaved more as passive respondents.

Source: Lois J. Einhorn, ''An Inner View of the Job Interview: An Investigation of Successful Communicative Behaviors,'' *Communication Education.*

Interviewees for a job must make a good first impression, which includes a neat appearance and a pleasant, confident manner.

Being Interviewed

Once you have researched the company, prepared your resume, and thought about the questions you are likely to be asked, you are ready for your interview.

Research suggests that the first few minutes of an interview are the most important, for it is then that many interviewers establish their biases and make their decisions.[4] Thus it is important that you make a good impression right from the start. Much of the good impression you convey is nonverbal: being on time, being dressed appropriately, and giving a firm handshake. It will also help if you can appear confident—even though you might not be feeling that way. Before you go into an interview, it would be useful to review the material in Chapter 5, "Nonverbal Communication." It would also be useful to have in mind a few topics of light conversation. You will appear more favorably if you are able to engage in small talk when you meet your interviewer.

SAMPLE EMPLOYMENT INTERVIEW

Like many other structured forms of communication, the employment interview has an opening, a body, and a closing. Let's look at some of the things you should do in an interview and apply them to an interview situation. In the following example, Pam Harris is being interviewed by John Lopez, the general manager of a radio station, for the job of radio news reporter.

THE OPENING

(Pam Harris is shown into Lopez's office by the secretary.)

JL: Hi. I'm John Lopez. You must be Pam. Come on in and have a seat.

PH: It's good to meet you. I've heard you a lot on the air and it's nice to see you in person. You have an attractive facility here. I hear that you have just moved into the building.

JL: Yes, we're finally getting settled down. I think it is going to work out well for us. We have a lot more space.

Notice that the beginning of this interview is mostly small talk. The purpose of small talk is to set up a friendly atmosphere and to enable both participants to feel comfortable. In this case, Harris takes the lead in suggesting a subject for small talk—the new building. By talking about this, she also suggests she knows something about the station.

THE BODY

JL: Do you know anything about our operation here?

PH: Well, I know that you operate on 5,000 watts and cover a two-county area. You seem to have a lot of news coverage. I have heard a lot of local news on your station.

Much of the body of the interview will concentrate on Harris's experience and what she knows. When she gets a question about what she knows about the station, she is able to answer because she has prepared for this interview.

JL: Yes, we have a lot of pride in our local news. We have two full-time reporters, and with this job we will be adding a third. What experience have you had?

PH: I've worked as a stringer on the station in my hometown. While I was in college, I covered radio news for the campus station, and in my senior year I was the radio news director. I have also done some reporting for the campus newspaper and television station, but I prefer radio.

Answers to questions in an interview should be thorough but to the point. When Harris is asked about her experience, she gives some details about her radio experience since that is what the job is all about. She briefly mentions her newspaper and television experience—just to show she has had additional reporting experience.

JL: Most people like television better. Why do you prefer radio?

PH: Radio is more exciting. If you have an important story, you can get it on the air right away. Newspapers and television are too slow.

JL: I agree. I always feel proud when we beat the newspaper on a story. What kind of technical experience have you had?

PH: I can run a simple radio board, and I know how to run cassette and cart machines. I don't feel intimidated by equipment. I like to figure out how it works.

JL: Have you had any experience with reel-to-reel recorders?

PH: Not very much. I have used them once or twice, but most of my ex-

Honesty is important. Harris admits to limited experience with

perience has been with cassette machines.

JL: Do you know how to splice tape?

PH: I did it once so I understand how it works; but I would need more experience before I got very efficient.

tape recorders and splicing. On the other hand, she says she is not apprehensive about working with unfamiliar equipment. Since the employment interview attempts to find an applicant whose experience and education will meet the needs of the job, some applicants will discover that they are not qualified.

JL: Have you done any mixing?

PH: I'm not sure. Could you be a little more specific? (Lopez explains mixing.)

Notice that Harris asks for clarification when she doesn't understand the question. Most people do not expect you to know everything. You often appear in a better light if you admit what you do not know.

JL: What do you think are your greatest strengths in working in radio?

PH: I seem to have a strong sense for a news story. While I was news director for the radio station, we scooped the local media several times.

When Harris is asked about her strengths, she answers with something that is really important for a reporter—her sense of news.

JL: What do you think your weaknesses are?

PH: I am not as fast as I would like to be. I've been picking up speed as a writer, but I'm still pretty slow with some of the technical stuff. I'm sure I'll get a lot faster when I work with it every day.

When she mentions her weaknesses, she indicates it is only a temporary problem that will be overcome with more experience.

JL: I guess we've pretty much covered all the facts. If we were to hire you, what would be your goals on this job?

PH: My main goal is to learn to cover stories faster and more efficiently. Once I have learned this, I would like to be a radio news director. Some day I would like to work in news in a big city.

Lopez is trying to find out how Harris will fit into the organization and to get some sense of her long-range plans. Most interviewers would not hire someone who was going to leave the organization in a short time. On the other hand, the interviewer might have a job that is basically for a beginner and might not want to hire someone who plans to stay in it forever.

THE CLOSING

JL: I think I've covered everything I need to know. Do you have any questions?

PH: Yes. I have a few questions about the station. (Harris asks the following questions, and Lopez responds to them:
Do you have any research on your audience for news?
Are most of your newscasts sponsored?
How well do you compare with other stations in the ratings?)

JL: Thanks for coming in. I will be making my decision by Monday. I will call you then.

PH: Thank you for the interview. I'm glad I have had a chance to meet you and look at the station. I'll look forward to hearing from you.

Note that Lopez asks Harris if she has any questions. Every interviewer is likely to do this. This is the time to ask some questions about the company or organization. In this interview, Harris asks some business-related questions—showing that she knows that news is just one part of a station's business.

At the end of the interview, the interviewer often mentions what will happen next. In this case, Lopez lets Harris know when he is going to be making his decision. If the interviewer does not raise this issue, the person being interviewed should. Like the opening of the interview, the closing will probably end with small talk.

Assessing the Interview

Once the interview is over, it's a good idea for you to do some personal assessment. Were there any areas of the interview that gave you difficulty? Did you present yourself as well as you could? Had you done the necessary homework about the organization? The answers to these questions will help you do better the next time. Since the employment interview is the most common way of getting a job, it should be approached with thought and preparation. But keep in mind that not every interview leads to a job offer. The more attractive the position, the greater the competition.

SUMMARY

An interview is a series of questions and answers, usually between two people, which has the purpose of getting and understanding information about a particular subject.

Our ability and success at perceiving others is likely to increase as we gain insight into the needs, desires, and motivations of others. For example, consider this illustration of one person's ability to see someone else's needs:

"During the great depression, a young man went to a telegraph office to apply for a job. As he walked into the lobby, he noticed that many other people—some even sitting on the floor—were filling out applications. He sat down, but only for a moment, and then jumped to his feet and walked into the inner office.

"A few moments later the receptionist announced that the position had been filled.

"'Why did that man get the job?' complained several of the other applicants. 'He came in after we did!'

"The answer was simple! While the others sat filling out applications, the young man *listened*. Someone in the inner office was tapping out the following message in Morse code: 'We need an operator. If you understand this message, the job is yours. Please come in.'"

Source: Nido R. Qubein, *Get the Best from Yourself.*

TRY THIS

The next time you have an interview, use this form to critique your performance. Use 3 for good, 2 for average, and 1 for needs improvement.

1. The opening
   a. Ability to engage in small talk _____
   b. Ability to establish rapport with interviewer _____

2. The body
   a. Ability to get to the point _____
   b. Ability to ask for clarification _____
   c. Ability to be honest in my answers _____
   d. Ability to respond with goals _____
   e. When asked for questions, I had several _____

3. Closing
   a. Feeling that I knew what I needed to know _____
   b. Ability to engage in small-talk _____

4. Overall communication skills
   a. Ability to express myself clearly _____
   b. Ability to look for nonverbal information _____
   c. Ability to listen well _____

Interviews can be used for a wide variety of purposes, including speeches, group projects, and research papers. Careful preparation is essential. The person conducting the interview should gather background information—both about the person being interviewed and about the topic. Questions should be prepared beforehand, and the interviewer should strike a balance between factual and thought-provoking questions.

Before the interview, the interviewer should decide whether he or she is going to use tape or take notes. Tape offers the advantage of greater accuracy and it frees the interviewer from note taking. The disadvantages of tape are that it is time consuming to listen to after the interview has been completed and that some interviewees will react differently if they are being taped.

When you are going for a job interview, you should also prepare yourself. You should provide information about yourself in the form of a resume, and you should do research about the company or organization that has the position. Typically, you will be asked about your job expectations, academic background, knowledge of the company, work experience, career goals, and strengths and weaknesses. You should also go prepared to ask questions about the company.

During the interview, you should remember to keep your answers thorough but to the point. It is also important that you answer honestly and ask for clarification if you don't understand something. Since the interview is likely to begin and conclude with some small talk, you should think about what you might talk about. After the interview is over, you should evaluate where you did well and where you could improve.

VOCABULARY

The following is a list of words you must know to understand the concepts in this chapter. You will find the words defined the first time that each is used in the chapter. All Vocabulary words also appear, with their definitions, in the Glossary at the end of the book.

closed questions	neutral questions
follow-up questions	open-ended questions
interview	primary questions
leading questions	

FURTHER READING

DONAGHY, WILLIAM C. The Interview: Skills and Applications. Glenview, Ill.: Scott, Foresman, 1984. Donaghy solidly grounds his book in current interviewing theory, but he emphasizes the acquisition of skills and the practical application of those skills in a variety of interviewing situations. He includes numerous exercises and activities in this very thorough textbook.

DOWNS, CAL W., G. PAUL SMEYAK, AND ERNEST MARTIN. Professional Interviewing. New York: Harper & Row,

1980. What are some of the most important decisions that need to be made in conducting interviews? The authors of this work provide some basic behavioral research findings useful to making decisions. This is a very thorough, skills-oriented textbook.

EINHORN, LOIS J., PATRICIA HAYES BRADLEY, AND JOHN E. BAIRD, JR. *Effective Employment Interviewing: Unlocking Human Potential*. Glenview, Ill.: Scott, Foresman, 1982. This textbook is designed to further the reader's understanding of fundamental communication principles that apply to the employment interview. The authors provide a thorough understanding of the principles and offer techniques for guided practice.

MEDLEY, H. ANTHONY. *Sweaty Palms: The Neglected Art of Being Interviewed*. Belmont, Calif.: Lifetime Learning, 1978. How do you conduct yourself in an interview? What do you do? How can you prepare? What will the interviewer ask? What should you say? What should you ask? What should you wear? This book helps interviewees overcome the fear of the unknown.

METZLER, KEN. *Creative Interviewing*. Englewood Cliffs, N.J.: Prentice-Hall, 1977. This is an especially valuable resource for those interested in information interviews. Metzler uses numerous examples, draws on a variety of sources, and offers exercises to help in coping with common interviewing problems.

ROBERTSON, JASON. *How to Win in a Job Interview*. Englewood Cliffs, N.J.: Prentice-Hall, 1978. This book provides fundamental information on the job interview. It offers insights into the tricks and techniques of professional interviewers. What are the criteria interviewers use to judge character and personality, self-image, enthusiasm, maturity, career objectives, and human relations and supervisory skills?

SINCOFF, MICHAEL Z., AND ROBERT S. GOYER. *Interviewing*. New York: Macmillan, 1984. This textbook is designed for the beginning student as well as the working manager of people. The authors begin with a systematic description of the process that is intended to result in communication, including the generation, transmission, and perception of messages and the evocation of desired meaning. They deal with both the event and the process of interviewing.

STEWART, CHARLES J., AND WILLIAM B. CASH, JR. *Interviewing: Principles and Practices*. Dubuque, Iowa: Brown, 1982. This is a complete, research-based textbook that includes information on both the general and specific aspects of interviewing. The authors offer a readable approach to preparing and structuring interviews.

part 3

COMMUNICATING IN GROUPS

212

9 *SMALL GROUPS*

CHAPTER OUTLINE

Why Discuss?
Characteristics of Small Groups
  Sharing a common goal
  Group size
  The meeting place
  Seating arrangements
  Group norms
  Group rules
  Cohesiveness

Discussion in Groups
  Recognizing the problem
  Analyzing the problem
  Deciding what your solution should accomplish
  Finding and evaluating solutions
  Putting the plan into effect
  Checking whether the plan is working

CHAPTER OBJECTIVES

After reading this chapter, you should be able to:

1. Describe the characteristics of a small group.
2. Describe the situations in which group decision making is superior to individual decision making.
3. Explain the physical setting that will make a group work better.
4. Distinguish between norms and rules.
5. Explain what contributes to group cohesiveness.
6. Describe and explain the steps in a group discussion.
7. Distinguish among questions of fact, value, and policy.

An issue of a small-town newspaper announces the following community events:

- The officers of the Bucktail Area High School Class of 1979 will meet to plan a class reunion.

- The executive board of VFW Post 1630 will meet in the post home.

- The Keystone Central Foundation will hold its annual meeting to choose representatives from each school district.

- Trainers for a baby-sitting course will meet at the Methodist Church.

- Officers of the Nittany Grange will meet in Lamar.

- The Sesquicentennial Executive Committee will meet to plan a week-long celebration.

These are only some of the meetings to be held in this small town. And the newspaper is announcing only meetings that might be of interest to the general public. All over the town people are also meeting in schools, businesses, and clubs. Regardless of the purpose of these meetings, they have something in common. They all bring together **small groups**—groups made up of three to thirteen members who meet to do a job or solve a problem.

Small groups are essential to helping society function efficiently, and many of us spend several hours each week communicating in such groups. We might take part in a seminar discussion, talk with a group of co-workers about improving job conditions, or discuss with family members how to make the household run more efficiently. Many of us belong to service or professional groups. Many of these groups are involved both with completing tasks and with social life.

Whatever groups we belong to, we want them to function efficiently. But participation should also be pleasurable; we want to meet, get on with the job, and then spend some time socializing with other group members.

This chapter and the next one discuss how groups work. In this chapter, we note the characteristics of small groups and how such groups go about solving a problem.[1] In the next chapter, we concentrate on how you can lead or participate in a group.

WHY DISCUSS?

When a group has a job to do, its main form of communication is discussion. Group members meet to exchange information and ideas in an effort to better understand a particular issue or situation. The Band Boosters group discusses

TRY THIS

List all the groups you are a part of right now. Then answer the following questions about each group:

1. Is the purpose of the group mostly social, or does it meet because it has a job to do?
2. What do you have in common with the other group members?
3. If you were to drop out of this group, how would your life change? Do you think the group would continue to influence you?
4. How would your life be different if you didn't belong to any group?

how to raise money for band uniforms; the tenants' committee discusses ways of improving the apartment complex; the social committee discusses security arrangements for the upcoming concert.

Not all people like discussion. Many find it time consuming and boring. What, then, is the value of discussion?

In a democratic society, one of the first assumptions is that no one person will make the decisions for everyone. Discussion is a way for everyone to participate and be heard. It is a forum where ideas are proposed and then modified in response to group feedback.

Group decision making is often superior to individual decision making. Those who study small groups have found that people who work in groups accomplish more than people who work alone.[2] In fact, some jobs are better done by groups. Take the case of the Band Boosters—the group that is getting new uniforms for the band. This is clearly a group project; no individual can do the job very well. First the group talks about how to raise the money. Then individual members help in the fundraising efforts. If this were left to one individual, it would be an overwhelming job.

If you have worked in a group, you probably have discovered that motivation increases when everyone works together.[3] If five roommates decide to redecorate their apartment, it is much more fun if everyone pitches in and helps. Also, the five roommates are likely to come up with more ideas about how to do things than if only one person takes on the project. People are also likely to be more motivated when others are depending on them.[4] If one roommate, for example, has to strip the window sills before the others can paint, he or she is likely to get the job done so the others can go ahead with what they have to do.

CONSIDER THIS

Japanese manufacturers have developed a system of small groups in their factories, involving the workers. These groups, called Quality Circles, have been so effective in Japan that the system has been adopted by many American businesses.

The theory behind Quality Circles is that if problems are occurring in production, workers are as well equipped as management to identify the problems and their causes. In fact, the workers are the real experts because they are closest to the problem. Workers meet in Quality Circles to identify problems, discuss solutions, and make recommendations to management. It is then up to management to put the solutions into effect.

Perhaps the main discovery of Quality Circles is that workers often have a solution—if somebody asks them for it.

When people work in groups, there are opportunities to ask questions when an idea or issue is not clear. As well as learning faster, group members are able to absorb more information.[5] Not only does more information become available, but group members can help to decide which information is important.

We can see how this works in a practical situation. Let's say the school board has decided to set up a study group to make recommendations about computer use in the school district. The board has asked the group to decide what computers should be bought and to develop some recommendations about how they should be used. Since this is a subject that requires a good deal of expertise, it is best dealt with by a group. Someone who has had experience with computers might be able to make recommendations about good buys. Someone else might be asked to look into the issue of software and to find out which programs would be most appropriate for schoolchildren. Another member of the group, perhaps a school principal, might want to concentrate on where the computers should be placed in a school and how students will have access to them. Yet another member might be asked to address the question of ethics—how children should be taught about computer piracy and privacy. Clearly, the whole problem of computers in the schools is too complicated for any one person. Setting up a group is an ideal way to attack the problem.

When you see how effectively a group can solve a problem, it's no surprise that groups are found in every aspect of life. When Thomas Peters and Robert Waterman set out to discover why certain American companies excel, they found that one answer was the use these companies make of small groups. In their book *In Search of Excellence* they write, "Small groups are, quite simply, the basic organizational building blocks of excellent companies."[6]

CHARACTERISTICS OF SMALL GROUPS

Sharing a Common Goal

A characteristic of all small groups is that they share a common goal.[7] Most groups get together in the first place because they have such a goal: they want to start a new organization, they want to solve a community problem, they want to make recommendations to a new supervisor. As long as the group shares a common goal, the group members feel a sense of purpose.

Group Size

Groups work best when all members in the group can communicate and interact with one another. For a group to be effective, it should be anywhere from three to thirteen members. Research indicates that an ideal size for a group is five members.

Often a group consists of so many members that it cannot work effectively to solve problems or do the job at hand. In such cases, the group should be broken up into smaller groups—each with a job to do. The student government, for example, is usually broken down into committees: the Social Committee, the Food Advisory Committee, the Constitutional Revision Committee, and so on. The committees then study the issues and make recommendations to the larger body, the student government.

One sign that indicates a group is too large is when all members do not have an opportunity to speak or when individual members do not participate in group decisions or actions. When this occurs, it is time to break the group into still smaller groups. With the student Social Committee, for example, some members could check out the availability of certain musical groups while other members could conduct a poll to see which musicians the students would like to have on campus.

Groups can also be too small. When there is a lot of information to gather or when the group requires specialization from its members, it is important to have enough members to do the job. The earlier example of the group that is going to make recommendations about computers for the schools is a good example of a need for members to specialize. The group might decide that there are so many different kinds of computers available that two people should research this area. The same might be true of software—it might take two people to look at all of it. Another member might assist the principals in working out schedules for computer use. Counting in the member assigned to investigate the question of computer ethics, this group will need at least seven members to do the job. If there are enough members, no single person will have too much to do.

CONSIDER THIS

Group Meetings in a Business Setting

These can be held over coffee, during a certain hour of the work week, or after hours. They must revolve around a plan, though, and that plan must be maintained. They should also be under the guidance of an effective leader who can draw out participants' thinking.

Such meetings can be the instrument of a series of discussions; for example, the scientific approach to management problems, what encourages high morale and cooperation among employees, the most pressing problem currently facing the department or firm.

Group meetings are also the place for trainees to practice public speaking, counseling and advising subordinates, getting ideas and instructions across clearly to another person.

Source: Ted Pollock, *Managing Others Creatively*.

The Meeting Place

The place where the group meets will often influence the general atmosphere of the meeting. A group that meets in a classroom or a conference room will probably be more formal than a group that meets in someone's room or apartment.

The group's meeting place can be chosen on the basis of who the group members are and what they want to accomplish. Group members who know each other well might want to meet in someone's home; when group members do not know each other well or if the group wants to continue to attract new members, the group would be better off meeting in a public place.

Sometimes the meeting place will be determined by what the group wants to accomplish. The local government study group, for example, has to meet in City Hall so members of the public can attend. The literacy council meets in the public library because it stores its materials there.

Seating Arrangements

The way group members will be seated in the room depends on the way the group is structured and the task it wishes to accomplish. A group sitting at a table is usually more formal than a group sitting in chairs around a room. And a group seated at a rectangular table might be more formal than a group seated

Is there a leader in this group? The seating arrangement gives a clue as to the answer.

at a round table. Quite often when there is a rectangular table, the person who sits at the head of it assumes the position of group leader.

Seating arrangements are particularly important at the first meeting. Once people arrange themselves, they are likely to continue with the same arrangement at subsequent meetings. Therefore it is important to consider what kind of structure you want the group to have before you arrange the chairs.

Group Norms

Norms are the expectations group members have of how the other members in the group will behave, think, and participate. These norms are informal—they are not written down. Members assume that others understand the norms and will follow them.

A college seminar is a good example of how norms operate. At the beginning of the semester, the instructor does not have to tell class members how to behave. He or she assumes that students will attend the seminar, speak in turn, buy the textbook, and generally act in a polite and responsible manner—in other words, that they will follow the norms of behavior for a seminar.

In familiar settings, we take group norms for granted. But if we join a group where the norms are not so obvious, we might just sit back and listen until we figure out what the group norms are.

TRY THIS

Think about some small group you have belonged to that had (or has) group norms and rules.

1. Can you sort out which are norms and which rules?
2. How did you learn the norms and the rules?
3. Did anything happen to members who did not follow the norms? The rules?
4. Did the group have any way of changing its norms or rules?
5. Did norms and rules lead to a more effective group? Why?

Norms are important because they give a group some structure. If members know how to behave, the group will function more efficiently. Also, outsiders can look at the group's norms to see whether they want to join the group. If, for example, you feel comfortable only in informal settings, you will probably not want to join a group that has lots of rituals and ceremonies.

Some groups are not very specific about their norms. It is assumed that because you join the group, you believe in the group's norms. You show that you believe in the group by attending meetings from time to time. Often task-oriented groups have no norms other than getting the job done.

Group Rules

Unlike norms, **rules** are formal and structured directions for behavior. In many cases, groups follow rules such as those in *Robert's Rules of Order*. These rules tell what jobs the members should do, how the meeting should be conducted, how motions should be introduced, and so on. The rules help the meeting to progress and ensure that everyone can be heard but that no one person will monopolize the meeting. Quite often a group will appoint a parliamentarian to see that these rules are properly interpreted and followed.

Cohesiveness

Cohesiveness is the feeling of attraction that group members have toward one another.[8] It is the group's ability to stick together, to work together as a group, and to help one another as group members. There are few more powerful and satisfactory feelings than the feeling of belonging to a group and of being loyal to that group. At one time or another, most of us have belonged to a group we felt particularly attached to. Even when the group's job was over, we were

CONSIDER THIS

One technique developed by Quality Circles is a way of getting everyone to talk. Whether the group is discussing an idea or considering a solution, the discussion goes around the circle, and each person contributes one idea. If someone does not have an idea, he or she says "pass." (People using this technique have found that people seldom pass more than twice.) The group continues to use this technique until everyone passes—then it is ready to go on to a new subject or to take a vote on the present one.

This technique is particularly useful if you have some unusually talkative or shy members.

reluctant to part from one another. This attraction and affection we felt for other members is an example of group cohesiveness.

Although cohesiveness is often a matter of group chemistry, an effective group leader can help cohesiveness to develop when the group meets for the first few times. A good leader will make certain that all members are introduced and, if appropriate, are given a chance to say something about themselves. Cohesiveness will also be helped if members have a chance to do a little socializing before and after the meeting. Finally, during the discussion, a good leader will try to draw out the quieter members. The more everyone participates, the better the chance for group unity to develop.

DISCUSSION IN GROUPS

Problem solving in groups works best if a logical sequence is followed.[9] Most groups use a sequence that is very close to the one you see in Figure 9-1. Let's look at each of these steps in some detail.

FIGURE 9-1 The Problem-Solving Sequence

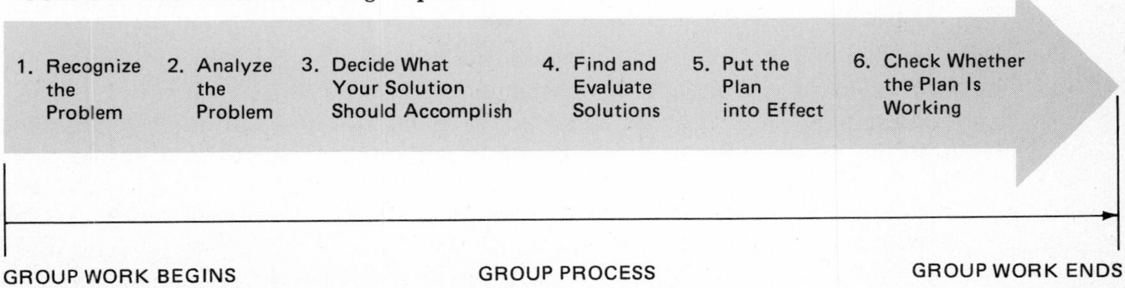

1. Recognize the Problem 2. Analyze the Problem 3. Decide What Your Solution Should Accomplish 4. Find and Evaluate Solutions 5. Put the Plan into Effect 6. Check Whether the Plan Is Working

GROUP WORK BEGINS   GROUP PROCESS   GROUP WORK ENDS

CONSIDER THIS

Sometimes group members will have so many ideas (or problems) that the group doesn't know where to begin. If this is happening in your group let each person vote for the top two or three things on the list. Then you will be able to eliminate some of the subjects only one or two people are interested in. After you have voted on the top two or three subjects, then, after some more discussion, you vote again—this time for the top choice.

Recognizing the Problem

If you are a member of a business, institutional, or community group, you are in this group because you already have a task to perform or a problem to solve. Since the problem already exists, this first step is not one you will have to deal with. When you are in a class, however, you are often given the assignment to pick a topic your group can discuss. How do you choose a topic? How do you choose a subject that all members of the group will find interesting?

Your first approach might be to look at your own school. Are there any problems or improvements your group might like to tackle? How's the food? Does registration run smoothly? Does the bookstore have fair prices? Is the library open at convenient times? Any of these questions might lead to an interesting discussion.

Take a look at the community. Are there any problems there? How do students get along with the local townspeople? Are students good neighbors? Do the banks cash out-of-town checks without adding a service charge? Do the local merchants realize how important students are to the economy of the town? Are there issues in the city council or county commissioner's office that might affect the school?

If your group is interested in attacking a broader social issue, the supply is almost limitless. Nuclear weapons, abortion, and federal spending are all issues that have been hotly debated through the years and will continue to be debated in the future. Discussing one of these topics in your group might be a good way for everyone to become informed about an important issue.

When a group cannot find a topic that all members consider interesting, it should try brainstorming. In **brainstorming** the leader should temporarily stop leading the group and let all members throw out ideas—however unstructured or even ridiculous the ideas might seem. The idea behind brainstorming is to let the group be as creative as possible. Suggestions should not be evaluated during the brainstorming session. If members fear that their ideas might be condemned, they are not as likely to be willing to share some of their wilder thoughts.

Quite often, group members will hear an idea during the brainstorming session that they all like. They are likely to respond with some variation of "That's it!" If this does not happen, the group leader should stop the brainstorming session when ideas seem to be drying up. Then the group can go back and discuss some of the ideas that have come out of the session.

Analyzing the Problem

Defining the Words

The first step in analyzing a problem is to define any word or phrase that might be ambiguous. For example, a classroom group decided that the campus mailroom took too long to deliver mail. Since members in the group defined "too long" in various ways, the group had to be more precise about the term. They agreed that "too long" was anything over 24 hours. A community group that wanted to start a program to teach illiterate persons how to read and write first had to define "illiterate." Did it apply only to people who could not read or write? What about a person who could do some reading and writing but not enough to function in ordinary society? From a practical point of view, was this person also illiterate?

Seeking Out Information

Often groups need to seek out information relevant to the problem. But the kind of information will vary. For example, the group trying to speed up the

TRY THIS

Here is a list of possible discussion topics. Which words and phrases need defining?

1. Should parents who send their children to private schools receive tuition tax credits?
2. Should welfare mothers receive federal money for abortions?
3. Should the government limit nuclear weapons?
4. Should the government prohibit broadcasters from showing violent programs on television?
5. Should affirmative action guidelines be allowed to discriminate against men?
6. Should the solid waste authority make use of the county's landfill?

Group problem solving often involves a division of responsibility. These two women are conducting library research on a problem of interest to their group.

campus mail will need to know why the mail is delayed—that is, the cause of the problem. However, the group that wants to teach illiterate persons to read and write doesn't need to concentrate on causes—it needs to find out how to teach these people to read and write.

When a group needs information, individual group members may each investigate a different aspect of the problem. In the case of the slow-moving mail, one person might go to the mailroom and talk to the person in charge. Another might observe how mail is sorted and distributed. Still another might mail notices from various parts of the campus to see how quickly each one reaches its destination. The group interested in literacy will probably begin its search for information in the library. They will look to see whether there is a national literacy organization or whether anyone in the state is doing work in literacy. After discovering names and addresses, group members will write to these organizations to get more information.

Deciding on the Final Wording of the Question

Once the problem is analyzed, it is a good idea to put it into words. Wording helps group members to agree about and focus on the problem. Most groups like to phrase their problem as a question. A question not only sounds more natural but also focuses on coming up with an answer.

Basically there are three kinds of questions: questions of fact, of value, and of policy. **Questions of fact** deal with what is true and what is false. Examples of these questions might be: "What is the most efficient fuel for heating a house: wood, coal, gas, or oil?" "Does alcohol consumption harm a fetus?" "How can our group invest its money to get the highest interest rate?"

Questions of value are questions of whether something is good or bad, desirable or undesirable. Examples are: "Are student foreign exchange programs desirable?" "Is it a good idea to permit freshmen to have cars on campus?" "Are coed dorms desirable?"

Questions of policy are about actions that might be taken in the future. Such questions are often asked in institutional settings such as schools, businesses, or organizations, and they usually include the word "should": "Should all students be required to take two years of a foreign language?" "Should employees be given longer vacations?" "Should the college build a new football stadium?"

Note that many questions of value also involve policy, and vice versa. For example, "Should the college build a new football stadium?" is a question of policy, but it also has a question of value built into it: "Is a new football stadium desirable?"

When a group is engaged in fact finding, it is most likely to use questions of fact. If some students, for example, are curious about how much money is spent on college athletics, some of their fact-finding questions might be: "What percentage of the student activity fee is spent on athletics?" "What percentage of the total college budget is spent on athletics?" "What percentage of salaries paid at the college goes to coaches?" These and other fact-finding questions will help them to gather information about how much money is budgeted for athletics.

When a group is going to make recommendations, it will use questions of value or questions of policy. A group considering the parking problem on campus might ask: "Should freshman be permitted to bring cars on campus?" "Should faculty and staff be given the first choice of parking spots?" "Should everyone be required to pay for parking stickers?" Research into these questions will help the group move to the point where it can make recommendations.

Deciding What Your Solution Should Accomplish

Before a group can look at solutions and evaluate them, it must decide what the group wants to accomplish. For example, when a faculty committee was set up to create a form to evaluate the university's president, the committee decided that no evaluation would be adequate unless it included feedback from three different groups on campus: students, staff, and faculty. By deciding on this criterion, the committee knew that any evaluation form that did not do this job should be eliminated.

In deciding what its solution should accomplish, the mail committee agreed that any solution was unacceptable that did not get the mail to its destination 24 hours after it was received in the mailroom. The literacy committee decided that it wanted to be able to offer all illiterate adults in the county a chance to learn to read and write. By deciding what its solution should accomplish, a group is better able to evaluate various solutions.

Finding and Evaluating Solutions

Often a group can find many solutions to its problem. Some of them, however, will have to be discarded because they are impractical. In the literacy group, for example, someone suggested that unemployed elementary-school teachers should be hired to teach illiterate adults. Although everyone agreed this was a good idea, no one could find a way to get the money to pay these teachers. Other times, groups are constrained by outside forces. The high-school band group wanted to put up a 40-foot sign promoting the band, but a city ordinance ruled out any signs over 15 feet. A group working in curriculum reform within the college found itself limited by the terms of the faculty contract. A group might also find that certain solutions have been tried and have not worked.

Every group must ask itself questions about proposed solutions. Typical questions include the following: Will the solution solve the problem? Is the solution practical? Does the solution require permission from anyone to put it into effect? Does the solution violate any law? Group members should subject the solution to hard scrutiny. If the solution doesn't pass such scrutiny, the group will have to keep working until it finds one that does.

Putting the Plan into Effect

The final step in a discussion is deciding how to carry out the solution or solutions endorsed by the group.

The test of a group's success is whether it can come up with ideas and a course of action that can be implemented. In the case of the campus mail problem, group members recommend a solution to the head of the mailroom. She expresses a willingness to try out the plan, and group members decide to check back in a month to see if it is working. The literacy group decides to start a literacy council in the county and to affiliate with a national organization. The national organization will supply a teacher to train members of the council in tutoring adults. This group knows it has been successful when, a year after its first meeting, it has 25 tutors working with students.

Checking Whether the Plan Is Working

Sometimes groups come up with plans that don't work. If a group finds that its plan is not working and there is still a problem, the group will have to

TRY THIS

Use the following list of questions to judge the success of the last problem-solving group of which you were a member:

1. Did you feel comfortable in this group?
2. Did everyone participate and interact?
3. Were the group sessions enjoyable?
4. Did you find the task of the group enjoyable?
5. Was the material adequately and efficiently covered?

Source: Adapted from William Fawcett Hill, *Learning Thru Discussion: Guide for Leaders and Members of Discussion Groups.*

meet again to consider some different solutions. For example, a group of Jaycee women decided to collect food for a local free lunch program by offering to compete with any other women's group in the community to see which group could collect the greatest number of canned goods. But when no other women's group accepted the challenge, the group had to find another way to collect food. This group found, as do many groups, that even good solutions do not always work.

SUMMARY

A small group is one whose members share a common goal. It must be small enough (three to thirteen members) so members can interact. If the group is to be successful, members must get along with one another.

All small groups use discussion. Research indicates that groups can solve problems more easily than individuals. Motivation increases when people are in groups, and most people seem to learn faster when they are members of a group.

Some practical factors that help small groups function better are the size of the group, the meeting place, and the seating arrangements. Psychological factors include group norms and rules and group cohesiveness.

Groups usually form in response to a problem. If the group has to come up with a problem, as in a classroom, the group should look to the campus and the community for ideas. Brainstorming is also a valuable technique for generating ideas.

When a group meets to solve a problem its first job is to analyze it. Typical steps in analysis include defining terms, gathering information, and stating the final wording of the question. In the next stage, the group evaluates the possible solutions by asking which one will best solve the problem. After a solution is agreed on by group members, they try it out. Many groups like to go back and look at their solution after it has been in effect for a while. This enables the group to decide whether the solution is working.

VOCABULARY

The following is a list of words you must know to understand the concepts in this chapter. You will find the words defined the first time that each is used in the chapter. All Vocabulary words also appear, with their definitions, in the Glossary at the end of the book.

brainstorming
cohesiveness
norms
questions of fact

questions of policy
questions of value
rules
small group

FURTHER READING

BARKER, LARRY L., KATHY J. WAHLERS, DONALD J. CEGALA, AND ROBERT J. KIBLER. *Groups in Process: An Introduction to Small Group Communication*, 2nd ed. Englewood Cliffs, N.J.: Prentice-Hall, 1983. The authors of this textbook present practical information on group functioning as well as communication techniques to increase the reader's value as a group member and leader. This concise, readable textbook emphasizes applied small group interactions.

BEEBE, STEVEN A., AND JOHN T. MASTERSON. *Communicating in Small Groups: Principles and Practices.* Glenview, Ill.: Scott, Foresman, 1982. This well-written, documented, and illustrated textbook covers the essentials of small-group processes and problem solving. The text includes chapters on theory, group formation, relating in groups, group climate, leadership, and problem solving.

FISHER, B. AUBREY. *Small Group Decision Making: Communication and the Group Process*, 2nd ed. New York: McGraw-Hill, 1980. Fisher emphasizes both decision making and communication. The book is intended for university students studying group discussion. This is a very thorough, well-constructed, well-researched approach to small-group decision making.

GOURAN, DENNIS S. *Discussion: The Process of Group Decision-Making.* New York: Harper & Row, 1974. This is a unique textbook because of its focus on group decision making alone. Throughout the book, Gouran has utilized scientific data to illustrate the means by which individuals can contribute more constructively in decision-making discussions.

HARE, A. PAUL. *Creativity in Small Groups.* Beverly Hills, Calif.: Sage, 1982. Hare develops various perspectives on social interaction, examines groups processes and structures, and summarizes his analysis of individual and group creativity with a flow chart of the steps involved in the process of creative problem solving.

HILL, WILLIAM FAWCETT. *Learning Thru Discussion: Guide for Leaders and Members of Discussion Groups.* Beverly Hills, Calif.: Sage, 1977. This is a 64-page how-to book for leaders and members of any type of group. Hill's LTD (Learning Thru Discussion) technique stresses time utilization, listening skills, and the ability to increase understanding and retention of material. Straightforward, practical advice is given.

JOHNSON, DAVID W., AND FRANK P. JOHNSON. *Joining Together: Group Theory and Group Skills,* 2nd ed. Englewood Cliffs, N.J.: Prentice-Hall, 1982. This 510-page paperback provides the theory and experiences necessary to develop an understanding of group processes and effective group skills. The authors stress an experiential approach to learning by including brief, clear theoretical explanations followed by exercises—more than eighty that supplement and illustrate the ideas discussed.

KELL, CARL L., AND PAUL R. CORTS, *Fundamentals of Effective Group Communication.* New York: Macmillan, 1980. Kell and Corts offer a brief, practical textbook examining the basics of small-group communication, members' roles as contributing participants in groups, and behaviors that should be both incorporated into and avoided in small-group communication.

NEWMAN, PAMELA J., AND ALFRED F. LYNCH. *Behind Closed Doors: A Guide to Successful Meetings.* Englewood Cliffs, N.J.: Prentice-Hall, 1983. The authors provide a guide for organizing and conducting business meetings. They cover how to prepare for a meeting, how to plan an agenda, how to conduct a meeting, and how to evaluate its success. This is a practical, readable book full of helpful advice.

SNELL, FRANK. *How to Win the Meeting.* New York: Hawthorn Books, 1979. Snell characterizes the meeting as a place of force and persuasion. He emphasizes preparation and directness, and he applies his ideas to school boards and political meetings, as well as community-action groups. This is a very readable book, full of useful, practical examples.

WILLIAMSON, JOHN N., ED. *The Leader-Manager.* Eden Prairie, Minn.: Wilson Learning Corporation, 1984. This collection of readings includes material on change, leadership, growth, mission, goals, feedback, rewards, and support. The volume offers a new lens through which to view the management of people. The focus is the importance of leadership.

ZANDER, ALVIN. *Making Groups Effective.* San Francisco: Jossey-Bass, 1982. Zander applies pertinent findings of current research on group dynamics to show how all types of groups can learn to solve day-to-day problems. He focuses on characteristics of effective groups, common obstacles to group effectiveness, as well as how managers and leaders can help groups function more productively. Zander provides realistic recommendations and guidance.

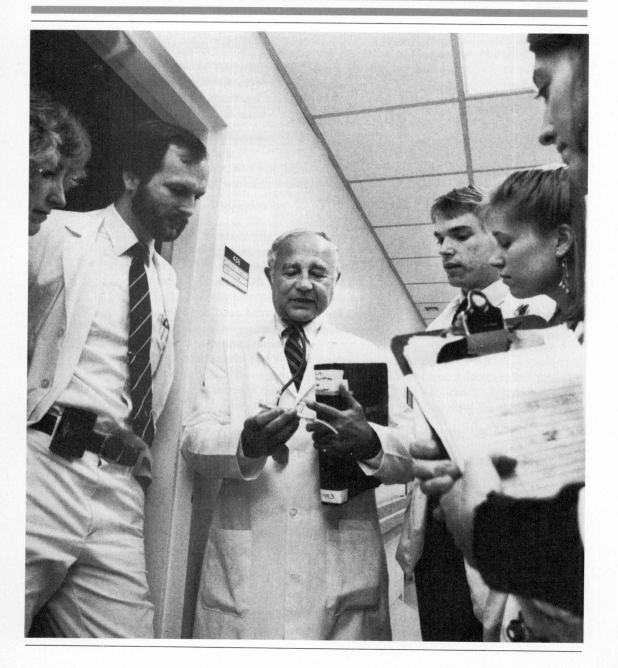

230

10 *LEADER AND PARTICIPANT RESPONSIBILITIES*

CHAPTER OBJECTIVES

After reading this chapter, you should be able to:

1. Describe the three ways people become leaders of groups.

2. Describe the three styles of leadership often employed.

3. Outline the procedures that should be established at the beginning of a group meeting.

4. Explain the ways in which the leader can help a group to progress.

5. Distinguish among task, maintenance, and negative roles, and give examples of each.

6. Describe the attitudes that help group discussion.

Imagine this scene. You are a member of the student government, and you are attending its first meeting. An agenda is handed out and the president calls the meeting to order. He begins with the announcements; by the time they are read, a half-hour has passed. He then proceeds to the items on the agenda. There is a treasurer's report, but someone complains that the report is not itemized so there is no clear idea of how the money has been spent. Several members get upset with the lack of itemization, and there is a long discussion on the responsibilities of the treasurer. No action is taken, however. By this time the meeting has gone on for an hour, and everyone is beginning to fidget—especially when they realize that several items still remain on the agenda.

The next items on the agenda are resolved more quickly. Then, under "New Business" there is an item that immediately arouses everyone's interest. The student government, which is responsible for the college vans, had loaned the vans to the soccer team. When the vans were returned, the vice president went to retrieve the keys and discovered that one of the vans had a big dent on the right-hand fender. Assuming that the van has been driven recklessly, she now proposes that van privileges be taken away from the team. Immediately there is a big uproar. There are two long speeches—one about carelessness and the other about responsibility. Several people point out, often repeating points already made, that there is no evidence that the van was driven carelessly—someone could have hit it while it was parked. Finally, after an hour of impassioned debate, a member of the government moves that van privileges be taken away from the team. The motion is defeated.

By now the meeting has lasted over two hours. Several members of the government have sneaked out the door; others are passing notes or are involved in conversations with their neighbors. Several actions still have to be voted on, but everyone is so bored that they pass all the motions in the next five minutes. Once the meeting is over, everyone looks relieved to escape.

Does this sound like any meeting you have ever attended? What has been described is a group process lacking control. The president, the leader of the group, made little attempt to keep the meeting moving along. He permitted points to be repeated, he was unaware of the boredom of the participants—or didn't know what to do about it—and he permitted the meeting to go on far beyond the time that it would hold participants' interest.

The leader, however, was not the only one at fault. The participants sat back and observed an ineffective and boring meeting without doing anything to make the meeting move faster or more efficiently. A group can function only as well as its leader and participants. What, then, are the responsibilities of the people who make up groups? Before answering this question, let's first focus on leaders—how they come to lead and their styles of leadership.

THE SELECTION OF LEADERS

People become leaders in basically three ways: they are imposed, they are elected, or they rotate into the leadership role.[1] When the boss appoints an

CONSIDER THIS

At the top was Doc; beneath him were Mike and Danny and also Long John in a somewhat anomalous relationship; beneath Mike and Danny were Nutsy and Angelo and Frank and a half dozen other followers. Doc was the focal point for the organization of the group. "In his absence," an observer reported, "the members of the gang are divided into a number of small groups. There is no common activity or general conversation. When the leader appears, the situation changes strikingly. The small units form into one large group. The conversation becomes general, and unified action frequently follows. The leader becomes the central point in the discussion. A follower starts to say something, pauses when he notices the leader is not listening, and begins again when he has the leader's attention. When the leader leaves the group, unity gives way to the divisions that existed before his appearance.

Source: James MacGregor Burns, *Leadership*.

employee to set up a study committee, this is an example of imposed leadership.

Where a formal structure exists, elected leadership is common. Thus many areas of government have elected leaders. Also, when a situation is highly controversial, it is a good idea to elect the leader. For example, when a group of employees meets to decide who gets to work for overtime pay, it would probably be a good idea if the leader were elected. The employees can then elect the person they believe to be the most fair.

When the group is informally structured, the leadership often will rotate among the members. The local chapter of the American Cancer Society, for instance, is made up of a core of members who do most of the work. So that the work does not become too much for any one person, the group rotates the presidency every two years among the core members—giving everyone a chance to be the leader.

Leadership is a role given by the group. A leader cannot function in that role without the group's permission. Occasionally a group will have a leader who it doesn't like or who is not functioning effectively. If this happens, another leader is likely to emerge—even though this person is never given the title of leader. If no other leader emerges, the group is likely to become ineffective and dissolve. If you look at the student government on your campus, you will probably notice that some years it is effective and other years it is not. When it's running effectively, the most likely reason is that it has an effective leader who works well with the rest of his or her cabinet and with the committees.

LEADERSHIP STYLES

There are many ways of leading a group.[2] The way the leader chooses to lead is termed leadership *style*. Different people have different styles—usually reflecting their own personalities and their own needs. Basically, there are three leadership styles: authoritarian, democratic, and laissez-faire.

The Authoritarian Leader

The **authoritarian leader** calls all the shots. He or she controls the group by deciding what it should talk about, who should talk, and who should not talk. Everything originates with the leader and is channeled back to him or her; group members have very little chance to interact with such a leader.

A typical authoritarian leader will often make decisions that might affect the group without consulting it. The student body president, for example, decides not to put the Social Committee on the agenda because she is afraid the committee is going to stir up controversy. Sometimes a group under an authoritarian leader can get more work done than other groups. Because the authoritarian leader does not tolerate other points of view, very little time is spent in discussion. If group members resent an authoritarian style, however, they may refuse to work at all.

The Democratic Leader

One who lets all points of view be heard is a **democratic leader**. Rather than deciding things personally, he or she will throw out ideas and let the group react to them. Ideally, such a leader keeps the discussion on track but makes a real attempt to let all members be heard. The group is never told what to do, though the leader may suggest a direction they can take. All members have a chance to contribute, and information can move among them as well as back and forth to the leader.

A democratic group provides more opportunity for originality and creativity. Since members share in the decision making, there is also greater motivation. Because members identify with the group, they are more interested in having the group achieve its goal.

The Laissez-faire Leader

The **laissez-faire leader** does very little actual leading. He or she might call the group together, but that's about it. Such a leader doesn't suggest any

A democratic or laissez-faire leader would prefer a seating arrangement like this. Every member of this group seems to be on an equal footing with the others and is expected to participate in the general exchange of ideas.

direction, nor does he or she impose any order on the group. Laissez-faire leaders really do not believe in leadership; they see leadership as a superior position—a position they feel uncomfortable with. If they communicate this attitude to the group, it is unlikely that any other leader will emerge. After all, who wants to say that he or she is superior to all the others in the group? It is no surprise that laissez-faire groups do not accomplish very much. The group is so unstructured that it is almost impossible to get anything done.

Democratic leadership is best for a group trying to get a job done because it permits all members to participate in decision making. There are times, however, where authoritarian and laissez-faire leadership have their place. If your group has a complex job to do and only two days to do it, authoritarian leadership will probably work best. In a self-help group—such as Alcoholics Anonymous—or in a group where the primary purpose is to express feelings, laissez-faire leadership will be the most appropriate.

Look at all the instructors from whom you are taking classes this semester or quarter, then answer these questions:

1. How would you classify the leadership of each in the classroom—as authoritarian, laissez-faire, or democratic?
2. What behaviors of the instructor indicate the particular leadership pattern he or she is following?
3. What style of classroom leadership do you feel most comfortable with?
4. Do you think that one leadership style is more appropriate than the others in a classroom setting? Which one? Why?

LEADING THE GROUP

The role of leader in a group is to help the group get the job done. To do this the leader must have a certain sense of detachment. He or she needs to look at the group from a different perspective than other members—the perspective of "Is the group functioning as well as it should be?" "Is the group making progress?" "What can I do to make the group work better?" Leaders can help groups work better when they establish procedures, help the group to keep moving, raise questions, focus on answers, delegate responsibility, and encourage social interaction.

Establishing Procedures

Every small-group meeting should be conducted according to a plan that organizes the group's work. This plan is called the group's *procedures*—or how the group should operate.

If the group is meeting for the first time, it's a good idea for the leader to let the members introduce themselves. If appropriate, the leader might also ask why the members have joined the group and what they want the group to accomplish.

Many groups will function more efficiently if someone is assigned to keep a record of what goes on in the meeting. This record can be formal minutes that will be read at the next meeting or a simple list of the topics the group has discussed that members can refer back to when necessary.

After the members have been introduced and someone agrees to take notes, the leader can briefly state what the group's work will be for that meeting. Once the work has been outlined, the discussion is ready to begin.

Many groups begin meetings with an **agenda**—a list of all the items that will be discussed during the group's meeting. In the previous chapter we discussed the problem-solving sequence, which included steps from defining the problem to putting the plan into effect. This is an excellent sequence for a group with a single problem to solve. Many groups, however, have a variety of items to handle during a meeting. These groups are more likely to use an agenda that begins with the reading of the minutes from the last meeting, announcements, old business, committee reports, and new business. Figure 10-1 shows a typical agenda.

Most groups exist because there is a topic to be discussed, a problem to be solved. In a classroom setting, however, students often must choose their topic. If there is no topic, this should be the first subject of discussion for the group. The role of the leader in such situations is to keep the group focused on this important job.

Throughout the meeting, the leader should give everyone a chance to participate. He or she can do this by paying attention to quieter members and asking them if they have anything to say. If the leader starts to do this at the very beginning of each discussion, it is a sign to all members that everyone will have a chance to participate.

Helping the Group to Progress

Groups cannot move ahead when members spend too much time dealing with trivia or with only a certain phase of a problem. An effective small-group leader will move the group toward another phase of the problem when a sufficient amount of information has been presented, when information is being repeated, or when the points discussed become too trivial. The leader might say, "I think we are beginning to repeat ourselves. Let's move along to the next issue."

FIGURE **10-1** An Agenda

1. Call to order
2. Reading, correction of, and approval of minutes of previous meetings
3. Reports of officers
4. Reports of boards and standing committees
5. Reports of special committees
6. Unfinished business
7. New business
8. Announcements
9. Adjournment

CONSIDER THIS

Think of vehicular traffic. When there is light traffic at an intersection, stop signs are adequate; when traffic is heavy in all directions, a great deal of skill is required to time your entry into (or across) the traffic flow, and accidents are more likely to happen. Some kind of signaling system, traffic lights or a policeman, ensures safety and also increases the rate of flow through the intersection. You heave a sigh when you discover a policeman at a busy intersection and don't have to poke the front part of your car into cross traffic and pray that the other cars will stop.

The same is true of a meeting. If you know someone is concerned with seeing that everyone is heard, that no one is attacked, that individuals can signal for entry into the conversational flow, you are relieved of a great deal of unnecessary tension. You can devote more of your energy to listening to others and thinking about what you want to contribute.

Source: Michael Doyle and David Straus, *The New Interaction Method: How to Make Meetings Work.*

Helping the group to move along requires some assertiveness on the part of the leader. Leaders must be willing to interject themselves and the group's agenda on its members. This requires some discretion and diplomacy because group members do not like to be bossed. A leader might say, for example, "Excuse me for interrupting you, Deb, but I wonder if we might hear what some of the others are thinking."

Summarizing is one good way to help the group progress. It alerts the group to where it has been, what it has accomplished, where it is now, and where it is going. A final summary is also a good way to close each group meeting. "Today we had a disagreement over whether we should lease our equipment to outsiders or permit only our own students to use it. At our next meeting I think we should work to resolve this issue."

Raising Questions

One of the ways a leader can be most helpful to a group is to raise pertinent questions. Sometimes, during discussion, it is easy for the group to lose sight of its original goal. A group of students, for example, might be discussing vandalism of the classrooms and get diverted to the subject of the unfriendly law enforcement officials. If the group leader says, "Is this directly related to the problem of classroom vandals?" the group will realize that it is not and will get back on the subject.

Sometimes a group will try to discuss a subject and will simply not have enough information. A group discussing faculty and student parking might realize that it doesn't know how many parking places are assigned to each group. A group leader can help a group discover the questions that still need to be answered.

Information that the group receives must be evaluated. Some information may be insignificant, irrelevant, or invalid. Appropriate questions include: How recent is the information? Who is the source? Might the source be biased? Facts and opinions should be scrutinized carefully for possible errors or misinterpretation.

Focusing on Answers

To accomplish its task, a group needs answers. If the function of the group is to solve a problem, members need to keep their attention on solutions. Effective group leadership involves focusing the members' attention on the need for answers and supporting members who work toward answers.

Focusing on answers involves evaluating solutions by considering their advantages and disadvantages. Some solutions rejected earlier in the discussion can be offered again, as new insights are gained and new combinations seen. A useful leadership role is played by members who ask such questions as: What are the consequences that are likely to occur? What are the costs going to be? What barriers have to be overcome? How serious are the barriers?

Sometimes solutions call for a plan of action. If you decided in your group that the only course of action is to demonstrate against the administration, your group would be faced with making plans for that demonstration. How are you going to publicize your grievances, get recruits, and carry out the protest effectively? Effective leadership helps the group to plan carefully for the action it has decided to take.

Delegating Responsibility

Many people do not want to become leaders because they think that leadership involves too much work. By the same token, they see a leader as the one who does all the work. This should not be true in any group. A good leader should be able to delegate responsibility to the group's members. If a group is going to do research, for example, the leader could assign some members to go to the library, some to interview experts, and others to coordinate and present the information to the group.

Some leaders do not delegate because they believe they are the only ones who can do the job right. If you are one of these people, you should consider taking a risk and letting some of the other people do some of the work. You might be surprised at how well they do it.

CONSIDER THIS

Skilled leaders—in business, politics or virtually any field—share traits that elevate them above the majority of managers. While most managers concern themselves with doing things right, leaders focus on doing the right thing.

In the past few years, I have studied 90 top leaders. At first, I was struck by their pluralism and diversity, but when I looked more closely I found that they have much in common:

They all have a compelling vision, a dream about their work. They are highly conscious at all times of what they want. They are the most results-oriented people I ever encountered. I discovered this in a funny way. Among those I interviewed was a conductor. When I asked one of his musicians what made this man remarkable, he replied, "He doesn't waste our time." And when I began observing this conductor rehearsing, he always seemed to know precisely what he wanted.

Source: "A Conversation with Warren Bennis: Effective Leadership—The Exception, Not the Rule," *U.S. News & World Report.*

Encouraging Social Interaction

Social interaction occurs in a group when people are recognized and accepted, when they feel secure, and when they feel they are valued by other members. The more friendliness, mutual trust, respect, and warmth exhibited, the more likely the members will find pleasure in the group and the more likely that they will work hard to accomplish the group's goals. The use of first names and the use of such words as "we," "us," and "our" will help group members feel a sense of belonging. The group leader can also strengthen social interaction by encouraging shy members to speak, praising worthwhile contributions, and praising the overall accomplishments of the group. Group leaders should also plan to leave a little time before and after a meeting so members can socialize.

PARTICIPATING IN GROUP DISCUSSION

Roles in Discussion

Although most groups have someone who is specified as leader of the group, the leader does not have the total responsibility for giving the discussion a direction or moving the group along. In most groups, individual members temporarily take over the leadership from time to time.

Individual group members continue to play the same roles in groups as they do in any other communication. A person who likes to take charge is likely to want the role of group leader. A person who is shy is going to be as shy in a group as in any other kind of communication. In addition to the roles we play in life, however, some roles are specific to small-group communication. Kenneth Benne and Paul Sheats, in a classic study, have divided group participation into three categories of roles: task, maintenance, and negative.[3] These roles can be played both by leaders and by group members.

Task Roles

Task roles are those that help to get the job done. Persons who play these roles help the group to come up with new ideas, aid in collecting and organizing information, and analyze the information that exists. Task roles are not limited to any one individual; they may be interchanged among the members as the group goes about its job. Here are some of the common task roles.

Initiators-Expediters Members who act as *initiators-expediters*—by suggesting new ideas, goals, solutions, and approaches—are often the most creative and energetic of the group. When the group gets bogged down, they are likely to make such statements as "What if we tried . . ." or "I wonder if . . . would solve our problem."

Initiators-expediters often can suggest a new direction or can prevent the group from losing sight of its objectives. They are not afraid to jump in and give assistance when the group is in trouble. Often they are the ones who hold the light so others can see the path.

Information Givers and Seekers Individual members may both seek information and give it. Since lots of information will lead to better discussion, many members will play these roles. *Information givers* are often the best-informed members of the group. They might have had more experience with the subject or even be experts on it.

The more complex the subject, the greater the group's need for *information seekers*. These are people who are willing to go out and research the subject. They might agree to interview experts or they might go to the library to do research. If the group has very little information on the subject, it might be necessary for several members to play the role of information seeker.

The roles of information giving and seeking are the most important in any group. The information the group gets provides the foundation for the entire discussion. The more group members who play these roles, the better the quality of group discussion.

Critics-Analyzers *Critics-analyzers* are those who look at the good and bad points in the information the group has gathered. These people see the points that need more elaboration, and they discover information that has been left out.

CONSIDER THIS

The winning football team is the one that seems able, at will, to break away for that critical score. It's perfectly put together to do its job, to force its will upon its opponents. But is that really what a championship team is, a single force that overcomes its competitors? No. Like any organized group, it's a blending of a number of individual talents, kicking just a little bit better, blocking a little bit better, passing better, running the ball better. When all these talents are put together, that complex unit called the "team" wins.

Source: Frank Snell, *How to Win the Meeting.*

The critic-analyzer is able to look at the total picture and see how everything fits together. People who play this role usually have an excellent sense of organization. Often they can help keep the group on track. "We have mentioned this point twice. Maybe we need to discuss it in more depth." "Maybe we should go back and look at this information again. Something seems to be missing."

Maintenance Roles

Maintenance roles focus on the emotional tone of the meeting. Since no one wants to spend his or her entire time being logical, gathering information, and doing the job, it is important that some emotional needs be met. People who play maintenance roles meet these needs—by encouraging, harmonizing, regulating, and being observant.

Encouragers Encouragers praise and commend contributions and group achievements. "You really did a good job of gathering this information. Now we can dig in and work."

The best encouragers are active listeners. They help in rephrasing points so as to achieve greater clarity. They do not make negative judgments about other members or their opinions. Encouragers make people feel good about themselves and their contributions.

Harmonizers-Compromisers Those who help to resolve conflict in the group, by settling arguments and disagreements through mediation, are the *harmonizers-compromisers*. People who play this role are skillful at discovering solutions acceptable to everyone. Good harmonizer-compromisers are especially effective when they can remind group members that group goals are more important than individual needs. "I know you would like the library to be open on Sunday morning, but we have to find the times that are best for everybody."

Regulators As their name implies, *regulators* help regulate group discussion—by gently reminding members of the agenda or of the point they were discussing when they digressed. "We seem to be wandering a little. Now, we were discussing . . ."

Good regulators also find ways to give everyone a chance to speak. "Jane, you haven't said anything. Do you have any feelings on this subject?" Sometimes the regulator has to stop someone who has been talking too much. "Jerry, you have made several interesting points. Let's see what some of the others think of them." A regulator who is too authoritarian, however, might find that others resent him or her. In this role, it is important that statements or questions be tactfully worded.

Observers *Observers* aid in the group's cohesiveness. They are sensitive to the needs of each member. "I think we have ignored the point that John just made. Maybe we should take some time to discuss it."

Negative Roles

The roles we have just discussed are positive ones. Unfortunately, group members often play **negative roles**—by being aggressive, seeking recognition or help, promoting special interests, or not contributing. When members play these roles, the group is often slowed down or hampered from achieving its goals.

Aggressors-Resistors *Aggressors-resistors* often attack others to make themselves look better. They try to get their own way, or they come to the group with a set position and refuse to change it. "I don't know why we're wasting our time discussing vandalism. Throughout history, students have destroyed school property. There's no reason to think they will change now."

Recognition Seekers and Self-Confessors *Recognition seekers* and *self-confessors* are not happy unless they can call attention to themselves. Often their contributions are irrelevant or so drawn out that the goals of the group are lost. "In my day students were expected to behave. The problem with kids today is they have no respect for property. If I were the president of this college I would . . ."

Help Seekers *Help seekers* often join groups to meet their own personal needs. They use the group to gain assistance, advice, or counsel. They may seek sympathy for their confusion, insecurity, or personal problems. "I was so unhappy when I was a student. Students are so cruel to each other. Why can't they get along with each other? My daughter is having the same problems. . . ."

Withdrawers People who make no contribution to the group at all are known as *withdrawers*. When asked for an opinion, they say they don't have one. Sometimes these people are so shy that they are afraid to speak up; other times they have so little interest in the group, they are too bored to make a contribution.

Countering Negative Roles

Much of a group's success will depend on how willing leaders and members are to play task and maintenance roles. These are the roles that will help the group function to solve problems. If your group is not proceeding well, it is important to ask yourself whether any members are playing negative roles. Until these roles are recognized and identified, it is difficult to do anything about their negative effects on the group.

What should you do when you are in a group where people are playing negative roles? Sometimes it may be productive to point it out tactfully. "Deb and Mark—you haven't said anything during the whole meeting. What do you think about . . . ?"

Occasionally groups have members who are in direct conflict with each other. Even though the conflict might be personal, it usually takes the form of

At the point where conflict between two members of a group arises, other members may have to step in, call for a vote, and then ask that the disputants accept the decision of the majority.

TRY THIS

Below is a list of statements that people might make in a group. In each case, decide whether the role indicated by the statement is a task, maintenance, or negative one.

1. "The idea to separate freshmen and sophomores from upperclassmen is a good idea, but I think it has several problems."

2. "I think this group has done a splendid job. We have a lot of good ideas and everyone has done his or her homework."

3. "According to the report from law enforcement, there have been 297 incidents of vandalism this year, with 63 percent of the problems occurring around midterm and finals time."

4. "There is only one solution to this problem: if a kid commits any vandalism, even writing on the wall with a pencil, he should be kicked out of school."

5. "I think we should stop and look at all the information we have gathered so far. We should analyze it and decide where to go from here."

6. "We are beginning to get off the subject. Could we go back to our agenda?"

7. "Even though we have two opposite views here, I think both of you are concerned about the same problem."

Answers: 1. task   2. maintenance   3. task   4. negative   5. task   6. maintenance   7. maintenance

fighting over an issue. If the conflict is growing to a point where the whole group is feeling tension, someone should suggest that a vote be taken on whatever subject is under dispute. Once the vote is taken, the group can move on.

When a group has more than one member playing a negative role, the group should consider setting specific rules and procedures. Once rules are established, it will be easier to keep control of unruly members. Such rules can be suggested by any member of the group. For example, someone might say: "Since we have all been arguing over this particular point, I suggest that each member explain his or her position. After everyone has spoken, then we can try to discuss the issue again."

What Attitudes Help Group Discussion?

When you approach a group discussion with the right attitude, you will find that you are better able to contribute to the group. The best benefit of a good group discussion is that you will feel you have spent your time well. The attitudes that contribute to a good group discussion are initiative, empathy, assertiveness, and patience.

Initiative

Quite often group members depend on the group leader for initiative—not realizing that the group might move more effectively if everyone showed initiative. For example, groups often forget their agenda and get off the subject. At such times, any person can help the group by tactfully pointing this out.

Empathy

When a group is working on an issue that is really controversial, some members might have widely diverse opinions. At the beginning of discussions about controversial topics, it is going to be very useful if you make up your mind to try to understand points of view that are different from your own. Why does a group member feel this way? Can you put yourself in his or her place? Even though you might not change your mind, can you understand why he or she feels this way?

Assertiveness

There are times in any group when members need to assert their own views. Quite often, shy members of the group will not be assertive enough. If you have trouble speaking up, set a reasonable goal for yourself. You might tell yourself, for example, that every time the group meets, you are going to make at least one contribution. Once you have met this goal and you are feeling more comfortable, you might be willing to contribute even more.

Patience

All group work takes time. People who make quick decisions and who are quick with words often have trouble when discussion drags on and on. If this happens to you, it might be useful to remind yourself that it is important that everyone be heard. Giving everyone a chance to participate is part of the group process.

SUMMARY

People become leaders in three ways: they are imposed, they are elected; or they rotate into a leadership role. In formally structured groups, leaders are usually elected; in informal groups, leadership usually rotates among the members.

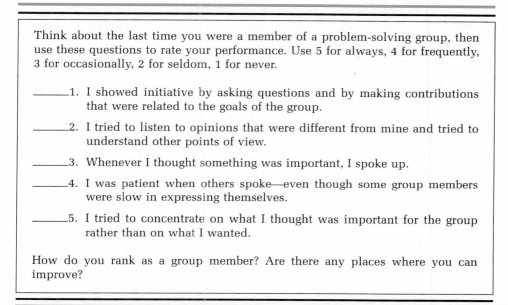

TRY THIS

Think about the last time you were a member of a problem-solving group, then use these questions to rate your performance. Use 5 for always, 4 for frequently, 3 for occasionally, 2 for seldom, 1 for never.

_____1. I showed initiative by asking questions and by making contributions that were related to the goals of the group.

_____2. I tried to listen to opinions that were different from mine and tried to understand other points of view.

_____3. Whenever I thought something was important, I spoke up.

_____4. I was patient when others spoke—even though some group members were slow in expressing themselves.

_____5. I tried to concentrate on what I thought was important for the group rather than on what I wanted.

How do you rank as a group member? Are there any places where you can improve?

The three leadership styles are authoritarian, democratic, and laissez-faire. In authoritarian leadership, all communication begins and ends with the leader; in democratic leadership, all members have an equal chance to participate. Laissez-faire leaders are essentially nonleaders—their groups are leaderless.

The group leader has six responsibilities: to establish procedures, to help the group keep moving, to raise questions, to focus on answers, to delegate responsibility, and to encourage social interaction.

Participants in group discussion play several roles. These roles are task-oriented (getting the job done), maintenance (being concerned with the emotional tone of the group), and negative (slowing down the progress of the group). The task and maintenance roles are productive; the negative roles are not. Group success is often determined by the attitudes members bring to the group. Helpful attitudes are initiative, empathy, assertiveness, and patience.

VOCABULARY

The following is a list of words you must know to understand the concepts in this chapter. You will find the words defined the first time that each is used in the chapter. All Vocabulary words also appear, with their definitions, in the Glossary at the end of the book.

agenda
authoritarian leader
democratic leader
laissez-faire leader

maintenance roles
negative roles
task roles

FURTHER READING

APPLBAUM, RONALD L., EDWARD M. BO-
DAKEN, KENNETH K. SERENO, AND
KARL W. E. ANATOL. *The Process of
Group Communication* Chicago:
Science Research Associates, 1974.
This textbook integrates theoretical
positions in the area of group communication with applications to
problems and situations. The authors offer a useful, understandable
approach to small groups.

BORMANN, ERNEST G. *Discussion and
Group Methods: Theory and Practice*, 2nd ed. New York: Harper &
Row, 1975. Drawing from theoretical
formulations from small-group
research conducted in speech
communications, social psychology,
industrial and educational psychology, psychiatry, and sociology—as
well as the program of research at
the University of Minnesota—Bormann presents a thorough integra-
tion of both general communication
theory and small-group theory.

BORMANN, ERNEST G. AND NANCY C. BOR-
MANN. *Effective Small Group Communication*, 2nd ed. Minneapolis,
Minn.: Burgess, 1976. This is a the-
ory-plus-methods handbook that includes material on the group tasks,
conflict management, listening,
groups in the organizational context,
norm development, and the influence of cooperation and competition
on small-group communication. The
book provides practical knowledge
without an in-depth study of all recent research.

BURGOON, MICHAEL, JUDEE K. HESTON,
AND JAMES McCROSKEY. *Small Group
Communication: A Functional Ap-
proach*. New York: Holt, Rinehart

and Winston, 1974. This textbook
integrates behavioral science findings in persuasion, conflict resolution, decision making, leadership,
and a number of other communication areas.

BURNS, JAMES MACGREGOR. *Leadership*.
New York: Harper & Row, 1978.
Burns presents a theory of leadership as involving reciprocity between ordinary people (followers)
and political and ideological leaders. According to Burns, leadership
thrives on conflict and demands no
consensus. Through creative scholarship, the author analyzes and syn-
thesizes the central role leadership
has played throughout history.

DEVILLE, JARD. *The Psychology of Leadership: Managing Resources and Relationships*. New York: New American Library, 1984. DeVille discusses
the patterns that affect performance
as well as the ways to manage different personalities. How do you
manage logically? Objectively? In-
spirationally? Supportively? He
concludes by offering a balanced
management style and offers suggestions for building a community of
achievers.

FISHER, B. AUBREY. *Small Group Decision
Making: Communication and the
Group Process*, 2nd ed. New York:
McGraw-Hill, 1980. This textbook
emphasizes decision making and
communication. Fisher's principal
interest is face-to-face interaction in
groups. Some of the areas covered
include group formation, task performance, social systems, decision
making, and social conflict.

GOLDBERG, ALVIN A., AND CARL E. LAR-

SON. *Group Communication: Discussion Processes and Applications.* Englewood Cliffs, N.J.: Prentice-Hall, 1975. Goldberg and Larson present a descriptive and analytical book. They draw on relevant research and scholarly literature to describe and explain group communication.

GORDON, THOMAS. *Leader Effectiveness Training—L.E.T.—The No-Lose Way to Release the Productive Potential of People.* New York: Bantam Books, 1977. Gordon has designed this book as a practical and specific guide for leaders of business or leaders of committees and clubs. He offers the problem-solving techniques and communication skills needed to encourage others to work, resolve conflicts, develop team spirit, run meetings, evaluate others, increase one's own influence, and raise productivity.

GOURAN, DENNIS S. *Making Decisions in Groups: Choices and Consequences.* Glenview, Ill.: Scott, Foresman, 1982. Gouran alerts readers to some of the pressures and influences that impair our ability to think and act rationally. He explores the ways in which these can interfere with reasoned choice, and he introduces the principles of disciplined inquiry that can facilitate efforts to contribute to informed decisions in groups. He focuses on discussion and the decision-making process.

GULLEY, HALBERT E., AND DALE G. LEATHERS. *Communication and Group Process: Techniques for Improving the Quality of Small-Group Communication,* 3rd ed. New York: Holt, Rinehart and Winston, 1977. With their primary focus on small-group decision making, the authors offer insight into the functions and operation of communication in small groups. They also provide ways for readers to become better group members—especially through becoming more effective communicators and listeners in small-group settings.

LEIDER, RICHARD J. *The Power of Purpose.* New York: Fawcett Gold Medal, 1985. This is a hands-on workbook to help people realize their expectations. There are self-assessment questionnaires, checklists, and exercises designed to help readers identify their talents, create an appropriate work environment, and take the risks that help them get what they want. Leider discusses the birth of purpose, living on purpose, working on purpose, tapping the power of purpose, living at risk, and the purpose connection.

SCHEIDEL, THOMAS M., AND LAURA CROWELL. *Discussing and Deciding: A Desk Book for Group Leaders and Members.* New York: Macmillan, 1979. The authors divide this book into three parts. The first gives an overview of the group discussion process. The second provides a step-by-step analysis of the process. The third part describes a number of special techniques and useful procedures for discussion groups.

TUBBS, STEWART L. *A Systems Approach to Small Group Interaction.* Reading, Mass.: Addison-Wesley, 1978. Tubbs emphasizes traditional problem-solving methods as well as interpersonal relations and personal growth. In addition he treats small-group theory and research while offering practical material on developing skills in small groups.

WAITLEY, DENIS. *The Winner's Edge: The Critical Attitude of Success.* New York: Berkley Books, 1980. If you can think of leaders as successful or as winners, then this book is about leaders. How are winners developed? What is the origin of self-honesty, self-esteem, self-image, and self-expectancy? How can they be developed? This book discusses the winning edge.

part 4

COMMUNICATING IN PUBLIC

11 *GETTING STARTED*

CHAPTER OUTLINE

Selecting a Topic
   Making a personal inventory
   Brainstorming
Testing the Topic
   Appropriate for the audience?
   Appropriate for you?
   Appropriate for the occasion?
Narrowing the Topic
Selecting a Purpose
   The general purpose
   The specific purpose
   The central idea

Analyzing the Audience
   The role of the speaker
   Audience knowledge
   Audience interest
   Audience attitudes and beliefs
   Audience demographics
Analyzing the Occasion
   Length of the speech
   The time of day
   Location of the speech

CHAPTER OBJECTIVES

After reading this chapter, you should be able to:

1. Choose a topic for a speech.
2. Assess whether the topic is appropriate for you, the audience, and the speech occasion.
3. Narrow the topic in such a way that it is manageable for you.
4. State a general purpose for your speech.

5. State a specific purpose for your speech.
6. State a central idea for your speech.
7. Distinguish between an informative and a persuasive speech.
8. Make some inferences about your audience's knowledge, attitudes, and interests.

Jerry, who is the sales manager for WWOW-FM, is putting together a sales presentation for his sales force. A month from now the radio station is going to change from a top-40 format to country and western. Since this new format will attract new and different kinds of advertisers, Jerry needs to persuade his salespeople that they will have to work harder for a while but that it will pay off in the end—with more money for the station and larger commissions for them.

Nancy is the home economist for the county cooperative extension office. She is working on a program about good nutrition that she will present to senior citizens next week. Along with her talk, she is going to demonstrate how to prepare three different dishes. Nancy knows it will be much easier to persuade her audience to take her nutritional advice if the food is tasty.

Bill's best friend is getting married on Saturday. The custom among his friends is to toast the bride and groom with short speeches about each of them. Bill has been asked to speak about the groom. Since the occasion is a wedding reception, he knows his remarks should be light and humorous.

Ben, the director of the community free lunch program, is preparing the budget for the year to come. He takes inflation into account and raises certain budget categories; he puts in a 5 percent increase in salary for himself and his staff members and adds an item for buying a new desk. Once the budget is put together, he copies it on a big piece of poster board. Tomorrow he will present the budget to the food program's board of directors for approval.

Sharon is president of the local branch of the Electrical Worker's Union. For several months the executive committee has been negotiating with management about a cost-of-living pay raise. The committee now realizes that management is not going to come through and that it is going to have to ask members for a vote to strike. Sharon will speak to her local branch to explain why a strike vote is necessary.

Kelly is working on a speech for her speech class. Her subject is "The Joy of Poetry," and she is putting together some short student-written poems to illustrate her main points. She hopes to inspire her audience enough so members will read poetry or even write some themselves.

Whether you are on the job, in school, or at a wedding reception, you might be asked to give a speech. People give speeches every day. They make presentations (to committees or boards of directors), hold workshops (for community members or professionals), or conduct seminars (for people who want to learn something). Whatever the purpose, all of these forms of speaking have a speaker and an audience.

Public speaking involves the same elements as other forms of communication: senders-receivers, a message, a channel, and feedback. The speaker is the main sender-receiver, although audience members will also respond as senders-receivers by providing nonverbal feedback or asking questions. The message in public speaking is the most structured of all communication. The speaker works on the message beforehand, carefully planning what he or she will say. Usually the channel is the voice and gestures, but some speakers enhance the channel by using graphics such as posters or slides. Feedback in a public speaking situation usually comes from the entire audience rather than from one or a few individuals. Typical feedback would be applause or laughter from the audience.

SELECTING A TOPIC

Most of the people in the examples at the beginning of the chapter did not have to select a topic for a speech—the topic grew out of the work they were doing. Sometimes people are asked to speak on their area of expertise, but the specific speech topic is left up to them. The Lion's Club asks Professor Cooper, an energy expert, to give a speech, and the professor chooses the subject of how to turn a front porch into a passive energy collector. Hank Jones, the county agricultural extension agent, is asked to speak to the garden club, and he decides to speak about the pruning and trimming of bushes.

Since you are in a speech communication course, you will have to make several speeches during the course of the semester, and the choice of topic will probably be left to you. Choosing the topic is one of the most difficult parts of making a speech, so let's take a look at how to go about it.

The most important consideration in choosing a topic is to find a subject that interests you. If the subject is one that you like, you are going to be more motivated to research it and your presentation will be more lively. How do you find a subject that is interesting and that would also lend itself to a speech topic? Let's look at some areas that you should investigate.

Making a Personal Inventory

The first place to look for a topic is within yourself. Making a **personal inventory** involves appraising one's own resources. What are you interested in? Would your interest make a good speech? Sometimes a hobby will lead to a good speech. A hobby can make you an expert about any number of subjects— stamp or coin collecting, refinishing furniture, sailing, skiing.

Another area you might examine is how you spend your free time. If you listen to music or play an instrument, you might have the basis for a speech. Are you interested in nutrition, or do you like to cook? Maybe you can tell your audience something about food that the members would find interesting.

Have you done anything unusual? One student gave a speech on how to teach a cat to do tricks—something most cats are reluctant to do. Have you been to any unusual places, or have you done something unusual in a usual place—such as living for a week in the woods?

Sometimes people have unique skills. Do you have the ability to make old cars run? Are you familiar with computers or word processors and how they work? Are you particularly good at entertaining children? Do you have any study skills you can share with others?

What are your interests? If you're fascinated by photography, as these students are, you'll be able to tap that knowledge for a speech topic and draw others into your speech by your obvious enthusiasm for the subject.

Often the books, magazines, and newspapers you read will offer possibilities for speech topics. Hundreds of thousands of articles are published in magazines and newspapers every year. Most of these articles are about what people are currently interested in and could lead to ideas for speech topics. To get some idea of the range of topics covered, take a look at the *Reader's Guide to Periodical Literature*. Here you will find hundreds of different subjects to choose from.

What newspapers and magazines do you read? What sections do you turn to first? Are there issues in these sections that might result in good speeches? For example, if you always read the sports section, you know that scores and accounts of games are unlikely to provide material for speeches. Well-written sports pages, however, also include stories on important issues in sports. Typical examples: "How is eligibility determined for college sports?" "How should we define 'amateur' athletes?" "Should the Olympics be held only in Greece to keep politics out of sports?"

Newspapers and magazines are also the best source of information for what is going on in your city or state, the nation, and the world. Even though you might not have a strong interest in this kind of news, take an hour or so some day and leaf through a big-city newspaper or a news magazine such as *Time* and *Newsweek*. What subjects catch your attention? What's going on in the community or in the nation that might affect you and the people you know? For example, what is the local zoning board up to? Do you know that this is the board that decides how many people can live in a single dwelling? This is certainly an issue that affects students, who often like to live with four or five others.

What is the state legislature up to? If you are attending a college or university supported by state money, this is an important question, since your state legislature will decide how much money your college will get and even how much tuition you will be paying. The federal government also makes many decisions that affect us all (nuclear power plants and defense spending) and many that affect college students in particular (draft registration and student loans).

Your college library probably subscribes to hundreds of magazines. Take a look at some of them you are not familiar with. Magazines such as *Science Digest, Psychology Today* and *Consumer Reports* cover dozens of subjects that could make good speech topics.

Sometimes the books you read can inspire speech topics. Generally, nonfiction books (which deal with facts and true stories) make better speech topics than works of fiction. Every year in this country, thousands of nonfiction books are published on subjects ranging from dieting to nuclear physics. If you were to pull out a card catalog drawer in the library, you would probably find dozens of book titles that would suggest good ideas for speech topics.

Whenever you seek a speech topic, you will do best with material you know something about. While you are making a personal inventory, your emphasis should be on discovering interests and skills that you have and would like to share with others. Figure 11-1 on the next page diagrams the various sources where speech topics might be sought.

Brainstorming

In an earlier chapter, we discussed brainstorming in groups. You can also brainstorm all by yourself. As we noted in Chapter 9, *brainstorming* is a technique of free association. You take a subject—cars, for example—and think of everything that might possibly be related to this subject. The goal of brainstorming is quantity—to come up with as many ideas as possible.[1]

When you are ready to brainstorm, it is a good idea to sit in a comfortable chair and relax with a paper and pencil by your side. Now, when you are comfortable, think about something you are interested in (maybe from your personal inventory) and write down everything that comes into your mind. Don't try to edit any of your ideas—in fact don't ever think about them. Work quickly and make your list as long as possible. After you have finished with one topic, try other areas that might seem promising. Some possibilities might include your major, your reading interests, school-related subjects, and so forth.

Let's say, for example, that we were going to brainstorm on the subject "cars." Our list might look something like this:

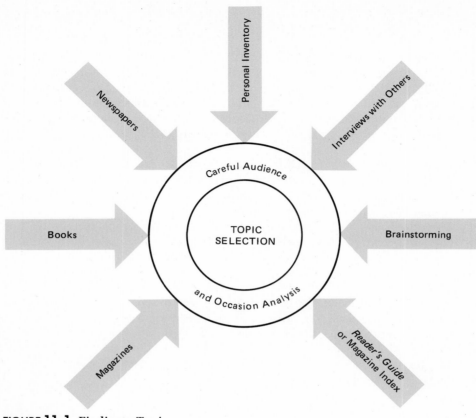

FIGURE 11-1 **Finding a Topic**

Antique
Cost of
Gas
Mileage

Japanese versus American
Safety
Front-wheel drive

After you have come up with a brainstorming list on a subject, you should go back and look at it with a more critical eye. If the topic doesn't look as though it will work, or if it is an aspect of the subject you are not really interested in, eliminate it from your list. In our list of car topics, for example, we might decide that we don't know anything about antique cars so we eliminate it from the list. Also the subjects of gas, mileage, and front-wheel drive do not seem meaty enough for a speech, so we eliminate them too. Now we are left with safety and Japanese versus American cars. So we decide to consider both of these areas as possible topics. Since "safety" is a broad concept, we brainstorm a little more to see what could come under this heading, and we come up with

Restraint systems (seat belts and airbags)

Safety records on large versus compact cars

Car color as a safety factor

In our brainstorming about cars, we emerged with two possible topics. Sometimes when you brainstorm, however, you might find that your list does not yield anything you want to talk about. In this case, take another subject and brainstorm again. It might take two or three brainstorming sessions before you find a topic you really like. Once you find a topic (or topics) you need to put it (or them) to the test to see which will work in a speech.

TESTING THE TOPIC

Now that you have some ideas for topics, you should put them to the test to see if they are really suitable for a speech. When choosing among possible topics, you should consider three questions: (1) Is the topic appropriate for your audience? (2) Is it appropriate for you? (3) Is it appropriate for the speech occasion?

Appropriate for the Audience?

Your first consideration should be whether the topic will be interesting to the audience and appropriate to the audience's level of knowledge. Some subjects are inherently interesting to audiences: making money, sex, and diet and fitness all seem to be perennial favorites. However, if the subject you are considering doesn't seem to have instant appeal, you should ask whether you can *make* it appealing. Most audiences will respond if the speaker can show how the subject affects them and their lives.

As well as making a subject interesting, you have to ask whether you can speak about it on a level the audience can understand. Does the subject require specialized or technical knowledge? Can you talk about this subject in a language everyone will understand? Does the audience have enough background to understand the subject? Answers to these questions will help you decide whether the topic will be appropriate to the audience.

Appropriate for You?

A topic is appropriate for you if it meets this test: Can you get involved in it, and is it interesting enough to motivate you to do the necessary research? A student majoring in air traffic control would probably have high interest in air disasters—especially those caused by mistakes on the part of traffic controllers.

CONSIDER THIS

In all such efforts, the speaker must take into account the character of the audience being addressed. A lecture on a given subject with a given end result in view should not be given to any audience at random. I have often been invited to talk on a particular topic to an audience for whom, in my judgment, it would be inappropriate to speak on the subject chosen. One must have a certain degree of confidence that the subject selected is one that holds some initial interest for the audience to be addressed and that their general background will enable one to enlarge that interest.

Source: Mortimer J. Adler, *How to Speak, How to Listen.*

A student studying restaurant administration would probably find it interesting to research the causes of food poisoning. Someone with a coin collection would be motivated to learn even more about his or her subject.

To give a good speech you are also going to have to speak with confidence and expertise. Do you know enough about the subject? Can you learn enough about it to give a speech? There is nothing worse than getting up before an audience and realizing that you don't know what you are talking about!

Appropriate for the Occasion?

The first consideration here is whether you are giving the right kind of speech for the occasion. An after-dinner speech, for example, should have a light touch and not be too long, since it will occur when members of the audience have just eaten and are not feeling at their most alert. On the other hand, if you are giving a speech at a seminar, this will be an opportunity to speak on a more complex topic. In a classroom setting, you will probably be given only a limited time to speak, so you have to decide whether you can cover your topic adequately in the time you have.

If you are speaking at a special occasion, you should tie at least some of the speech into the occasion itself. If the speech is for some kind of ritual occasion such as graduation or a bar mitzvah, certain conventions are expected of the speaker. At a graduation, for example, a speaker typically has some words about the future for graduates. At a bar mitzvah, a Jewish ceremony initiating a boy into religious adulthood, it would be appropriate to praise the young man and his parents.

Another consideration is whether you can fit the speech into the time limits of the occasion. Usually the speaker is given some idea of how long he or she should speak. In a speech class, this is always true. You must consider

TRY THIS

Go back and look over the list of topics you developed during your brainstorming session. Following the above guidelines, ask yourself for each topic, whether it is appropriate for your speech classmates, for you, and for the occasion. Which topics should be eliminated from your list? Why?

whether you can cover your topic or whether you need to narrow it down in such a way that you can cover it adequately within the time allowed.

For many of us, making a final decision about a topic is difficult—especially when we are faced with several good options. When you are deciding on a topic for your speech class, however, it is important that you make up your mind well ahead of the date the speech is due. If you don't do this, you will waste a lot of time doing odds and ends of research on several topics—time you could have spent better in developing a single topic. If you have three topics that seem equally good and meet the tests for appropriateness and you still can't make up your mind, put all the topics in a hat and draw one out. Now that you have the topic, stick with it!

NARROWING THE TOPIC

A common mistake of beginning speakers is trying to cover a topic that is too broad. If you wanted to talk about a social issue such as crime, racial equality, or educational reform, you would discover so much material on these subjects that you would not even be able to read and research everything that is available, let alone cover it in a single speech. If you tried to do so, your coverage would have to be so superficial that the speech would not be very meaningful. Let's say you wanted to speak on the subject of education. One could probably divide education into 100 or more different subsections. Do you want to talk about elementary schools or high schools? special education? adult education? If you choose elementary education, there are still many possibilities. Do you want to talk about how children learn? about curriculum? about educational games? about audiovisual aids?

Narrowing the topic is the process of finding some specific aspect of a subject and speaking about that. Let's see how three different students narrowed their subjects for speeches.

Amy is a radio-television major and wants to talk about some aspect of broadcasting for her speech. She can't decide precisely what she wants to talk about, so she goes to the library to look at card catalog entries under "Broadcasting" and "Radio-television." Much to her surprise, she discovers almost half a drawer of entries devoted to broadcasting. Some of the entries include:

- Effects of Broadcasting
- European Broadcasting
- American Broadcasting
- History of American Broadcasting
  Noncommercial radio
  Rise of commercial radio
  Rise of television
- Economics of Broadcasting
  Advertising
  Economics and station operations
  Networks and advertisers
- Broadcast Programs

As Amy looks through the entries, she decides that "Effects of Broadcasting" sounds interesting. She notices several cards under "Effects"—on children, on homemakers, on older adults. She decides to concentrate on children. When she discovers there are at least 50 books on this subject, she decides to narrow her subject even further. She then finds two books about the effect of television cartoons on children. Amy remembers watching cartoons when she was a kid. She decides that this will be her choice. She has narrowed the topic in such a way that it is manageable. The material she has found is enough to cover the subject adequately but not so much as to overwhelm her.

Jeff knows that he wants to talk about some aspect of football. He uses brainstorming to narrow down his topic. He writes "football" at the top of the page and writes down everything he can think of under this heading. His final list looks like this:

Football
    College
    Professional
    Ethical aspects
    Organization and administration
    Injuries
    Photography
    Rules
    Super Bowl
    Televising of

Although this list might not cover every aspect of football, it covers Jeff's main interests. He now studies this list and looks for something he can talk about. Since he is a photographer and always takes his camera to football games, he decides that "photography" is the aspect that interests him most. His speech topic will be "How to Take Good Action Photographs." He has narrowed his subject in such a way as to be able to present information that will be useful and interesting to his audience.

Sherri, a mother of two pre-school children, has returned to school to get her degree. Because she has had so many problems in arranging for baby-sitters she knows she wants to give her persuasive speech on some aspect of child care for preschool children. She goes to the library and finds several articles about child care. Some focus on psychological problems: others discuss working mothers as role models; yet others deal with professional standards in child-care institutions. Sherri finds these articles interesting but decides that she wants to focus on practical information that will help others who face her problem. Finally she asks herself, "What would be the ideal child-care arrangement for me and my children?" Her answer to the question becomes the topic of her persuasive speech: "Colleges Should Provide Child Care for Student Parents."

By starting with a subject they found interesting, Amy, Jeff, and Sherri were able to work with it and narrow it in such a way that it would be manageable for a speech. Now they are ready to start thinking about the purpose for which they will be giving the speech.

SELECTING A PURPOSE

Whenever you give a speech you should have a good idea of the purpose or the reason you have for giving the speech. Having this purpose in mind beforehand is very much like planning a trip: if you know where you're going, you are able to plan the route ahead of time. In the same way, if you have a purpose for your speech, the purpose will help you to look for materials, organize and outline the speech, and adapt the speech to the needs and interests of the audience.

There are three stages in working out the purpose for your speech: (1) selecting the general purpose, (2) selecting the specific purpose, and (3) stating the central idea.

The General Purpose

Your first goal in giving a speech is to decide whether your general purpose is to inform or to persuade. **Informative speeches** generally concentrate on explaining—how something works, what something means, or how to do something. A speaker who gives an informative speech usually tries to give his or her audience information without taking sides. For example, if a speaker is giving an informative speech about using animals for research, he will not state whether he is for or against it; he will let members of the audience make up their minds. When the subject is controversial, the speaker will present all sides of the issue. In an informative speech about running for fitness, for example, you could give the advantages (physical fitness and feeling good) and the possible disadvantages (shin splints and heart attacks).

In a **persuasive speech** the speaker takes a particular position and tries to get the audience to accept and support that position. For example, a speaker tries to persuade her audience that it should oppose the nuclear freeze movement. Someone else tries to persuade the audience to support ERA or to join the move to save the whales. In a persuasive speech, the speaker concentrates on looking for the best information available to support his or her point of view.

Often the same subject could lead to either an informative or a persuasive speech—depending on your wording of the topic and your approach. Say your subject is the ethics of abortion. If you choose as your topic "The Ethical Issues of Abortion" and cover the ethics on both sides of the issue, the wording of your topic and your approach are appropriate for an informative speech. But if your topic is "Abortion: The Wrong Choice," you clearly have a persuasive speech, because you have made up your mind and are in favor of one particular side of the issue. Here are some other subjects that are phrased first as informative (*I*) and then as persuasive (*P*) topics:

I: Using a Computer at Home
P: Home Computers Can Save You Money

I: Breeds of Dogs That Make Good Pets
P: Every Child Should Have a Dog

I: The Coupon Craze in the Supermarket
P: Coupon Saving Can Take Dollars off Your Supermarket Bill

Sometimes it's difficult to fit a speech firmly into an informative or persuasive slot. In a persuasive speech, informative material is often an important part of the material the speaker uses. If you are speaking in favor of a political candidate, it is natural to use information about his background and voting record. In an informative speech, even when you try to present both sides, one side might seem more persuasive than the other to some audience members.

The Specific Purpose

After you have decided whether the general purpose of your speech is to inform or to persuade, you must then decide on a **specific purpose**. Your specific purpose statement will help you focus on precisely what you want to accomplish—that is, it will help you state exactly what you are going to inform or persuade your audience about. In deciding your specific purpose, you should follow four guidelines.

1. *State your purpose clearly and completely.* Examples of a purpose statement would be:

TRY THIS

Here is a list of speech topics. In each case, state whether the purpose of the speech is informative (*I*) or persuasive (*P*).

1. Voting for the Democrats in the Next Election
2. Learning One New Vocabulary Word Every Week
3. Nutrition and Caloric Content in Fast Food
4. Soybean Products as Meat Substitutes
5. Giving Up Watching All Television Entertainment Programs
6. Money-making Ideas for College Students
7. Advantages of Going Abroad During College
8. Going Abroad During One Semester of Your College Career
9. Performance Principles for High Achievers
10. Robotics and the Job Market

Answers: 1. *P* 2. *P* 3. *I* 4. *I* 5. *P* 6. *I* 7. *I* 8. *P* 9. *I* 10. *I*

To inform my audience how a record gets on a top-40 chart.

To explain to audience members how to make their own videos.

To persuade audience members to return their library books.

To persuade audience members to vote for Nancy Jones.

2. *State your purpose in terms of the effect you want to have on your audience.* What do you want the members of your audience to think or do after your speech is over? If you are giving an informative speech, probably the main effect you are looking for is for them to remember the information. In a persuasive speech, however, the effect you might want is for audience members to take direct action:

To persuade my audience to start a recycling project here on campus.

To persuade my audience to contribute to the fund to have the bell restored.

3. *Limit your purpose statement to one idea.* Keeping your purpose statement limited to one idea will help you to narrow your topic and keep it specific. Notice that the above examples all have one idea. If the first example had been "To inform my audience how a record gets on a top-40 chart and how to become a disk jockey," the speaker would have had two topics to cover rather than one.

4. *Use specific language in your purpose statement.* The more precise your language, the clearer the ideas will be in your mind. For example, "To persuade my audience against nuclear power" is too vague. Do you mean bombs? Nuclear power plants? You could rephrase your purpose like this:

To persuade my audience that stockpiling nuclear bombs is likely to lead to a war that will destroy the world.

or

To inform my audience about the risks of nuclear-produced electric power.

Once you have determined your statement of purpose, you should subject it to some tests. Does it meet the assignment? You might discover, for example, that your opinions on a subject are so strong that you are unable to talk about it without favoring one side over the other. This means your subject is better for a persuasive speech than for an informative one. If you have been assigned an informative speech, then you should keep this subject for a later time.

Another important test is to ask whether you can accomplish your purpose within the time limits of the speech. If your speech purpose is too broad for the allotted time, you will have to either narrow the topic further or find a new topic. One speaker discovered, for example, that her purpose, "To inform my audience about physical fitness," was too broad; too many issues were involved. She rephrased her purpose: "To inform audience members how daily exercise can improve their health."

The Central Idea

Whereas the specific purpose is a statement of what we want to accomplish when we give the speech, the **central idea** statement represents the main thrust of the speech. Everything in the speech relates to the central idea. In an informative speech the central idea contains the information you want the audience to remember; in a persuasive speech, it tells audience members what you want them to do.

The difference between a specific purpose and a central idea statement is illustrated in the following examples. Notice that the central idea explains the *why* or the *how* of the specific purpose.

Specific Purpose: To persuade my audience to eat less salt.
Central Idea: Excess levels of salt in the body can lead to heart problems, depression, and irritability.

Specific Purpose: To inform my audience of what to look for in terms of safety features in buying a car.

Central Idea:	When you buy a car, look for three safety features: color, weight, and restraint systems.
Specific Purpose:	To inform my audience of the dangers inherent in "selling" political candidates through television commercials.
Central Idea:	When we base our choice of candidates on television commercials, we put greater emphasis on the image of the candidate than on the issues he or she stands for.

The central idea should be stated in a full sentence, contain one idea, and use precise language. Sometimes it is not possible to come up with a central idea statement until you have finished organizing and outlining the speech. When you start working on your speech, you should have a tentative central purpose in mind; when you have finished organizing and outlining the speech you can refine it.

Joe decided on a speech topic and a specific purpose right away. When he was a child he had lost an arm in an accident. Because so many people had reacted to this loss with odd and irritating remarks, Joe decided to give a speech with the specific purpose "To inform my audience about how to talk to the handicapped." Joe knew that his central idea would contain advice about appropriate ways of talking to the handicapped, but these specific ideas did not emerge until he had a rough outline:

I. Many people do not know what to say to people with handicaps.

II. Some people make handicapped people feel bad by showing pity toward them.

III. Some people react to the handicapped as if the handicapped were mentally retarded or hard of hearing.

Once Joe had completed his outline, he knew what his central idea would be: "When you see a handicapped person, ignore the handicap and talk to him or her as you would to anyone else."

ANALYZING THE AUDIENCE

Virginia Story, an expert on forest preservation, works for the state forestry department. Because of her expertise and her public speaking ability, her office sends her out to make speeches all over the state. Ms. Story speaks to all kinds of audiences: on Monday she might talk to sixth graders in a middle school, on Wednesday to a group of women from garden clubs, on Thursday to a businessmen's organization, on Friday to a group of forestry professionals.

In her speeches Ms. Story always talks about forestry. However, she does not make the same speech to each audience. Instead, she *adapts* her material to make it appropriate for each particular group. Before she makes the speech to sixth graders, she finds out from their teacher what the children already know. She discovers that they are presently studying a unit on trees in their science class so they have some basic knowledge. She decides to concentrate on telling the children what people can do to protect their forests. Knowing that sixth graders have a shorter attention span than adults, she brings a short film on the subject so they won't have to listen to her all the time.

When Ms. Story speaks to the businessmen, she assumes that most of them have forgotten much of the science they learned in school, so she plans a speech that will give them basic scientific information about problems in forests. Because she wants the businessmen to have an active interest in the state's forests, she plans her speech to show several ways that business and government can cooperate in the conservation movement.

When Ms. Story speaks to the garden club, she assumes that many of the members will be well informed about botany. With them, she speaks about the similarity between gardens and forests. Finally, in presentation to her forestry colleagues, Ms. Story speaks on the newest research on tree diseases. Since they are all experts in the field, she has no hesitation about using highly technical language to talk about the subject.

The Role of the Speaker

In all of the above examples, Ms. Story was playing the role of the speaker. Whenever you play this role, the audience has certain expectations of you. When an audience comes to hear you, it expects that you will be knowledgeable about your topic and that you will present what you know in an interesting way. Ms. Story is an able speaker not only because she knows her subject but also because she knows her audiences.

What Ms. Story has done with her four audiences is to adapt her subject matter to each individual group through audience analysis. **Audience analysis** is the process of finding out what the members of the audience already know about the subject, what they might be interested in, what their attitudes and beliefs are, and what kinds of people make up the audience. In your role as speaker you should spend time on audience analysis.

Audience Knowledge

One important aspect of audience analysis is to take into account how much the audience is likely to know about a subject. In a practical sense, we can make only an educated guess about our audience's knowledge. We can assume that if we are talking to a lay audience and we pick a topic related to a specialized field of knowledge (electronics, radar, nuclear medicine, behavioral psychology), we will have to do a lot of explaining and defining of basic terminology before we can go into the subject in any depth. For example, when

CONSIDER THIS

An accurate assessment of the communication situation, and especially of the audience, may play a significant role in the success of the speech, whether we evaluate success from the standpoint of the speaker's purposes or from the standpoint of how much the audience profited from hearing the speech. Careful planning of communication strategy may contribute as much or more to the realization of the audience's goals as it does to those of the speaker.

Source: Theodore Clevenger, Jr., Audience Analysis.

Sam spoke to his class about word processors, he had to explain such terms as "file," "format," "memory," and "buffer" before he could talk about anything else.

On some subjects we can assume that audiences have a base of general knowledge. If we are speaking on vitamins, we can assume most people know that vitamins are good for us and even that vitamin C is particularly good when people have colds. But a general knowledge about other vitamins should not be taken for granted.

Speakers should realize that although people have general information about many subjects, they usually don't know the specifics. Most people know, for example, that the Constitution guarantees us the right to free speech. Yet if you were to ask them what free speech means, they would probably be a little fuzzy on a definition or on what is encompassed by the term. Would they know, for example, that the courts regard ringing a bell or waving a flag as a form of free speech?

To give another example, when speaking to a college audience about her recent trip to mainland China, the speaker assumed that most of her listeners would know approximately where China is located and that most of them would know that China is ruled by a Communist government. She figured, however, that most of them would not know much about such important Chinese ideas as communal farming or the Cultural Revolution, so she took some time to explain these ideas. Once she had given this background information, her speech and slides about what she saw and did made much more sense.

In a college speech class, you can get some idea of how much is known about your subject by asking your friends and classmates what they know. If you have been asked to speak before a group you belong to, you can ask a couple of members what they know about the subject. If they don't know very much, you can assume that your audience won't either and that you will have to start by giving basic information. Often the program chairperson who is responsible for finding speakers will be able to give you some information about the level of knowledge of members of the audience and also about what is likely to interest them.

Audience Interest

Some subjects seem to be inherently interesting. Books on the best-seller list usually are about diet, exercise, and money. If you look at the topics covered by popular magazines, you will discover that self-help or self-improvement is the category of articles that appears most often. However, most of us do not want to be limited to speaking about physical fitness, diet, and self-help. Instead, we have to find a way to make other subjects interesting to our audiences.

One way to interest an audience in a topic is to point out that it has importance and relevance to them. Jan, an English major and a tutor in the Writing Center, wants to give a speech on the importance of writing skills. She knows that most students would like to improve their grades, but she also knows that most of them do not want to listen to a lecture on English composition. So she calls her speech "Five Tips for Better Grades on Papers" and concentrates on giving specific and practical advice.

Another way to get an audience's interest is to get it involved in the subject. Judy wants to persuade her audience that the government should spend more money on food stamps. She starts her speech with examples of three children in three different families who are not getting enough to eat. Even though her audience might not have had an interest in the subject to begin with, her examples are so compelling that she creates an interest.

Since you will be speaking on a subject that interests you, it might be useful to spend some time thinking why you find this area so interesting. What things about it caught your attention in the first place? If you can recreate your own enthusiasm for a subject, you will have a better chance of getting your audience interested too.

Audience Attitudes and Beliefs

When planning your speech, you also need to consider your audience's attitudes and beliefs about your subject. Often you will be speaking before an audience that has the same beliefs as you do—as when you speak before your club or your church group. The Sierra Club (a conservation group) will approve of a speech on how to preserve the desert. Animal lovers will support a proposal to establish a local SPCA. Fellow employees will be interested in a speech about improving working conditions. College students will favor a proposal requiring instructors to state their grading policies at the beginning of the semester. These subjects tie into the attitudes and beliefs of the audience members.

TRY THIS

Assume that you are going to speak to three different audiences: a college speech class, a group of senior citizens, and a group of eighth graders. Take one of these topics and adapt it to each of these audiences with reference to the members' level of knowledge about the subject, their interest in the subject, and their attitudes toward it.

- Cigarettes Are Harmful to Your Health.
- All States Should Have a Returnable Bottle and Can Law.
- Everyone Should Have a Daily Exercise Program.

Your audience, however, may not have any particular attitudes or beliefs about your subject. They may not have had enough information to make up their minds, or they may not care enough to have an opinion. The latter will be especially difficult to deal with. If you want to appeal to an indifferent audience you will have to try especially hard to make your listeners feel that the speech has relevance and importance to them. Bob, for example, wanted to speak to his class about the importance of voting in the student government election. He knew that most of his audience members believed that voting was a good idea but that when election day came, few of them would actually vote. In order to motivate them, he began his speech by pointing out that student government controls three areas of high interest to students: concerts, athletics, and the food services.

Sometimes your own beliefs can run contrary to those of your audience, and your speech can be met with hostility. If you think your audience may be opposed to your ideas on a subject, you have to plan your speech very carefully. Deb, for example, knew that her classmates would be opposed to the idea of a tuition increase. Yet by researching her topic carefully and presenting the reasons for the increase, she was able to show that the increase was necessary. Her audience might not have been happy about the increase, but they had a better understanding of the reasons for it. In his speech, John set out to persuade members of his speech class that the college should drop its entire football program. Since football is a part of college life, he could expect his audience to be hostile to the idea. John, however, was able to show that attendance at games was declining, that football took an enormous cut out of the athletics budget, and that the money could be better used if it were applied to intramural programs that would benefit all students. Not all of his classmates were persuaded; but after the speech was over, several of them told John that his ideas were worth considering.

Since people's attitudes and beliefs will affect how your speech is received, it is absolutely essential that they be considered when your speech is in the planning stage. Important clues to people's attitudes and beliefs can be discovered through audience demographics—to which we now turn.

Audience Demographics

Even if you have no specific information about your audience's knowledge of, interest in, and attitudes toward the subject, certain factual information about the audience members can tell you a great deal. **Demographic analysis** reveals data about the characteristics of a group of people, including such things as age, sex, education, occupation, race/nationality/ethnic origin, geographic location, and group affiliation.

When we look at demographic information, we are generalizing about the *entire audience;* our generalizations might not be true of individual members. For example, we might generalize that the age of our speech class audience is between 18 and 27—even though one member is in his fifties. In the same way, we can make generalizations about the class's educational level or about

This audience is quite diverse demographically. Members are male and female, young and old, and from a variety of ethnic backgrounds. What would you need to do to adapt a topic to such an audience?

its racial composition. And on the basis of such generalizations, we can make some predictions about what might interest the people in this audience and what they might be knowledgeable about. Let's consider each of the demographic characteristics in turn.

Age

As a speaker you need to have a sense of the age range of your audience, because interests differ with age. College-age people are usually interested in school, future jobs, music, and interpersonal relationships. Young parents are often interested in subjects that might affect their children, such as school bus safety and school board policy. People in middle age tend to be focused on their jobs, while older adults tend to be interested in issues related to retirement. However, not all subjects are age-related. Computers, elections, and world and national news, for example, have interest for most age groups because they affect all age groups.

Sometimes the same subject can be of interest to various age groups if it is adapted in a way that will appeal to the particular age group. Take the subject of nutrition. If you were speaking to an elementary school audience you would probably not go into detail about vitamins and minerals because you would have problems keeping the attention of the children. Instead, you might use puppets (one who eats junk food and the other who eats good food) or put your speech into a story with characters the children could identify with. If you talked about nutrition to pregnant mothers, you could adapt your speech to the needs of the fetus, assuming that every mother-to-be has a high interest in having a healthy baby. When you speak to older adults, you could talk about their particular nutritional needs, such as calcium to avoid bone injuries.

Gender

The gender of audience members can also be important. In a speech that's open to the public, you will probably have both males and females in your audience. If you have either an all-male or all-female audience, it will probably be because you are talking to some kind of club or organization whose members are all of one sex. The topic of your speech will then be more influenced by the organization itself than by the sex of its members. For example, the American Association of University Women (AAUW) has long been interested in education. If you were speaking to this group, its interest in education would be more important than the fact that the group is all-female.

Education

The audience's level of education is important to a speaker because it gives some idea of the group's knowledge and experience. We can assume that the more education people have, the more specialized their knowledge. Lawyers, doctors, and Ph.D's all have specialized knowledge; however, they might have little information about subjects other than their own. Your main consideration when you prepare a speech is whether your audience has the same knowledge you have or whether you will have to start with the basics. For example, if you are a psychology major, don't assume that your speech class will know what the terms "paranoid" and "schizophrenic" mean. Even though people use these terms loosely, they often do not know the proper scientific definitions.

Occupation

The occupation of audience members may influence how you approach some topics. Sometimes occupation indicates the area of specialized knowledge: paramedics and nurses know about the human body; lawyers know about human rights; social workers know about social problems. Occupation can also indicate interest in a subject. Most professional groups would probably be interested in a speech about ethics in their profession. Factory workers might be interested in the workings of the union or how to form a union. If you are speaking to a group made up of one occupation, see if you can adapt your speech to that audience's occupational interests.

Race/Nationality/Ethnic Origin

Politicians are the people most likely to have whole audiences made up of a single race or ethnic group. To identify with these groups, they eat knishes in Jewish neighborhoods, burritos with Hispanics, and soul food with blacks. When they speak to one of these groups, they try to identify with its goals and aspirations.

If you are speaking to a group with diverse backgrounds, you should be particularly careful in your use of language. If your audience includes foreign students, they may have problems understanding slang and colloquial expressions. If you are in a class with different ethnic groups, some groups might not understand experiences that are typical of your own group. For example, not everyone has gone to summer camp and not everyone has eaten burritos.

You should always be careful in any speech not to offend the feelings of others. Have you ever thought that Polish jokes might be offensive? One speaker learned this when several Polish exchange students and Polish-Americans walked out on his speech. Stereotypes of any group, or jokes that hold an ethnic group up to ridicule, are always inappropriate.

Geographic Location

Awareness of the geographic location of your audience can help in adapting your speech. If the federal government is giving money to improve airport runways, find out if some of this money is coming to the local airport. If the nation has been hit with a crime wave (or a heat wave), has this been a problem in your local area? If you have a chance to speak in a town or city other than your own, the audience will be pleased if you know something about its area. Ralph Nader, the consumer advocate, always does some geographical research before he speaks. When he spoke before an audience in Pennsylvania, for example, he came armed with information about Three Mile Island (which took place in Harrisburg, Pennsylvania) as well as information about chemical spills that had happened in the city where he was speaking.

Group Affiliation

Knowing the clubs, organizations, or associations that audience members belong to can be useful because people usually identify with the goals and interests of their organizations. If you speak to a group, you should be aware of what the group stands for and adapt your speech accordingly.

If you speak to the local historical society, its members will expect you to speak on a subject that has some historic angle. The campus journalism society will be interested in a speech dealing with the theory (e.g., freedom of the press) or practice (e.g., using video display terminals) of journalism. Some groups have particular issues or themes for the year, and they look for speakers who can tie their speeches into these themes.

TRY THIS

Looking at your speech class, what demographic information can you come up with?

- *Age*: What is the age range? What is the average age?
- *Sex*: How many females? How many males?
- *Education*: What is the level of education? Mainly freshmen and sophomores or juniors and seniors?
- *Occupation*: Do your classmates work? What kinds of jobs?
- *Race/nationality/ethnic origin*: What races, nationalities, and ethnic groups are represented in the class? Is everyone a native English speaker?
- *Group affiliation*: What groups do your classmates belong to? Can you determine any attitudes and beliefs they might hold from their group affiliations?

ANALYZING THE OCCASION

When planning your speech, as well as doing audience analysis, you need to consider the occasion. Factors to take into account when analyzing the occasion include the length of the speech, the time of day, and the location of the speech.

Length of the Speech

Always stick to the time limit set for the speech. If you are giving a speech in class, you will probably be told the amount of time you can speak. It you are asked to give a speech to a group or organization, you should ask how long you will be expected to speak. When the audience has an expectation of the length of your speech, it will get restless if you go on too long. If your speech topic is too complicated to be covered in the allotted time, you should narrow your topic or find something else to speak on.

More than one speaker hasn't known when to stop. Mortimer J. Adler has written of the time he was giving lectures on philosophy to college students. Student interest in the subject was great, but not great enough to sit through each of Adler's two-hour lectures! When Adler returned the next year to deliver another series of lectures, the students hid alarm clocks in the lecture hall. After an hour, all of them went off. At the second lecture, a student pulled the main switch and blacked out the lecture hall after an hour. Adler got the message; he cut his remaining lectures to a listenable length.[2]

The Time of Day

The time of day should also be a consideration when choosing your topic. In a classroom setting, students seem to be less alert in the early morning and late afternoon. If you are in a class that meets at one of these times, you have to pay special attention to audience interest in your topic. An interesting topic or a topic handled in an interesting manner can get the attention of even a sluggish audience. Probably most public speeches occur at night. Since people are usually somewhat tired, the speaker has to take special care to find material that will be interesting to the audience.

Location of the Speech

The place where the speech will be given might also be a consideration. If you are not familiar with the room, you might want to go and take a look at it before your speak. Is the podium where you want it? Are the chairs arranged the way you want them? Is there a public address system? Do you need one? It is easier to make changes before the audience arrives.

Comfort should also be considered in a location. Many a politician has given a speech from the courtyard steps, where there was no place for the audience to sit. If you are in a location where the audience cannot be comfortable, be prepared to give a short speech and get to the point before you lose your audience.

SUMMARY

Whenever you are scheduled to make a speech, it is important to find a topic that interests you. Two techniques will help you discover topics: making a personal inventory, which means taking a careful look at what interests you, and brainstorming, which is a method of generating ideas through free association.

Once you have an idea for a topic, you should test whether the topic is appropriate for the audience, whether it is appropriate for you, and whether it is appropriate for the occasion.

Whatever you plan to speak on, you should narrow the topic so that it can be adequately covered within the time set for your speech. Narrowing the topic means taking some specific aspect of the subject and speaking about that.

Every speech should have a general purpose, a specific purpose, and a central idea. The general purpose relates to whether the speech is informative or persuasive. The specific purpose focuses on what you want to inform or persuade your audience about. The central idea captures the main idea of the speech—the idea you want your audience to retain after the speech.

An important step in giving a speech is analyzing the audience. Before you speak to any audience you should have some sense of what it knows, what it is interested in, and what it believes in. You can get general information about the audience through demographic analysis. The factors in demographic analysis include age; sex; education; occupation; race, nationality, and ethnic origin; geographic location; and group affiliation.

As well as analyzing the audience, you should also consider various aspects of the occasion: the length of the speech, the time of day, and the place where the speech will be given.

VOCABULARY

The following is a list of words you must know to understand the concepts in this chapter. You will find the words defined the first time that each is used in the chapter. All Vocabulary words also appear, with their definitions, in the Glossary at the end of the book.

audience analysis	personal inventory
central idea	persuasive speech
demographic analysis	specific purpose
informative speech	

FURTHER READING

ADLER, MORTIMER J. *How to Speak, How to Listen.* New York: Macmillan, 1983. Written from a layman's perspective, this book discusses the sales talk, lectures and discussion, conversation, as well as question and answer sessions. The book is full of examples and practical suggestions.

I Have Spoken: American History Through the Voices of Indians. Compiled by Virginia Irving Armstrong. Chicago: Swallow, 1971. This anthology includes speeches and fragments of speeches made by Indians on problems of concern to them. Some of the speeches go back to the seventeenth century.

KLOPF, DONALD W., and RONALD E. CAMBRA. *Speaking Skills for Prospective Teachers.* Englewood, Colo.: Morton, 1983. This textbook specifically addresses the speaking behaviors typical of the school environment. The authors clearly and practically answer the question, "What are the communication processes, factors influencing, and skills useful in classroom speaking?"

LINKUGEL, WIL A., R. R. ALLEN, and RICHARD L. JOHANNESEN. *Contemporary American Speeches: A Sourcebook of Speech Forms and Principles,* 5th ed. Dubuque, Iowa: Kendall/Hunt, 1982. The authors address the question of why speeches should be studied. They provide bases for speech analysis. Finally, they offer sample speeches that impart knowledge, affirm propositions of fact, value, and policy, create concern for problems, and intensify social cohe-

sion. This is an excellent anthology of speeches by a wide range of speakers on a very broad range of topics.

MACRORIE, KEN. *Uptaught.* New York: Hayden, 1970. Student speakers often find it difficult to avoid obvious ideas, shopworn clichés, and trivial thinking. Macrorie challenges students to find something worthwhile to express. Although his book is concerned with writing, the same problems face speakers looking for speech content.

MICALI, PAUL J. *How to Talk Your Way to Success: The Secrets of Effective Business Communication.* New York: Dutton, 1983. Micali, president of the Lacy Sales Institute, is a noted expert in the field of sales and management. In a clear and direct manner, using numerous examples from the world of business, he shows readers how to master the simple skills needed to make effective sales presentations.

SMITH, ARTHUR (ed.). *Language, Communication, and Rhetoric in Black America.* New York: Harper & Row, 1972. This collection of articles by various writers about the communication experiences of black Americans ranges from discussion about dialect to rhetorical case studies.

STEVENS, LEONARD A. *The Ill-Spoken Word.* New York: McGraw-Hill, 1966. This interesting and readable book discusses the spoken word. The writer looks at the history of speaking and asks some provocative questions about the role of speech in contemporary life.

12 *FINDING SPEECH MATERIAL*

CHAPTER OUTLINE

Researching Your Topic: Where to Look
    Personal experience and observation
    Interviewing
    Using the library
Supporting Material: What to Look For
    Comparison
    Contrast
    Examples

    Narratives
    Statistics
    Quotations and testimony
    Polls
    Studies

Adapting Support Material to the Audience

CHAPTER OBJECTIVES

After reading this chapter, you should be able to:

1. Use some of your own experiences as part of your speech.
2. Gather speech information by interviewing.
3. Research your speech in the library.
4. Use the various reference tools in the library.
5. Recognize the various kinds of supporting materials.
6. Use the supporting materials that are most appropriate for your topic.
7. Use the supporting materials that are most appropriate for your audience.

Karen was desperate. She had to give a speech and she hadn't found a topic yet. As she sat with her friends in the student union, she said, "Come on, you guys. Help me find a topic for my speech." One of them who was reading his horoscope said, "What about astrology? Everyone's interested in that." Karen said, "That's a great idea. Students are always talking about their signs." Karen didn't have much time to prepare a speech, but she knew that she should start in the library. She checked out the card catalog under "Astrology" and found a few book titles. But once she had located the books in the stacks, she realized she didn't have time to read them. However, she did find two magazine articles that were useful.

Later that night when she put together her speech, she found she didn't have much material at all. When it was organized and she tried it out, she found it was only three minutes long—and that was only when she paused a lot. However, it was too late to do anything about it. When she gave the speech the next day, Karen's audience listened closely at first but soon lost attention. Since it was clear she had little information, they asked no questions. The speech was barely mediocre, and Karen felt embarrassed about the whole experience.

In another speech class a second student, Tim, was planning to give a speech on the same subject. Tim was an astronomy major, and he had read in one of his textbooks that astrology was an early form of astronomy. This idea was so interesting that Tim thought it might be a good speech topic, so he went to the library to see what he could find. He found several books and articles on the subject and was able to put together lots of note cards of information. As he was reading, he also discovered that astrological signs are now being charted by computer. He decided to organize his speech around the history of astrology—beginning with the days it was considered a science and ending with computers.

The audience listened to Tim's speech with obvious interest. It was clear that he had done some research and knew quite a lot about his subject. After the speech was over, several people asked him questions, and at the end of class someone even asked where to go to get a computer horoscope. By doing his research and carefully planning his speech, Tim had come across as a *credible*—that is, believable—speaker.

No doubt you would like to have the same reaction from the class as Tim had. You would like to be thought of as credible, as knowing your subject. The key to having this happen is in the research you do for your speech. The more diligent you are about finding relevant material and adapting it to your audience, the more successsful you are going to be when you give your speech.

RESEARCHING YOUR TOPIC: WHERE TO LOOK

Once you have decided on the topic and purpose of your speech, it is time to begin finding material on your subject. The sources you can draw on for material are your own personal experience and observation, interviews, and the library. Let's look at each of these areas.

Personal Experience and Observation

If you have chosen a topic in which you have a strong interest, the first thing you should ask yourself is whether you have had any direct experience with the subject. Your own experience can provide some of the most interesting and valuable material. For example, when Dan spoke to his speech class on the subject "Preventing Fires in Your Home," he drew heavily on his experiences as a volunteer firefighter. Not only did he describe the tragedy of a family being burned out of its home, he also gave some facts and figures on the causes of home fires that he had learned during this training period.

When Kelly spoke of the danger of drunk drivers, she too gave facts and figures: how many innocent victims are killed each year by drunks on the road. Then she stunned her classmates by telling them that her own sister was one of those victims. Because Kelly spoke out of personal experience, her example became much more vivid and real than if she had used only statistics from a book or an article.

Sometimes we do not put enough value on personal experience; we think that if it happened to us, it can't be important. However relating our own experiences to the subject of our speech can often provide the most interesting material of all.

Interviewing

Interviews can be an excellent source of speech material. Because you can talk directly to decision makers, interviews are one of the best ways of gathering material on such campus-related topics as why tuition has gone up or why women's sports get more money than men's. Interviews are also a good way of getting up-to-date information. For example, if a war breaks out in the Middle East, you can interview the person on campus who is knowledgeable in this area. Another advantage of interviewing is that if the subject is complicated, you can ask questions about any areas you don't understand. Chapter 8 deals with the subject of interviewing, and if you are considering gathering material through an interview, you might find it helpful to look at that chapter again.

Using the Library

Depending on how well you know your way around, the library can be one of the richest sources of material or it can lead to total frustration.[1] Any library—whether large or small—has millions of pieces of information. Fortunately for

CONSIDER THIS

It is natural enough for beginners to feel disconcerted—lost and lonely—in a strange library. You can quickly overcome this feeling by making up your mind to learn your library. Regardless of size, all libraries have common features that the experienced researcher looks for at once. After you have conquered a few of these strongholds you will realize that to master one library is to master them all.

Source: Jacques Barzun and Henry F. Graff, *The Modern Researcher.*

us, all libraries organize their information in essentially the same way, so once we learn how to use one library we can use this skill in any library. The goal of this section is to help you use your campus (or public) library to find information that will be useful in preparing speeches.

Looking for Books

Books provide some of the best speech material. They usually cover a subject comprehensively and are written by experts. The main disadvantage of using books is that they are long; and if you want several different views of the subject, it is time consuming to look through several books. The problem can often be solved by using one or two books together with some magazine and newspaper articles.

When you are looking for books in a library, the card catalog is the place to begin. Most commonly it is housed in a large, many-drawered cabinet in a central location in the library. In some libraries the card catalog is also computerized, and you get the information you want by typing your request onto a computer terminal.

Whatever form the card catalog takes, it provides information on every book in the library. The cards in the catalog are classified three ways: by author, by title, and by subject. If you want a particular book and you know who wrote it, you can look it up by author. If you know only the title, you can look it up by title. If you don't know any authors or titles but are interested in a particular subject, you can look in the subject catalog. Figure 12-1 shows the same book—classified by author, title, and subject.

As shown in Figure 12-1, the upper left-hand corner of every card has a number. This, the book's call number, corresponds to where the book can be found in the library. Somewhere in a prominent position in the library you will see a large chart telling where the call numbers can be found. It might say, for example, numbers beginning with AC are on the first floor; those beginning with PN, on the second. If you use both public and academic libraries, you might notice that their call-number systems are different. Most

Ball, Donald W.

GV
701
.S64

Sport and social order : contributions to the sociology
of sport / [edited by] Donald W. Ball, John W. Loy.
- - Reading, Mass. : Addison-Wesley Pub. Co., c1975.
xiii, 574 p. : ill. ; 25 cm. - -
(Addison-Wesley series in the social significance of sport)
ISBN 0-201-00408-9

1. Sports- -Addresses, essays, lectures.

GV
701
.S64

Sport and social order : contributions to the sociology
of sport / [edited by] Donald W. Ball, John W. Loy.
- - Reading, Mass. : Addison-Wesley Pub. Co., c1975.
xiii, 574 p. : ill. ; 25 cm. - -
(Addison-Wesley series in the social significance of sport)
Includes bibliographies.
ISBN 0-201-00408-9

1. Sports- -Addresses, essays, lectures. I. Ball, Donald
W. II. Loy, John W.

SPORTS - - ADDRESSES, ESSAYS, LECTURES.

GV   1975
701
.S64

Sport and social order : contributions to the sociology
of sport / [edited by] Donald W. Ball, John W. Loy.
- - Reading, Mass. : Addison-Wesley Pub. Co., c1975.
xiii, 574 p. : ill. ; 25 cm. - -
(Addison-Wesley series in the social significance of sport)
ISBN 0-201-00408-9

1. Sports- -Addresses, essays, lectures.

FIGURE 12-1 Card Catalog: The Same Book Classified by Author, Title, and Subject

college and university libraries use the Library of Congress system, whereas most public libraries use the Dewey Decimal System. Library of Congress call numbers begin with a letter, Dewey Decimal listings with a numeral.

The catalog card not only tells you where to find the book, it also gives you some general information about the book and what it is about so that you can decide whether it is likely to be useful. Look especially at the bottom of the card. In Figure 12-1, for example, the cards indicate: "Sports—addresses, essays, lectures." Also, check the date the book was published. If you are researching history, this date might not be important. However, if you want up-to-date information on your subject, the date of publication will be very important.

Since catalog card entries about a book are so brief, some people use the catalog merely to find out where books on a particular subject are shelved in the library and then go directly to the shelf to pick out what they want. Books in library stacks are grouped by topic and subtopic. Sometimes a trip to a stack or topic area can yield valuable results. Such a trip provides the opportunity to flip though various volumes for information or resources. The best way to discover whether a book will be helpful is to look at its table of contents and index.

The card catalog will also tell you which periodicals (newspapers, magazines, and journals) are held in the library, including those that are on microfilm. The catalog, however, does not list the articles in these periodicals. For these you will have to look in the periodicals section of the library.

Looking for Articles

Periodicals Periodicals—the inclusive name for magazines, journals, and newspapers—have the latest available information on a subject, so they are often used as source material for speeches. If you want to know, for example, what the American president said to the Soviet premier yesterday, the newspaper is your best source, for it will have the latest information. Magazine articles typically cover such subjects as the latest trends in food, sports, or movies. Journals cover the latest research.

Because newspaper and magazine articles are brief, they are very useful as material for speeches. You can easily read several articles to get various points of view. If you were to do that with books, it would take you weeks— even months.

In most libraries, periodicals have a room or section to themselves. The current issues (the last six months or so) are organized in alphabetical order on the shelves. In most libraries, the current issue is on display and if you lift up the shelf you will find the earlier issues underneath. Issues that go back more than six months are either bound into large volumes or are put onto microfilm. The card catalog will tell you where to find the periodicals as well as what issues are available in the library (see Figure 12-2).

micr.

Newsweek, the magazine of news significance. v. 1 —
    Feb. 17, 1933—
New York [etc.] Weekly publications, inc. [1933—
    v. illus. (incl. ports.) 29 cm.
Title varies: 1933—   News–week, the illustrated news–magazine
    (1933–Aug. 1935, lack subtitle)
                            Newsweek, the magazine of news significance.
Editors: 1933–Feb. 20. 1937. S. T. Williamson.–Feb. 27–June 1937,
    Raymond Moley.–July 1937—   Malcolm Muir, Raymond Moley
    (with Rex Smith,   –Oct. 13, 1941; with J. B. Phillips, Oct.
    20, 1941—   and others.
    Publication office, Dayton, O.; editorial and executive departments,
New York.
    Absorbed Today (1933–37) with Feb. 27, 1937, issue.
    I. Williamson, Samuel Thurston, ed. II. Moley, Raymond, 1886–
ed. III. Muir, Malcolm.   1885—   ed. IV. Smith, Rex, 1900–
ed. v. Phillips, Joseph   Becker, 1900—   ed.
AP2.N6772   051   35—9615
Library of Congress   [68r43z2]

FIGURE 12-2 Card Catalog: Card for a Magazine

Libraries are always short of space, so many of them have material (especially periodicals) on microfilm or microfiche. Microfilm and microfiche differ only in the method by which pages are put on the film. *Microfilm* looks like film used in a movie camera, with one page following another on the roll. In *microfiche*, a large number of pages are put on the same piece of film, which looks like a small note card. The machines needed to read each one are different. Don't let the machines scare you away. Someone in the library will show you how to use them.

Since hundreds of thousands of magazine and journal articles are published every month, you will need an index to find the particular articles you need, and your library is likely to have several such indexes. Like the card catalog, these indexes are classified by author, title, and subject.

However, you should be aware that your library will not have all of the periodicals referred to in the index. College and university libraries usually have the major general interest periodicals as well as those related to the majors the school offers. Once you have found the articles that might be of interest, you can see if the library has the periodicals by checking the card catalog under the periodical name. Libraries also have a centralized listing of the names of periodicals. Check with one of the librarians for its location.

The Reader's Guide to Periodical Literature is the main index to popular magazines. This is an index of articles appearing in the kinds of magazines you are likely to subscribe to or to find at your local newsstand. *Reader's Digest, Playboy, and Redbook* are typical of the kinds of magazines to be found

Learning to use a microfiche machine such as this is not difficult—just ask a library staff member for help. Some libraries also have the facilities to photocopy the material you'll find using such a machine.

in this index, and if you are looking for information on a general topic, it's a good index to begin with.

Most libraries also have several specialized indexes covering particular subjects. They list periodicals that wouldn't be known by or be of interest to the general public. For example, the *Social Science Index* covers anthropology, economics, environmental science, geography, law and criminology, the medical sciences, political science, psychology, public administration, and sociology.

If you are interested in education, consult the *Education Index*. It covers preschool, elementary, secondary, and higher education; teacher education; vocational education; counseling and personnel service; teaching methods and curriculum; the arts; audiovisual education; international education; computers in education; the language arts; library and information sciences; psychology; mental health; and religious education.

Students interested in technology should take a look at the *Applied Science and Technology Index*. Here there is information on aeronautics and space science, chemistry, computer technology, energy resources and research, engineering, food and food industry, geology, oceanography, plastics, transportation, and many other subjects. Other indexes that might be useful to you include

Essay and General Literature Index

Art Index

Index to Periodical Articles by and about Blacks

Humanities Index

The Industrial Arts Index

Book Review Index

Books in English: Authors, Subjects, Titles

Public Affairs Information Service Bulletin

Business Periodicals Index

Monthly Catalog of United States Government Publications

Consumer's Index

Newspapers Most libraries have the local newspaper, papers from around the state, and a few of the important big-city newspapers. Generally, the big-city papers deal comprehensively with international and national issues while the local papers cover information of importance to the particular area. Practically every college has the *New York Times*. This paper is particularly useful for research, since it publishes an index of many of the articles it carries. The *New York Times* is also one of the few newspapers to carry partial or full texts of such documents as Supreme Court decisions, legislation, and speeches (especially presidential ones).

If you are looking for certain newspapers and don't see them on the newspaper rack, check the card catalog. Some libraries have newspapers and magazines on microfilm in order to save space.

Finding Reference Works

Every library has a reference section or a reference room. The reference section is basically a huge repository of information about every subject under the sun. If you know how to use this room you can probably find everything you ever want to know about anything.

Encyclopedias Encyclopedias are an important part of any library's reference collection, and most libraries have several different sets. Encyclopedias contain short articles written by experts, and they are a very good way to get basic information on a subject you don't know much about. They work best as a starting point. Once you have the basic knowledge, you can do further research in other sources. Most encyclopedias are arranged in alphabetical order by subject. Some of the best known are *The American Academic Encyclopedia*, *The Encyclopaedia Britannica*, *World Book Encyclopedia*, *Collier's Encyclopedia*, and *The Encyclopedia Americana*.

Almanacs Almanacs are compilations of factual material. Although they do not contain enough material on which to base a speech, they are very useful for checking out factual information. If you want to know who won the World Series in 1964 or how many people were executed in 1981 or how much the federal government spends on defense, you'll find it in an almanac. Some of the most popular almanacs are *The World Almanac, Information USA, Reader's Digest Almanac, Guinness Book of Records,* and *Information Please.*

Biographical Sources Biographical information can be useful in many contexts and is essential for a speech of introduction. If the person is well known, several biographical sources are available, of which the *Who's Who* series is the best known. There are the broad, general ones—*Who's Who in the World, Who's Who in America*—and there are the more specific ones: *Who's Who in Finance and Industry, . . . of American Women, . . . in American Politics, . . . in Government,* and *. . . in Science*—to name just a few. The entries, listed alphabetically by last name, typically list birth date, names of spouse and children, school attended, and accomplishments. Other biographical sources include: *Current Biography, Dictionary of National* [English] *Biography, Dictionary of American Biography, New York Times Biographical Service,* and *The Biography Index.*

Figure 12-3 shows entries for Stephen King, the novelist, from several biographical sources.

Government Documents Documents pertaining to city, state, and federal government are an important part of the collection in most libraries. Many of these documents describe how government is run. If you are doing a speech on any aspect of government policy, it would be useful to check out this information. Typical city (or county) information will cover such subjects as budget allocations, social service agencies, and maps and surveys. Many state governments publish yearly almanacs, which contain such information as the number of people in the state, the longest river, per capita income, and so on. Most states also publish information about state law and state tax structure. Often libraries also carry tourist and promotional information about the state. Since state and local governments differ in how they publish and organize information, ask the reference librarian for help if you want to use this material.

The United States government is the biggest publisher in America. To find out what it is publishing, check the *Monthly Catalog of United States Government Publications.* This is an index to articles about various federal departments. Here are some of the departments covered:

Agricultural Cooperative Service

Census Bureau

Centers for Disease Control

Civil Rights Commission

KING, STEPHEN EDWIN, novelist; b. Portland, Maine, Sept. 21, 1947; s. Donald and Nellie Ruth (Pillsbury) K; m. Tabitha Jane Spruce, Jan. 2, 1971; children: Naomi, Joe Hill, Owen. B.S., U. Maine, 1970. Tchr. English, Hampden (Maine) Acad., 1971–73; writer in residence U. Maine at Orono, 1978–79. Novels include Carrie, 1974. Salem's Lot, 1975. The Shining, 1976. The Stand, 1978. Firestarter, 1980. Danse Macabre, 1981. Cujo, 1981. Different Seasons, 1982. The Dark Tower: The Gunslinger, 1982. Christine, 1983. Pet Sematary, 1983; short story collection Night Shift, 1978; author numerous other short stories. Mem. Author's Guild Am., Screen Artists Guild, Screen Writers of Am., Writer's Guild. Democrat. Office: Press Relations Viking Press 625 Madison Ave New York NY 10022

Who's Who in America, 1984–1985

Stephen King has built a big name and a small fortune writing novels about the occult and other chilling phenomena that make readers' flesh creep. "I like to scare people. I really do," he says devilishly.

Mr. King, 32 years old, once had quite a scare himself — he thought that no one would ever publish his novels. That was in the early 1970's, when he and his wife were living in a trailer in Maine and he was bringing home all of $6,400 a year teaching high-school English. "I was really depressed. I began to think that only cousins of editors get books published."

Life in the trailer ended in 1973 when Doubleday bought one of his novels, "Carrie," for a $2,500 advance. Hardcover sales were not spectacular, but the paperback sales — boosted by the film of the novel — were nearly 4,000,000 copies. "The movie made the book, and the book made me," Mr. King says. Since "Carrie," he has written four more novels, all published by Doubleday, that later became softcover best sellers. The least successful sold 1,400,000 copies. One, "The Stand," had a short run on the hardcover bestseller list and sold 65,000 clothbound copies . . .

New York Times Biographical Service 1979

KING, Stephen (Edwin) 1947–

PERSONAL: Born September 21, 1947, in Portland, Me,; son of Donald (a sailor) and Ruth (Pillsbury) King; married Tabitha Spruce (a poet), January 2, 1971; children: Naomi, Joseph Hill, Owen. *Education*: University of Maine, B.Sc., 1970. *Politics*: Democrat.
CAREER: Writer. Has worked as a janitor, laundry worker, and in a knitting mill; Hampden Academy (high school), Hampden, Me., English teacher, 1971–73; University of Maine at Orono, writer-in-residence. 1978–79. *Member*: Authors Guild, Authors League of America. *Awards, honors*: Hugo Award nomination from World Science Fiction Convention, 1978, for *The Shining*; Balrog Awards, second place in best novel category for *The Stand*, and second place in best collection category for *Night Shift*, both 1979.
WRITINGS—Novels, except as indicated; published by Doubleday, except as indicated: *Carrie*, 1974, movie edition, New American Library, 1976; *Salem's Lot*, 1975, television edition, New American Library, 1979; *The Shining*, 1977, movie edition, New American Library, 1980; *The Stand*, 1978; *Night Shift* (short stories), 1978; *The Dead Zone*, Viking, 1979; *Firestarter*, Viking, 1980; *Stephen King's Danse Macabre* (nonfiction), Everest House, 1981. Author of numerous short stories; also author of screenplay "The Stand," based on his novel of the same title
SIDELIGHTS: Stephen King is one of the most successful writers of modern horror fiction working in the genre today. His books have sold over ten million copies, and several of his novels have been produced as popular motion pictures . . .

Contemporary Authors 1981

King, Stephen [Edwin]

Sept. 21, 1947 — Writer. Address: h. RFD 2 Kansas Road, Bridgton, Me. 04009

Beginning with *Carrie* in 1974, Stephen King's seemingly inexhaustible imagination has produced seven novels of heart-stopping terror in as many years. Each of his macabre novels has been a best seller, and at one point in 1980, he became the only American writer ever to have three different books—*Firestarter, The Dead Zone,* and *The Shining*—on the lists at the same time. Following the pattern of its predecessors, King's most recent novel, *Cujo*, leaped to the top of the New York Times's best-seller list within days of its publication in August 1981.

By 1981 there were considerably more than 22,000,000 copies of Stephen King's nine books in print, most of them in paperback. Two of them, *Carrie* and *The Shining*, have been filmed; two more, *The Stand* and *The Dead Zone*, have been scheduled for motion picture production in the near future; and his *'Salem's Lot* became a successful miniseries on CBS–TV in 1979 . . .

Current Biography, October 1981

FIGURE **12-3** **Biographical Sources**

Congress

Education Department

Environmental Protection Agency

Fish and Wildlife Service

Indian Affairs Bureau

Justice Department

National Center for Health Statistics

National Portrait Gallery

State Department

Supreme Court

Since federal government publications are so extensive, few libraries carry all of the articles listed in the *Monthly Catalog*. If your library does not have the material, you have two choices: you can write away for the material (the catalog tells how to do this) or you can ask your librarian for the location of the nearest federal depository library. A federal depository library is a regular library, but it is also one in which the federal government has chosen to put all of the documents it publishes. There are 1,350 federal depository libraries in the United States, so there is probably one not very far from where you live. (Your own library might be one.)

The Vertical File If you need more information on a subject or if you need a subject for a speech, see if your library has a vertical file. Most libraries receive hundreds of publications from consumer groups, business, industry, and the consumer divisions of state and federal government. To make these available, libraries file them alphabetically by subject matter in filing cabinets called the **vertical file**. If you opened a drawer of your library's vertical file, you might find the following subjects:

Silicon

Silicosis

Silk

Silk screen printing

Silos & silage

Silver

Silver plating

Silverware

Singapore

Singing

Single people

Sinkholes

Sinus disease

Sisal

Skateboards

Skeletons

Skibobbing

Skiing

Skin

Miscellaneous Material In addition to the reference material discussed above, every library has a miscellaneous collection of material of interest to its patrons. For example, many libraries have telephone books from around the country, annual reports from corporations, historical and genealogical information that is used for researching a family tree, and books about local history.

Using Interlibrary Loan

When your own library doesn't have a book or article you need, it can obtain the material from some other library. Each library has a specific procedure for requesting books through interlibrary loan, so check with one of the librarians. You will have to plan ahead if you want to use this service. A photocopy of a magazine article will take about ten days; a book might take three or four weeks.

Using the Library Staff

Whatever the size of a library, its librarians are the single greatest resource. All their education and experience has been devoted to finding and organizing information, and because of this training they are able to help you find anything you want to know. Although you should be able to do most of your library work on your own, you should not be afraid to ask for help when you need it.

Taking Notes

Since library research is time consuming, there is no sense in having to do it twice. Careful note taking will help you use your time efficiently. Make sure to copy information completely and accurately. This will help you if you should need to find the material again. Also, if you are asked about any of the sources you have used, you can tell someone where to find the information.

CONSIDER THIS

A good Reference Librarian can be your best assistant in preparing your speeches. If you give speeches fairly often, it would be worth your time to go to your library and meet the Reference Librarian in person. Generally, he or she is someone who enjoys digging out obscure bits of information. Such specialists get a kick out of finding out the real name of that famous movie star, or the cost of our first aircraft carrier, or how high in the sky those satellites are that relay our TV programs.

Source: Leon Fletcher, *How to Speak Like a Pro.*

TRY THIS

Take your speech topic and try to find at least one item of information in each of the following: an encyclopedia, an almanac, a biographical index, and one of the other sources mentioned above.

Which sources do you predict will be most useful? Why?

Whether it is for footnotes, endnotes, or bibliography, make certain you copy the author's full name correctly. In addition, for a book, copy the title of the book, place of publication, name of publisher, publication date, and page numbers you have used; for an article, copy the title of article, title of periodical, volume numbers, date, and page numbers of the article. Figure 12-4 shows sample note cards.

SUPPORTING MATERIAL: WHAT TO LOOK FOR

Once you have learned where to look for material, your next project is to find material that will work in your speech. To do this you begin by stating the purpose of your speech. Let's say you want to talk about robots in the automobile industry, and your specific purpose statement is: "To inform the audience about the role of robots in manufacturing automobiles." Now you have to find material that will help you achieve your goal of informing the audience about robots—supporting material.

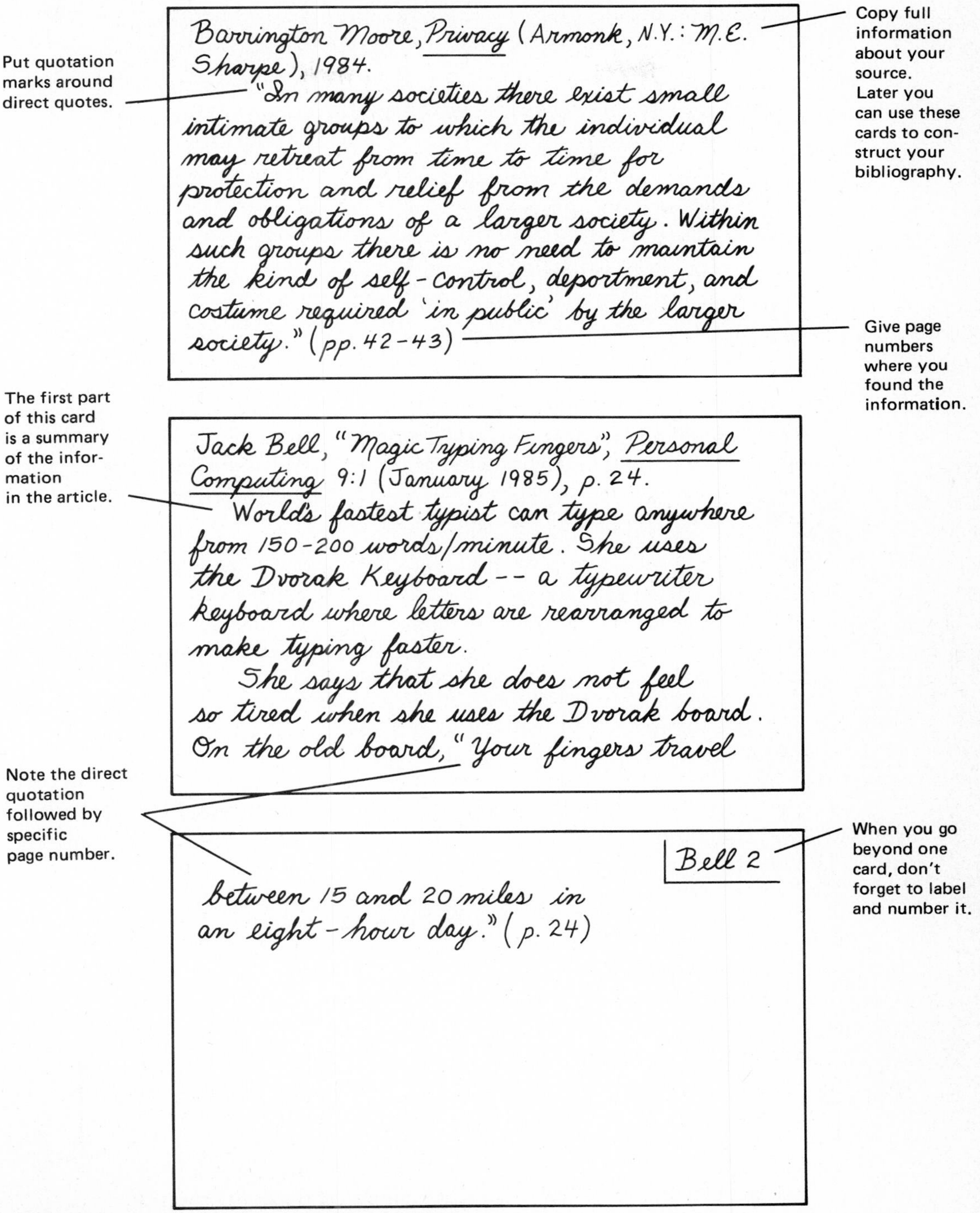

Put quotation marks around direct quotes.

Copy full information about your source. Later you can use these cards to construct your bibliography.

Barrington Moore, *Privacy* (Armonk, N.Y.: M.E. Sharpe), 1984.

"In many societies there exist small intimate groups to which the individual may retreat from time to time for protection and relief from the demands and obligations of a larger society. Within such groups there is no need to maintain the kind of self-control, deportment, and costume required 'in public' by the larger society." (pp. 42-43)

Give page numbers where you found the information.

The first part of this card is a summary of the information in the article.

Jack Bell, "Magic Typing Fingers", *Personal Computing* 9:1 (January 1985), p. 24.

World's fastest typist can type anywhere from 150-200 words/minute. She uses the Dvorak Keyboard -- a typewriter keyboard where letters are rearranged to make typing faster.

She says that she does not feel so tired when she uses the Dvorak board. On the old board, "Your fingers travel

Note the direct quotation followed by specific page number.

Bell 2

When you go beyond one card, don't forget to label and number it.

between 15 and 20 miles in an eight-hour day." (p. 24)

FIGURE 12-4 Taking Notes: Sample Note Cards

Before you begin to look for such material you should think about what might work in your speech and make some notes to yourself of what to look for. Your notes might look something like this:

I wonder how many automobile plants are using robots.	Look for statistics
I bet most people don't know what a robot is. I had better tell them.	Define robot
It will be interesting to find what a robot can do that a man can't, and vice versa.	Look for comparison between man and robot

By thinking out the speech beforehand, you are saving yourself time. You won't have to read everything about robots. You have a good idea of what you are looking for and can pass over information that does not serve your purpose. Sometimes you might find some interesting material you hadn't thought about. If it fits into your speech, use it.

Every speech you put together should have supporting material, which will provide the main content of your speech. Some of the material you will find through library research; other material can come from your personal experience or from interviews.

In the section that follows, we are going to discuss some types of supporting material. Each time you are preparing a speech, you should decide which type will work best for your particular speech.

Comparison

Comparisons point out the similarities between two or more things. For example, one student who spoke about the need for the Soviet Union and the United States to cooperate said:

> For years we have been assuming that these two countries are different. Yet both countries are made up of human beings, and humans are the same all over the world. They want their families to prosper, they want their children to have a future, and they want to live in a country they are proud of.

Comparisons are often useful if you need to clarify something. A student comparing a word processor and a typewriter said:

> The mechanics of using a word processor and a typewriter are pretty much the same. The keyboards look alike, the letters are in the same place, and the tab and shift keys function the same way. Both machines show you what you are typing. The only difference is that you see it on a screen when you use a word processor.

CONSIDER THIS

One year I gave a lot of speeches in support of building an educational television station in a city I used to live in. The total cost, a half-million dollars, is a mighty big figure, especially to educators who are used to worrying about budget items of a few hundred dollars. But that $500,000 became memorable when I did a few calculations and was able to tell them—accurately:

The cost of our half-million dollar TV station works out to less than what most of our students spend in a year on just paper and pencils!

That specific comparison was the one fact most remembered in my speeches. It was quoted repeatedly in articles reporting my speeches. That data was memorable. (And that station was built!)

Source: Leon Fletcher, *How to Speak Like a Pro.*

Sometimes a comparison can show us a new way of looking at something. We have often heard the United States referred to as a "melting pot" of different races and nationalities. Wanting to use the same concept but not the same cliché, the Rev. Jesse Jackson found a new comparison:

America is not like a blanket—one piece of unbroken cloth, the same color, the same texture, the same size. It is more like a quilt—many patches, many pieces, many colors and many sizes, all woven and held together by a common thread.[2]

Contrast

Contrasts point out the differences between two or more things. A contrast might tell how baseball is different from softball or how a three-speed bike is different from a ten-speed. One student who was speaking on the subject of keeping a diary made this contrast:

Men's and women's diaries are very different from each other. In most cases, men's diaries concentrate on their public life; women, on their private life. Men seldom write of wives and children; women have numerous entries about their families. Most important, women write of their feelings; men write of their deeds.

It can be effective to contrast the familiar with the unfamiliar. This student, just back from an exchange program in England, informs her class of the differences between an American (familiar) and an English (unfamiliar) college education.

A college education is not available for every student in England. Students take a series of examinations throughout their elementary and secondary schooling. How they do on these exams will determine whether they go to college at all or whether they go to a university or a teacher training institution. In this country every student who has graduated from high school has a chance to go to college—even though it might not be the college of his or her choice. In England, students study one or two subjects in great depth. In the United States students are more likely to have a broad, general education and study several subjects.

Examples

An **example** is something that is used to illustrate a point. It is often an experience, sometimes drawn from our own life, that supports a generalization. Good examples draw the audience in and get members involved in the subject. Let's see how they work.

Generalization: Inflation is a problem that applies to all of us.

Example: Last year at this time I bought five notebooks for $2.50 each. This year when I went to the bookstore, these same notebooks were $2.65—75 cents more than what I paid last year.

Generalization: In a few more years no one will be able to afford college tuition.

Example: My parents started saving money for me to go to school when I was just a baby. In deciding how much to save, they took into account inflation and rising college costs. However, they never could have guessed how much the costs would go up. Eighteen years later, when I was ready for college, they had enough money saved to pay for only two-thirds of my tuition for the four years.

Not all examples have to be drawn from your own life or the lives of people you know. A student speaking on rising medical costs might use as an example material from a magazine article read as part of his research. For example:

Rosa Smith, a 63-year-old cleaning lady, was diagnosed as having cancer. Although her cancer was detected early and was cured, her illness wiped out her entire life savings. Mrs. Smith had been planning to retire in two years. Now she won't be able to.

Sometimes people use **hypothetical examples**—examples that are made up to illustrate a point. These examples are often told in narrative (story) form. One student, explaining the need for infant car seats, used a hypothetical example to bring his point home to the audience. To make his hypothetical people seem more real, he gave them names:

Jerry and Marcie Kaplan were bringing their new baby, David, home from the hospital. Marcie was holding the baby in her arms. It was in mid-January, the car skidded on an icy patch on the road, and Jerry slammed on the brakes. The baby was thrown against the windshield and was badly bruised. A half hour after the Kaplans had left the hospital, they were back in it—getting emergency care for the baby. This would not have happened if the baby had been properly restrained.

When you use hypothetical examples, make sure they are things that really could have happened. Although hypothetical examples are useful, examples that have happened to you or somebody you know are the most effective. Nothing beats, "I know what I am talking about because I have been there."

Narratives

Narratives are extended examples told in the form of brief stories. They are usually told about people in particular situations, with the intent of getting the audience to identify with these people. A student speaking about drinking and driving used this narrative:

Five years ago, I was a senior in high school. One night my best friend Jeff called and asked if I wanted to go out to the lake and have a few beers. Since I had planned to see my grandmother, who was in the hospital, I told him I couldn't go but to be sure to check me out the next time.

There was no next time. That night Jeff and three of my other friends were killed in an accident. According to the police report, they hit a tree while going 75 miles an hour. All of them had high levels of alcohol in their blood.

I like to party as well as the next guy, but I never drink and drive, nor do I ride with anyone who has been drinking. I am here today to beg all of you to do the same.

Such narratives are powerful because of high-level speaker involvement. They should be used sparingly, however, because they are so emotionally vivid. You don't want them to draw audience attention away from the main point of your speech.

Statistics

Statistics—which are facts in numerical form—have many uses in a speech. Being factual material, they are a convincing form of evidence. Quite often, a speaker who uses statistics is seen as one who has done his or her homework.

Sometimes statistics can support your speech in a way no other information can. Bob, for example, wanted to persuade his class that, contrary to popular opinion, high schools are improving. He had examples that he could use from his own experience and those of his friends. This, however, did not give him enough information to generalize that all high schools in the country are improving. When he went to the library to research the subject, he discovered a newspaper article which stated that this year's high-school students had scored an average of 4 points higher on the SAT than last year's—the largest gain in 20 years.[3] This was a statistic that Bob could use to prove his point.

Statistics are easy to find. A single issue of a newspaper will have hundreds of statistics, and books and magazines will have thousands more. Since you don't want to overwhelm your audience with numbers and you want to present information that is reliable as possible, there are some rules you should follow whenever you use statistics:

Rules for Using Statistics

Use the Best Possible Sources If you see the headline, "Peanut Butter Causes Half of all Heart Attacks," it will be much more believable if it comes from the *New York Times* than from one of the newspapers that are by the checkout stand in your local supermarket. Pick your statistics from well-respected sources.

Be Wary of Surveys **Polls,** or surveys, are a good source of statistics. They study what a selected number of people think, feel, or know about a subject. You have to be careful, however, to make sure that a survey really is representative of what people are thinking. For example, let's say you want to take a random survey of what students on your campus think of the way the bookstore is run. If your survey is really random, *every student on the campus must have an equal chance of being chosen.* That is what a random survey means. If someone states in a speech that she did a random survey by standing in front of the student union building and interviewing students who came along, her survey was not random—everyone didn't have an equal chance of being chosen.

Whenever you read the results of a survey in a newspaper or magazines, there should be information about how the researchers got their data. In writing up one of its surveys, for example, the *New York Times* wrote: "This June, 1,593 Americans were surveyed at random by the *New York Times*/CBS News Poll."[4] The purpose of this information is to let you know how the data were collected, and it should be available with every poll or survey. If it isn't, don't use those statistics.

Make Sure the Information Is Up to Date Figures on military spending in 1973 are useless—unless you want to compare them with the figures for the current year.

Use Statistics That Show Trends We can often tell what is happening to an institution or even a country if we have information from one year to another. For example, one student wanted to show how attitudes toward euthanasia were changing in this country. She cited a poll that had been taken in three different decades:

> *This question was asked in a poll of Americans: "When a person has a disease that cannot be cured, do you think doctors should be allowed by law to end a patient's life by some painless means if the patient and his family request it?" In 1947, 37 percent of those asked said yes. By 1973 slightly over half agreed, and by last year, 63 percent said yes.*[5]

Use Concrete Images When your numbers are large and might be hard to comprehend, using concrete images is helpful. For example, one student spoke about the problem of increasing amounts of garbage. Since she knew that audience members would have difficulty imagining figures such as a million tons, she used a visual image that she found to convey the information:

> *There is enough [garbage] to fill the New Orleans Superdome from floor to ceiling twice a day including weekends and holidays. In eight years there will be enough national garbage to fill the same stadium three times a day.*[6]

Use Visual Aids If you are going to use several sets of statistics, you should consider using a visual aid. If the statistics aren't very complicated, you can probably write them on the blackboard. If they are more detailed and you don't have the time to write them all on the board, make up a poster beforehand.

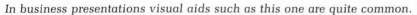

In business presentations visual aids such as this one are quite common.

Quotations and Testimony

Many speakers like to use quotations from others to support points they are making. A **quotation** is a passage cited as evidence or illustration. Historic or well-known sources are favored because quotations from these sources can lend authority to a speech. Speaking to a Christian group, you might want to quote from the Bible. Speaking about American freedoms, you might want to quote someone like Thomas Jefferson. Many of the lines written by Shakespeare are highly quotable. For example, a student on the problems of the generation gap used this quotation from Shakespeare: "Crabbed age and youth cannot live together."

Not all quotations have to come from the famous or have historic importance. Often people we interview will say something interesting or phrase something in such an unusual manner that they should be quoted. For example, when a student was interviewing the dean about a tuition increase, the dean said: "If the legislation does not give us more money we are going to go right down the drain." The student used this quote as part of her speech.

Testimony is using another person's statements or actions to give authority to what you are saying. Experts are best for testimony. Suppose you are planning to speak about nutrition and you go to the local cooperative extension office to get information from the home economist who works there. When you use this information in your speech, tell your audience where it came from. Because the information has come from an expert, your speech will have more authority and be more convincing.

Another form of testimony is to show that people who are prominent and admired believe and support your ideas. For example, if you are going to try to persuade your audience that they should take up running for fitness, it might be useful to mention some of your audience's heroes and heroines who are also runners. If you want people to sign your petition to build a new city park, mention the people in the city who are also supporting this park.

Testimony is often made up of direct quotations. However, be careful when you use quotations and testimony not to spend too much time quoting other people, since your speech could end up sounding like everyone else rather than yourself. Limit yourself to material that supports your points clearly. If you have information from a source that is long and wordy, put the material into your own words. Use direct quotes only for those people whose way of expressing themselves is as unique as what they are saying. In all cases, whether you quote directly or paraphrase, you should give credit to the person you are quoting.

Polls

Polls, as we noted above, are a good source of information about people's thinking. Quite often polls are conducted on controversial subjects. If you want to know how the American public feels about abortion, nuclear arms control, or environmental issues, you will probably be able to find a poll.

National polls also can provide useful information as to what particular segments of the population think about an issue. For example, the *New York Times*/CBS News poll on euthanasia mentioned earlier not only found what the American public as a whole believed on this issue; it also analyzed the responses according to sex, age, income level, educational level, race, political leaning, and geographical location (see Table 12-1).

TABLE 12-1

PROLONGING LIFE BY MACHINE

"Medical technology now enables doctors to prolong the lives of many people who are terminally ill. Do you believe doctors should stop using these techniques if the patient asks, even if that means the patient will die?"

	Yes	No	Don't know
Total	**77%**	**15%**	**8%**
Male	78	15	7
Female	77	14	9
18-44 years old	80	14	6
45 and older	73	16	11
$12,499 or less	69	19	12
$12,500-$24,999	75	17	8
$25,000-$34,999	84	12	4
$35,000-$49,000	83	11	5
$50,000 or more	83	13	4
Not high school graduate	66	20	14
High school graduate	78	15	7
Some college	87	9	4
College grad	81	13	5
Lives in Northeast	75	16	9
Midwest	77	16	7
South	73	17	9
West	85	8	7
Whites	80	13	7
Blacks	60	30	9
Liberal	86	11	3
Moderate	77	15	8
Conservative	76	17	7

Poll of 1,593 adults interviewed from June 23 to 28.

Source: *New York Times*, September 23, 1984, p. 56.

If you are interested in how people think on national or state issues, look at some of the polls that are available in your library. The best-known polls are those conducted by such groups as Roper, Gallup, and Harris.

Studies

As the term implies, a **study** is an in-depth investigation of a subject. The subject might be anything—from how white rats run mazes to how newspapers present political news. Studies are found in popular magazines such as *Psy-*

TRY THIS

Now take a topic that you have chosen for a speech and try to develop some ideas for supporting material by answering the following questions:

- *Definitions:* Is there anything in your topic that needs defining? Would it be useful to trace the history of the word?
- *Explanations:* What kinds of explanation does your topic need? Is there any material that is so technical or specialized that your audience might not understand it?
- *Comparison and Contrast:* Is there anything your subject can be compared with to make it more understandable? Is there something the audience might be familiar with that would provide a basis for comparison? What about a contrast? Can you show how your subject is different from something in order to explain it?
- *Examples:* What examples can you draw from your own life to help your audience understand the topic? Can you think of any examples that would promote audience empathy or sympathy?
- *Narratives:* Do you have any good stories—ones that illustrate a point—that you could use with this topic? If you don't have any, do you think it's possible to find some either from people you know or from library sources?
- *Statistics:* Are there any statistics available on your topic? If you used them would they make your speech better?
- *Quotations and Testimony:* Will quotations and testimony be useful in this speech? Are there any people you can quote that might help you to prove your point? Can you find any expert testimony?
- *Polls and Studies:* Have any polls or studies been done on your subject? Can you fit them into your speech? Can you explain them in such a way that they will be interesting to the audience?

chology Today, but they are more common to academic journals. If you are interested in finding out what research has been done in a particular field, generally the best place to start is with the journals published in that field. In the speech field, for example, the prominent journals are *Human Communication Research*, the *Quarterly Journal of Speech*, *Communication Education*, and *Communication Monographs*. All of these journals, as well as several regional ones, will have articles on the most recent research in the field of speech communication.

ADAPTING SUPPORTING MATERIAL TO THE AUDIENCE

Because the supporting material you use may work better with some audiences than with others, you should keep your audience constantly in mind when choosing it.[7]

First, you should analyze the level of knowledge of the audience. Consider, for example, a speech about microwave ovens. If you were going to speak to a group of potential customers, you would probably give examples of how it cooks food quickly. Comparing and contrasting the microwave to a standard oven would also be interesting to your audience. You could, however, speak on microwave ovens to an audience that has completely different expectations. Say that a group of environmental experts is concerned that microwave ovens are dangerous, and you have been asked to speak to the group. In this situation, you should assume that members of your audience are knowledgeable about the subject—that is why they are concerned. To get anywhere with this audience you are going to have to use studies and expert testimony proving that the oven is safe.

Second, you need to consider the attitudes of the audience toward your topic. If you have an audience that is suspicious of you or your message, you will probably do best with facts and figures and with quotations and testimony from people your audience respects. If people are shown *evidence* in the form of statistics and facts, you will have a better chance of persuading them to accept your point of view.

Finally, you should consider what kind of supporting material will hold your audience's attention. If you are speaking to a young and potentially restless audience, examples and narratives will probably hold its attention best.

Often audiences are not so homogeneous that one form of supporting material is better than another. If you have an adult audience with different levels of knowledge and different attitudes, you should use a variety of supporting material. In the following extract, the speaker begins with a statistic and then goes on to give an example:

A California study of 3,000 divorced couples found that one year after the divorce, the woman's income had dropped 73 percent while the man's had increased 43 percent.

Karen Jackson is one of these women. Last year she was living with her three children in a comfortable middle-class neighborhood. Now she is living in a slum and needs food stamps to feed her children.

Having a variety of supporting material is like having a variety of fruit in the fruit bowl. Some will like the grapes and others will like the peaches, but everyone will be pleased that there is something there to appeal to them.

SUMMARY

When you are putting together material for your speech, you should see whether you can draw on three areas: your own experience, interviews with others, and research in the library. Depending on the topic, one of these sources might provide better information than the others.

Library material is organized into three categories: books, periodicals, and reference works. Book titles, authors, and subjects can all be found in the card catalog. Magazine and journal articles can be located through periodical indexes. Reference material includes encyclopedias, almanacs, biographical information, government documents, and vertical files.

Supporting material forms the main content of every speech. Supporting material includes the following: comparisons, to point out similarities between two or more things; contrasts, to point out differences; examples, which are used to illustrate points; narratives, which are extended examples told in the form of brief stories; statistics, which are facts in numerical form; quotations, which give us the words of other people on the subject; testimony, in which the statements or actions of others are used to give authority to the speech; polls, which indicate what a selected number of people think, feel, or know about a subject; and studies, which are in-depth investigations.

When choosing supporting material for a speech, you should consider which kinds will be appropriate for the audience. To make this choice, consider the audience's level of knowledge about and attitude toward your topic, and ask which material will best hold the audience's attention.

VOCABULARY

The following is a list of words you must know to understand the concepts in this chapter. You will find the words defined the first time that each is used in the chapter. All Vocabulary words also appear, with their definitions, in the Glossary at the end of the book.

comparison	hypothetical example
contrast	narratives
example	periodicals

polls   study
quotation   testimony
statistics   vertical file

FURTHER READING

LUCAS, STEPHEN E. *The Art of Public Speaking*, 2nd ed. New York: Random House, 1986. Lucas offers students a balanced approach. He uses classical and contemporary theories of rhetoric but keeps his eye on practical skills as well. His Chapters 5 and 6, "Gathering Materials" and "Supporting Your Ideas," are especially useful and applicable.

MILLS, GLEN E. *Putting a Message Together*, 2nd ed. Indianapolis: Bobbs-Merrill, 1972. Mills's book examines the preparation of messages and the role played by messages in communication. He places his analysis within the context of principles, theories, and motives of communication. His textbook is knowledgeable, witty, and succinct, designed for the specialist.

NEWMAN, ROBERT P., and DALE R. NEWMAN. *Evidence*. Boston: Houghton Mifflin, 1969. This book is designed for those who wish to support their speeches with evidence. The first part discusses supporting goals, positional statements, and predictions. The authors offer a technical, but thorough, examination.

RIEKE, RICHARD D., and MALCOLM O. SILLARS. *Argumentation and the Decision Making Process*, 2nd ed. Glenview, Ill.: Scott, Foresman, 1984. This textbook is designed to help students with little or no background in argumentation to understand the basic concepts of the process. For our purposes, the chapters on support (5, 6, and 7) that treat evidence, values, and credibility are especially useful and complete.

SAMOVAR, A., and JACK MILLS. *Oral Communication: Message and Response*, 5th ed. Dubuque, Iowa: Brown, 1983. This very complete textbook on public speaking offers a concise statement of basic principles and theories of good speech communication with an emphasis on clarity, usefulness, and improvement. Chapter 6, "Evidence: The Foundation of Your Ideas," is relevant in this context.

SPRAGUE, JO, and DOUGLAS STUART. *The Speaker's Handbook*. San Diego, Calif.: Harcourt Brace Jovanovich, 1984. The authors provide a compendium of principles, examples, and exercises that cover all the topics students confront when preparing and delivering speeches. Chapter 4, "Research," discusses library usage; Chapter 12, "Supporting Materials," discusses the other material in our chapter. This is a succinct handbook.

TAYLOR, ANITA. *Speaking in Public*, 2nd ed. Englewood Cliffs, N.J.: Prentice-Hall, 1984. This is a comprehensive, well-written textbook on speech. Chapter 6, "Preparing Speeches: Finding and Adding Supporting Materials," is the one that applies most to our presentation in this chapter.

WILSON, JOHN F., and CARROL C. ARNOLD. *Public Speaking as A Liberal Art*, 5th ed. Boston: Allyn and Bacon, 1983. The authors approach public speaking as an art and discuss some general problems—rhetorical invention, style, delivery, and the like. Chapters 4–6, on invention, are cogent and relevant.

13 ORGANIZING AND OUTLINING THE SPEECH

CHAPTER OUTLINE

Principles of Organization
Relate points to your specific purpose and central idea
Distinguish among the introduction, body, and conclusion
Distinguish between main and minor points
Phrase all points in full sentences
Give all points a parallel structure

Patterns of Organization
Time order
Spatial order
Cause and effect
Problem-solution
Motivated sequence
Topical order

The Speech Introduction
Stating your purpose and main points
Getting attention
Additional tips for introductions

The Speech Conclusion
Summarize your main ideas
Use a quotation
Inspire your audience to action
Additional tips for conclusions

Speech Transitions
Additional tips for transitions

Preparing an Outline
The outline format
Full-sentence and key-word outlines

The Bibliography
A Sample Outline

CHAPTER OBJECTIVES

After reading this chapter, you should be able to:

1. Distinguish among the introduction, body, and conclusion of the speech.
2. Organize your speech into main and minor points.
3. Explain the six patterns of organization for a speech.
4. Explain the function of an introduction and be able to write one.
5. Explain the function of a conclusion and be able to write one.
6. Explain how transitions help listeners, and be able to write them.
7. Make an outline of your speech—both full-sentence and key-word.

Kelly got up early because she had lots to do that day. After she had eaten breakfast, she finished making up the grocery list. As she put together her list, she had a mental picture of the store's layout so she could make out her list according to the aisles in the store. Before she left the house she wrote a note to her 12-year-old son: "If you don't mow the lawn today, don't plan on getting your allowance."

As Kelly set out to do her errands, she was thinking how she could move around most efficiently in the city traffic. She decided to pick up some prescriptions (even though she didn't need them yet) because the supermarket was next to the drug store. She also dropped off some shoes to be repaired, since the shoe repair shop was located in the next block.

While driving to the supermarket, she mentally went over the list of what she still had to do. In the afternoon she had to clean up the house because company was coming for dinner that night. Was there anything she had to do for dinner? The salad greens were washed, she had made a pie yesterday, her husband was picking up the steaks. As she reviewed the list, she remembered she had to pick up sweet corn.

Once Kelly's errands were done and she had solved all her immediate problems, she started thinking about the speech course she was taking at the nearby community college. She reminded herself that some time during the weekend she had to work on an outline for her speech. She wasn't looking forward to it. The last time she had outlined something had been when she was in high school, and she remembered the experience as difficult and unpleasant.

What Kelly didn't realize was that the skills she needed for organizing and outlining her speech were the same skills she had been using all morning. When she reviewed what she had to do, she set priorities—what things had to be done right away and what could wait. She organized her grocery list by the way the store was laid out. She planned her errands (supermarket, drug store, and shoe repair) by geographical area. Although Kelly did not plan it that way, her errand list even resembled an outline:

Shoe Repair

Drug Store
     Prescriptions
     Cotton balls

Supermarket
     Oranges
     Sweet corn
     Flour
     Baking soda
     Sour cream
     Eggs

As you can see, then, organizing and outlining are not mysterious processes used only in academic settings. They are part of the skills that we all know and use. Let's see how we can apply these skills to the job at hand—organizing and outlining a speech.

PRINCIPLES OF ORGANIZATION

When you are putting together a speech you must organize it so it will make sense both to you and to your audience.[1] As you organize it, you should follow the principles of organization discussed below.

Relate Points to Your Specific Purpose and Central Idea

The points you make in your speech should relate directly to your specific purpose and central idea. In this speech titled "Checking Out Charities," notice that all of the main points do this.

Specific Purpose: To inform my classmates about the need to check out charities before giving them money.

Central Idea: Don't give your money to a charity without checking it out first.

Main Ideas:
I. Find out the purpose of the charity.
II. Ask what the charity has accomplished.
III. Ask about the charity's method of collecting money.
IV. Find out how the charity will use your money.

Distinguish Among the Introduction, Body, and Conclusion

All speeches should have three main parts: an introduction, a body, and a conclusion. The word **body** refers to all the material between the introduction and the conclusion, and it consists of all the major and minor points in the speech.

Distinguish Between Main and Minor Points

When organizing your speech, you should distinguish between main and minor points. If you do this, the speech will flow and will seem logical to your listeners. The main points are all the broad, general ideas and information that support your central idea; the minor points are the specific ideas and

CONSIDER THIS

There remains much merit in the old advice to the public speaker: Tell them what you're going to say; say it; and tell them what you've said. It may help you to resort to numbering your points: *The Supreme Court erred in three ways. First, it distorted the statute; second, it trampled upon the Constitution; third, it trespassed upon the power of Congress.* You would then go on to expand upon these offenses, taking them in the same order.

Source: James J. Kilpatrick, *The Writer's Art.*

information that support the main points. Say that the purpose of your speech is to persuade your audience to cut down on fast foods. The central idea of your speech is that many fast foods violate the rules for good nutrition. Your main point will have this broad, general idea: "Fast food restaurants do not provide good nutrition." Your minor points will be any points that explain the main point in more specific terms. Examples might be: "(1) fast food is high in salt content; (2) fast food has too much fat; (3) fast food contains little fiber." All of these minor points help to explain the ways in which fast food is not nutritious.

If you have difficulty distinguishing between major and minor points, write each of the points you want to make in your speech on a separate index card. Then spread all the cards out in front of you and organize them by main points, with minor points coming under them. If one arrangement doesn't work, try another. This is the advantage of having each point on a separate card.

Phrase All Points in Full Sentences

Phrasing all your points in sentences helps to flesh out the outline. Complete sentences will also help you to think out your ideas more fully. Once your ideas are set out in this detailed way, you will be able to discover problems in the organization that might need more work.

Give All Points a Parallel Structure

Parallel structure means that each of your points will begin with the same grammatical form. For example: "The first way to lose weight. . . . The second way to lose weight. . . ." and so on.

TRY THIS

For each of the following sets of sentences, identify the main point with an *M* and the minor or supporting point(s) with an *S*.

_____1. There are thousands of different kinds of dolls.

_____2. Nesting dolls is the term for dolls that fit inside each other.

_____3. Baby dolls resemble infants.

_____1. Don't wear anything that glitters.

_____2. Don't wear all-black or all-white clothing.

_____3. If you are appearing on television, be careful what you wear.

_____1. The amount of agricultural land under cultivation does not support the population.

_____2. Famine can occur for many reasons.

_____3. Population exceeds the food sources.

_____4. Unusual weather, such as drought, occurs.

In each of the next sets there are *two* main points. Find them and match them with the correct minor points.

_____1. Certain signs indicate that your pet is too fat.

_____2. Cut back food by one-third.

_____3. It tires easily after a little exercise.

_____4. Put your pet on a diet.

_____5. Use low-calorie fillers such as rice or cottage cheese.

_____6. It looks fat (or everybody calls it butterball).[2]

_____1. Some studies indicate that people who drink coffee in large amounts are more prone to heart disease.

_____2. Caffeine can cause birth defects such as cleft palate and bone abnormalities.

_____3. Decaffeinated coffee is a good alternative to coffee with caffeine.

_____4. If you want to break the caffeine habit, do it by a cup or two a day.

_____5. People who drink large quantities of coffee may be endangering their health.

_____6. You can break the coffee-caffeine habit.

Answers: The main points are:
- There are thousands of different kinds of dolls.
- If you are appearing on television, be careful what you wear.
- Famine can occur for many reasons.
- Certain signs indicate that your pet is too fat.
- Put your pet on a diet.
- People who drink large quantities of coffee may be endangering their health.
- You can break the coffee-caffeine habit.

PATTERNS OF ORGANIZATION

After deciding on your statement of specific purpose, your next step is to decide on an organizational pattern for your speech. This organizational pattern will mainly affect the body—the main part of the speech. (Introductions and conclusions are discussed later in the chapter.)

The body of the speech is made up of main points, numbered I, II, III, and so on in the outline. Most classroom speeches should not have more than four or five main points, and many of them will have no more than two or three. Your choice of how many main points to use will depend on your topic. If you want to cover it in depth, you will use fewer main points. If you want to give a broad, general view, you might want to use four or five main points.

You have several choices in deciding how to arrange the main points in your speech. The choice you make should depend on what best suits your material. In this section we will discuss six possible arrangements: time order, spatial order, cause and effect, problem-solution, motivated sequence, and topical order.

Time Order

Time order, or chronological order, is used to show development over time. This order works particularly well when you want to use a historical approach. For example, in a speech about the development of the circus, the speaker arranged her main points in chronological order:

Specific Purpose: To inform my audience about the development of the circus.

    Central Idea: The circus went through four major stages of development.

    Main Points: I. The circus began in Rome thousands of years ago.
                    II. The modern circus developed in England during the 1700s.
                 III. The earliest circus in America was established in 1792.
                IV. The golden age of the American circus began in the late 1800s.

Time order is often used to explain a process. The process could be anything from how to wrap a gift to the steps in applying for a student loan. This student used time order for describing the process of making a pot:

Specific Purpose: To inform my audience of how a pot is made.

    Central Idea: Making a pot involves four steps: wedging, shaping, glazing, and baking.

In explaining the process of using a life jacket, this airline steward would probably use time order. His main points would be the steps in putting it on, inflating it, and using it as a flotation device.

Main Points: I. In the first step the potter gets the air bubbles out of the clay in a process called wedging.

II. In the second step the potter shapes the pot on the potter's wheel.

III. In the third step the potter glazes (puts a color finish on) the pot.

IV. In the fourth step the potter bakes the pot in a kiln.

Spatial Order

Spatial order is especially useful when you want your audience to see how the parts make up the whole. To help your audience visualize your subject, you explain it by going from left to right or from top to bottom, or in any direction that best suits your subject.

In this speech, a student explains the use of solar heating elements in building a new house. His spatial order is organized around the different parts of the house: the roof, the windows, the walls, and the floors. He could have proceeded outside to inside but he chose top to bottom.

Specific Purpose: To inform my audience about several ways in which solar heating elements can be built into a house.

Central Idea: Solar heating elements can be built into a house in a number of ways.

Main Points:
I. Solar panels built into the roof will gather the sun's heat.
II. Banks of south-facing windows can bring solar heat into the house.
III. Solar storage units built into the walls will absorb heat on sunny days and release it into the house at night.
IV. Floors made of concrete or stone can be placed to absorb solar heat and release it into the house.

Spatial order works particularly well when the speech focuses on a chart or diagram. When using the visual aid, the speaker naturally moves from top to bottom or from left to right. For example, when a student decided to speak on the topic "Who Makes Decisions on Campus," he used a spatial order and worked from top to bottom on a flow chart showing who the bosses were and what they were responsible for.

Specific Purpose: To inform my audience about who makes decisions on campus.

Central Idea: Campus business is divided into two branches: the administrative branch and the academic branch.

Main Points:
I. The president is the chief administrative officer of the college; the two vice presidents report directly to him.
II. The academic vice president is responsible for everything that concerns classes, such as curriculum and faculty.
III. The administrative vice president is responsible for all nonclass activity, such as law enforcement, revenues, and payroll.

Cause and Effect

Speakers using **cause-and-effect order** divide their speech into two major parts: cause (why something is happening) and effect (what impact it is having). In this speech the speaker is using a cause-and-effect arrangement to talk about teen-age eating disorders:

Specific Purpose: To inform my audience about teen-age eating disorders.

Central Idea: Teen-age eating disorders can be so serious that they can lead to death.

Main Points: I.   (Cause) Teen-age eating disorders are usually caused by psychological problems such as a lack of self-esteem or the need to control one's parents.

   II.   (Effect) A typical victim of an eating disorder is anywhere from 15 to 30 pounds under her normal weight and, in extreme cases, may starve herself to death.

You do not always have to start with the cause and end with the effect. In this speech about eating disorders, the order could have been reversed: the speech could have begun with examples of eating disorders and then gone on to say what caused the problem. This order might have been more effective in capturing the audience's attention.

Problem-Solution

As with a cause-and-effect arrangement, speakers using a **problem-solution order** divide their speech into two sections: one dealing with the problem, the other dealing with the solution. For example:

Specific Purpose: To inform my audience how to protect themselves from shopping-mall crime.

Central Idea: You can protect yourself from shopping-mall crime by parking close to elevators, sending parcels home, accompanying small children at all times, and carrying as little cash as possible.

Main Points: I.   Shopping malls attract muggers, car thieves, child molesters, drug peddlers, and pickpockets.

   II.   Shoppers can take several precautions to protect themselves from shopping-mall crime.

Here is another example:

Specific Purpose: To persuade my audience that everyone should be taxed only on income.

Central Idea: If federal income tax were based solely on income, taxes would then be fair and equitable.

Main Points: I.   Current tax laws favor the rich and put a heavy tax burden on the middle class and the poor.

   II.   A tax based solely on income would ensure that everyone paid his or her fair share of taxes.

Motivated Sequence

The **motivated sequence,** developed by Professor Alan H. Monroe in the 1930s,[3] is also a problem-solving pattern of arrangement. The sequence is designed to persuade listeners to a point of view and then motivate them to take action. The full pattern has five steps:

1. *Attention:*   The speaker calls attention to the topic or situation.

2. *Need:*   The speaker develops the need for a change and explains related audience needs. This is the problem-development portion of the speech.

3. *Satisfaction:*   The speaker presents his or her solution and shows how it meets (satisfies) the needs mentioned.

4. *Visualization:* The speaker shows what will result when the solution is put into effect.

5. *Action:*   The speaker indicates what kind of action is necessary to bring about the desired change.

Any persuasive problem-solving speech can be adapted to the motivated sequence. Notice how this speaker uses the pattern:

Specific Purpose: To persuade my audience of the need to vote in the next student election.

Central Idea: If all students vote in the next student government election, it will be a way of telling the government that we care about what they are doing.

Main Points: I. (Attention) This year our student activity fee went up 100 percent. Even though our fee has doubled, there has not been a single extra service.

II. (Need) Student government has consistently ignored student wishes because so few students have shown an interest in student government.

III. (Satisfaction) If we all go out and vote in the next election, it will be a way of telling the officers and the senators that we care about what is happening in government.

IV. (Visualization) If the officers and senators realize that the entire student body has put them into office, they, in turn, will be more responsive to the needs and wishes of the students.

V. (Action) Tomorrow is voting day. The voting booths are in the lobby of the student center and they will be open from noon until 4:00 P.M. Get out there and vote!

Topical Order

When your speech does not fit into any of the patterns so far described, you will probably use a topical pattern of organization. You can use a **topical order** whenever your subject can be grouped logically into subtopics. Here are some examples: four ways to save money for college, good dogs for house pets (group by breed), traveling by bicycle (group by places you could travel to or by helpful hints), or three reasons to give up eating meat.

In this next speech, the student uses a topical order to explain how to improve term papers. Topical order is the only order she could use for this speech. Time order wouldn't work because there are no steps to follow; nor would spatial order. And since she doesn't state a problem, neither the problem-solution nor the motivated sequence would apply. The topical order works because she wants to talk about five things—all related to the central idea of improving term papers.

Specific Purpose: To inform my audience how to get better grades on essay tests and term papers.

Central Idea: There are five things you can do to get better grades on your essay exams and term papers.

Main Points:
I. Don't get information only from books—use interviews too.
II. Give some indication in your paper or exam that you are enthusiastic about the topic.
III. Paraphrase as many quotations as possible.
IV. Don't pad your paper; make your point and quit.
V. Have your paper typed by a good typist and proofread it before you hand it in.

In a persuasive speech on the importance of fluoride, this student's topical pattern was organized around reasons for using fluoride:

Specific Purpose: To persuade my audience that all drinking water should contain fluoride.

Central Idea: Fluoride in drinking water prevents tooth decay and bone loss.

Main Points:
I. Children who grow up drinking fluoridated water have two-thirds fewer cavities than children who don't.
II. Osteoporosis, the breakdown of bones in old age, is less common in communities that have fluoridated water.
III. There is no evidence that fluoride is linked to any disease.

TRY THIS

Which organizational pattern might you use for each of the following speech topics?

1. Overcoming the problem of adult illiteracy
2. Reading a road map—what those red and blue lines really mean
3. Three ways to fight the flu
4. Building an inexpensive bookcase for your room
5. Industrial pollution: a problem for the future

Answers: 1.   problem-solution or motivated sequence   2.   spatial order   3.   topical order   4.   time order.   5.   cause-and-effect order

THE SPEECH INTRODUCTION

The **introduction** of a speech is extremely important. It gives audience members their first impression of you. It lets them know if you have confidence, if you know what you're talking about, and if you have prepared your material. From this first impression, those in the audience will decide whether they like you and whether they want to listen to you.

The introduction also gives an idea of what the speech is going to be about so the audience can focus and follow the speech more easily. Another important job of the introduction is to arouse audience curiosity and interest—so that people will listen to the speech with full attention.

Stating Your Purpose and Main Points

In most speaking situations the speaker will say in the introduction what he or she is going to talk about. When the speaker does this, the audience can turn its attention to the topic and begin to concentrate. Although you do not have to mention the topic in your very first words, you shouldn't wait too long. By the time you reach the end of your introduction, your audience should know what you intend to accomplish and the central idea of your speech. By including this information in your introduction, you are providing a signpost as to the direction you will be taking. For example:

> *The physical abuse of children is a serious problem in this country, and today I want to talk about how bad the problem is and some of the things we can do about it.*

In your introduction, you might also want to preview your main points. Not only does this give members of the audience a sense of your direction, it also helps them to follow your speech more easily. The student speaking on the physical abuse of children previewed her main points this way:

> Since this problem covers such a broad area, I would like to limit my talk to three areas: parental abuse of children, social agencies that deal with abuse, and what the ordinary citizen can do when he or she suspects a child is being abused.

Getting Attention

As well as letting your audience know what you are going to be talking about, your introduction should also arouse attention and interest. Attention is not just a matter of getting the audience members to listen to your first words—they would probably do that anyway. Attention is a matter of creating interest in your subject. You want your audience members to think, "This really sounds like an interesting subject" or "I am going to enjoy listening to this speech."

Through the test of time, certain techniques have been found to work as attention getters. Let's look at them and at the functions they serve. Note that sometimes a speaker might use more than one of these techniques.

Use Some Humor

When the speaker is a stranger to the audience, a humorous introduction can create good will. This is how a speaker began her speech for Senior Recognition Day:

> Greetings to you, seniors, who invited me to address you today and who soon will be able to decide whether that was a mistake. Greetings to you, colleagues, and to you, freshmen, and most special greetings to anyone who came even though you were not required to.[4]

Use an Anecdote

Anecdotes are short, interesting accounts of some happening. They can be personal examples or they could have happened to someone else. Sometimes they are humorous. A student used this anecdote to spark interest in her speech:

> Gilbert is 42 years old. He has three children, ages 17, 10, and 4. Gilbert never read to his two oldest children nor helped them with their schoolwork. If they asked for help with reading, Gilbert's reply was "Ask your mother." Last week everything changed. Gilbert read The Cat in the Hat to his 4-year-old. It was the first time Gilbert had ever read to one of his children. In fact, it was the first time Gilbert had read anything at all.

Most after-dinner speakers use humor and anecdotes to warm up their audience and to keep members' attention.

Gilbert had been illiterate. For the past four months he has been learning to read through a program in the literacy council. I am Gilbert's teacher.

Refer to the Occasion

If you are asked to speak for a special occasion or if a special occasion falls on the day you are speaking, make a reference to it, as in the following:

I am very honored to have been asked to give a speech for Founder's Day. This occasion has a special meaning for me because, one hundred years ago, when this college began, many people said the college would never succeed. Now this college is the lifeblood of this town.

Show the Importance of the Subject

Showing the audience that the subject is important to their own lives is a good way of getting and keeping attention. This student not only lets his audience know how important the subject is to it, he also keeps his audience's attention by building suspense.

I would like to speak on a topic that affects all of us. It raises the price of every product we buy. It often makes us feel inadequate because we are not beautiful enough, thin enough, or young enough. It makes us go in debt because we buy things we cannot afford. It comes uninvited into our homes, and it interrupts us every ten minutes or so. What is this thing that has such a negative influence on our lives? It's television advertising.

Use Startling Information

Using information that startles or surprises your audience is a good device for gaining attention. In a speech about the national debt—not the most fascinating topic to a college audience—this speaker was able to "hook" his audience with this introduction:

We have all heard about the national dept but what exactly does it mean? It means that this year it will cost the federal government an estimated $100 billion to pay just the interest on the national debt. Every ten minutes the government owes about another $2 million dollars in interest due.[5]

Use Questions

Questions get the audience involved right away because often it will mentally answer the questions as you ask them. Sometimes questions can be used to build suspense. Here's how one student began her speech about buying a secondhand car:

How do you shop for a secondhand car? Do you look for a particular model, or do you go in to see what's available? Is there any kind of research you can do before you go to the car lot? Is there any way of knowing what a particular car is worth? Are secondhand cars ever under warranty by the dealer? These are some of the questions many of us ask when we go to buy a secondhand car. Today, I am going to try to give you some answers.

Use Personal Experiences

Don't be afraid to refer to your own experiences when you can tie them into your subject. Personal experiences make a speech stronger because they are a way of showing that you know what you're talking about. This speaker used his own experience to begin a speech about dropping out of school:

Seven years ago I was a teen-age dropout. I went away to college because my parents wanted me to. I moved into a dorm, made lots of friends, and began to have a wonderful time. A time that was so wonderful that I only occasionally went to class or studied for an exam. The college, realizing that freshmen take time to adjust, only put me on probabtion for the first year. In the second year, however, I had to settle down.

I tried to study, but I didn't have any idea of what I was studying for. I didn't have a major and I had no idea of what I wanted to do with my life. Finally I asked myself, "What am I doing here?" I could come up with no answer. So after finishing the first semester of my sophomore year, I dropped out of school. It was the second-best decision I ever made. The first-best was to come back to school—at the grand old age of 24.

Sometimes your personal experience helps to tell your audience why you are qualified to speak on the subject. If the audience thinks you have some experience or expertise, you will have more credibility as a speaker.

Today I am here to persuade you never to take up smoking. You might think it is a case of the pot calling the kettle black. You have all seen me smoke at every possible opportunity. All I can say is that if I had one wish, I would like to be a nonsmoker. Why do I want to give it up? Let me tell you what you might not know. Every morning I cough for half an hour when I get out of bed. I have thrown away countless clothes because I have burned tiny holes in them with cigarette sparks. The windows of my house and car are covered with a greasy yellow film from smoke. Worst of all, my favorite cat won't sit in my lap because she hates smoke.

Why haven't I given it up? Because it is a powerful addiction that is very hard to break.

Use a Quotation

Sometimes you can find a good quotation that will get your speech off to a good start. It can also give credibility to your speech. In urging her audience to learn about computers, one student said:

John Naisbitt, the author of the best-selling book Megatrends, has said, "To be really successful, you will have to be trilingual: fluent in English, Spanish, and computer."[6] *Today I want to talk to you about becoming fluent in computer.*

Additional Tips for Introductions

When you are writing an introduction to a speech, remember these points as well:

1. Although you might want to build curiosity about your speech topic, don't do this for too long. The audience will get annoyed if it has to wait too long to find out what you're going to talk about.

2. Don't spend too much time on your introduction. The body of your speech contains the main content, and you shouldn't wait too long to get there.

3. In planning your speech you will have adapted the topic to the occasion and to the audience. Now you should ask yourself whether there is

---

TRY THIS

What kinds of introductions do you think would work well for the following speech situations?

- You are asked to give the annual Lincoln Day speech at the local high school. You will be speaking on Lincoln's Birthday.
- You are speaking about child abuse to a group of local social workers who work with delinquent girls. You want to stress the point that children who have been abused will grow up to abuse their own children.
- You are going to speak about the value of jogging. As you plan your speech you remember how difficult it was for you to learn and how many times you were tempted to give up.

---

anything in the situation that you did not anticipate and need to adapt to. For example, did someone introduce you in a particularly flattering way? Do you want to acknowledge this? Did your audience brave bad weather to come and hear you talk? Do you want to thank them?

THE SPEECH CONCLUSION

Like introductions, conclusions have specific functions. They give the audience the feeling that the speech is coming to an end. A good **conclusion** should not introduce any new ideas—rather it should tie together all the ideas of the speech.

If you have not had very much experience in public speaking, it is especially important that you plan your conclusion carefully beforehand. There is nothing worse than knowing that you have said all you have to say but not knowing how to stop. If you plan your conclusion, this won't happen to you.

As with introductions, there are certain kinds of conclusions that are used time and time again. When you are working on your conclusions, consider one of these. Note that even though the conclusions are of different types, they all have an inspirational quality to them. They make the audience feel that the speech was terrific and that they would like to hear this speaker again.

Summarize Your Main Ideas

If you want your audience to remember your main points, it helps if you go back and summarize them in the conclusion of your speech. The student whose topic was "Five Tips for Improving Term Papers" concluded her speech this way:

> Let me briefly summarize what you should do whenever you write a term paper. Use interviews as well as books, show enthusiasm about the subject, paraphrase quotations, don't pad your paper, and have your paper typed by a good typist. If you follow these hints you are certain to do better in the next paper you write.

Use a Quotation

If you can find a quotation that fits in with your subject, the conclusion is a good place to use it. A quotation gives added authority to what you have said, and it can often help sum up the main ideas of your speech. In his speech trying to persuade the audience not to make political choices on the basis of television commercials, this student used a closing quotation to reinforce his point:

> An executive in the television industry once wrote, "Television programming is designed to be understood by and to appeal to the average 12-year-old." If that is the opinion that television executives have of the typical American, I would suggest that we fight back. There is only one way to do that. Turn off the television set.

Inspire Your Audience to Action

When you are giving a speech, especially a persuasive one, your goal is often to inspire an audience to some course of action. If this has been the goal of your speech, you can use your conclusion to tell audience members precisely what they should do. In this example, a student has been trying to persuade members of her audience to join campus organizations. Notice how she motivates them to take this action.

> We often hear that college is not part of "real life." Real life, however, is made up of clubs and organizations—all which function to make decisions about our community, our lives, and even the course of democracy. This campus has 159 different clubs and organizations. If you are not a member of one of them. I encourage you to join today. If you join one of them you become part of campus life. If you start working with an organization, you are preparing yourself for life in the "real world." On the table by the door there are lists of all of these organizations along with their telephone numbers. Please pick up a list on your way out. I'm sure you will find that at least one organization has something for you.

Additional Tips for Conclusions

1. Work on your conclusion until you feel you can deliver it without any notes. If you feel confident about your conclusion, you will feel more confident about your speech.

2. If you tell your audience you are going to conclude, do it! Don't set up the expectation that you are finished and then go on to talk for several more minutes.

3. Don't let the words "thank you" take the place of a conclusion.

4. Give your conclusion and sit down. If you don't do this, you will ruin the impact of your conclusion and perhaps even your entire speech.

SPEECH TRANSITIONS

Your speech will also require **transitions** from one point to another to tell your audience where you have been and where you are going. Transitions are a means of getting from one point to another smoothly. For example, if you are going to show how alcohol and tobacco combine to become more powerful than either acting alone, you might say:

> We all know, then, that cigarette smoking is hazardous to our health and we all know that alcohol abuse can kill, but do you know what can happen when the two are combined? Let me show you how these two substances act synergistically—each one making the other more powerful and dangerous than either would be alone.

Now you are set to speak about their combined effect.

Additional Tips for Transitions

In writing transitions, you should also pay attention to these points:

1. Use a transition to introduce main heads and to indicate their order: "First, . . . Second, . . . Third, . . ."; "The first matter we shall discuss . . ."; "In the first place, . . ."; "The first step . . ."; "Let us first consider . . ."; and the like.

2. Write out your transitions and include them in your speech outline. Often, a transition that is written out and rehearsed is more likely to be used.

3. If in doubt as to whether to use a transition, *use it*. Since speech is a one-time event, listeners cannot go back. Anything you can do to make the job of listening easier and more accurate should be done.

PREPARING AN OUTLINE

An **outline** is a way of organizing material so you can see all the parts and how they relate to the whole. Outlines are very useful in helping to discover where there might be problems in structure.

The Outline Format

Your speech will be organized into an introduction, a body, and a conclusion (with transitions connecting them). Since the introduction and the conclusion deal with so few points, they are usually not outlined. (However, some speakers like to write out the introduction and conclusion and include them as part of the outline.)

Main and Supporting Points

The outline deals with the major portion of the speech—the body—and it shows the organization into main and supporting (minor) points. The broad, general statements are the main points; minor points contain the more specific information that elaborates on and supports the main points.

Using the Standard Symbols and Indentation

All outlines use the same system of symbols. The main points are numbered with Roman numerals (I, II, III) and capital letters (A, B, C). Minor, more specific, points are numbered with Arabic numerals (1, 2, 3) and lower-case letters (a, b, c). The most important material is always closest to the left-hand margin; as material gets less important, it moves to the right. Note, then, that the outline format moves information from the general to the more specific through the use of numbers, letters, and indentation.

I. Vegetables
   A. Root Vegetables   B. Leafy Vegetables
      1. Carrots   1. Spinach
      2. Potatoes   2. Collard greens
      3. Parsnips   3. Lettuce

Another thing you should note about the outline format is that there should always be at least two points of the same level. That is, you can't have just an A and no B; you can't have just a 1 and no 2. The only exception to this is that in a one-point speech, you would have only one main point.

Full-Sentence and Key-Word Outlines

There are two major types of outlines: full-sentence and key-word. A *full-sentence outline* is a complete map of what the speech will look like. All the ideas are stated in full sentences. In a full-sentence outline it is easy to spot problem areas and weaknesses in structure, idea support, and idea flow. This type of outline is very useful when you are planning and developing your speech.

Key-word outlines give only the important words and phrases; their main function is to remind the speaker of his or her ideas when delivering the speech. Sometimes speakers will add statistics or quotations to key-word outlines when such information is too long or too complicated to memorize. Some speakers prepare a full-sentence outline on the left and a key-word outline on the right, as in the following example. The key-word outline enables the speaker to avoid having to look at his or her notes all the time.

Produce should be carefully washed before you eat it.	Wash produce.
Breads without preservatives should be refrigerated.	Refrigerate bread
Meat should not be eaten raw.	No raw meat.

The main points (whether presented in full sentences or by key words) are sometimes put on cards—one to a card. We will discuss the reasons for this in the next chapter.

THE BIBLIOGRAPHY

At the end of your outline you should have a **bibliography** of all the material you have used in preparing the speech. This bibliography should include everything you have read (books, newspapers, magazines) and all the people you have interviewed. Figure 13-1 on the next page shows how items should be listed in a bibliography. At the end of this chapter, following the sample speech, you will find a sample bibliography.

Bibliographies should have items stated in a specific way. Since books, magazines, and interviews are the most common sources for speeches, an example is given of how each should appear in the bibliography.

Items in the bibliography should be listed alphabetically by author.

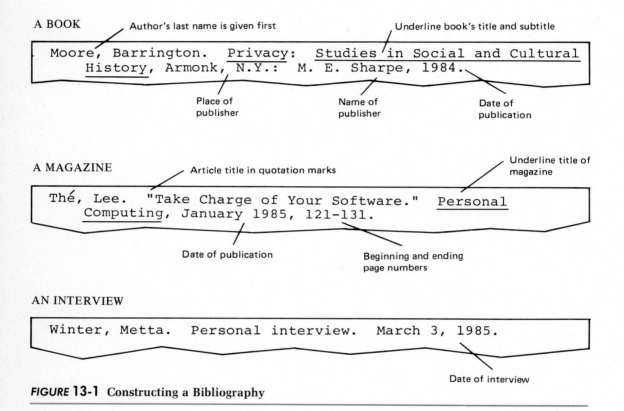

A BOOK — Author's last name is given first — Underline book's title and subtitle

Moore, Barrington. Privacy: Studies in Social and Cultural History, Armonk, N.Y.: M. E. Sharpe, 1984.

Place of publisher — Name of publisher — Date of publication

A MAGAZINE — Article title in quotation marks — Underline title of magazine

Thé, Lee. "Take Charge of Your Software." Personal Computing, January 1985, 121-131.

Date of publication — Beginning and ending page numbers

AN INTERVIEW

Winter, Metta. Personal interview. March 3, 1985.

Date of interview

FIGURE **13-1** **Constructing a Bibliography**

SAMPLE OUTLINE

To help you do your own outline, here is a sample speech done in outline form. Note that the speech follows a topical pattern of organization. The topical outline works well for this particular speech because all the main points are illustrations of the central idea—that television news is biased. The speech outline appears on the left, our commentary on the right.

Title: Television New Bias
Specific Purpose: To inform my audience how television news can be distorted.

By stating your specific purpose and central idea you will be able to keep on track while you are doing your outline. Whenever

Central Idea: Television news is distorted in four ways.

you add a new main point, ask yourself whether it ties in directly with your purpose and central idea.

Introduction

Every time a poll is taken about where people get their news, the majority of Americans answer "television." This means that every night most of us are getting our picture of the world and what is happening in it from our television set.

By mentioning the poll, the speaker is showing that television news is important.

Are we being well served by television news? Does it give us an accurate picture of the world? Does it make us better informed citizens? To answer these questions I would like to talk about bias in news. From my experience in working in campus TV news and from my research, I have found four ways in which television news can be biased or distorted. I would like to talk about these now.

These questions are a way of involving the audience, since some audience members will be answering them in their minds.

The speaker tells the audience of the direct experience she has had with TV news. This makes her more believable. Notice that she also directly mentions her specific purpose in this introduction.

Body

I. Television news is little more than a headline service.
  A. If a half-hour newscast were put into newspaper print, it would not even fill the front page.
  B. Because television news is so brief, it can cover stories only superficially.
    1. Last night's story on Lebanon got 20 seconds.
    2. President's new economic policy—30 seconds.
    3. War between Iraq and Iran—25 seconds.

The speaker develops the first main point under Roman numeral I. Note that this point is stated as a full sentence.

Subpoints A and B are also stated as full sentences. However, items below this level—those with Arabic numbers—do not have to be stated in full sentences.

Transition: Television news producers are always on the lookout for stories that will look good on television.

The transition is stated in a full sentence and serves the function of moving smoothly from one point to the next.

II. Television news always looks for the visual angle.
   A. Stories with action are chosen over nonaction stories.
      1. In last night's newscast, there were four fire stories—two of them on vacant lots.
      2. Only two minutes was spent on an important school board decision.
   B. Because of the emphasis on a visual angle, TV news is biased toward stories that have violence such as riots and combat.
   C. Most important decisions made by local, state, and government bodies have no visual angle, so they are covered superficially—if at all.

The second main point is stated in a full sentence, as are sub-heads A,B,C.

Transition: One thing you may never have thought of is that news—whether it's printed or broadcast news—is also biased toward a certain class.

III. All television news is biased toward the upper middle class.
   A. According to Donald Murray of the *Boston Globe*, reporters for print and broadcast news are "predominantly white, college-educated, and members of the professional class."
   B. Herbert Gans, a sociologist who has observed news operations, says that reporters report stories that show the values of their own class.
   C. Television reporters interview the most articulate spokespersons—leaving out those who do not express themselves well.
      1. Working-class people are seldom interviewed about major issues.

Under this main point the speaker uses the names and titles of two authorities to support her main point. She thus makes this point more believable and more interesting.

2. Television news favors the expert for interviews.

Transition: Not only are certain people never covered by TV news, but it also ignores entire cities and geographical regions.

IV. Most television news is shot in specific American cities.
   A. Generally networks have camera crews in New York, Los Angeles, Chicago, and Washington.
      1. It is easier to schedule a story where you already have a crew.
      2. It's cheaper to shoot in a city where you have a crew. One assignment editor said, "If we had to choose between covering a demonstration in Chicago or Little Rock, we'd choose Chicago because that's where we have a crew."
   B. Places that are hard to get to or are out of the way will not be in the news unless a story of such importance occurs there that it cannot be ignored.

Again, the speaker uses an authority to reinforce her point.

Conclusion

When I speak of the bias in television news I do not do so with the goal of asking you to turn off your television set. If you are going to be an intelligent consumer of news it is important for you to know that television news is biased: it's superficial, it focuses on action stories, it's biased toward the upper middle-class, and it covers only certain geographical areas. Once you know this you can make your own decisions about what to believe and whether you should check out your TV news against other sources such as newspapers and maga-

Here, in the conclusion, the speaker summarizes her main points. She also mentions again her central idea—that television news is biased. Rather than only listing the problems of TV news, she also suggests a solution.

zines. The important thing to realize when you watch the news is that you are probably not getting the whole picture. If you know that, then you will be able to look elsewhere to make the stories more complete.

Bibliography

Epstein, Edward Jay. *News from Nowhere.* New York: Random House, 1973.

Gans, Herbert J. *Deciding What's News.* New York: Pantheon Books, 1979.

Morton, John. "And That's the Way It Could Be. . . ." *Washington Journalism Review,* May 1983, pp. 16, 58.

Murray, Donald. *Writing for Your Readers.* Chester, Conn.: Globe Pequot Press, 1983.

Simon, Paul. "Throwing Stones." *Columbia Journalism Review,* July–August 1984, pp. 56–57.

This bibliography lists all of the sources the speaker used in preparing the speech. If she (or anyone else) wants to check her information, the bibliography will tell where to look.

SUMMARY

The principles of organization include selecting information that relates to the specific purpose and central idea; distinguishing among the introduction, body, and conclusion of the speech; distinguishing between main and minor points; and phrasing all points in full sentences with parallel structure.

Six patterns of organization work well for organizing speeches: time order, using a chonological sequence; spatial order, moving from left to right, top to bottom, or in any direction that will make the subject clear; cause-and-effect order, showing why something is happening and what impact it is having; problem-solution, explaining a problem and giving a solution; motivated sequence, following the steps of attention, need, satisfaction, visualization, and action; and topical order, arranging the speech into subtopics.

The purpose of the introduction is to set the tone for the speech, introduce the topic, and get the audience's attention. Some attention-getting devices are humor, anecdotes, referring to the occasion, showing the importance of the subject, using startling information, using questions, using personal experiences, and using quotations.

Speech conclusions should give the audience the feeling the speech is over and should tie all the ideas together. In their conclusions, speakers often summarize main ideas, use quotations, and inspire the audience to further actions.

Speech transitions help an audience follow where a speaker is going. They introduce main heads and may be written into a speech outline.

An outline is a way of organizing material so you can see all the parts and how they relate to the whole. In a speech outline, the body of the speech is what is outlined—the introduction and conclusion are handled separately.

The outline shows the organization into main and minor points, through the use of standard symbols and indentation. Many speakers like to construct two outlines: a full-sentence outline for organizing the speech and a key-word outline to summarize the main ideas and to function as notes during delivery of the speech.

VOCABULARY

The following is a list of words you must know to understand the concepts in this chapter. You will find the words defined the first time that each is used in the chapter. All Vocabulary words also appear, with their definitions, in the Glossary at the end of the book.

anecdote
bibliography
body (of speech)
cause-and-effect order
conclusion (of speech)
introduction (of speech)
motivated sequence

outline
problem-solution order
spatial order
time order
topical order
transition

FURTHER READING

BOYD, STEPHEN D., and MARY ANN RENZ. *Organization and Outlining: A Workbook for Students in a Basic Speech Course.* Indianapolis: Bobbs-Merrill, 1985. This workbook can be used by individuals without direction. It helps develop proficiency by systematically providing principles, frequent examples, sample exercises, and possible answers. It begins by discussing points of focus of speeches and ends with the complete outline.

GIBSON, JAMES. *Speech Organization: A Programmed Approach.* San Francisco, Calif.: Rinehart, 1971. Gibson provides a simple, developmental approach to acquiring organizational skills.

HAYNES, JUDY L. *Organizing A Speech: A Programmed Guide,* 2nd ed. Englewood Cliffs, N.J.: Prentice-Hall, 1981. In her book Haynes begins with a review of the elements of outlines. She then discusses the structuring and sequencing of ideas as well as the finishing touches. She offers a step-by-step method for acquiring the essential skills.

WALL, K. WAYNE. *Fundamentals of Outlining: A Self-Teaching Program.* Dubuque, Iowa: Kendall/Hunt, 1983. This is a well-designed program that develops outlining skills. In a useful and instructive way, Wall discusses types of outlines, the appearance of outlines, coordinate and subordinate ideas, supporting material, and common problems.

14 DELIVERING THE SPEECH

CHAPTER OUTLINE

Characteristics of Good Delivery
    Attentiveness
    Conversational quality

Types of Delivery
    Impromptu speaking
    Speaking from a manuscript
    Speaking from memory
    Extemporaneous speaking

How You Look
    Appearance
    Body movement
    Eye contact
    Facial expressions
    Gestures
    Posture

How You Sound
    Volume
    Pace
    Pitch and inflection
    Enunciation

Using Visual Aids
    Types of visual aids
    Rules for using visual aids

Controlling Nervousness

Practicing the Speech
    Preparing the speech
    Trying out the speech
    Practicing actual delivery

Evaluating and Trying Again

CHAPTER OBJECTIVES

After reading this chapter, you should be able to:

1. Explain how to achieve attentiveness in a speech.
2. Explain how to achieve a conversational quality in a speech.
3. Distinguish among the four types of delivery.
4. Explain how movement (body movement, eye contact, gestures) can help a speech.
5. Give the reasons for articulation problems.
6. Distinguish between pitch and inflection.
7. Explain how visual aids can help a speech.
8. Describe the various types of visual aids and what each one can do.
9. Outline the steps you should follow in practicing your speech.

Ginny DeVries had been out of college for two years. She had majored in social work and was now working for the Department of Social Services. Most of her work involved finding foster homes for problem children and helping these children make adjustments to these homes. Ginny loved her work, and when the Social Work Club at her alma mater asked her to speak she was excited by the opportunity. She decided to speak on the subject "Foster Care for Problem Kids," and she hoped to inspire some of the future social work graduates to choose the area of foster care for their own careers.

In preparing her speech, Ginny gathered facts and figures about foster care in the state. She prepared two charts: one with a list of characteristics that make up a good foster home; the other a graph showing the percentage of children who stay out of trouble once they have been in a foster home. As well as her factual and statistical material, she had a large number of examples and anecdotes based on her own experience. She organized all this material into a full-sentence outline—choosing items she thought would be particularly interesting to her audience.

Ginny had not done any public speaking since her speech class in college, but she remembered that it had been very helpful to practice her speech beforehand. So once it was organized, she gave the speech in her living room—pretending it was filled with an audience. On the first run-through she discovered it was 20 minutes long whereas she had been asked to speak for only 15. She set herself to cutting it back, and she also added a couple of transitions to make the speech run more smoothly. When she had finished her editing and revising, she tried giving the speech again—this time in front of a mirror. She found her speech was the right length and the transitions worked very well, but she wasn't using enough gestures. She noted on the margin of her note cards that she should move around a little more and use more gestures. This she would practice in her next run-through. Feeling satisfied with her progress, she went to bed.

The next morning she woke up with a new idea for the introduction. She made a few notes and then went off to work. During her lunch hour, she shut the door of her office and ran through the speech again. As she was giving it, she made an effort to add gestures and to move around. The speech went so smoothly that she felt confident about it and went back to her work.

That evening, on her way to give the speech, she was feeling a little nervous; but she told herself that she was in good shape: the speech was well prepared and she knew she could deliver it well.

When she arrived in the room where she was to give the speech, she was still feeling a little apprehensive, so she took the remaining time to look over her note cards again.

When she stood up to speak, she started with a humorous anecdote, thus winning the complete attention of the audience. Ginny felt that she was off to a good beginning and that this was going to be a good speech. As she spoke, she remembered to look around the room—particularly toward the back row and back corners. She looked at individual audience members. When she was two-thirds through the speech, she noticed some restlessness, so she added an anecdote. Immediately she had the audience's attention again.

When the speech was over, the chairperson asked if there were any questions. With barely a pause, several hands went up. Ginny answered dozens of questions—all of them dealing with different aspects of her work. The questions went on for so long that the chairperson had to call a halt—campus security had come to lock up the room. As the audience left the room, the chairperson told Ginny that this was the best speech the Social Work Club had heard all year. She added, "We'll be sure to invite you back next year." As Ginny drove home, she felt very good about herself. She thought, "I would like to do this again. It was a lot of work but it really paid off."

CHARACTERISTICS OF GOOD DELIVERY

A good speech can bring a lot of satisfaction to the speaker (and to the audience). There is nothing quite like the experience of communicating your ideas, having them understood, and having an entire audience respond to you in a positive way. Yet the experience of speaking to an audience does not come naturally; it is a skill you have to learn. By now it is assumed that you have begun to master the skill of finding material and putting the speech together. Here the focus shifts to delivering the speech.

Attentiveness

You might consider strange the idea that you might be inattentive to the speech you are giving. Yet it's quite possible to be there and functioning as a body while not being there in spirit. When Deb's friend complimented her on the speech she had given in speech class, Deb replied: "You know, it's almost like I wasn't there at all. I don't remember looking at anyone and I barely remember what I said."

Not being attentive to your own speech is really a matter of psychological noise: you are so overcome with the mechanics and anxiety of giving a speech that you forget this is basically a human encounter between a speaker and listeners.

Attentiveness means focusing on the moment. It means saying to yourself that you are here to tell your listeners something important and that you are going to do your very best to communicate with them. It is also a matter of being aware of and responding to their needs. When you have the goal of being attentive to an audience, there are several things you can do:

1. *Pick a topic that is important to you.* If you are speaking on something of high interest and importance to you, it is likely that you will communicate this interest and enthusiasm to your audience. Also, if you can get involved in your subject, you are likely to feel less anxiety about giving the speech.

2. *Do all the work necessary to prepare the best speech possible.* If you work on your speech, organize it, and practice it, you will be much more confident about it and will feel less anxious when the time comes to give it. Then you will be able to concentrate on delivering your speech.

3. *Individualize your audience members.* Try to think of your audience as individual human beings rather than as a mass of people. As you give the speech, think: "I am going to talk to Kathy who sits in the second row. Kevin always looks like he is going to sleep. I am going to give a speech that will wake him up."

4. *Focus on the audience rather than on yourself.* As you speak, look for audience feedback and try to respond to it. The more you can focus on the audience members and their needs, the less likely you are to feel anxiety.

Ginny, for example, had this experience when she gave her speech. She selected a topic, "Foster Care for Problem Kids," that was important to her; she did the work necessary to prepare the best speech she could; she looked at individual audience members; and she focused on the audience rather than on herself. At one point, noting some restlessness in her audience, she even added an anecdote to her speech.

Conversational Quality

Some of our models for public speaking come from orators who address huge audiences. Their voices rise and fall dramatically, their gestures are large and expansive, their voices big and booming. Although this might be an effective speaking technique for some occasions (political rallies and religious revivals), the trend is toward a conversational quality in public speaking.

A conversational quality in speaking means talking before an audience in much the same way we talk when we are having a conversation with another person.[1] The value of a conversational tone in public speaking is that it has the feeling of talking *to* an audience rather than *at* it. Notice how this speaker uses a conversational tone and the word "you" to involve his audience:

> *Have you ever felt embarrassed—I mean really embarrassed—where you never wanted to show your face in public again? Has your face ever turned red when lots of people were watching you? I would guess that you have had this experience once or twice in your life—I know I have. But—have you ever wondered what happens to us physically and psychologically when we are embarrassed?*

How do you achieve a conversational tone in speaking? The most useful way is, while you are planning your speech, to imagine giving your speech to

TRY THIS

Take the following information that has been written in a rather formal style and, using the guidelines suggested for being conversational, try to adapt the material for oral delivery in a conversational style:

> I am not a very funny person although I think I have a reasonable sense of humor. I do enjoy laughing and laughter; however, I have a very difficult time remembering jokes. When I try to tell them to other people— my friends, for example—I either get the information out of sequence or I forget the punch line. I really find the best kind of humor that which flows directly and naturally from the situations in which I find myself. More than anything else, I have found, having a sense of humor involves my willingness to laugh at myself and at life. I think all of us take life, and even ourselves, too seriously. We need to loosen up a bit and just enjoy life for all of its richness, pleasure, and especially—fun!

one person or to a small group of people. Have a mental picture of this person or persons, and try to talk directly to them in a normal, conversational manner. This will help you to achieve the right tone.

However, a conversational tone doesn't mean being casual. A speech occasion is more formal than most conversations. Even though you're aiming for a conversational tone, you don't want long pauses or such conversational fillers as "O.K." or "you know." You should also avoid some of the slang or "in" jokes or expressions you would use in casual conversation.

Here are a few additional hints on how to achieve a conversational quality:

- When you give your speech, imagine you are giving it to someone you know.

- Use contractions such as don't, can't, isn't, and weren't.

- Use words everyone will understand.

TYPES OF DELIVERY

Picture some speeches you have heard. Do you remember how the speech was delivered? From notes? From a manuscript? Was it memorized? Was the speaker making a few brief, off-the-cuff remarks?

Speakers have four ways of delivering a speech: impromptu, from a manuscript, memorized, and extemporaneous.

Impromptu Speaking

Impromptu speaking requires you to give a speech on the spur of the moment. Usually, there is little or no time for preparation. Sometimes your instructor might ask you to give an impromptu speech in class. Other times you might be asked to give a toast or offer a prayer at a gathering, or you may make a few remarks at a meeting.

If you are asked to give an impromptu speech, the most important thing is not to panic. Your main goal is to think of a topic and organize it quickly in your head before you start to speak.

In finding a topic, look around you and at the occasion. Is there anything you can refer to? Formal occasions always occur for a reason. They often honor someone or something, and the person or thing being honored can provide a focus for your speech: "I am delighted to be at this yearly meeting of documentary film makers. Documentary film making is one of the noblest professions. . . ." Other times you might want to refer to the place or the people: "I am happy to be here in Akron again. The last time I was here . . ." or "I am very much touched by the warm reception you have all given me. . . ."

In impromptu speaking it's essential to keep your remarks brief. No one expects you to speak for more than a minute or two. The audience knows that you are in a tight spot, and it doesn't expect a long and well-polished speech.

Speaking from a Manuscript

Speaking from a manuscript involves writing out the entire speech and reading it to the audience. When you read a speech you can get a clear idea of how long it is, so manuscript speaking is a good method when exact timing is necessary. Because a manuscript also offers preplanned wording, political leaders often favor this method when they speak on sensitive issues and want control over what they say. When Jane, for example, decided to run for pres-

---

TRY THIS

Imagine that you are attending a meeting of the student government. The main item for discussion is what entertainment activities the student government should support this year. After an hour or so of debate among student government members, someone says that there should be input from a student who is not in the goverment. The president points to you and asks what you think of the whole issue. How will you respond?

ident of the student government, she prepared a five-minute speech in manuscript form for her appearance on the campus television station with the other candidates. Jane knew that having a manuscript would help her stay within her time limit and would also help her say exactly what she wanted to say. Manuscript delivery also allows for the distribution of copies of the speech and lessens the possibility of being misquoted.

When speaking from a manuscript, speakers find that one problem is trying to sound spontaneous; if listeners think they are being read to, they are more likely to lose interest. Experienced speakers who use manuscripts are often so skilled at delivery that the audience is not aware the speech is being read. Beginning speakers, however, have difficulty making a manuscript speech sound spontaneous and natural.

Feedback is another problem in speaking from a manuscript. If the audience becomes bored and inattentive, it is difficult to respond and modify the speech; the speaker is bound to the manuscript. A manuscript also confines a speaker to the lectern—because that's where the manuscript is.

Speaking from Memory

Speaking from memory involves writing out the entire speech and then committing it to memory word for word. It has the same advantages for speakers as the manuscript method: exact wording can be planned, phrases and sentences can be crafted, and potential problems in language can be eliminated. Also, the speech can be adapted to a specific, set, inflexible time limit. Jess, who was running against Jane in the student election, decided to memorize his speech. He decided this was a good idea because he wanted exact wording but he also wanted the freedom to move around. Feedback was not a problem to Jess because he was speaking to a television audience. In other situations, however, responding to feedback can be a problem because it is difficult for the speaker to get away from what he or she has memorized.

A memorized speech can put considerable pressure on a speaker. Not only does the speaker have to spend hours memorizing the speech, but he or she is also likely to feel anxiety about possibly forgetting it. In addition, making a memorized speech sound natural and spontaneous requires considerable acting talent.

Extemporaneous Speaking

Using the **extemporaneous speaking** method, speakers deliver their speeches from notes. They might commit the main ideas of the speech to memory—possibly also the introduction and conclusion—but they rely on their notes to remember most of the speech.

The extemporaneous method has several advantages. It permits flexibility; speakers can adjust to the feedback of listeners. For example, if the speaker

CONSIDER THIS

The best impromptu speech I ever heard was by Dr. Gordon Lippitt of Organizational Renewal, Incorporated, in Washington, D.C. Dr. Lippitt was a poor man's Jonathan Winters as he grabbed a few markers and began drawing diagrams while presenting his topic. I was so impressed I went to hear him a few weeks later. As a matter of fact I drove through a snowstorm to see what kind of impromptu talk he would give this time, and he gave essentially the same "impromptu" speech I had heard previously. At first I felt as though Lippitt might be putting something over on his audiences. Later I realized what a good speaker he actually is. He has the skill to mix in stories, illustrations, and examples spontaneously.

Source: Terry C. Smith, *Making Successful Presentations: A Self-Teaching Guide.*

CONSIDER THIS

Rosalynn Carter writes of her fear of giving speeches. This fear surfaced when her husband, Jimmy, was governor of Georgia and she was often asked to speak. She writes how she overcame her fear when she discovered the extemporaneous speech:

I went to the luncheon at a downtown hotel armed with my card with six or eight words on it. I tried to appear nonchalant, as though I did this every day with great ease. I carried on a conversation with my hostesses in a conscious effort to keep the speech out of my mind. I even ate my lunch. Finally I was introduced. I stood up to speak and looked out over the crowd and pretended they were all tourists. Suddenly they all looked like tourists—all strangers, all looking at me, just as they did at the mansion—and while I was enjoying the thought because that made it easier, I began to talk about the Governor's Mansion . . . and it was easy. They were listening attentively, and when I got through, they wanted to hear more. So I answered questions with no problem, no problem at all.

The speech over, I said my good-byes, walked calmly from the room, then ran to find a telephone. I couldn't wait to tell Jimmy. I called him at his office: "I did it! I did it!" And Madeline, my secretary, still remembers that day when I got back home: She was in the ballroom looking over the tables being set for a big dinner party that evening when my car drove up, the door opened, and I burst in, saying, "I did it! I did it!"

I had done it. It was a wonderful feeling and quite a breakthrough for me. Although I have never gotten completely over my nervousness, I have been making speeches regularly ever since.

Source: Rosalynn Carter, *First Lady from Plains.*

sees that several audience members do not understand something, he or she can stop and explain. If the audience looks bored, the speaker can try moving around or using a visual aid earlier than planned. The extemporaneous method is the one that comes closest to good conversation because speakers can be natural and responsive to their listeners.

One disadvantage of the extemporaneous method is that the speaker may stumble over or grope for words. However, much of this problem can be overcome by rehearsing the speech beforehand. Sometimes speakers want to use exact words or phrases. Although in extemporaneous speaking the speech as a whole is not memorized, there is nothing wrong with memorizing a particularly important sentence—or having it written down and reading it from a note card.

For the beginning speaker, the extemporaneous method is the best type of delivery. As well as eliminating heavy burdens for the speaker (writing out and/or memorizing the speech), it provides a natural and spontaneous style of speaking. It also makes the listeners a central element in the speech, for the speaker is able to respond to them throughout the speech.

HOW YOU LOOK

Appearance

On days when you are going to make a speech it is a good idea to look your best. Not only does looking good give you a psychological boost, it also gives the audience a positive impression of you. Looking your best doesn't necessarily mean dressing up in your best clothes. If you wear a suit and tie, for example, and everyone else is wearing T-shirts and jeans, you are going to stand out a little too obviously. Looking your best means wearing the top of the line of what everyone else is wearing. This means the new jeans—not the shabby old ones with holes in the knees that bring you luck at final examination time.

Body Movement

Movement usually causes a response. Turn signals on a car attract more attention than tail lights; most of us prefer motion pictures to still photos; the most interesting commercials show the products working. By the same token, a speaker who uses some movement is likely to attract more attention than a speaker who stands absolutely still.[2] When Bill gave his first speech to the class, he discovered that every time he moved he got the audience's complete attention. For his second speech, he decided to move at every transition point—reasoning it was there he had to regain audience attention.

CONSIDER THIS

In his book *You Are What You Wear*, William Thourlby says there is one simple thing you can do that can alter and thereby dramatically change your life:

> *You can change your appearance, by packaging yourself to achieve specific goals, and become happier, more successful, and even richer. . . . It doesn't take too long to conclude that there is a factor operating in success stories that isn't rational, isn't idealistic, and has largely escaped notice. That factor is the tremendous influence our appearance has on others.*

Source: William Thourlby, *You Are What You Wear.*

As well as attracting and keeping attention and helping to make transitions, moving about when you are speaking in public can also help to punctuate the important points in your speech or provide an outlet for your nervous tensions. On the other hand, your movements can also be so distracting to the audience that it loses track of what you are saying. Too much movement that is repetitious or movement that is random or unrelated to what is being said can divert audience attention.

No speaker will be able to engage in much movement if he or she is too tied down with notes. If you have to move back to the lectern constantly to see your notes, you are as limited as a dog on a short leash. The better you know your speech, the more you will be able to experiment with gestures.

Many effective speakers move their entire bodies when they speak. They move from behind the lectern when they want to be informal; they move to the left or right when making a major point; they move away from the audience when they are showing strong emotion.

When you are planning how to deliver your speech, you should consider whether to plan deliberate body movements. If you leave these movements to chance, you might not move at all or move in a way that would be distracting to your listeners. When Susan planned her speech about abused children, she decided to stay behind the lectern when she talked about policy but to move toward the front of the lectern when she talked about individual children. So she wouldn't forget, she made notes about moving on her note cards.

Eye Contact

In our culture, it is considered extemely important to look into the eyes of the person we are talking to. If we don't, we are at risk of being considered dishonest or of having something to hide. Public speaking is no exception. Speakers are expected to scan the audience and to look directly into the eyes of individual audience members.[3]

Eye contact is also an important way of gauging audience reaction to your speech. In her speech explaining how to get coupon refunds, Lynn noticed at one point that some of her audience members were confused. Because of this eye contact she was able to clarify the point she was making.

Ideally, a speaker should be looking directly at the audience 90 percent of the time. If audience members know a speaker is looking at them, they are much more likely to pay attention. Also, a speaker should look at all members of the audience—not just at those in some parts of the room. When you are speaking, work out some sort of plan for eye contact. For example, you could start in the front row, go to the back, and then cut across the room in two diagonals. This way you would look at the entire audience.

Although the idea of this much eye contact may be scary to you, it can have positive benefits. Every audience includes members who look sympathetic and interested in what you are saying. Once you realize you are getting a positive response, you will begin to feel much more confident.

Facial Expressions

Facial expressions are the most difficult movements to change. We seldom have a chance to see our own faces, so it is difficult to know what we are expressing. Generally, however, this is an area of movement that you don't have to worry about *unless you get some negative reaction*. For example, if someone remarks that you looked bored to death while you were giving the speech, this is an area you should work on for your next speech.

Gestures

In speaking, most gestures are made up of hand and arm movements. We usually use gestures to express or emphasize ideas or emotions. Most of us are too stiff when we speak and could benefit by using more gestures. The best way to add more gestures to your speech is to practice in front of a mirror. Always aim for gestures that look spontaneous and that feel natural to you.

Posture

Posture is a matter of how we walk and stand. It can give the audience all sorts of messages. If you drag your feet or slouch, you could be communicating that you are lazy, sick, tired, or depressed—none of which you would want to communicate when giving a speech.

CONSIDER THIS

Shakespeare wrote that all orators give two speeches at the same time: the one which is heard and the one which is seen. You can't *not* communicate. Whether you smile or maintain a blank face, look straight ahead or down at the ground, reach out and touch or hold back, you are communicating and others will attach meaning to that communication.

Source: Alan Garner, *Conversationally Speaking.*

It should also be remembered that the way you sit in your seat, rise and walk to the lectern, and return to your seat after the speech can leave as much of an impression as the posture you use during your speech.

When giving a speech, we usually don't have a very good idea of our eye contact, facial expressions, or general body movement. Because we don't have

Spontaneous gestures that underline a point can be very effective in conveying the message of your speech.

a very good sense of how we look to others, a speech class is a great opportunity to get some feedback. Try to listen to critical remarks from your instructor and classmates without feeling defensive. If you can learn from your mistakes you will improve every time you give a speech.

HOW YOU SOUND

When members of a speech class have a chance to see themselves on videotape, most of them react more negatively to how they sound than to how they look. Very few people really like their own voices.

Our voice reveals things about us that might be far more important than the words we speak.[4] How loud, how fast, how clear and distinct the message—all are part of the information we send about ourselves.

The voice is also a powerful instrument of communication. Because it is so flexible, you can vary it to get the effect you want. You can speak in a loud voice and then drop to a mere whisper. You can go through basic information quickly and then slow down to make your point. You can even use your voice to bring about a change of character. Notice how many different voices your favorite actress or comedian uses.

We have some idea of how we look to other people because we can look into a mirror. However, very few of us have any idea of how we sound, and once we find out, most of us would like to make some changes. Again, your speech class is the place to find out where you need to improve your voice. What follows is a discussion of those aspects of the voice that seem to present the greatest problems to speakers.

Volume

Volume, as we noted in Chapter 5, is how loud you speak. In a public speaking situation, you have to speak loudly enough so that people in the back row can hear you. Because your voice-producing mechanism is so close to your ears, you probably think you are speaking louder than you really are. This means that you probably need to speak in a louder voice than you feel comfortable with.

Always check out the back row to see if people can hear you there. Generally you can tell if they are straining to hear you, and often they will give you some nonverbal sign (e.g., leaning forward) that you need to speak louder. If the place in which you are speaking is unusually large, you could even ask if people in the back can hear.

If people have to strain to hear you, they probably will not make the effort unless you have something extraordinary to say. Also, you should remember that in this society, a weak and hard-to-hear voice implies that the speaker has little confidence. You don't want people to think that about you!

Pace

Like volume, pace is easy to vary. **Pace** refers to how fast or how slowly you speak. If you speak too fast, you may be difficult to understand. If you speak too slowly, you risk losing the attention of your audience. If audience attention seems to be drifting away, try picking up your pace. Usually you don't know that you have been going too fast until someone tells you so after your speech is over. If you are told this, guard against the mistake in the future: in your next speech write reminders on your note cards to slow down.

Ideally the speaker varies his or her pace. Speaking fast and then slowing down help keep the attention of the audience. Also, don't forget the benefits of pausing. A pause before or after a dramatic moment is a highly effective technique. The next time you are watching a comedian on television, watch how he or she uses pauses.

Pitch and Inflection

As we also noted in Chapter 5, pitch is the range of tones used in speaking. **Inflection** is a related concept. It refers to the change in pitch used to give certain words and phrases emphasis. The person who never varies his or her speaking voice is said to speak in a **monotone.** Generally a low-pitched voice is considered more pleasant than a high-pitched one.

Sometimes a person's voice might not seem very interesting because of lack of inflection. If you listen to professional newscasters or sportscasters, you will discover that they use a lot of inflection. By emphasizing certain words and phrases, they help direct the listeners' attention to what is important. Emphasis can also bring about subtle changes in meaning. Try reading the following sentence emphasizing a different word each time you read it. You should be able to read it in at least eight different ways.

You mean I have to be there at seven, tomorrow?

The best way to get inflection in your voice is to stress certain words deliberately—even to the point where it seems as though you are exaggerating. Try taping something in your normal voice and then in your "exaggerated" voice. You might be surprised to find that your "exaggerated" voice is more interesting.

Enunciation

Enunciation is made up of articulation and pronunciation. **Articulation** is the ability to pronounce the letters in a word correctly; **pronunciation** is the ability to pronounce the whole word. Good enunciation is not only important so people will understand us, it is also the mark of an educated person. Most of

TRY THIS

You can practice correct articulation by saying each of the following tongue twisters three times, rapidly.

1. She sells seashells on the seashore.
2. Rubber baby buggy bumpers.
3. The little lowland lubber was a lively lad, lucky, liberal, and likable.
4. The theme is there for them.
5. Betty battled bottles for thirty days.
6. Fanny Finch fried five floundering fish for Frances Fawlie's father.
7. While we waited for the whistle on the wharf, we whittled vigorously on the white weatherboards.
8. Meaninglessly meandering Melina managed to master Monday's memory work.
9. We apprehensively battled with the bragging apprentices, but they broke away from our blows and beat a poor retreat.
10. Grass grew green on the graves in Grace Gray's grandfather's graveyard.

Source: Adapted from Glenn R. Capp, G. Richard Capp, and Carol C. Capp, *Basic Oral Communication.*

our articulation problems go back to the people from whom we learned the language. If our parents, teachers, or peers pronounced words incorrectly, we probably will too.

Three common causes of articulation problems are sound substitution, omission of sounds, and slurring. Sound substitution is very common. Many people say "dere," "dem," and "dose" for "there," "them," and "those." In this case a *d* has been substituted for the more difficult *th* sound. If an American can't get a glass of water in a foreign country it is probably because he or she is asking for "wader" rather than "water." The substitution of a *d* for a *t* in the middle of a word is widespread in American English. If you need any proof, try pronouncing these words as you usually do: "butter," "thirty," "bottle." Unless you have very good articulation, you probably said: "budder," "thirdy," and "boddle."

Some people believe they have a speech defect that makes them unable to produce certain sounds. This can be easily checked. For example, if you always say "dere" for "there," make a special effort to make the *th* sound. If you are able to make it, you have a bad habit, not a speech defect.

TRY THIS

Below is a list of paired words that sound somewhat alike. Read them so that they can be told apart.

accept	except
access	excess
adapt	adopt
amplitude	aptitude
are	our
Arthur	author
ascent	accent
axe	ask
comprise	compromise
consecrate	confiscate
consolation	consultation
disillusion	dissolution
immorality	immortality
line	lion
martial	marital
Mongol	mongrel
pictures	pitchers
statue	statute
vocation	vacation
wandered	wondered

Source: John P. Moncur and Harrison M. Karr, *Developing Your Speaking Voice.*

We also commonly omit sounds. For example, we sometimes say "libary" for "library," dropping the first r sound. And we frequently omit sounds that occur at the ends of words, such as "goin" or "going" and "doin" for "doing."

Slurring is caused by running words together. We use such phrases as "Yawanna go?" and "I'll meecha there." Slurring, as with other articulation problems, is usually a matter of bad speech habits, and it can be overcome with some effort and practice.

Once you are aware of a particular articulation habit, you can try to change it. Changing a habit is not easy, since it probably has been a part of you for many years. Sometimes it helps to drill, using lists of words that give you trouble. It also helps to have a friend remind you when you mispronounce a word. Once you become accustomed to looking for the problem, you will catch yourself more often. If you have several articulation problems, do not try to solve them all at once. Work on one sound at a time; when you can handle that sound, then attempt another one.

Pronunciation is a matter of saying words correctly. Most of us have a bigger reading vocabulary than speaking vocabulary, but we don't know how to pronounce many of the words we read. If you are in doubt about how to pronounce a word, check it in the dictionary.

USING VISUAL AIDS

Visual aids are devices such as charts, graphs, and slides that help illustrate the points you are making in a speech. Visual aids serve three functions in a speech: they help to hold the attention of the listeners, they provide information in the visual channel, and they help the audience to remember what you've said. A study has shown that if members of an audience are given only verbal information, after three days they will remember only 10 percent of what they were told; if they are shown material without verbal communication, they will remember 35 percent. However, if both verbal and visual information is provided, they will remember 65 percent after three days (see Table 14-1). Just because you have a visual aid, however, does not mean that your audience will automatically give you its attention. You may remember sleeping through all the films you were ever shown in elementary school. An audience can sleep through visual aids as easily as it can sleep through the speech itself.

Types of Visual Aids

Visual material should be chosen to help make your topic lively and interesting to the audience. There are numerous types of visual aids to choose from. In making your choice, you should ask yourself which kind of visual material would best illustrate your topic.

TABLE 14-1

RETENTION OF VERBAL/VISUAL INFORMATION

	Percentage of Retention After	
	3 Hours	**3 Days**
Tell only	70	10
Show only	72	20
Show and tell	85	65

CONSIDER THIS

Around 10,000 B.C., during the last period of Paleolithic culture, humans drew leaping bison on the walls of a cave near Altamira, Spain. Today, historians wonder why. Possibly there was some early religious significance. Or maybe prehistoric persons painted merely for their own enjoyment. Well, as long as opinions are being ventured, I'll advance one of my own. Perhaps it was a training session, and the prehistoric presenter had found that the use of visuals added an entirely new dimension to explanatory grunts.

Farfetched? It seems as good an explanation as the others. Why not? Almost 12,000 years later, training experts would be laboring over drawings of their own—curves and bar charts that can increase comprehension and retention by as much as 500 percent.

Source: Terry C. Smith, *Making Successful Presentations: A Self-Teaching Guide.*

The Actual Object

Sometimes it is useful to use the thing you are talking about as a visual aid. An audience likes to see what you are talking about—especially if the object is not familiar to them. One student brought his butterfly collection to illustrate the different types of butterflies found in North America. Another, explaining how to make minor adjustments on one's car, brought a carburetor. Still another borrowed a skeleton from the biology department to illustrate a speech on osteoporosis, a bone disease.

Models

A model is a replica of an actual object, and it is used when the object itself is too large to be displayed (e.g., a building), too small to be seen (e.g., a cell), or inaccessible to the eye (e.g., the human heart). A model can be a very effective visual aid because it shows exactly how something looks. It is better than a picture because it is three-dimensional. Although models are useful, they are not always available. Around colleges and universities, models of various parts of the human body seem to be the most commonly available.

Graphic Charts

Graphic charts—those that use diagrams—are easy to prepare and can be used to condense a lot of information into a useful, understandable form. Perhaps most important, everyone can make a chart. It does not require any special skills.

The most commonly used graphic charts are organizational charts, bar graphs, pie graphs, and line graphs. The last three are all excellent ways of recasting statistical material into visual form.

Organizational Charts If you are talking about the administrative setup of a corporation or institution, you will find an *organizational chart* useful. Figure 14-1 is an example. In this chart, you can easily see how the top person in the organization relates to everyone else. A student describing decision making on campus might use this organizational chart to explain the divisions of authority.

Bar Graphs A *bar graph* is used to show comparisons. It might compare the gross national product of various countries or salaries for new college graduates entering the work force. Whatever it compares, the bar graph is a visual way of making comparisons very clear. One student, speaking on the subject of grade inflation, used a bar graph to show how many students got A's, B's, and so on (see Figure 14-2 on the next page).

Pie Graphs A *pie graph* illustrates how the parts make up the whole. Unlike a bar graph, the parts in a pie graph have to add up to 100 percent. A student who was making a speech about mental health on campus went to the infirmary to get statistics on what mental health problems students reported. He discovered that 40 percent complained of depression; 25 percent, anxiety; 10 percent,

FIGURE 14-1 Organizational Chart of a College

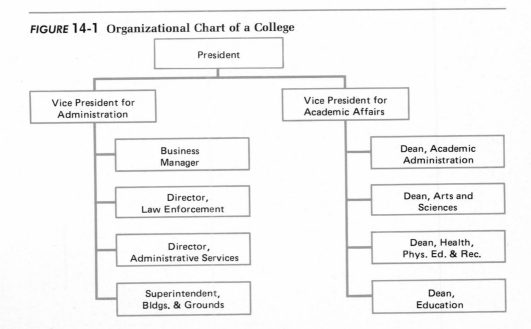

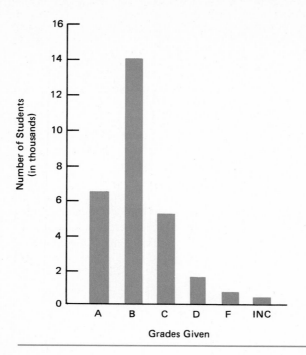

FIGURE 14-2 Bar Graph: Grading of Students in One University

stress; and 25 percent, miscellaneous problems. Rather than read off these statistics in his speech, he put them all into a pie graph labeled "Mental Health on Campus" (see Figure 14-3).

Line Graphs A *line graph* is best for illustrating a trend—a tendency over a period of time. Figure 14-4 illustrates the generally downward trend in SAT scores over a 20-year span. Line graphs have many uses. One student used a line graph to show how student vandalism had decreased over the last ten years. Another student used a line graph to show both a trend and a comparison. In his graph he used two lines: one to show that liberal arts majors were increasing; one to show that education majors were decreasing. He made the lines different colors to make this information clearer.

Other Types of Charts

Charts do not always have to be graphic. Sometimes speakers use charts to list the key points they want the audience to remember. A student whose topic was "Dress for Success" used a chart that listed the following points:

1. Decide on a basic color.

2. Buy basics at one store.

3. Buy accessories at sales.

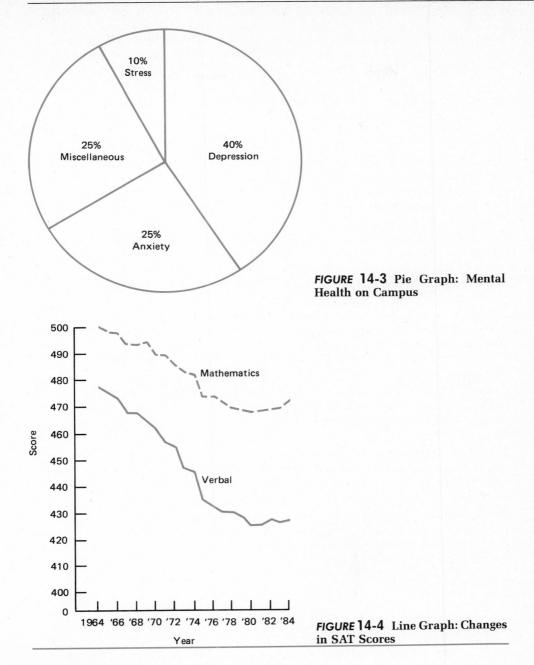

FIGURE 14-3 Pie Graph: Mental Health on Campus

FIGURE 14-4 Line Graph: Changes in SAT Scores

Not only did this chart provide the audience with a way to remember the points, it also gave, in visual form, the general outline of the speech.

Charts can also take the form of pictures. One student, speaking of the new styles in cars, used pictures to show the latest model of cars. Another used pages from magazines to illustrate how advertisements for products are designed to appeal to our fantasies. You don't always have to use someone else's pictures. Try drawing your own. You will find that even simple stick figures can be effective. One student found that stick figures were adequate to illustrate the proper arm positions for golf swings.

Projected Material

Movies, videos, slides, and other projected material are useful visual aids. When you are using projected material, remember that it should enhance, not replace, your speech. Most classroom speeches are too short for movies. Showing just a segment of a movie is a possibility, but it would probably be more trouble than it is worth.

Videos have interesting potential as visual aids. If your college has video facilities or if you have your own equipment, you could easily make your own video. One student made a video tape illustrating four basic karate moves for his speech. Because the video is so easy to work with, he was able to stop it, talk about the move, then go on to the next one. Another student, speaking about a dangerous crossing on the campus, made a short video of students trying to cross the street. Her video was an effective way of persuading her audience of the need for a traffic light.

You may have slides you could use in a speech or you may have access to a set of slides that have been commercially produced. Since you are giving a speech rather than a slide show, however, you should limit the number of slides you use. One student who had traveled to China decided to limit her slides to those of the Great Wall. She figured this scene would be of the greatest interest to her audience.

Overhead projectors are a very easy way of showing visual material. With an overhead, a page from a book can be shown enlarged on a movie screen— which is much less complicated than copying from the book onto a chart. With an overhead projector you can also draw your information on an ordinary-sized piece of paper since it will appear enlarged on the screen.

Whatever projection equipment you use, make sure you know how to use it. Try out the procedure and time it before you have to give your speech. You might also want to consider having someone run the equipment for you— leaving you free to concentrate on your speech without having to worry about technicalities.

Other Types of Visual Aids

Besides those mentioned above, there are other possibilities for visual aids. Maps can help to illustrate a speech. For example, the student who spoke on China could have used a map to show where the Great Wall is located. And don't overlook the blackboard—it is accessible and easy to use.

Handouts are still another possibility. When material is a bit complex or when there is a lot of it, listeners may need it right in front of them. Make certain you have enough copies for everyone. Keep in mind, however, that using something that needs to be passed among audience members can be a source of distraction. Speakers need to maintain control. If handouts are used, you should think of ways to regain attention and control. One way might be to say, "Now, would everyone please turn the chart (handout) over?" Another would be to hand out the material only at the close of the speech.

Rules for Using Visual Aids

You want a visual aid that will really work for you. The wrong one could detract from your speech and make it much less effective.

When you are considering a visual aid, subject it to the following rules:

1. *Use the visual aid to supplement, not replace, the speech.* The visual aid should not become the whole show. It should be a useful addition to support the speech.

2. *Choose visual aids for areas that need more explanation.* Look over your speech and decide which details could be better explained by a visual aid. Is there a particular statistic you want to stress? Will something be more easily understood if your audience can see it? Will it help your speech to show your main points visually?

Visual aids such as an easel or tape shown on a monitor can enhance a speech providing that they are interesting and well integrated with your presentation.

3. *Show the visual aid only when you are ready for it.* Put the visual in an inconspicuous place; then, when you are ready to use it, take it out. When you are finished with it, put it away. You don't want it to compete with you for attention.

4. *Make sure everyone can read the visual aid.* When making a chart, use a dark marker with a thick tip so you can draw bold lines that will show up. If you have any doubts, check it out beforehand. Set it up in the front of the room and stand in the farthest corner to see if you can read it. If you can't read it easily, fix it so you can.

5. *Before your speech, check out the room to see if your visual aid can be easily displayed.* If you are using projection equipment, find the electrical outlets and see if the room has blackout curtains. If you are hanging a chart, decide how to hang it. Are you going to need tape or thumbtacks?

6. *Practice with your visual aid before the speech.* If you are using a chart, be careful not to block it with your body. if you are using any kind of equipment, make sure you know how to use it. If you are using something complicated such as projection equipment, consider having a classmate run it for you. If you do this, practice with him or her. When practicing with your visual aid, check to see how much time it takes. If it is going to take too much time, decide how you will cut back.

7. *Talk to the audience, not to the visual aid.* Visual aids can be looked at occasionally, but speakers must remember to maintain eye contact with the audience.

8. *Maintain control of the speech situation.* Since visual aids can distract audience attention away from you, keep them simple.

TRY THIS

The next time you use a visual aid, subject it to the following check:

1. Can everybody see it?
2. Is it short and simple? Did you use color, dark lines, and heavy letters?
3. Will you need a pointer?
4. Is there a place to put the visual aid before and after it is needed?
5. Does the visual help to make the speech better?
6. Do you need anything to mount the visual aid?
7. Do you know how much of your speech time using the visual will take?

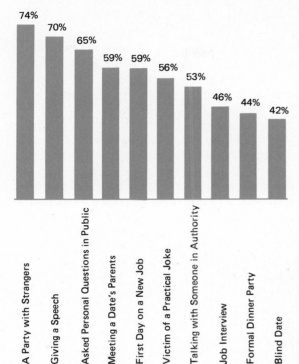

74%

70%

65%

59% 59%

56%

53%

46%
44%
42%

A Party with Strangers

Giving a Speech

Asked Personal Questions in Public

Meeting a Date's Parents

First Day on a New Job

Victim of a Practical Joke

Talking with Someone in Authority

Job Interview

Formal Dinner Party

Blind Date

FIGURE **14-5 Situations Causing the Most Anxiety***
In surveys of several hundred men and women, these situations were reported as producing the most anxiety.
* The research was done by Warren Jones at the University of Tulsa and Dan Russell at the University of Ohio College of Medicine.

CONTROLLING NERVOUSNESS

We all experience times in our lives when we feel nervous about performing. As you can see in Figure 14-5, many people feel nervous when they are going to give a speech.

You might be surprised to learn, however, that nervousness is not always a negative factor; it can make you feel more alert and energetic. One student commented, after her speech was over, that she felt her nervousness had helped her to feel especially aware of the audience and how it was responding to her. Another student said, "I could feel strength surging in me. Things I practiced by myself came out with so much more force, life, and spirit than I thought I had."

Your reaction to nervousness should not be to try to eliminate it but to control it. When you enter a situation in your speech class that makes you feel nervous, it is important to remember that you are not expected to be perfect; your instructor does not expect it, nor do your classmates. A speech communication class is structured in such a way as to give you maximum support. Its aim is to build skills; you start with easy tasks and work up to the harder ones.

Another key to controlling nervousness is to recognize that you are not alone. Although they might not show it, even seasoned performers are not immune to nervousness. Entertainers, U.S. presidents, sports personalities— almost all communicators experience it. Ask an experienced teacher if he or she feels nervous when facing a new class at the beginning of the semester. The answer is sure to be yes. It might also help to remember that most of your classmates are feeling as nervous as you are.

Physical activity helps to control nervousness because it provides a channel for releasing excess energy. Shortly before you are going to give a speech, try working off some of this energy through physical activity such as running, biking, or a series of exercises.

As you gain in experience, although you may still feel nervous, you will find yourself more in control. You will find that people didn't even notice when you made little fluffs. Perhaps more important, you will discover that most people didn't notice how nervous you were. If you don't tell them, other people won't know that your mouth was dry or your knees were shaking.

Finally, practicing a speech will help you to control your nervousness. You will gain confidence if you know what you're going to say and when you're going to say it. How to practice, then, is the next point to consider.

PRACTICING THE SPEECH

This section outlines a method for practicing your speech. You might feel some resistance about going through this kind of practice session—probably because you feel silly talking to an empty room. Yet if you go into a store and buy a new item of clothing, you probably will spend a lot of time in the dressing room looking at it from all angles. By practicing, you are doing the same thing with a speech. You are trying it on to see if it fits you; if it doesn't, you will have time to make the necessary alterations.

How can you practice delivery so you will feel comfortable with the content and language and yet not get so locked into the speech that it sounds memorized or mechanical? Here is a plan that seems to work well for most speakers.

Preparing the Speech

Before you give your speech in a practice session, you should do the following:

1. Prepare the content thoroughly. Your speech will be no better than what you've put into it. Do you have a clear statement of purpose? Do the materials you collected support this statement of purpose? Have you done enough research to provide support for each of your main points?

CONSIDER THIS

Of course, the more common way to communicate with your people is to talk to them as a group. Public speaking, which is the best way to motivate a large group, is entirely different from private conversation. For one thing, it requires a lot of preparation. There's just no way around it—you have to do your homework. A speaker may be very well informed, but if he hasn't thought out exactly what he wants to say *today, to this audience,* he has no business taking up other people's valuable time.

Source: Lee Iacocca with William Novak, *Iacocca: An Autobiography.*

2. Organize your content into a full-sentence outline. Have you made the proper distinction between main idea and supporting points? Does your outline flow clearly and logically? Are you quite clear about what you are going to say in your introduction and conclusion? Is your conclusion worded in such a way that you can end the speech and sit down without feeling awkward?

3. From your full-sentence outline, prepare a key-word or short-phrase outline that you can use for rehearsal and while you give your speech. Put your key-word outline on one side of a 3 × 5 card. Can you follow the speech from this outline? Have you written out phrases or quotations that you want to quote precisely? Can you read the cards easily?

Trying Out the Speech

During the tryout session, emphasis should be on the content of the speech and whether it is working the way you imagined it in your head. (There is often a big difference between the way we imagine something will sound and the way it really sounds.) In this session you want to actually say the words—stopping to clear up imprecise language, maybe adding a transition, trying out the conclusion. In this practice session, it will take you a while to get through the speech because you will be making corrections as you go along.

Practicing Actual Delivery

The next stage is to actually deliver the speech. As you practice your delivery, try to imagine an audience.

CONSIDER THIS

Some of the world's greatest orators were not born with the talent to speak. Paul J. Micali cites the example of Demosthenes, a famous Greek orator:

Demosthenes . . . was born with a weak voice. He lisped, enunciated poorly, and couldn't pronounce the letter r. Yet determination helped him overcome these handicaps. He practiced with pebbles in his mouth, shouted over the roaring breakers on the shores of Phaleron, recited while running uphill, striving to deliver more and more lines with one breath, and rehearsed before a mirror to improve his gestures.

In spite of all these efforts he failed a number of times to win over his listeners. They laughed at him and he was crushed, but not so crushed that he gave up the whole idea. In fact, he actually built an underground chamber where he could project his voice and perfect his delivery without interruption. And for three months at a time he would shave one half of his entire head so that he would resist the temptation to desert his training program and mingle with his friends in "pleasurable pursuits." He overcame all obstacles and became one of the world's greatest orators.

Source: Paul J. Micali, *How to Talk Your Way to Success: The Secrets of Effective Business Communication.*

1. Stand against one wall and look over your "audience." Try to establish eye contact with all other parts of the room.

2. Check your beginning time. In this practice session you want to find out how long your speech is.

3. Deliver the speech all the way through without stopping. As you are speaking, remember to look at your "audience."

4. When the speech is over, check your end time.

5. Now ask yourself these questions: Did any parts of the speech give you difficulty? Did the speech seem clearly organized? Check over your outline. In giving the speech, did you leave anything out? Was your outline clear and easy to follow? How about time? Did you need to add or delete any material to make the speech the proper length?

6. Make the necessary changes and practice the speech again.

You should practice delivering the speech until you feel comfortable with it. As you practice, try to use wording that sounds natural to you. Every time you speak, your wording should be a little bit different—otherwise your speech will sound mechanical. Also, during your practice sessions you should become less and less dependent on your notes. See if you can get away from them as much as possible.

If you feel that you need a lot of practice to feel comfortable with your speech, it is better not to do all the practice sessions at one time. Put the speech away for a few hours or even overnight. The next time you approach it, you might be surprised to find fresh ideas or ways of solving problems that you couldn't solve before.

EVALUATING AND TRYING AGAIN

Many speakers feel their work is done after they speak the final words of their conclusion. However, some of the most valuable work begins after the speech is over. This is the time to ask whether you reached your goal and to discover what effect you had on your audience.

These questions can be partly answered by the feedback you received during your speech. While you were giving the speech, how did the audience respond? Did you get attention at the beginning of the speech and lose it later? If so, why? You may be able to answer some of these questions even while you are giving the speech, but you can probably best discover the answers after the speech is over.

Some of your most useful feedback will come with the discussion and questions following the speech. Questions often indicate whether the audience followed the speech and understood what you were saying. Lively discussion is usually a sign that you have stimulated thinking among audience members. Everyone does not have to agree with you to make the speech successful. The most negative feedback may be no feedback at all—an apathetic audience that has no questions and no comments.

The classroom situation provides an unusual opportunity for speech analysis. During the students' first speeches, the instructor (and perhaps the class) will spend a lot of time discussing each speech—particularly with regard to delivery. We would all like to think that we have delivered a perfect speech, but that doesn't always happen—especially the first time. You will be receiving some criticism. Sometimes this criticism may seem threatening, so it is important to remember that the comments refer only to the speech—its content and the way you delivered it—they are not directed at you as a person. If you can accept criticism in this spirit, it will prove very useful. You will be able to change bad habits and to become aware of some problems you may not have known about. Once you are aware of your problems, you are ready to try again. By the time you give your last speech in class, you might be close to giving a perfect speech.

SUMMARY

Good delivery in a speech involves attentiveness—focusing and paying attention to giving the speech. It also involves achieving a conversational quality in your speech.

The four ways of delivering a speech are speaking impromptu, with very little preparation; speaking from a manuscript; speaking from memory; and speaking extemporaneously, from notes. For the beginner, extemporaneous speaking is the best type of delivery because it permits the speaker to depend on notes and still sound spontaneous.

All speakers should be aware of how they look and what they can do to look better. Speakers should concentrate on what they wear, their body movement, eye contact, gestures, and posture so that they appear at their very best.

How the speaker sounds is also an important consideration in public speaking. Speakers should pay special attention to volume, pace, pitch and inflection, and enunciation. If they find they have a problem with one of these areas, they should work to improve it.

All speakers should consider using visual aids in their speeches. Visuals help to hold attention and to clarify information in the speech. Some of the most common visual aids include the actual object, models, charts, and projected material. When using visual aids, make sure that they can be easily read and that they enhance the speech rather than take over.

Most people are nervous at the thought of giving a speech. This nervousness can be a positive force because it makes the speaker feel especially alert and energetic. The best way to get nervousness under control is to recognize that most people are nervous in a similar situation. Physical activity and practice before a speech can help reduce nervousness.

The final step in getting ready to deliver a speech is to practice it. Your practice should include rehearsing delivery of the speech, imagining an actual audience, checking the speech for clarity and organization, and checking its length.

The speech class is the best place to learn how to give a speech. Listen and learn from the criticism of your speech. That is how you will improve.

VOCABULARY

The following is a list of words you must know to understand the concepts in this chapter. You will find the words defined the first time that each is used in the chapter. All Vocabulary words also appear, with their definitions, in the Glossary, at the end of the book.

articulation	monotone
enunciation	pace
extemporaneous speaking	pronunciation
impromptu speaking	visual aids
inflection	

FURTHER READING

BRADSHAW, PETE. *Personal Power: How to Build Self-Esteem and Improve Performance.* Englewood Cliffs, N.J.: Prentice-Hall, 1983. We recommend this book because of the close relationship Bradshaw establishes between power and self-esteem. He considers power from a personal, individual perspective and develops several models for observing and thinking about power.

COOPER, MORTON. *Change Your Voice, Change Your Life.* New York: Macmillan, 1984. Cooper provides a plan that requires everyday practice to acquire a natural, dynamic voice that will influence others and improve your self-image.

DONALDSON, LES. *Conversational Magic: Key to Poise, Popularity and Success.* West Nyack, N.Y.: Parker, 1981. This is a very practical book on expanding your personality, improving conversation, and understanding others. Donaldson includes a chapter that outlines techniques of telling interesting stories, developing humor, and joining any conversation without preparation—useful for those who must give impromptu speeches.

FLETCHER, LEON. *How to Speak Like a Pro.* New York: Ballantine Books, 1983. This is a practical, how-to approach to speaking. Every chapter includes lists of methods for accomplishing any task associated with public speaking. It is a comprehensive, lively handbook.

GARNER, ALAN. *Conversationally Speaking.* New York: McGraw-Hill, 1981. Garner identifies several specific skills vital for social effectiveness. These skills build self-confidence and can be transferred naturally to public-speaking situations.

HAHNER, JEFFREY C., MARTIN A. SOKOLOFF, SANDRA SALISCH, and GEOFFREY D. NEEDLER. *Speaking Clearly: Improving Voice and Diction,* 2nd ed. New York: Random House, 1986. This is a readable and helpful textbook for those taking a voice and diction course. The book concentrates on materials and approaches that have proved themselves in the classroom. It includes material for numerous drill exercises and an excellent special chapter on dealing with nervousness.

MICALI, PAUL J. *How to Talk Your Way to Success: The Secrets of Effective Business Communication.* New York: Dutton, 1983. Micali focuses essentially on presentation skills. From the basics, he discusses bad habits, vocabulary, nervous tension, physical tension, creating impact, the need to look for a public platform, and gaining the upper hand.

NELSON, ROBERT B. *Louder & Funnier: A Practical Guide for Overcoming Stagefright.* St. Paul, Minn.: Pragmatic Publications, 1984. Nelson first explains the nature of stage fright, then the reasons why we fear, and his model for overcoming it. In addition, he offers other methods for overcoming stage fright and controlling its symptoms. He includes a separate chapter on "Overcoming Stagefright During Delivery."

WYDRO, KENNETH. *Think on Your Feet: The Art of Thinking and Speaking Under Pressure.* Englewood Cliffs, N.J.: Prentice-Hall, 1981. This is one of the few books written especially for those facing impromptu speech situations. Useful and enjoyable, it is a practical, skills-oriented book full of examples, suggestions, and specific guidelines.

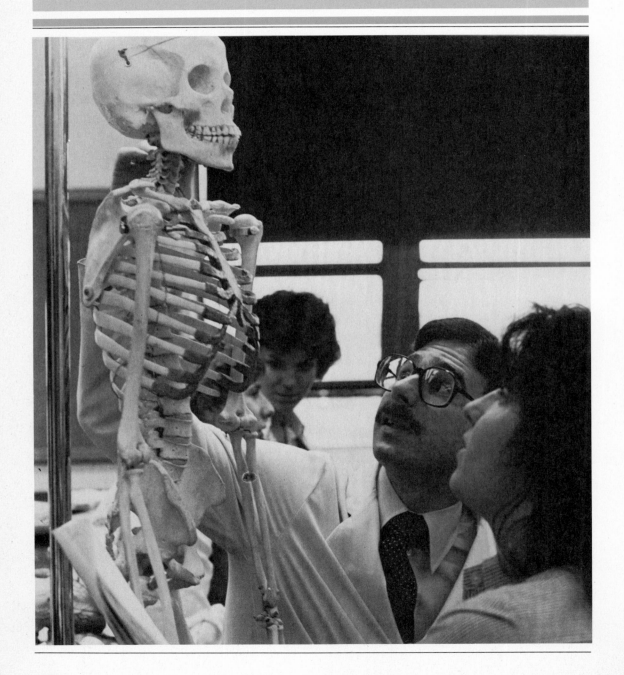

15 *THE INFORMATIVE SPEECH*

CHAPTER OUTLINE

CHAPTER OBJECTIVES

After reading this chapter, you should be able to:

1. Get the attention of listeners.
2. Increase listener understanding.
3. Help aid listener retention.

4. Use specific strategies in informative speeches.

Mike is studying to be a dietician. Since he works in the college cafeteria to help pay for his education, when he is assigned to give an informative speech he decides to explain to his classmates how the college food service plans and readies meals. In preparation for the speech, he interviews the head dietician at the college, finds several books on diet and nutrition in the card catalog, and even writes a letter to the American Dietetic Association for more information.

Susan is taking a course in robotics, so her informative speech is about how robots are being used to build television sets. Like Mike, she looks for books and articles in the library. She also arranges to spend some time observing robots at work on the assembly line at a local factory. Although Susan's presentation will be concerned mostly with the technical aspects of robotics, she is also interested in the human problem. Before she leaves the factory, she interviews the union president and asks whether robots are considered to be a threat to jobs.

Kevin is a student worker in the audiovisual department of the university. Now that fall classes are starting, he is going to hold several training sessions for the students who run movie projectors. He knows he is going to have to do a thorough job, for once the projectionists start showing films all over the campus, he is not going to be there to help them. As he plans his training sessions, he writes down a list of steps that have to be gone through to load a film in the projector. Once he has figured out the steps, he is going to have the list duplicated so that each projectionist can have a copy.

Lori, the manager of the campus radio station, is preparing notes for a meeting with her advertising staff. The main subject of the meeting will be the new system of logging, selling, and playing commercials. Lori prepares some facts and figures about the amount of money made on advertising over the past year and how much she predicts can be made this year if the system is changed. She feels confident that when her staff members see the reason for the change, they will accept it.

Mike, Susan, Kevin, and Lori all have something in common: they are preparing information. Like a majority of people in the United States, much of what they do is concerned with producing, processing, and distributing information.

If these students had been in school 30 or 40 years ago, they might not have been so involved with information. In 1950 only about 17 percent of the population worked in information jobs. Now, however, almost 60 percent of us work with information.[1] What are these information jobs? They include programmers, teachers, clerks, secretaries, accountants, stock brokers, managers, insurance people, bureaucrats, lawyers, bankers, technicians, doctors and nurses, and journalists—to name just a few.[2]

This increasing emphasis on information demands greater skill in our ability to produce and deliver it. Although some of this information is delivered in written form, much of it is oral: the teacher before the class, the radio or television reporter broadcasting to an audience, the professional sharing ideas with colleagues, the employer explaining policies to employees—all of them need oral skills to convey information.

The informative speech—one that defines, clarifies, instructs, and explains—is a common phenomenon in our society. If we are going to prosper in the information society, the ability to give an informative speech is going to be a very useful skill.

GOALS OF THE INFORMATIVE SPEECH

With so much information available, it is surprising that listeners don't topple from information overload. When listeners are so overloaded with information, we face a serious problem as speakers. We have to ask ourselves: "How can I, as an informative speaker, make *my* information stand out?"

Getting Attention

The first goal of the speaker is to get the attention of the audience members. In most public speaking situations there are many distractions: people come

If you plan a career in business, you will have many occasions to present information to groups—to plan a project, report on finances, summarize the results of a marketing study, and so on. Learning informative speaking skills now will be an asset to you.

in late, the air conditioner fan turns on and off, a fly is buzzing around the room, the microphone is giving off feedback.

Once you have attention, there is no assurance that you will keep it. Attention spans are short. You have probably noticed that as you listen to a speech or lecture, your attention wanders—even when you are very interested in the speaker's message. Since this pattern of wandering attention is characteristic of most listeners, as a speaker you have to work to get attention back again.

The best way to get and keep attention is to create a strong desire to listen to your material. Ask yourself whether the material is *relevant*. Does it apply to the people in your audience? If it doesn't, how can it be adapted to them?

One speaker, informing his audience about the protective tiles that cover the space shuttle, had a unique opportunity to make his topic relevant to his listeners:

> These protective tiles are made from the thinnest glass fibers ever made. They are so thin that one pound of them, laid end to end, would stretch for about 10 million miles. You say, "So what?" Do you know who invented these glass fibers? Dominick Labino. You say, "So what? Who's he?" Did you know that he lives and works within ten miles of where we are sitting? Some of you have heard of him? Did you know that within 50 feet of where we are right now, there is a popular glass sculpture that you have all seen, that was made by Dominick Labino?[3]

Notice how the speaker told the listeners first that the tiles are being made in the local area. Notice, too, how he mentioned they were sitting in close proximity to one of the glass sculptures. Both of these devices made the speech more relevant to the audience.

If the audience perceives the information as *new*, it is more likely to pay attention. New doesn't necessarily mean a subject no one has ever heard about—it might be a matter of a new perspective or a new angle. Certain topics are going to provoke a "ho hum" reaction from the audience. You don't want your audience to think, "Not another speech about jogging . . . or saving money . . . or stopping smoking." When one student decided to speak on physical fitness, he wanted to give a new perspective to an old topic. Knowing that physical fitness had already been the subject of other speeches (as well as countless articles and books), he talked about how to tailor a physical fitness program to each individual's needs, and he concentrated on the importance of finding a program that is safe. He started this way:

> For years, Jim Fixx has been the guru of the joggers. He has urged housewives to leave their pots and pans, and sedentary executives to take up their shoes and run. Fixx showed the way. He wrote the books on jogging and practiced what he preached. Every day he was out there running—burning up the pavement as he covered mile after mile for physical fitness.

One warm morning Fixx was out on his usual run. Although no one was there to watch him get ready, we can assume that he followed his regular routine; he did his stretching and warm-up exercises and set out running on one of his favorite New England roads. Although we don't know how his run began, some of us have heard how it ended. Fixx's body was discovered on the road by a motorist. He had died of a massive heart attack while running.

Although audience members knew this speaker was going to speak on physical fitness, most of them did not expect such a speech to begin with a story about the death of a runner.

Increasing Understanding

Since the goal of an informative speech is to give the audience new or in-depth information on a subject, it is particularly important that speakers put together a speech that audience members will understand. Several things will help understanding: language choice, organization, and illustrations and examples.

Language Choice

In a highly technological world, many of us are speaking a language that is understood only by people in the same field. Because we are so accustomed to this language, we often don't realize that other people don't know what we are talking about. If you are giving a speech that uses a technical or specialized vocabulary, you must take the time to stop and define your terms. Or consider whether you can avoid technical terms altogether.

Organization

Organization not only helps you to put your speech together, but it also helps listeners understand what you are talking about. A good organizational pattern will show the relationship of ideas to each other as well as help you move from one idea to another. Recent research has found, in addition, that listeners give higher ratings to better-organized speeches.[4]

Illustrations and Examples

Probably the greatest key to understanding is an ample supply of illustrations and examples. If you are going to explain a principle that might be unfamiliar to your audience, use an example to show what it is or how it works. For example, a student who was explaining three basic body types held up pictures to illustrate each type. When he held up the related picture, a term such as "ectomorph" was immediately clear.

Helping Retention

An important goal of informative speaking is to have your listeners remember what you said once the speech is over. Listeners are more likely to remember speeches where they had some kind of emotional involvement. This involvement might range from sympathy when they hear about an adult who can't read to high interest in a speech about how to get a better job. For the speaker, then, the goal is to involve the listeners by speaking about subjects they can identify with or that have an impact on their lives.

When you want people to remember certain points, it is useful to give these points a special emphasis. Sometimes this can be done with verbal cues: "This is my most important point" or "If you remember only one thing I said today, remember this." Sometimes you can use a cue after a point: "Now let me show you how important what I just said can be to you." Points can be emphasized, too, by repeating them, by changing your pacing of the speech when you need emphasis, or by using a pause just before the point to be emphasized.[5]

STRATEGIES FOR INFORMATIVE SPEECHES

There are different types of strategies for informative speeches. Each type requires a special skill. Sometimes all of these types can be found in a single speech; usually at least two will be used.

Defining

Richard M. Weaver, one of the best-known teachers of the art of public speaking of our time, gave "definition" a place of prime importance. He regarded definition as the most valuable type of development because it builds from the essential nature or essence of things.[6]

How do speakers go about the task of establishing clear definitions in their listeners' minds? They have six ways to do this: etymology, classification, synonym, example, comparison, and function. Again, more than one method can be used in a speech.

Etymology

Etymology, study of the origin and development of words, can be used as a basis for definition. For example, when discussing romantic love and the intense feelings that occur, one speaker pointed out that the word "ecstasy," which is a common label for emotions during the time of romantic love, is derived from a Greek word meaning deranged—a state beyond all reason and self-control.[7] She went on to show that the word "deranged" accurately describes the state of mind that exists early in romantic relationships. The *Oxford English Dictionary* provides the best source for word etymologies.

Classification

Classification means arranging things according to some systematic division. By classifying things we give them boundaries.

Chapter 13, on organization, discussed topical order—breaking down the topic into subtopics, or various aspects of the subject—as one way of arranging things. For example, in a speech about fundamentalist politics, a speaker divided her speech into two subtopics: (1) that such politics were exclusionary and (2) that they polarized the political system.[8] This is one way to classify in a speech. Another way is by time sequence. In a speech about building a house, the speaker started by discussing the foundation and concluded with painting the interior.

Synonym

A **synonym** is a word that has the same or nearly the same meaning as another of the same language. An **antonym** has the opposite meaning. These two, synonyms and antonyms, make up the most popular ways of defining. "What does she mean by 'cumbersome'?" one person asks. "Awkward and hard to manage," another replies. We hear such explanations often.

In her speech "David: And a Whole Lot of Other Neat People," provided in full at the end of this chapter, Kathy Weisensel quoted the synonyms used by E. Milo Pritchett to establish the difference between mental retardation and mental illness:

> *Mental retardation is a condition of impaired, incomplete, or inadequate mental development. . . . Mental retardation is NOT mental illness. Mental illness is a breakdown of mental functions which were once normal. Specialized care and treatment may restore the person to normalcy. Retardation is a condition for which there is no cure.*[9]

Pritchett uses "impaired mental development," "incomplete mental development," and "inadequate mental development" as synonyms. He makes it clear that we should not use the term "mental illness" when we mean "mental retardation."

Example

An example is something that is used to illustrate a point. When using an example, the speaker often either points to an actual thing or points out something verbally. For example, in a speech about finding the correct colors for a wardrobe, a speaker draped members of her audience with actual pieces of fabric so audience members could see what colors worked best.

Another student used a verbal example. Speaking on proposed cutbacks in student aid, he said, "The new changes in student loans would mean that one-third of the people getting loans on this campus would no longer be eligible." Notice that both of these examples make the speech come to life by providing material the audience can relate to.

Comparison

Comparisons point out the similarities between two or more things. This is how Ralph Baruch compared two schools of thought regarding our future:

> There is a school of thought that believes "the more things change, the more they stay the same." There is another school across the street that regards the dynamism of cultural and technological change as a very real force in shaping human destiny.
> I got my diploma from that second school. I admit that I am addicted to the future. I see change not only as inevitable, but desirable.[10]

Baruch's entire speech is based on defining change as desirable. He establishes the desirability of change at the outset through comparison, then develops his speech from there.

Function

Function involves how things perform or how they can be used. Sometimes, function is more important than etymology or classification. For example, etymology or classification would not be very useful in defining BASIC, a computer language. However, it is useful to define it in terms of its function:

> Most personal computers come with some kind of BASIC language. BASIC is a programming language that interprets English-like instructions in a computer program. You can use the BASIC in your professional computer to write your own programs or, more commonly, use programs written by others in BASIC for your computer.[11]

Defining ideas with respect to function provides a practical base with which listeners can identify. Speakers can stress an object's usefulness, advantages, benefits, convenience, or service.

Describing

In using descriptions, speakers attempt to provide a clear and vivid mental impression. They try to get listeners to see what something looks like or how the parts fit together. To describe is to picture in words. To describe effectively, then, speakers must use careful and precise wording. In the following extract, Daniel R. Crary uses description to portray an automobile accident:

TRY THIS

For each of the following ideas, decide which kinds of definitions would work in a speech: etymology, classification, synonym, example, comparison, or function.

love	*in loco parentis*
inflation	unbeatable bargain
educational opportunity	intimate relationship
a movie beyond comparison	alcoholic
aerobics	job skills

In Los Angeles, California, during rush hour on a heavily traveled, fog-shrouded freeway twelve lanes wide, a woman's car blew a tire, careened to the side of the lane and stopped. But out of the fog came another car which could not stop in time, and it struck the first . . . and another and another until one of the worst automobile accidents in history had involved a string of 200 cars, over a mile long.[12]

When describing things to an audience, a speaker's descriptions can cover any or all of the following areas: size or quantity, shape, weight, color, composition, age, and fit.

Size or Quantity

In the preceding quotation, Crary used "twelve lanes wide," "200 cars" and "over a mile long," to describe the accident. In another speech, the speaker referred to size when he said, "I came from a very small street, in a very small town, in the very heart of this huge country."

Shape

In a speech on "Bigfoot" one college student used description in his quotation from an article in *Science Digest*. Notice the emphasis on shape:

What people usually report is something seven to eight feet tall with an extremely heavy build—about eight hundred pounds—and covered with a fairly dense coat of brown or black hair two to four inches long. Its face has less hair or is naked; it looks somewhat like a gorilla's face, but much longer. Its shoulders are large and high, so that the mouth and chin are below shoulder level, which is a very apelike characteristic. But it walks on two legs in a human manner, with the walking hinge, the hip joint, about mid-height.[13]

The student emphasized shape with words like "extremely heavy build," a face that looks longer than a gorilla's face, shoulders that are large and high, and its human manner of walking.

Weight

People have a hard time visualizing large numbers. So speakers need to relate them to something from the listeners' own experience. One speaker was trying to impress her listeners with how much a million was. She said that a class in Des Moines, Iowa, collected 1 million bottle caps. According to the speaker, these caps weighed 2½ tons. "They were put into 200 bags and the bags were so heavy it required a moving van to take them away."

Color

Color is an obvious component of description and serves quickly to call up mental pictures. In his speech on "Bigfoot" the speaker described Bigfoot's hair as being brown or black. Look at the emphasis placed on color by books such as *Color Me Beautiful* and *Color for Men.*[14] It is an important descriptive element.

Composition

Composition refers to the make-up of a thing. Describing the composition of something helps call up a clearer, more accurate mental picture. Examples are "the craggy Maine coast" or "a person whose wrinkles have been chiseled into his face like a time-worn monument." In the speech on "Bigfoot," can you visualize "a fairly dense coat of brown or black hair two to four inches long"? That is effective description.

Ralph Zimmerman used composition effectively in his speech "Mingled Blood." He was talking about the need for blood:

> *Your blood, dark and rich, rich with all the complex protein fractions that make for coagulation—mingled with the thin, weak, and deficient liquid that flows in his [the hemophiliac's] veins.*[15]

Age or Newness

Notice how Adlai E. Stevenson worked "newness" into his eulogy of Lloyd Lewis:

> *I think it will always be April in our memory of him. It will always be a bright, fresh day, full of the infinite variety and the promise of new life.*[16]

TRY THIS

Using any of the aspects of good description just discussed (size or quantity, shape, weight, color, composition, age or newness, and fit), describe one of the following:

A movie you saw recently.   An accident you witnessed.
A trip you have taken.   A place you like to go.
A dream you have had.   A book you have read.
A walk to the library.   An experience you have had.

Stevenson connected memories of Lewis to newness through his use of "April," "bright," "fresh," and "new life." Sometimes subtlety helps description because it asks audience members to complete images, to fill in details, and to determine meanings for themselves.

Fit

Fit refers to the way parts belong together or the relationship among parts. A mental picture emerges when listeners can fit all the parts into a proper relationship.

Say you are speaking about the campus newspaper and you want to explain how all of the parts fit together. You talk about the responsibilities of the editor, then of the jobs of the features, news, and sports editors and what their relationship is to the editor. Next you talk about the roles of the business manager and advertising department and the relationship these people have to the editor. If you discuss how all of these people fit into the overall structure, your audience will have a good idea of how the newspaper works.

Explaining

Almost everything that we know how to do was explained to us at one time or another. We were not born knowing how to do such things as cook or play volleyball—someone told us how to do them. Many of the questions we ask have to do with asking for explanations. What does this concept mean? How does this work? How do I get there? Explaining, then, is the process of making something clear.

Much of explaining is made up of analysis. Analysis is breaking up a whole into its parts and then examining the nature and function of these parts and the relationship of the parts to the whole. Not all subjects are analyzed

TRY THIS

Take one of the following topics and list the main points you would make in preparing a speech on it:

Using the library.

Writing a book report.

What makes a good sportswriter?

Selecting a movie for a date.

Using time efficiently.

Playing a game.

the same way. If you are explaining a process (for example, how to build a house) you will probably talk about each step chronologically; it makes more sense to begin by talking about the foundation than about the roof. In a speech on the causes of teen-age pregnancy, it will probably make sense to develop each cause separately (topical order).

Connecting the Known with the Unknown

When listeners have limited knowledge or experience of a subject, the speaker can help them to understand it by connecting the new idea to something the listeners already know about. For example, when a British student wanted to explain the game of cricket to her American classmates, she started out by listing the ways that cricket was similar to baseball. Another student, explaining how a word processor works, started out comparing it to a typewriter. In both cases, after explaining how the two were similar, the speakers then went on to point out the differences.

Repeating and Reinforcing Ideas

Repetition in a speech is important because it helps the listeners to remember the points. However, if it is overdone, the speaker runs the risk of boring the listeners. Let's look at a format that will enable you to spread out the repetition and reinforcement in a speech.

In your introduction, *tell your listeners what you plan to tell them.* In her speech "Creating a More Effective Voice," Michelle listed the main points in her introduction: "Today I want to talk about the three main steps for changing your voice. These steps are analysis, discipline, and production."

In the body of your speech, *tell your listeners* (i.e., explain your points). In Michelle's speech, she explained each of her steps:

The first step in creating a more effective voice is analysis. You need to find your best pitch and a balanced tone and you can do this only through an analysis of your own voice.

The second step is discipline. By disciplining yourself to practice your natural, right voice in exercises and everyday conversation, you can use your voice to best advantage.

The third step in creating your best voice is production. You need to ease slowly and gradually toward producing the same pitch level whenever you speak.

In your conclusion, *tell your listeners what you told them.* This is the place to summarize your main ideas. Michelle concluded her speech by saying:

Now you can see how you can go about creating a more effective voice. You need to analyze your voice, to discipline yourself to practice, and to work on producing a pitch that will show your voice at its best.

Arousing Interest in Your Topic

So many things compete for the listener's attention that even though we might get attention, it is not always possible to keep it. You probably have had the experience of half-listening to a speaker while you were wondering what was for lunch, were mentally preparing a grocery list, and so on. What can you, as a speaker, do to compete?

Arouse Curiosity

One way to make sure the audience will listen to you is to create a desire to learn about your subject by stimulating listeners' curiosity. For example, one speaker began her speech with "Have you ever wondered why you get so tired?" Another began his speech with "Do you know how to stop procrastinating?" Another started, "The real name of Captain Kangaroo is Bob Keeshan. The name of the river that flows over the Holland Tunnel is the Hudson. Five states border on the Pacific Ocean. Ever wonder why we are so fascinated by trivia?"

Introduce Anecdotes

Of course getting attention in your speech is only one of your problems; you also have to keep it. Thus when you plan your speech, you should put in attention-getting devices throughout the speech. One effective technique is to introduce anecdotes. Since anecdotes usually involve individual people, most listeners find them very interesting.

Build Anticipation

One way to build anticipation is to preview your points in the introduction. You could say, for example, that you are going to talk about the way to get the best buy on anything: haggle. Then say:

> I want to give you some rules to sharpen your bargaining skills—rules like doing your homework, resisting the urge to make the first offer, avoiding a bid in round numbers, taking your time, and being creative.

The audience is then more likely to listen for each of these points.

Build Suspense

Building suspense is one of the best ways of keeping attention. One student started his speech this way:

> When he was only 26, John began to go into kidney failure. Although he went for dialysis three times a week to clean the wastes from his body, it was clear that this was a stopgap measure and that he would eventually need a kidney transplant. He discovered, however, that his insurance did not pay for it and that the cost of the transplant would be $60,000. If John were going to have this operation, he would have to raise the money.

The speaker went on to tell of organ transplants, what they cost, and how they are paid for. Throughout his speech he referred to John and his problems with raising money. It was not until the conclusion, however, that he revealed that John had raised the money, had had the operation, and was now living a normal life.

Getting Listeners Involved

Get the Audience to Participate

In a speech on aerobic exercises, the speaker had listeners try several of them. In a speech on self-defense, a speaker had the class practice a few simple moves. In a speech on note taking, the speaker had listeners taking notes, and as she did so, she taught them some short cuts and simplified procedures.

As every magician knows, choosing someone from the audience to participate in an act is a good technique for keeping attention. Speakers can do this too. In a speech on the proper method to use in cardiopulmonary resuscitation, the speaker called for a volunteer from the audience. For a speech titled "Appearance Sells," one student asked three classmates to come to class dressed in a certain way: one was to dress casually, another in dressy clothes, and the third in a businesslike way.

Ask Rhetorical Questions

Some speakers keep their listeners involved by asking rhetorical questions (questions answered in the mind rather than aloud): "How would you have approached that same situation?" "Does appearance mean anything to you?" "Do you see how this applies in your life?" "Can you see why I'm committed to this idea?"

Solicit Questions from the Audience

Another device is to solicit questions from the audience following the speech. A question-and-answer session encourages listeners to get involved. You might even tell your listeners at the beginning that you will take questions when you finish, which may encourage them to pay attention so as to be able to ask questions.

There are, however, some useful guidelines if you plan to solicit questions from your audience. First, make sure you listen to the full question before answering it. Sometimes speakers will cut off a questioner or will focus on irrelevant details and not on the main thrust of the question. Second, if a question is confusing, ask the questioner to rephrase it. If you are still confused, rephrase it yourself before answering it. For example, say, "Let me make sure I have heard you right; what you are asking is . . . Am I right?" Finally, in responding to questions, try to keep your answers brief and to the point. This is no time for another speech. As a final check, it's also a good idea to ask, "Does that answer your question?"

SAMPLE INFORMATIVE SPEECH

The following informative speech was written and presented by Kathy Weisensel in a speech class at the University of Wisconsin, Madison.* The speech uses a topical order of presentation. Here is the full speech, with our commentary on the right:

Title: David: And a Whole Lot of Other Neat People

Specific Purpose: To increase the understanding of class members about the nature of mental retardation.

* The speech appears in *Contemporary American Speeches*, 5th ed., pp. 80–83.

Central Idea: There are three important misconceptions regarding mental retardation.

1. There is a problem which is shared by millions of people in the United States. It knows no barrier to age, sex, or social class. Yet, it is a problem that for years was hidden in society's darkest closet. Only recently has the closet door begun to open. That problem is mental retardation.

Kathy's introduction builds anticipation. She builds it by mentioning her topic only in the final sentence of the paragraph.

2. One out of thirty-three persons is born mentally retarded. It is the most widespread permanent handicap among children. It is among the least understood handicaps of adults. In Wisconsin alone, there are 120,000 retarded people.

To establish the extent of the problem, Kathy introduces statistics. She keeps them short, and she adapts them to her audience by citing some from Wisconsin.

3. My involvement with mental retardation has been lifelong and deeply personal. For you see, David, my older brother, is mentally retarded.

Kathy establishes her own credibility through her use of personal experience.

4. As our family adjusted to David's problem, we became aware of a number of misconceptions which cloud the public's vision. Among these misconceptions are: that mentally retarded people are mentally ill and therefore dangerous; that mentally retarded people are ineducable; and that mentally retarded people are incapable of leading happy and productive lives. Since these misconceptions are socially harmful and painful to the retarded and their families, it is important that they be corrected.

She builds on her personal experience to outline three important misconceptions. These three points will form the structure of her speech. Once again, she builds anticipation for her ideas. As presented here, she offers listeners a preview of her main points.

Notice that in this paragraph she also explicitly explains the purpose of her speech—the correction of the misconceptions.

5. How do you correct the notion that retarded people are somewhat crazy and therefore not really to be trusted? It may be helpful to start with a definition. According to Dr. E. Milo Pritchett:

Kathy introduces the discussion of her first main point with a rhetorical question. She begins to answer that question, starting with a definition—by an expert.

THE INFORMATIVE SPEECH   385

Mental retardation is a condition of impaired, incomplete, or inadequate mental development.
. . . Mental retardation is NOT mental illness. Mental illness is a breakdown of mental functions which were once normal. Specialized care and treatment may restore the person to normalcy. Retardation is a condition for which there is no cure.

The definition is part synonym, part comparison.

6. But let's extend that definition with a series of contrasts. Mental retardation is subnormal intelligence; mental illness is distorted intelligence. Mental retardation involves deficient cognitive abilities; mental illness involves emotional impairment of cognitive abilities. Mental retardation is manifested early; mental illness may occur anytime in life. The mentally retarded person is behaviorally stable; it is the mentally ill person who is given to erratic behavior. The extremely mentally retarded person is submissive and mute; the extremely mentally ill person may be violent and criminally dangerous. Thus retarded people are retarded, and no more. We need no longer place them in pens with the criminally insane, as was the custom in medieval societies.

Kathy's use of contrasts extends the definition, but it is also a form of emphasis through reinforcement.

Notice that she ends the list of contrasts with a final classification.

7. OK, the skeptic says, so what if they aren't mentally ill—they're still ineducable. Those who favor this misconception have, in the words of Dorly D. Wang, formerly of Woods School in Pennsylvania, "one-dimensional views of the retarded." They fail to "distinguish degrees of retardation" and tend to perceive "all the retarded with one image"— and that image is of the intellectual vegetable, more appropriately

Kathy begins this paragraph with a brief summary of her first main point and a transition to her second main idea.
To develop her second main point, she once again turns to expert opinion.
Notice at the end of this paragraph how she subdivides her second main idea into three subpoints. Once again, she uses the technique of preview to alert her listeners: she builds anticipation

planted in a cell or ward than in the school classroom. But retarded people are not all alike. Most psychologists identify three subgroups of mentally retarded people: the educable, the trainable, and the custodial.

by offering her listeners the points she plans to discuss.

8. The educable mentally retarded have IQ's ranging from 75 to 50. In the nation's schools, they are placed in a curriculum with a special classroom base, but are encouraged to enter the curricular mainstream whenever it is possible. Most of these students share with normal students instruction in home economics, physical education, shop, and music.

This is a brief explanation of "educable" based on Wang's definition. It is definition by classification.
She paces her speech by keeping discussion of each of her points brief.

9. The trainable mentally retarded's IQ is usually 50 to 30. In the schools, these students are not found in any normal classes. Rather, they work exclusively in special classrooms under the direction of teachers who understand their needs. In these classes they learn self-care, and they train for social and economic usefulness. Three percent of the present school population is made up of the educable and trainable mentally retarded.

This explanation is developed as a parallel to the preceding paragraph.
Note the additional use of statistics here to support the point.

10. The custodial mentally retarded have IQ's below 30. They are usually confined to institutions such as Central Colony, just across Lake Mendota from this University. These people experience little mental development. Few exceed the intellectual acuity of a normal three year old.

Brevity is important to Kathy's pacing in this section.
Her reference to Central Colony keeps the speech relevant to her audiences.

11. Thus, the mentally retarded are not a faceless, hopeless mass. While not all of them may profit from schooling, many will. Careful and loving

Kathy uses an internal summary as a transition to her third main idea—the second misconception. ("Thus" is a useful transitional word.)

teachers will eventually be rewarded by what one teacher of the retarded has called "the smile of recognition."

12. But to say that the mentally retarded person is not mentally ill and is not ineducable is not enough. It does not destroy the myth that one must be of average mentality to be socially productive and happy. In a society characterized by speed, change, competition, and progress, it is difficult for us so-called "normals" to understand that retarded people can live happily and productively in a life pattern alien to our own.

Again, notice the emphasis on organization. She summarizes once again—mentioning both of her previous ideas—before progressing to the third misconception.

Audience identification is fostered through her use of "us"—in "us so-called 'normals.'"

13. Bernard Posner, Deputy Executive Secretary of the President's Committee on Employment of the Handicapped, has captured society's dilemma in coming to grips with the mentally handicapped. He commented:

In using expert opinion here, see how Kathy fully establishes Posner's expertise before quoting him.

> . . . ours are norms in which change is a way of life. In the United States, we change jobs every five years and homes every seven years. We say that to stand still is to regress. Where do the retarded fit in, those without the capacity for constant change?
>   . . . ours are norms of competition. We compete in school, at play, at love, at work. Where do the retarded fit in, those who can go to school, can play, can love, can work, but who cannot always come out on top in competition?
>   . . . ours are norms of discontent. Life becomes a series of steppingstones leading who knows where? Each of life's situations is not to be enjoyed for itself, but is to be tolerated because it leads elsewhere. Where do the retarded fit in, those who can be happy with a stay-put existence?

The quotation provides useful contrasts and questions to hold listener attention. Notice the parallel construction.

Although Kathy chose an unusually long quotation, it contributes to her pacing. The quotation is written in a style that would be easy to deliver powerfully.

The repeated question: "Where do the retarded fit in?" serves to reinforce Kathy's specific purpose and is a useful retention feature as well.

14. But retarded people do fit in and do lead useful and rewarding lives. A few years ago, I worked with a girl who is educably mentally retarded. Mary went to my high school and attended two normal classes—home economics and physical education. She had a driving desire to become a waitress. Her determination was evident as I tutored her in addition, subtraction, making change, and figuring sales tax. She is working today in a small restaurant—happy and self-supporting.

Kathy answers the question posed repeatedly in the quotation.

Kathy's personal experience with Mary is a powerful attention device.

15. My brother David is another example. Under Wisconsin law he was entitled to school until age twenty-one, and he spent all those years in a separate special class. There he learned the basic skills of reading, writing, and mathematics. After graduation he was employed by the Madison Opportunity Center, a sheltered workshop for the retarded. He leaves home each morning on a special bus and returns each evening after eight hours of simple assembly-line work. While he is by no means self-supporting and independent, he loves his work, and he is a happy man and a neat person with whom to share a family.

A second personal experience is with her brother David. She makes David real for her listeners by describing his development in detail.

Notice, as Kathy describes her personal experiences, how she makes heavy use of concrete data—she ties her ideas down to specific and exact settings.

16. As a final example, I give you Jeff, age 14. He is custodially mentally retarded at Central Colony. In the three years that I have worked with him, I have found him to be incredibly happy and content in his "permanent childhood." He enjoys toys, writing letters of the alphabet, and watching Sesame Street. This last summer he was especially proud to be selected as a jumper in the Special Olympics. To tell you the truth, he was chosen because he was one

"As a final example" is a transition. Kathy's examples have reinforced and underscored her clear organizational scheme. Her first example, Mary, was educable; her brother David, trainable; and Jeff, custodial.

of the few kids in the ward who could get both feet off the floor at the same time. But Jeff doesn't know that the competition wasn't keen, and he's proud and happy.

17. While misconceptions are slow to pass away, they must surely die. Our nation's retarded are not mentally ill, totally ineducable, or incapable of happy and productive lives. I know, in a deeply personal way, the pain that these misconceptions inspire. But I also know that the world is changing. I have a deep faith that you and others of our generation will reject the senseless and destructive stereotypes of the past. As Bernard Posner has said:

. . . the young people of the world seem to be forging a new set of values. It appears to be a value system of recognizing the intrinsic worth of all humans, retarded or not . . . a value system of acceptance: of accepting life as it is, and people as they are.

18. Thank you for your acceptance.

Kathy begins her conclusion. Notice that she first summarizes her ideas. She then becomes personal—and slightly emotional. This is likely to have a significant impact on her listeners—holding their attention, gaining their understanding, and ensuring their retention.

Finally, she uses expert opinion once again. Her quotation is likely to have strong appeal to her classmates because it pats their generation on the back and makes them feel good about themselves.

Her closing comment drives home her purpose: to gain listener understanding of mental retardation—and through understanding, acceptance.

SUMMARY

Information is becoming increasingly important in our society. Sixty percent of the American people work in information jobs. In an information society, knowing how to give an informative speech is a very useful skill. An informative speech is one that defines, clarifies, instructs, and explains.

When giving a speech, the speaker's goals should be to get and keep attention by using information that is relevant and interesting to the audience. The speaker should work to increase understanding by making careful language choices, having the speech organized, and using illustrations and examples. Finally the speaker should aim to have the audience retain the information, through emphasis and repetition.

Strategies for informative speaking include defining important terms and concepts by using etymology, classification, synonym, example, comparison, and function. Description—made up of size and quantity, shape, weight, color, composition, age and newness, and fit—is also useful in an informative speech.

Explanation, yet another useful strategy, is the process of making something clear and is often made up of analysis. Analysis involves breaking up the whole into parts and examining these parts in relationship to the whole.

Other strategies for informative speaking include connecting the known with the unknown, repeating and reinforcing ideas, arousing interest in the topic, and getting listeners involved.

VOCABULARY

The following is a list of words you must know to understand the concepts in this chapter. You will find the words defined the first time that each is used in the chapter. All Vocabulary words also appear, with their definitions, in the Glossary at the end of the book.

antonym	etymology
classification	function
composition	synonym

FURTHER READING

HART, RODERICK P., GUSTAV W. FRIEDRICH, AND BARRY BRUMMET. *Public Communication*, 2nd ed. New York: Harper & Row, 1983. This book has an excellent unit on "The Informative Challenge in Public Communication," which includes material on making ideas substantive, intense, coherent, and graphic.

MINNICK, WAYNE C. *Public Speaking*, 2nd ed. Boston: Houghton Mifflin, 1983. We recommend this textbook, with its chapter on informative speaking, because of its clear style and no-nonsense approach.

PATTON, BOBBY R., KIM GIFFIN, AND WIL A. LINKUGEL. *Responsible Public Speaking*. Glenview, Ill.: Scott, Foresman, 1983. This well-written textbook on public speaking has two excellent chapters on informative speaking—one on helping listeners understand and the other on developing the informative speech.

SAMOVAR, LARRY A., AND JACK MILLS. *Oral Communication: Message and Response*, 5th ed. Dubuque, Iowa: Brown, 1983. This popular public-speaking textbook includes a chapter on informative speaking within Part 3, "Having an Influence."

SMITH, TERRY C. *Making Successful Presentations: A Self-Teaching Guide*. New York: Wiley, 1984. Smith offers a how-to book on planning, organizing, developing, and delivering presentations. His useful and practical book is a step-by-step guide supplemented by artwork showing charts, slides, and room setups. Also helpful are his checklists.

SPRAGUE, JO, AND DOUGLAS STUART. *The Speaker's Handbook*. New York: Harcourt Brace Jovanovich, 1984. This is a compendium of principles, examples, and exercises covering all the topics commonly confronted in preparing and delivering a speech.

TAYLOR, ANITA. *Speaking in Public*. Englewood Cliffs, N.J.: Prentice-Hall, 1979. Taylor provides specific information on clarification, amplification, explanation, narration, comparison, and repetition. The book is useful and practical.

WALTER, OTIS M. *Speaking to Inform and Persuade*, 2nd ed. New York: Macmillan, 1982. In a 164-page paperback, Walter provides the essentials. After an overview of exposition, he looks at support, or what he calls the tactics of exposition, and then at main ideas, or the strategy of exposition. It is an interesting and valuable guide.

WILLIAMS, FREDERICK. *The Communications Revolution*. Beverly Hills, Calif.: Sage, 1982. We talked in this chapter of the information explosion. Better than most other books, Williams' work clearly portrays the communications explosion—the means that will bring information within easy reach. It is a book designed for those interested in the future of communication.

16 THE PERSUASIVE SPEECH

CHAPTER OUTLINE

Speaker Credibility
   Expertise
   Dynamism
   Trustworthiness
   Ethics
Appealing to the Audience
   Logical appeals

   Emotional appeals
Structuring the Speech
   Questions of fact, value, and policy
   One-sided versus two-sided arguments
   Order of presentation
A Sample Persuasive Speech

CHAPTER OBJECTIVES

After reading this chapter, you should be able to:

1. Explain the four factors that make up credibility.
2. Use logical appeals and emotional appeals in a speech.
3. Explain how questions of fact, value, and policy can be used in a persuasive speech.
4. Explain when to use one-sided versus two-sided arguments.
5. Organize a speech using each of the following: problem-solution, comparative advantages, and the motivated sequence.

Professor Robert Carney is the chairperson of the foreign language department. In order to recruit students for foreign language study, he visits all the freshman composition classes. He tells them of the advantages in studying a foreign language, explains the college's foreign language requirement, and tells them about programs abroad, where students can fulfill their language requirement in one semester. He also points out that students can study in Madrid, Paris, or Mexico City for no more than it costs to stay on campus. At the end of his speech, he gives his audience his office location and a telephone number where he can be located. He is so successful with this speech that several students come to inquire about the program.

Kim Campbell is editor of the student newspaper. Since the paper needs more reporters, she decides to visit all the introductory journalism classes. When she gets there she talks about what is involved in reporting for the paper and promises to personally help any beginner. She also mentions the advantages of regularly writing for the paper. Not only do students improve their writing skills, she says, but they also gain status on campus by being associated with the paper. She tells the time and place of the next staff meeting. At the next meeting 15 people from the classes show up.

Nancy Good gives a speech to her speech communication class about her own experiences with alcoholism. She points out that it is entirely possible to be an alcoholic at 19—she is one herself. She tells the class of the warning signs of alcoholism and urges them to get help if they or anyone they know is in difficulty. After her speech, she gives out a dittoed sheet with the telephone

CONSIDER THIS

A rational person is not only open to persuasion; he also recognizes that no single dogma contains all the truth, that in most cases there is something to be said on both sides, that even the "absolutes" we believe in must be tempered by the admission that all men are fallible and all human answers are tentative and provisional.

People who are locked into their beliefs, no matter what they be, soon suffocate from a lack of intellectual oxygen; they begin breathing in their own air and lose contact with reality. This manifests itself by chronic use of the same stale epithets for those who disagree with them—a trait as prevalent among Marxist fundamentalists as among religious fundamentalists.

Life is too short, and time too precious, to engage in debate with these people. The sad fact is that even when they happen to be right—which is rarely—they are wrong, because they are convinced that there is only one way to be right.

Source: Sydney Harris, "Strictly Personal," *Toledo Blade.*

numbers of all the Alcoholics Anonymous branches in the city and the names of several drug and alcohol counseling centers. Although Nancy cannot assess the impact of her speech directly, she senses that her audience is paying careful attention. After the speech is over, several students tell her she made a real impression.

All these speakers are engaged in the act of persuasion—the process of trying to get others to change their attitudes or behavior. Most of you are engaged in some sort of persuasion every day of your life. You try to persuade someone to join you for lunch or to join your study group. Others are involved in trying to persuade *you*: radio commercials exhort you to buy, telephone salespersons offer bargains on a variety of goods and services, professors try to persuade you to turn in your papers on time, and students running for student government try to persuade you to vote for them.

Since persuasion runs through every aspect of our society, it is important to study how it works. Understanding persuasion will help you to evaluate better the persuasive techniques of others. Studying persuasion will also help you to develop your own persuasive messages in the most effective way possible.[1]

TRY THIS

In what ways does persuasion touch your life? Which of the following have the power to persuade you?

- Advertising
- Sales pitches
- Speeches
- Friends' communications
- Family communications
- Editorials in newspapers
- Members of groups you belong to
- Letters
- Teachers
- Religious leaders

Of these, which touch you the most directly? Which ones can change your attitudes or behavior? Why are some more powerful than others?

SPEAKER CREDIBILITY

Much of persuasion comes about because of the person doing the persuading. You can probably think of people in your own life who are particularly persuasive. Why are some people more persuasive than others? Research on persuasion says we are more likely to be effective as persuaders if listeners consider us to be credible. **Credibility,** or believability, consists of four qualities: expertise, dynamism, trustworthiness, and ethics. Let's look at each of them.[2]

Expertise

You are looking at the news one night and you see a woman who is talking about the effects of long-term exercise on health. In the introduction to the speaker, you learn she is a medical doctor from Johns Hopkins Medical School who has been studying the effects of exercise. The results of her study are interesting so you listen closely. The next day you hear a student speaker trying to persuade students of the value of exercise. His speech, however, contradicts some of what you heard on the evening news. Which speaker do you believe? In this case there isn't much doubt. You believe the medical doctor because she is an expert.

Expertise Based on Personal Experience

When you are a speaker trying to persuade an audience, it will help your credibility if you can show some expertise on your subject. **Expertise** is having the experience or knowledge of an expert—one who is very skilled, highly trained, or well informed. One way to do it is to use your own personal experience. Nancy, for example, speaks of her own experience with alcoholism.

> One night I went to a party. I remember the early part of the evening but that's about all. The next thing I remember was waking up in my own bed. I have no recollection of the end of the party or how I got home. When I woke up that morning and realized I didn't remember anything, I knew I was in serious trouble.

You don't always have to have such a dramatic experience as Nancy's. One student who had done volunteer work with the Red Cross persuaded classmates to serve as volunteers. Another student persuaded several classmates to petition the dean of students for better food in the cafeteria. She knew that the food was poor, as did many members of her audience. Thus she used both her experience and the experience of audience members to make her point.

Expertise Based on Commitment

Another way to show expertise is through establishing your commitment to your topic. Listeners are more inclined to believe speakers who have taken actions in the past that support their position. If you can show that you have donated blood, you are more likely to persuade others to donate. If you can point out that you have been a scout or have worked with scouts for many years, people are more likely to take you seriously on this subject.

Expertise Through Research

Expertise can also be built through research. By interviewing and reading articles and books, you can quote sources who will be acknowledged as experts, thereby making your speech more credible. When you are using information derived from experts, make that clear in your speech with such references as:

> According to Dr. John Smith, a noted authority in this area . . .
>
> From an article in last week's U.S. News & World Report . . .
>
> As noted in Lee Iacocca's best-selling book Iacocca. . .

Dynamism

Dynamism, another aspect of credibility, concerns the amount of enthusiasm and energy speakers have for their subject. For example, when a student tried to get students to become more politically active, he spoke of his own work in a local politician's primary campaign as if it was one of the most exciting times of his life. He described his experience so vividly that the audience was able to feel his excitement.

It's easy to be dynamic about a subject you're enthusiastic about. When Jane spoke about the Australian exchange program, she started this way:

> When your classmates are fighting snow and ice, you will be on the sunny beaches of Australia. When it's winter here, it's summer there. You'll have a chance to talk with people who speak your language. You'll have a chance to see how a different political system works, and you'll have a chance to visit spaces that are more wide-open than you've ever dreamed of. A semester in Australia will change your life.

Much of the dynamism in a speech will be created nonverbally. A speaker who stands up straight, projects his or her voice to the back of the room, and doesn't hesitate will be seen by the audience as more dynamic than one who doesn't do these things. Watch for the most dynamic speakers in your class and make some mental notes on how they convey their energy and enthusiasm nonverbally.

Trustworthiness

Trustworthiness is a matter of being perceived as reliable and dependable. These qualities are often based on the past experience we have had with people. For example, if you worked on a committee with Deb and she always did her share of the work, you will regard her as dependable. If Todd, however, was on the same committee and never did anything, you would not consider him as very reliable. Because of your negative experience with Todd, you are less likely to trust him if he tries to persuade you to do something the next time he gives a speech.

Ethics

Listeners often base their judgment of a persuasive message on what they think of the ethics underlying the message. **Ethics** means conforming to acceptable standards of conduct. You might listen with some reservations to a vacuum cleaner salesman's talk on how wonderful his vacuum cleaner is. After all, he has a lot to gain if you buy the vacuum cleaner. Is he telling the truth? Presenting the facts correctly? Telling you *all* you need to know? In the same way, audiences for persuasive speeches could be thinking: "This speaker is

Leaders must have the trust of those they seek to influence, or their words will not be persuasive. But trust must be earned.

TRY THIS

Among all the persuaders you have heard recently, select one who has tried to persuade you of something. Is this person someone you know well or is he or she a stranger?

Using the concepts of expertise, dynamism, trustworthiness, and ethics, evaluate this person's credibility. Is this person credible? Do you accept what he or she says? Why or why not? Are you willing to question his or her credibility? Why or why not?

Do you think there is a way this person could increase his or her credibility? How?

How important is this person's credibility to his or her daily life? To his or her occupation? To his or her contact with others?

trying to persuade me. Is she being honest? Does she have anything to gain by persuading me?''

Speakers can deal with these questions by paying careful attention to their own ethical behavior. If speakers have something to gain from the speech, they should let audience members know at the beginning of the speech. A student government president did this with his audience:

I am asking you to vote to extend the office of student government president to two years. I want you to know that this will work to my benefit because it means I will serve another year. However, I also want you to know that it will work to your benefit, too.

Speakers also have an ethical obligation to use the best possible evidence and to present it fairly. Don't distort your quotations or take them out of context. Not only is this wrong, but if someone finds out you did this, the word will spread and you won't be trusted the next time you give a speech. It's also important that you distinguish between what is yours and what belongs to someone else. For example, if you use statistics, let your audience know where you found them. If you find a terrific quote, make sure you give its source.

APPEALING TO THE AUDIENCE

Audiences can be persuaded in many different ways. Persuasion is very complex, and what persuades some listeners may have no effect on others. What may encourage one student to sign a petition to get the administration to buy more science equipment may cause another student to think that the money should go for library books instead. While one person might be persuaded to join a group dedicated to banning nuclear weapons, another person might want to look at much more evidence before joining. This section discusses some of the different kinds of persuasion and when it might be appropriate to use a particular method.

Logical Appeals

A **logical appeal** is one that relates to our reasoning ability. Reasoning involves how we approach topics as well as the evidence we accumulate in support of those topics.

Every persuasive speech should use evidence. Evidence can be made up of examples or statistics or any other supporting material that will help persuade the audience. Chapter 12 develops, in detail, the kinds of supporting material.

Deductive Reasoning

Good evidence depends on the kind of reasoning you use. You might want to use **deductive reasoning**, which moves from the general to the specific. When this student gave his speech, he argued deductively:

> *Acid rain is a problem throughout the entire northeastern United States.*
> *Pennsylvania is a northeastern state.*
> *Pennsylvania has a problem with acid rain.*

Care is needed, however, with this pattern of reasoning. Have you ever heard someone say, "It's dangerous to generalize"? A faulty generalization is really faulty deductive thinking—as in this example:

> *All college students procrastinate.*
> *Mary is a college student.*
> *Therefore, Mary procrastinates.*

Inductive Reasoning

Another logical technique is **inductive reasoning**—reasoning from the specific to the general. Usually when we use inductive reasoning we move from a number of facts to a conclusion. In this speech a student tried to persuade her audience that the college should require everyone to take a foreign language. To do this she used inductive reasoning:

In some parts of the United States, you need to understand Spanish to get by.

Americans are traveling more and more to countries where a language other than English is spoken.

The mark of an educated person is that he or she can speak, write, and read at least one other language.

Conclusion: Everyone should learn another language.

When you use inductive thinking in a speech, you can organize it in a way that best suits the material. Sometimes it will work best to give the facts and then draw the conclusion; in other cases you might want to start with the conclusion and then support it with facts.

Causal Reasoning

Another way to reason is causally. **Causal reasoning** always uses "because"—either implied or explicitly stated. "I failed the class because I didn't complete the assignments" or "The basketball team is losing because it has an incompetent coach." This latter example points out some of the problems of causal reasoning. That the coach is incompetent may be a matter of opinion. The team might be losing because it doesn't have good players or because the other teams have taller players or because there is no way of recruiting good players. The causal pattern can be used for presenting evidence as well as for organizing an entire speech. Cause and effect is one of the ways to organize a speech discussed in Chapter 12.

Reasoning by Analogy

Finally, you can also reason by **analogy**. In this case you compare two similar cases and conclude that if something is true for one it must also be true for the other. One student used analogy to argue that since the school supported men's sports, it should give equal money to women's sports.

Often speeches of policy use analogy. Advocates of a policy will look to see if the policy has been tried elsewhere. This student argues, for example, that the United States should follow the English policy in treating heroin addicts:

The English do not treat heroin addicts as criminals. If someone is addicted to heroin in England, he or she can get the drug with a prescription from a doctor. Because heroin is available it is less desirable. The English addiction rate has changed very little over the past few years.

Emotional Appeals

An **emotional appeal** is concerned with listeners' needs, wants, desires, and wishes. Most persuasion is based on a mixture of logical and emotional appeals. Speakers who use emotional appeals are concerned with motivation: what will impel listeners to change attitudes and behaviors. For example, a person looking for a job would be more motivated to listen to a persuasive speech titled "Improving Interview Skills" then would someone who has a secure job.

Appealing to Needs

Because emotional appeals deal with psychological needs, they do not operate the same way with all people. Psychological needs are rooted in people's brains and may be unique for each individual. A speech trying to persuade people to buy insurance would be more persuasive to a mother with small children than a student who is single. A speech trying to persuade parents to give their children music lessons would probably be more appealing to parents who have felt a need in their own lives for some kind of artistic expression than to those who have not felt such a need.

The psychologist Abraham Maslow has proposed a model that arranges people's needs from relatively low-level physical needs to higher-level psychological ones. This model, referred to as a **hierarchy of needs**, is shown in Figure 16-1. Let's take a look at the needs in the hierarchy and see how they can help us decide what emotional appeals we can put in our persuasive speeches.

As you can see from Figure 16-1, the first needs all human beings have are *physiological needs*. Starving people do not care about freedom; their need for food is so great that it outweighs all other needs. Therefore, physiological needs must be taken care of before other needs can be met. We usually assume that basic needs are taken care of, so they are generally not a basis for a persuasive speech.

Safety needs are next in the hierarchy. The whole area of safety needs can be useful in persuasion, since all of us have these needs in varying degrees. Notice how this speaker appeals to his student audience's need for safety:

> In the last three months there have been six assaults on this campus. Where have they occurred? All in parking lots with no lights. When? At night, after evening classes are over. Does this mean that you can't take any more evening classes without fearing for your life? Should you leave your car at home so you can avoid the campus parking lots?

Belongingness and love needs, the next level, also have a potent appeal. If you doubt this, turn on your television set and note how many commercials are making a direct pitch for the need to be loved.

This student used the need to belong to urge freshmen to join "The Way"— a religious group on campus:

> The freshman year is the hardest year of college. You are in a new environment and are faced with a bewildering array of choices. I felt this way when I was a

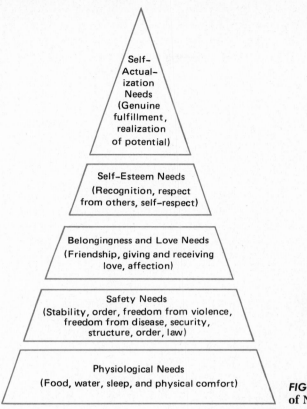

FIGURE 16-1 Maslow's Hierarchy of Needs

freshman. Then I met someone from "The Way" who invited me to one of its meetings. The minute I walked in the door several people met me and made me feel welcome. Today some of these people are my best friends.

Self-esteem needs involve feeling good about ourselves. We see a lot of persuasion with this end in mind in self-help books. Typical themes are that you'll feel good about yourself if you change your fashion style, learn how to climb mountains, practice meditation, and so on. This student appealed to the self-esteem need when she gave a speech called "Try Something New":

I have a friend who, at the age of 35, decided to learn how to play the flute. She had never played an instrument before, but she loved music and thought it would be interesting to give it a try. Now that she has been studying for two years, she told me, "I will never be a great player but this has been a wonderful experience. I enjoy my records even more because I know what the musicians are doing because I understand so much more about music. It's wonderful to try something new." I am here today to urge you to try something new yourself. To see what you can discover about yourself.

At the top of his hierarchy, Maslow puts *self-actualization needs*—the need to recognize one's potential. This need involves our desire to do our best with what we have. An admissions director for a community college gave this speech when she talked to a group of older women in an attempt to persuade them to go to college.

> I'm sure that many of you look back at your high-school days and think "I was a pretty good writer. I wonder if I still could write." or "I really liked my business courses. I would like to try my hand at bookkeeping again." I believe one of the saddest things that can happen to us is not to be able to try out things that we are good at, things that we have always wanted to do. Our new college program for returning adults will give you a chance to do just that—try out the things you are good at.

You have the best chance of choosing the right emotional appeal if you have done a thorough job of researching your audience. Let's take safety needs and look at them only from the viewpoint of the age of audience members. Safety needs are probably going to be important to families—especially those with young children. On the other hand, younger audiences such as college students are generally focusing in their own lives on belonging, love, and self-esteem needs. If you were going to focus on a safety need such as buying IRA's or bonds, a college audience probably wouldn't find it very interesting. Self-actualization needs probably appeal most to an older audience. Adults who are approaching mid-life are the most likely to ask themselves whether they have made the right choices for their lives or whether they should consider making some changes. Age, of course, is only one factor to consider in emotional needs. The more information you have about your audience, the better the chance of selecting the right emotional appeals.

Appealing to Other Emotions

Appeals can also be made on the basis of other emotions that all of us feel. In each of the examples that follows, the speaker is appealing to a common emotion.

In persuading her audience to be more aggressive in filing tax returns, this speaker used the emotion of fear:

> When April rolls around, there is nothing the American taxpayer fears more than the Internal Revenue Service. I am here to tell you there is nothing to fear. I have been audited five times, and each time I have come out the winner.

In the next example, the speaker wanted audience members to consider taking a foster child. She used compassion as a way of getting them to feel sympathetic to the children:

> What happens when a child has no home? When he is shunted around to five different foster homes in four years? This happens to thousands of American children every year. There is no place they can call home.

In this speech, the speaker used the emotion of anger to get her classmates to sign a petition to student government.

> *Every year each student pays $50 in student activity fees. What do we get for this money? Concerts by groups we have never heard of. Support for athletic teams that never win a game. A student newspaper that is written by illiterates. I am fed up and you should be too.*

You don't always have to use emotions with negative associations. This student urged students to attend an honors convocation by appealing to their pride:

> *The most unsung heroes and heroines of this campus are those who have academic achievements. Do you know that 15 students from this school have scholarships to medical school next year? That for the past six semesters students from this campus have gone on highly competitive federal internships? That we are ranked as number four in the nation for our writing program?*

When you are going to give a persuasive speech, think about the emotions you can appeal to that are suitable to your subject. Emotions are powerful tools in persuasion. If you can find a good way of using them, they will add strength and power to your speech.

STRUCTURING THE SPEECH

Questions of Fact, Value, and Policy

Chapter 9 discussed using questions of fact, value, and policy when we are involved in group discussion. Now let's see how these questions can be used for persuasive speeches.

Questions of Fact

A *question of fact* deals with what is true or false. One student used a question of fact when he spoke on the question "Do Unidentified Flying Objects Really Exist?" The purpose of his speech was to persuade the audience that they did.

Questions of Value

Questions of value are concerned with some aspect of moral values: whether something is good or bad, right or wrong, beneficial or detrimental, and so on. In this speech a student used a question of value to discuss the topic of moderate drinking.

Specific Purpose: To persuade my audience that even moderate drinking is unsafe.

Central Idea: Moderate drinking is unsafe because it interferes with interpersonal relationships and health.

Main Points: I. Moderate drinking interferes with work.

   II. Moderate drinking interferes with interpersonal relationships.

   III. Moderate drinking harms one's health.

Questions of Policy

Questions of policy deal with specific courses of action and usually contain such words as "should," "ought," or "must." Here is the outline for a speech based on a question of policy:

Specific Purpose: To persuade my audience that business should grant sabbaticals to administrators.

Central Idea: Sabbaticals are an effective solution to attracting and keeping workers, dealing with job stress and burnout, and broadening professional skills.

As the leader of an organization, you will have many opportunities to speak on questions of policy. Your skill in persuasive speaking will be of service.

Main Points: I. Sabbaticals are an effective way to attract and keep workers.

II. Sabbaticals are an effective way to deal with job stress and burnout.

III. Sabbaticals are an effective way for workers to broaden their professional skills.

IV. Sabbaticals should be granted to administrators.

One-Sided Versus Two-Sided Arguments

Should persuaders present one side or both sides of an issue? When you know your listeners basically support your ideas, one side may be sufficient. For example, when a member of the literacy council went out to promote literacy in the community, she knew she didn't need to convince people of the need for literacy. Her audience members already knew how important it was to read and write. She could focus, then, on persuading audience members to support the council financially.

There are occasions, however, when speakers should present both sides of the argument. Often the presentation of both sides will help speaker credibility: a speaker who presents both sides is likely to be perceived as more fair and rational. When an issue of public importance is controversial, it's a good idea to present both sides, since most people will probably have heard something about each side. When a student spoke on nuclear energy, he presented both sides because he knew there were strong feelings for and against. Another speaker chose to present both sides of the sex education issue. She thought sex education should be taught at home, but she wanted to let her audience know that others preferred it to be handled in the schools.

There has been extensive research comparing the one-sided versus two-sided speech. The results seem to indicate that (1) a two-sided speech is more effective when the listeners have completed at least a high-school education; (2) the two-sided speech is especially effective if the evidence clearly supports the thesis; (3) the two-sided presentation is more effective when listeners oppose the speaker's position, but the one-sided approach is more effective when listeners already support the thesis.[3]

Order of Presentation

Certain ways of organizing speeches seem to work particularly well for persuasion. As we discussed in detail in Chapter 13, the *problem-solution order* works well for persuasion. It lets the speaker build tension by describing the problem and getting listeners involved in it; then the speaker can relieve the tension by providing a solution.

TRY THIS

Consider the following topics and see if you can frame an argument for each side. Are there subjects where you are so firmly committed to one side that you can't even think of opposite argument?

abortion	capital punishment	rock music
astrology	grades	seat belts
communism	exercise	prayer in schools
feminism	racism	organ transplants
freedom of speech	reincarnation	

Another organization pattern that works well for persuasion is the **comparative advantage order**. This order allows persuaders to compare the advantages of one solution over another:

Our entire activity fee goes to student government, which decides how it should be spent. One of these decisions is how much money should go to the student newspaper. I maintain that the newspaper should be funded separately, and there are three ways this could be done: (1) give a percentage of money from the activity fee to the newspaper; (2) assess students an extra fee for the newspaper; (3) let the administration fund the newspaper directly. What are the advantages of each of these solutions?

The *motivated sequence*[4] was discussed in some detail in Chapter 13, but because of its popularity and usefulness for persuasion, it is reviewed here. The five steps of the motivated sequence, which is based on the problem-solution form, suggest five specific main points for developing a speech. Any problem-solving speech can be adapted to this form.

1. The *attention* step's purpose is to gain the attention of the audience. You do this by following the suggestions in the section "The Speech Introduction" in Chapter 13.

2. The *need* step points out a problem that affects audience members. In this step you create a sense of urgency about this problem.

3. The *satisfaction* step gives relief to the audience by providing a solution to the problem.

4. The *visualization* step lets the audience see how much better things would be if this solution were put into effect.

5. The *action* step urges the audience to go out and take some action that will help solve the problem.

Since the motivated sequence follows the human thought process, it is extremely easy to use. In fact, you might be using it without even knowing it. Here's how Marie tries to persuade her roommate to go to Bermuda instead of Florida over spring break:

Attention: I have a great idea. Let's go to Bermuda instead of Florida for spring break.

Need: You know Florida is really the pits at this time of the year. Everything is so crowded that you can't get a room, you have to wait in line if you want anything, and the guys are getting more immature every year.

Satisfaction: I have just found a terrific package deal for Bermuda. For only $299 we can get a room just for the two of us. I hear that Bermuda attracts more mature guys.

Visualization: Just think of those white sandy beaches. The moon on the water. I bet we'll meet some guys we'll really like.

Action: I have the form right here where we sign up. Let's do it.

Now see how one student speaker developed a persuasive speech using the motivated sequence:

Specific Purpose: To persuade my audience that the campus newspaper should be funded directly by the activity fee rather than by student government.

Central Idea: When student government funds the newspaper, it often tries to control the news.

Main Points: I. Attention: This week the student government says it will stop funding the newspaper unless it stops criticizing the government.

II. Need: This has been a problem for a long time. Whenever the government doesn't like what the paper says, it closes the paper down.

III. Satisfaction: The only way to solve this problem is to fund the paper directly with money from the student activity fee. If government doesn't control the funding, it can't control the newspaper.

IV. Visualization: The newspaper will be able to play its proper role as watchdog of government, and all of you will no longer find that the paper has not come out because the government has closed it down again.

V. Action: I have a petition here to the president of this university. I hope that all of you will sign it.

TRY THIS

Take one of the following speech topics and see if you can sketch out an outline for the speech following the motivated sequence:

- Public television should be subsidized by the federal government.
- High schools should offer courses in love, marriage, and parenthood.
- Food additives are harmful and their use should be banned.
- Males under the age of 21 should not be permitted to drive cars.
- Schools should give funding to athletic teams on the basis of their win-loss records.

SAMPLE PERSUASIVE SPEECH

The following persuasive speech was written and presented by Kathy Atkinson in a speech class at Bowling Green State University. The speech centers on a question of policy and is arranged according to the motivated sequence. A full transcription of the speech appears on the left, our commentary on the right.

OBESITY: A SOCIAL ILL IN THE UNITED STATES TODAY

Specific Purpose: To persuade my audience that obesity should be overcome.

Central Idea: Obesity, a serious problem with numerous causes and effects, must be solved through diet and exercise.

1. How many of you consider yourself overweight? Too many Americans today are finding themselves overweight, but not so many of us are trying to do something about it. I believe that obesity is a serious problem in our society and that something should be done about it.

    Kathy gains the attention of her audience with her opening question. Knowing her listeners, she can anticipate a significant response from them. Note that her attention step includes a preview of her central idea.

2. Obesity has become commonplace in American society. It is a serious

    This is a transition between the attention and need steps.

problem because so many of us are unwilling or don't care to attack the problem. Obesity is a problem that should be dealt with for many reasons. I want to explain some of these reasons now.

3. Obesity is being not overweight but overfat, though we use the term overweight. It is having more fat than is healthy for your body—this is, having more than 25 percent fat than is normal.

Kathy's need step begins with a description supported by statistics. She first establishes facts.

4. Women, on the average, should have about 20 to 25 percent body fat. Men should have a little less. When the condition has increased to 50 percent above normal, the person is labeled as morbidly obese. These people are risking death because of their obesity. According to the *Saturday Evening Post*, there are about 1 million of these morbidly obese people in the United States. And, to quote the *Post*, "While much of the world is starving, most Americans are eating too much." *U.S. News & World Report* says that the United States is the most overweight country in the world. Think about it. Can you even count how many overweight people you've seen today? Can anyone say there isn't one obese person in their family? We see obesity everywhere.

Notice how Kathy incorporates her sources into her speech. By indicating her research efforts, she is adding to her credibility.

Notice how Kathy relates her need step to her listeners.

5. The causes of obesity include food intake, lack of exercise, hormonal conditions, heredity, or emotional causes.

Here Kathy previews each of the subpoints she intends to touch on. She wants to establish the fact that there may be several causes for obesity—not just one.

6. Let's consider food intake first. If you eat more than you burn off, you will gain fat. Many people eat after they are satisfied because they were taught it was sinful to leave food on their plate.

7. But it's not just that Americans are overeating; it's what we're eating too. Much of what we eat is fast food, processed food, or junk food. These foods are almost always high-fat, high-calorie-content foods, especially fried food. According to *Current Health*, fried foods are high in cholesterol and saturated animal fat.

8. However, many people are obese not because they eat more than average but because they don't exercise properly. You have to exercise to burn off calories. What you don't burn, your body turns to body fat.

9. Because obesity is related to hormonal conditions, the problem increases with age. Many people don't realize that the calories used at rest under standard conditions (your metabolic rate) decrease as you get older. As you age, you lose muscle mass. Muscle weighs more than fat; you may weigh the same at 50 as you did at 20, but you have lost muscle and gained fat. You burn less as you get older, so you don't eat the same way you once did.

Kathy continues to give her listeners some background information on her topic. Although some of her information is a bit technical, it is interesting and holds attention. This is partly because her choice of topic was good: many listeners are concerned about obesity.

10. Heredity as a cause of obesity is rare. It is more likely to be a family problem. Fat parents tend to have fat children. This could be genetic, but it is more likely because fat parents tend to overfeed their children. Also, children who are overfed as infants or are given sweets as rewards develop dangerous eating patterns. They will probably always be fat.

11. A study at Rockefeller University comparing groups of rats, one overfed from birth, another fed normally, showed the overfed rats

Also, Kathy has selected some very good supporting material—for example, the study she cites here from Rockefeller University.

gained weight quickly and kept it; they also had three times as many fat cells. The *Saturday Evening Post* put it this way: "[Those] who become obese in adulthood have larger fat cells, but not an increase in number; once the cells appear in infancy, they don't disappear." In other words, people who were overfed as infants gain weight easily and have trouble losing it.

12. Finally, there are emotional causes. The satiety center of the brain—the mechanism that makes you feel satisfied and stop eating—can be disturbed by emotional pressures or damaged by infection, injury, or tumor, causing the person to eat continually. Emotional overeating is common. Anxiety, loneliness, frustration, stress, and depression are major causes. In the words of *Current Health* magazine, many people "confuse hunger with an emotion."

13. Now that I have discussed some of the causes, let's look at some of the effects of obesity.

Having completed her list of causes, Kathy places a transition here.

14. The effects of obesity include medical effects, economic effects, prejudice, and psychological problems.

Here, Kathy previews some of the effects she will discuss.

15. Consider the medical problems. Obesity can be a major cause of high blood pressure, hypertension, diabetes, varicose veins, and heart and blood vessel disorders—to name just a few. *Current Health* states that "the primary cause of heart attacks and strokes is the accumulation of fat in the artery walls," a condition known as atherosclerosis.

16. In addition, obesity makes surgery dangerous and treatment for other

problems difficult. Arthritis is made more painful because of the weight of fat on the joints.

17. As for economic effects, it might be of interest to some of you to know that the high-calorie foods of fatness cost more than good food.

18. But being fat is not only costly in health and economic terms; it can also spoil your chances in life. Because, to quote Dr. Faith T. Fitzgerald, "condemnation of fat people is one of the few remaining sanctioned prejudices in this nation freely allowed. . . . The fat are denied jobs, promotions, educational opportunities and, recently, challenged in their right to adopt a child until they lose weight."

19. But perhaps the worst part of being obese is the psychological problems it entails. Obese people usually have a low opinion of themselves. They have low self-worth and low self-esteem as well. One overweight woman, quoted in *U.S. News & World Report*, said, "I relate my problems—depression, anxiety—to being overweight."

20. Now that we have looked at the seriousness of the problem, how can we solve it?

    Solving the problem of obesity involves two things: diet and exercise.

This transition moves listeners from the need step to the satisfaction step. Kathy begins her satisfaction step with a preview of the two subpoints she plans to discuss.

Notice that the satisfaction step is used to present listeners with the solution to the need that has been developed.

21. Diet is important. Steps must be taken to prevent obesity. We can teach our children and ourselves good eating habits.

22. *Glamour* magazine advises: "Eat only when you're hungry and only as much as you really want."

23. A diet is not something you try for a week until you lose weight and

then go back to your usual way of eating; it must be a permanent change to lose weight and keep it off. Fad diets and starvation diets can be very dangerous, often resulting in malnutrition or starvation itself. You should eat a nutritious diet from the four basic food groups.

24. To cut back your calorie intake, develop these important habits:

    • Eat smaller portions.

    • Put your food on a smaller plate to make it look like more.

    • Eat slowly, taking smaller bits.

    • Enjoy your meal and focus on it; don't eat in front of television.

    • Set small goals you can feel good about achieving. Reward yourself—but not with food. Do something special.

    • When hunger strikes, stick to low calorie snacks like carrot and celery sticks.

Kathy's suggestions are practical. Those members of her audience who want to will be able to apply her information directly to their lives.

25. Exercise is important. *Glamour* tells us that "Exercise is the best all-around way to curb your appetite."

26. According to Dr. Lawrence E. Lamb, in his book *Metabolics: Putting Your Food Energy to Work*, good exercise builds active cells (muscle) and keeps you from being fat and fatigued.

27. You shouldn't jump right into a vigorous exercise program if you're out of shape, though, since it can put strain on your heart.

28. Start out easy—like walking. *Vogue* points out that "as the time spent walking lengthens, weight and body-fat reductions become more dramatic."

Notice that Kathy begins the second subpoint of the satisfaction step in the same way as the first one. This parallel construction helps listeners follow her speech.

29. Watch out for distractions from proper diet and proper exercise.

30. Fad diets are dangerous and usually result in malnutrition.

31. To quote Dr. Lamb again: "Appetite suppressing pills perhaps have some use under controlled circumstances, at least to motivate the person to start on a diet." But, he adds, "We should avoid all the advertised weight-reducing regimes."

32. Almost all miracle diet and exercise programs are gimmicks—they don't work. In sweating diets, for instance, you merely sweat off water and salts that your body needs to replace. You lose weight. But drink water, and you gain it back.

33. By following a healthy diet and exercise plan, you *will* lose weight. You'll feel healthier and you'll look healthier, too.

34. If you continue to eat more than you burn, you only stand to gain weight. You need to picture the ideal you: What do you want to look like? Keep that image—that mental picture—in your mind as your goal. Then work step by step, with proper exercise and diet, to meet that goal.

35. If you succeed in following the plan, you can lose weight. *Consumer's Digest* says that "people see important health and status benefits from looking and feeling fit." You'll look better and feel better, and it can make a great difference in your life.

36. I hope I've convinced you of how serious a problem obesity has become. America has developed dangerous eating and exercising patterns. I want you all to realize the

Now Kathy comments on diet and exercise together, warning her listeners against distractions. Hers is a plea for reason and good sense in following proper programs to control obesity.

Notice the number of positive impressions that Kathy projects in her visualization step.

Kathy makes a transition by summarizing what she has said. Notice how direct and personal she gets here.

health risks you take when you develop these habits and become obese. It can be emotionally and physically as well as economically harmful to become overfat.

37. If you really have trouble maintaining a diet and exercise program, see a physician or visit a free program like Overeaters Anonymous. There are available outlets right here in our city.

38. Please think seriously about what I've said, and consider the path you're taking. Obesity is a problem we should solve.

In her action step, Kathy offers her listeners two specific options. When she mentioned these options, she wrote each of them on the blackboard. This visual aid provided strong reinforcement to her message.

Bibliography

ANDEREGG, KAREN. "Are We Fatness Crazy?" *Vogue* 172 (March 1982): 399.

Consumer's Digest, November–December 1984, pp. 30–32.

Current Health, January 1981, pp. 28–29.

Glamour, December 1984, pp. 24–27.

KAPLAN, NORMAN M., M.D. "The Bottom Line About Fat." *The Saturday Evening Post* 255 (April 1983): 18–23, 100.

LAMB, LAWRENCE E., M.D. *Metabolics: Putting Your Food Energy to Work.* New York: Harper & Row, 1974.

Science News, April 26, 1980, p. 266.

U.S. News and World Report, December 22, 1980, pp. 61–62.

"Vogue's Health Style." *Vogue* 174 (November 1984): 486.

SUMMARY

Persuasion is part of everyday life. Not only do we engage in persuasion, but other people are constantly trying to persuade us. A knowledge of persuasion helps us to put together better persuasive speeches and to understand the persuasive messages of others.

For a speaker to persuade an audience, he or she must have credibility. Credibility comes from four areas: expertise, dynamism, trustworthiness, and ethics. Expertise involves doing research and being informed on a subject.

Dynamism is a matter of delivering a message with energy and enthusiasm. Trustworthiness depends on past experience; if you have been reliable in the past, people are more likely to trust you. An ethical speaker tells the audience if he or she has something to gain from the persuasion. The ethical speaker also looks for the best evidence, presents it fairly, and identifies its origin.

A persuasive message is usually made up of a combination of logical and emotional appeals. Logical appeals present evidence through deductive reasoning, inductive reasoning, causal reasoning, and reasoning by analogy. Emotional appeals play on the need for safety, the need to be loved and to belong, and the needs for self-esteem and self-expression. The speaker can also build emotional appeals into a speech by appealing to emotions we all feel such as fear, pity, anger, and pride.

Structure is important to a persuasive speech. Some speakers like to organize their speeches around questions of fact, value or policy. When the speaker is gathering supporting material for the speech, he or she must decide whether to present one side or both sides of the issue. Generally two-sided arguments work best when the audience is educated and the subject is controversial.

Ordering the presentation depends on the subject. In persuasive speaking, speakers commonly use a problem-solution order, an order that gives comparative advantages, or the motivated sequence. The motivated sequence involves five steps: attention, need, satisfaction, visualization, and action.

VOCABULARY

The following is a list of words you must know to understand the concepts in this chapter. You will find the words defined the first time that each is used in the chapter. All Vocabulary words also appear, with their definitions, in the Glossary at the end of the book.

analogy	ethics
causal reasoning	expertise
comparative advantage order	hierarchy of needs
credibility	inductive reasoning
deductive reasoning	logical appeal
dynamism	trustworthiness
emotional appeal	

FURTHER READING

BETTINGHAUS, EDWIN P. *Persuasive Communication*, 3rd ed. New York: Holt, Rinehart and Winston, 1980. Bettinghaus takes a behavioral approach to persuasion. The basic data for this textbook are derived from the literature of the behavioral sciences. The literature he discusses comes from scientific research in communication, psychology, social psychology, sociology, psycholinguistics, and anthropology. This is a solid, theoretical approach to persuasion.

BOSTROM, ROBERT N. *Persuasion*. Englewood Cliffs, N.J.: Prentice-Hall, 1983. This is a well-researched and written, comprehensive approach to persuasion. In this primarily theoretical textbook, Bostrom relates persuasion to communication, then treats it in the public setting. In addition, he looks at it in the small group, in bargaining and negotiation, in organizations, and in our personal lives. It is an enjoyable textbook.

CIALDINI, ROBERT B. *Influence: How and Why People Agree to Things*. New York: Quill, 1984. Cialdini has organized his book around the principles of consistency, reciprocation, social proof, authority, liking, and scarcity. Each of these is discussed in terms of its function in society, how it is used, and the results that occur.

CLARK, RUTH ANNE. *Persuasive Messages*. New York: Harper & Row, 1984. Clark has one goal: to aid readers in constructing persuasive messages. She focuses on public speaking and provides strategies designed to enlarge the range of alternatives available to persuaders.

GILBERT, MICHAEL A. *How to Win an Argument*. New York: McGraw-Hill, 1979. Gilbert shows how to argue and reason more effectively. He discusses the art of argument, the ways of argument, and the arguments. He includes sample arguments, with annotations by the author, to indicate good and poor techniques. The book is understandable to the average reader and full of specific, practical advice.

ILARDO, JOSEPH A. *Speaking Persuasively*. New York: Macmillan, 1981. Ilardo wrote this book for upper-level students taking courses in persuasion and persuasive speaking. The book is grounded in current theory, but Ilardo relies on traditional wisdom and practical experience as well. This is a thorough, readable textbook.

O'DONNELL, VICTORIA, and JUNE KABLE. *Persuasion: An Interactive-Dependency Approach*. New York: Random House, 1982. O'Donnell and Kable emphasize both the persuader and "persuadee." They have taken a realistic approach that combines theories with techniques. They emphasize that sometimes persuasion fails in spite of our best efforts. These authors help us understand that persuasion cannot always succeed and help us understand why.

REARDON, KATHLEEN KELLEY. *Persuasion: Theory and Context*. Beverly Hills: Sage, 1981. Reardon treats persuasive discourse as an invaluable tool not only for selling aspirin or political causes, but also for defining one's social identity and desirability. In this largely theoretical volume, Reardon embraces the rule-following model as the best way for dissecting the persuasion process.

ROSS, RAYMOND S., and MARK G. ROSS, *Understanding Persuasion*. Englewood Cliffs, N.J.: Prentice-Hall, 1981. Here is an introductory textbook on persuasion that is readable, interesting, practical, and relevant to students.

SIMONS, HERBERT W. *Persuasion: Understanding, Practice, and Analysis*. Reading, Mass.: Addison-Wesley, 1976. Simons helps readers understand the process of persuasion, practice persuasion effectively, and analyze the persuasive discourse of others. Practical suggestions are placed in a research context. In this well-written book, Simons describes theories, cites studies, and offers cautionary comments.

NOTES

Chapter 1

1. Edgar H. Schein, *Career Dynamics: Matching Individual and Organizational Needs* (Reading, Mass.: Addison-Wesley, 1978), p. 77.
2. Peter F. Drucker, *People and Performance* (New York: Harper College Press, 1977), pp. 262–263.
3. David K. Berlo, *The Process of Communication: An Introduction to Theory and Practice* (New York: Holt, Rinehart and Winston, 1960), p. 24.
4. Albert Mehrabian, *Silent Messages: Implicit Communication of Emotions and Attitudes,* 2nd ed. (Belmont, Calif.: Wadsworth, 1981), pp. 76–77.
5. See Carol Wilder, "The Palo Alto Group: Difficulties and Directions of the Transactional View for Human Communication Research," *Human Communication Research* 5 (Winter 1979): 171–186.

Chapter 2

1. Chris L. Kleinke, *Self-Perception: The Psychology of Personal Awareness* (San Francisco, Calif.: Freeman, 1978).
2. Muriel James and Dorothy Jongeward, *Born to Win: Transactional Analysis with Gestalt Experiments* (Reading, Mass.: Addison-Wesley, 1971), pp. 68–100.
3. Robert K. Merton, *Social Theory and Social Structure* (New York: Free Press, 1957).
4. Dean C. Barnlund, "Toward a Meaning-Centered Philosophy of Communication," *Journal of Communication* 12 (1962): 197–211.
5. For an excellent review of perception in interpersonal communication, see Alan L. Sillars and Michael D. Scott, "Interpersonal Perception Between Intimates: An Integrative Review," *Human Communication Research* 10 (Fall 1983): 153–176.
6. Abraham H. Maslow, *Toward a Psychology of Being,* 2nd ed. (New York: D. Van Nostrand, 1968), p. 46.

Chapter 3

1. Sperry Corporation, *Your Personal Listening Profile* (n.p.: Sperry Corporation, 1980), p. 4.
2. See Lyman K. Steil, Larry L. Barker, and Kittie W. Watson, *Effective Listening: Key to Your Success* (New York: Random House, 1983); and Florence I. Wolff, Nadine C. Marsnik, William S. Tacey, and Ralph G. Nichols, *Perceptive Listening* (New York: Holt, Rinehart and Winston, 1983).
3. Vincent DiSalvo, David C. Larsen, and William J. Seiler, "Communication Skills Needed by People in Business," *Communication Monographs* 25 (1976): 274.
4. Neville Moray, *Listening and Attention* (Baltimore: Penguin Books, 1969), p. 23.
5. Paul G. Friendman, *Listening Processes: Attention, Understanding, Evaluation* (Washington, D.C.: National Education Association, 1978), p. 274.

6. Wesley N. Shellen, "Measurement of Listening Achievement: The Role of Perceived Interest and Extrinsic Incentives," paper presented at the International Communication Association, Chicago, 1975 (ERIC ED 105 539).
7. Stanford E. Taylor, *Listening* (Washington, D.C.: National Education Association, 1964), p. 13.
8. Sperry Corporation, *Your Personal Listening Profile.*
9. Bert K. Pryor, K. Phillip Taylor, Raymond W. Buchanan, David U. Strawn, "An Affective-Cognitive Consistency Explanation for Comprehension of Standard Jury Instructions," *Communication Monographs* 47 (1980): 69.
10. Ibid.
11. Gerald I. Nierenberg and Harry Calero, *Meta-Talk* (New York: Simon and Schuster, 1973), p. 12.
12. See J. Dan Rothwell, *Telling It Like It Isn't: Language Misuse & Malpractice: What We Can Do About It* (Englewood Cliffs, N.J.: Prentice-Hall, 1982); and Peggy Rosenthal, *Words and Values: Some Leading Words and Where They Lead Us* (New York: Oxford University Press, 1984).

Chapter 4

1. Benjamin L. Whorf, "The Relation of Habitual Thought and Behavior to Language," *Language, Thought and Reality* (Cambridge, Mass.: MIT Press, 1956), pp. 134–159.
2. Neil Postman, *Crazy Talk, Stupid Talk* (New York: Delta, 1977), p. 9.
3. Erving Goffman, *Relations in Public* (New York: Basic Books, 1971), p. 62.
4. Esther Blank Greif and Jane Berko Gleason, "Hi, Thanks, and Goodbye: More Routine Information," *Language in Society* 9 (1980): 159–166.
5. Marsha Houston Stanback and W. Barnett Pearce, "Talking to 'the Man'; Some Communication Strategies Used by Members of 'Subordinate' Social Groups," *Quarterly Journal of Speech* 67 (1981): 24–25.
6. Faye Crosby and Linda Nyquist, "The Female Register: An Empirical Study of LaKoff's Hypothesis," *Language in Society* 6 (1977): 313–314.
7. Chris Kramer, "Women's Speech: Separate but Unequal," in *Language and Sex: Difference and Dominance,* Barie Thorne and Nancy Henley, eds. (Rowley, Mass.: Newburg House, 1975), p. 47.
8. Crosby and Nyquist, "The Female Register," p. 314.
9. Nancy De La Zerda Flores and Robert Hopper, "Mexican Americans' Evaluation of Spoken Spanish and English," *Speech Monographs* 42 (1975): 91–98.
10. Mary Rhodes Hoover, "Community Attitudes Toward Black English," *Language in Society* 7 (1978): 65–87.
11. Robert Hopper, "Language Attitudes in the Em-

ployment Interview," *Communication Monographs* 44 (1977): 346–351.

12. Dale T. Miller, "The Effect of Dialect and Ethnicity on Communication Effectiveness," *Speech Monographs* 42 (1975): 69–74.

13. Gerald I. Nierenberg and Harry H. Calero, *Meta-Talk* (New York: Simon and Schuster, 1973), p. 12.

14. Cyra McFadden, *The Serial* (New York: Knopf, 1977), p. 14.

Chapter 5

1. Albert Mehrabian, *Silent Messages: Implicit Communication of Emotions and Attitudes*, 2nd ed. (Belmont, Calif.: Wadsworth, 1981), pp. 76–77.

2. Mark L. Knapp, *Nonverbal Communication in Human Interaction*, 2nd ed. (New York: Holt, Rinehart and Winston, 1978).

3. Mark L. Knapp, *Essentials of Nonverbal Communication* (New York: Holt, Rinehart and Winston, 1980), p. 237.

4. Loretta A. Malandro and Larry Barker, *Nonverbal Communication* (New York: Random House, 1983), p. 9.

5. Ibid., p. 280.

6. Mehrabian, *Silent Messages*, pp. 42–27. See also "Communicating Without Words," *Psychology Today* 2 (1968): 53.

7. James MacLachlan, "What People Really Think of Fast Talkers," *Psychology Today* 13 (November 1979): 113–117.

8. Paul Ekman and W. V. Friesen, "The Repertoire of Nonverbal Behavior: Categories, Origins, Usages, and Coding," *Semiotica* I (1969): 49–98.

9. Ernst Kretschmer, *Physique and Character: An Investigation of the Nature of Constitution and of the Theory of Temperament* (New York: Cooper Square, 1970), pp. 18–35.

10. William H. Sheldon, *The Varieties of Temperament* (New York: Hafner, 1942).

11. W. Wells and B. Siegel, "Stereotype Somatype," *Psychological Reports* 8 (1961): 77–78. Their work was confirmed by K. T. Strongman and C. J. Hart, "Stereotyped Reactions to Body Build," *Psychological Reports* 8 (1968): pp. 77–78.

12. Knapp, *Nonverbal Communication*, pp. 153–161.

13. Ellen Berscheid and Elaine Hatfield Walster, *Interpersonal Attraction*, 2nd ed. (New York: Random House, 1978).

14. Lawrence B. Rosenfeld, "Beauty and Business: Looking Good Pays Off," *New Mexico Business Journal*, April 1979, pp. 22–26.

15. "Clothes Make the Person," *Psychology Today* 18 (January 1984): p. 17; as originally reported in *Public Opinion* 6, no. 4 (August–September 1983).

16. Edward T. Hall, *The Silent Language* (Greenwich, Conn.: Fawcett, 1959); and Edward T. Hall, *The Hidden Dimension* (Garden City, N.Y.: Anchor Books, 1969).

17. Hall, *The Hidden Dimension*, pp. 116–125.

18. As cited in R. Winter, "How People React to Your Touch," *Science Digest* 84 (March 1976): 46–56.

Chapter 6

1. Alan H. Wurtzel and Colin Turner, "What Missing the Telephone Means," *Journal of Communication* 27, no. 2 (1977): pp. 48–57.

2. John Powell, *Why Am I Afraid to Tell You Who I Am?* (Allen, Texas: Argus Communications, 1969), p. 44.

3. William C. Schutz, *The Interpersonal Underworld* (Palo Alto, Calif.: Science and Behavior Books, 1966), pp. 18–20.

4. Ralph Keyes, *Is There Life After High School?* (New York: Warner Books, 1977).

5. Schutz, *The Interpersonal Underworld*.

6. Ibid.

7. Thomas F. Cash and Louis H. Janda, "The Eye of the Beholder," *Psychology Today* 18 (December 1984): 46–52.

8. Steven W. Duck, *Personal Relationships and Personal Constructs: A Study of Friendship Formation* (New York: Wiley, 1973), p. 20.

9. See Charles R. Berger and Richard J. Calabrese, "Some Explorations in Initial Interaction and Beyond: Toward a Developmental Theory of Interpersonal Communication," *Human Communication Research* 1 (1976): 99–112.

10. Sam Keen, "Why We Love Gossip," *Family Weekly*, June 5, 1983, pp. 4–8.

11. Lawrence R. Wheeless and Janis Grotz, "The Measurement of Trust and Its Relationship to Self-Disclosure," *Human Communication Research* 3 (Spring 1970): 250–257. Wheeless and Grotz explain the relationship between trust and self-disclosure.

12. Joseph Luft, *Group Process: An Introduction to Group Dynamics*, 2nd ed. (Palo Alto, Calif.: National Press, 1970), pp. 11–12.

13. Lawrence Rosenfeld, "Self-Disclosure Avoidance: Why I Am Afraid to Tell You Who I Am," *Communication Monographs* 46 (March 1979): 63–74.

14. For a discussion of the relationship between liking and disclosure, see John H. Berg and Richard L. Archer, "The Disclosure-Liking Relationship," *Human Communication Research* 10 (Winter 1983): 269–281.

Chapter 7

1. Mark L. Knapp, *Interpersonal Communication and Human Relationships* (Boston: Allyn and Bacon, 1984), pp. 35–44.

2. Paul H. Wright, "Self-Referent Motivation and the Intrinsic Quality of Friendship," *Journal of Social and Personal Relationships* 1 (March 1984): 115–130.

3. Mary Anne Fitzpatrick and Patricia Best, "Dyadic Adjustment in Relational Types: Consensus, Cohesion, Affectional Expression, and Satisfaction in Enduring Relationships," *Communication Monographs* 46 (1979): 167–178.

4. Rebecca J. Cline and Bonnie McD. Johnson, "The Verbal Stare: Focus on Attention in Conversation," *Communication Monographs* 43 (1976): 1–10.

5. Jack Gibb, "Defensive Communication," *Journal of Communication* 11 (1961): 141–148.

6. See Joseph P. Folger and Marshall Scott Poole, *Working Through Conflict: A Communication Perspective* (Glenview, Ill.: Scott, Foresman, 1984). See also Toni Brougher, *A Way with Words: How to Improve Your Relationships Through Better Communication* (Chicago, Ill.: Nelson-Hall, 1982).

7. G. H. Morris and Robert Hopper, "Remediation and Legislation in Everyday Talk: How Communicators Achieve Consensus," *Quarterly Journal of Speech* 66 (1980): 266–274.

8. See Roger Fisher and William Ury, *Getting to Yes: Negotiating Agreement Without Giving In* (Boston: Houghton Mifflin, 1981).

9. William Anthony Donohue, "An Empirical Format for Examining Negotiation Processes and Outcomes," *Communication Monographs* 45 (1978): 247.

10. Deborah Weider-Hatfield, "A Unit in Conflict Management Communication Skills," *Communication Education* 30 (1981): 265–273.

11. William K. Rawlings, "Negotiating Close Friendship: The Dialectic of Conjunctive Freedoms," *Human Communication Research* 9 (Spring 1983): 255–266.

12. Patricia Sternberg, *Be My Friend: The Art of Good Relationships* (Philadelphia: Westminister Press, 1983).

Chapter 8

1. For an overview of the various types of interviews, see Michael Z. Sincoff and Robert S. Goyer, *Interviewing* (New York: Macmillan, 1984).

2. Oriana Fallaci, *Interview with History* (Boston: Houghton Mifflin, 1976), p. 157.

3. Ronald B. Adler, *Communicating at Work* (New York: Random House, 1983), pp. 159–162.

4. Charles J. Stewart and William B. Cash, Jr., *Interviewing: Principles and Practices* (Dubuque, Iowa: Brown, 1982), pp. 188–189.

Chapter 9

1. For a thorough overview of small group communication, see B. Aubrey Fisher, *Small Group Decision Making: Communication and the Group Process*, 2nd ed. (New York: McGraw-Hill, 1980); Francis L. Ulschak, Leslie Nathanson, and Peter G. Gillan, *Small Group Problem Solving* (Reading, Mass.: Addison-Wesley, 1981); and Rodney W. Napier and Matti K. Gershenfeld, *Groups: Theory and Experience*, 2nd ed. (Boston: Houghton Mifflin, 1981).

2. John E. Baird, Jr., and Sanford B. Weinberg, *Communication: The Essence of Group Synergy* (Dubuque, Iowa: Brown, 1977), p. 126.

3. Elizabeth W. Flynn and John F. LaFaso, *Group Discussion as a Learning Process* (New York: Paulist Press, 1972), pp. 102–103.

4. Baird and Weinberg, *Communication*, p. 125.

5. R. Victor Harnack, Thorrel B. Fest, and Barbara Schindler Jones, *Group Discussion: Theory and Technique*, 2nd ed. (Englewood Cliffs, N.J.: Prentice-Hall, 1977), p. 14.

6. Thomas J. Peters and Robert H. Waterman, Jr., *In Search of Excellence: Lessons from America's Best-Run Companies* (New York: Harper & Row, 1982), p. 126.

7. Marvin E. Shaw, *Group Dynamics: The Psychology of Small Group Behavior*, 2nd ed. (New York: McGraw-Hill, 1976), pp. 6–12.

8. Steven A. Beebe and John T. Masterson, *Communicating in Small Groups: Principles and Practices* (Glenview, Ill.: Scott, Foresman, 1982), p. 89.

9. For an analysis of small-group interaction, see Marvin E. Shaw, *Group Dynamics: The Psychology of Small Group Behavior*, 3rd ed. (New York: McGraw-Hill, 1981).

Chapter 10

1. Cecil A. Gibb, "Leadership," in *The Handbook of Social Psychology*, 2nd ed., vol. 4, G. Lindsey and E. Aronson, eds. (Reading, Mass.: Addison-Wesley, 1969), pp. 205–282.

2. See Ralph White and Ronald Lippitt, *Autocracy and Democracy* (New York: Harper & Row, 1960) for a discussion of leadership styles.

3. Kenneth D. Benne and Paul Sheats, "Functional Roles of Group Members," *Journal of Social Issues* 4 (1948): 41–49.

Chapter 11

1. Alex Osborn, *Applied Imagination: Principles and Procedures of Creative Thinking* (New York: Scribner's, 1979).

2. Mortimer J. Adler, *How to Speak, How to Listen* (New York: Macmillan, 1983), pp. 71–72.

Chapter 12

1. Robert B. Downs and Clara D. Keller, *How to Do Library Research*, 2nd ed. (Urbana: University of Illinois Press, 1975).

2. Jesse Jackson, Excerpts from text of Jesse Jackson's remarks prepared for the Democratic Convention, *New York Times,* July 18, 1984, p. 12.

3. "High School Seniors' Scores Rise 4 Points on College Apptitude Test," *New York Times,* September 20, 1984, pp. A1, B12.

4. "Many See Mercy in Ending Empty Lives," *New York Times,* September 23, 1984, pp. A1, A56.

5. Information derived from ibid., p. 56.

6. Derived from *Toledo Blade,* October 30, 1978, p. 21.

7. See Jo Sprague and Douglas Stuart, *The Speaker's Handbook* (San Diego, Calif.: Harcourt Brace Jovanovich, 1984), for an excellent sourcebook for material on the principles of speech communication.

Chapter 13

1. Judy L. Haynes, *Organizing a Speech: A Programmed Guide*, 2nd ed. (Englewood Cliffs, N.J.: Prentice-Hall, 1981).

2. Denise Foley, "Shape Up Your Pet!" *Prevention,* August 1984, pp. 58–63.

3. Douglas Ehninger, Alan H. Monroe, and Bruce E. Gronbeck, *Principles and Types of Speech Communication*, 8th ed. (Glenview, Ill.: Scott, Foresman, 1978), pp. 142–161.

4. Rebecca C. Jann, "What They Should Have Told Me When I Was a Senior," *Vital Speeches of the Day,* November 1, 1983, p. 51.

5. Fred Shaw, "The Federal Deficit," *Vital Speeches of the Day,* April 15, 1984, p. 405.

6. John Naisbett, *Megatrends* (New York: Warner Books, 1982), p. 76.

Chapter 14

1. See Alan Garner, *Conversationally Speaking* (New York: McGraw-Hill, 1981). Also see Les Donaldson, *Conversational Magic: Key to Poise, Popularity and Success* (West Nyack, N.J.: Parker, 1981).

2. Timothy G. Hegstrom, "Message Impact: What Percentage Is Nonverbal?" *Western Journal of Speech Communication* 43 (Spring 1979): 134–142.

3. Evan Marshall, *Eye Language: Understanding the Eloquent Eye* (New York: New Trend, 1983).

4. See Jeffrey C. Hahner, Martin A. Sokoloff, Sandra Salisch, and Geoffrey D. Needler, *Speaking Clearly: Improving Voice and Diction*, 2nd ed. (New York: Random House, 1986).

Chapter 15

1. John Naisbett, *Megatrends: Ten New Directions Transforming Our Lives* (New York: Warner Books, 1984), p. 14.

2. Ibid., pp. 14–15.

3. Dominick Labino is an artist and glass researcher who lives and works in Grand Rapids, Ohio. The speech was given at Bowling Green State University. The glass sculpture by Labino is called *Icosahedron,* dated November 6, 1976, and it is displayed in the main hallway on the second floor of the Math-Science Building on the Bowling Green campus. The speech was given in a classroom in that building. The student listed the *Toledo Blade,* May 2, 1981, as the source for his facts.

4. Douglas G. Bock and Margaret E. Munro, "The Effects of Organization, Need for Order, Sex of the Source, and Sex of the Rater on the Organization Trait Error," *Southern Speech Communication Journal* 44 (1979): 364–372.

5. Ray Ehrensberger, "An Experimental Study of the Relative Effects of Certain Forms of Emphasis in Public Speaking," *Speech Monographs* 12 (1945): 94–111. See also, N. L. Gage and David C. Berliner, *Educational Psychology* (Chicago: Rand McNally, 1975), p. 457. Planned repetition can help increase comprehension. See O. L. Pence, "Emotionally Loaded Argument: Its Effectiveness in Stimulating Recall," *Quarterly Journal of Speech* 40 (1954): 272–276. See also Harry Lorayne and Jerry Lucas, *The Memory Book* (New York: Ballantine Books, 1974), p. 6.

6. Richard L. Johannesen, Rennard Strickland, and Ralph T. Eubanks, "Richard M. Weaver on the Nature of Rhetoric: An Interpretation," in *Contemporary Theories of Rhetoric: Selected Readings,* Richard L. Johannesen, ed. (New York: Harper & Row, 1971).

7. Mark L. Knapp, *Interpersonal Communication and Human Relationships* (Boston: Allyn and Bacon, 1984), p. 195.

8. Patricia Roberts Harris, "Religion and Politics: A Commitment to a Pluralistic Society," *Vital Speeches of the Day,* November 1, 1980, pp. 50–53. Reprinted in *Contemporary American Speeches: A Sourcebook of Speech Forms and Principles,* 5th ed., Wil A. Linkugel, R. R. Allen, and Richard L. Johannesen, eds. (Dubuque, Iowa: Kendall/Hunt, 1982), p. 282.

9. E. Milo Pritchett, quoted in Kathy Weisensel, "David: And a Whole Lot of Other Neat People," in *Contemporary American Speeches,* 5th ed., p. 81.

10. Ralph M. Baruch, "Lifestyle Revolutions in the Television Age," in ibid., p. 48.

11. Gary Gagliardi, *Professional-Personal Computers* (New York: Bantam Books, 1983), p. 13.

12. Daniel R. Crary, "A Plague of People," in *Contemporary American Speeches,* 2nd ed., Wil A. Linkugel, R. R. Allen, and Richard L. Johannesen, eds. (Belmont, Calif.: Wadsworth, 1969), p. 221.

13. Patrick Huyghe, "The Search for Bigfoot," *Science Digest* 92 (September 1984): 56.

14. Carole Jackson, *Color Me Beautiful* (New York: Ballantine Books, 1980); Carole Jackson, *Color for Men* (New York: Ballantine Books, 1984).

15. Ralph Zimmerman, "Mingled Blood," *Winning Orations, 1956* (Evanston, Ill.: Interstate Oratorical Association, 1956). Reprinted in *Contemporary American Speeches,* 2nd ed., p. 201.

16. Adlai E. Stevenson, "Farewell to a Friend," in *American Short Speeches,* Bower Aly and Lucile Folse Aly, eds. (New York: Macmillan, 1968), p. 123.

Chapter 16

1. See Mary John Smith, *Persuasion and Human Action: A Review and Critique of Social Influence Theories* (Belmont, Calif.: Wadsworth, 1982) for a comprehensive overview of persuasion.

2. See Ruth Ann Clark, *Persuasive Messages* (New York: Harper & Row, 1984) for an up-to-date review of credibility in persuasion. See also James C. McCroskey, *An Introduction to Rhetorical Communication,* 4th ed. (Englewood Cliffs: Prentice-Hall, 1982).

3. Wayne N. Thompson, *Responsible and Effective Communication* (Boston: Houghton Mifflin, 1978), p. 209. According to Thompson, research supporting these generalizations has been extensive. The original study was by Carl I. Hovland, Arthur Lumsdaine, and Fred Sheffield, *Experiments on Mass Communication,* vol. III of *Studies in Social Psychology in World War II* (Princeton, N.J.: Princeton University Press, 1949), pp. 213–214.

4. Douglas Ehninger, Alan H. Monroe, and Bruce E. Gronbeck, *Principles and Types of Speech Communication,* 8th ed. (Glenview, Ill.: Scott, Foresman, 1978), pp. 145–161.

GLOSSARY

Abstract symbol A symbol that stands for an idea rather than a thing.

Active listener Someone who is able to think about and evaluate what a person is saying.

Adaptors Nonverbal ways we have of adapting to the communication situation.

Affection The feeling of warm emotional attachment to other people.

Agenda A list of all the items that will be discussed during a group's meeting.

Aggression A physical or verbal show of force.

Analogy In reasoning, comparing two similar cases and concluding that if something is true for one it must also be true for the other.

Anecdote A short, interesting account of some happening.

Antonym A word with an opposite meaning.

Articulation The ability to pronounce the letters in a word correctly.

Assessment Evaluating communication after it is over.

Audience analysis Finding out what your audience knows about a subject, what they might be interested in, what their attitudes and beliefs are, and what kinds of people are in the audience.

Authoritarian leader A leader who controls a group by deciding what should be discussed and who will do the talking.

Avoidance In relationships, refusal to deal with conflict or painful issues.

Bibliography A list of sources (books, magazines, interviews, newspapers) used to prepare a speech or report.

Body In a speech, all the material between the introduction and conclusion.

Body movement See kinesics.

Brainstorming Coming up with as many ideas as possible without attempting to evaluate them until the ideas run out.

Causal reasoning Reasoning that uses "because"—either implied or explicitly stated.

Cause-and-effect order Organization of a speech around why something is happening (cause) and what impact it is having (effect).

Central idea The main idea of the speech.

Channel The route traveled by a message as it goes between the senders-receivers.

Classification Arranging things according to some systematic division.

Closed questions Questions that are worded in such a way that they restrict the answer.

Cohesiveness The feeling of attraction that group members have toward one another.

Commitment A desire by both parties in a relationship for the relationship to continue.

Communication A process in which people share information, ideas, and feelings.

Comparative advantage order An order of arranging a speech that enables the speaker to compare the advantages of one solution over another.

Comparisons Similarities between two or more things.

Composition The make-up of a thing.

Conclusion The closing remarks in a speech.

Conflict resolution Negotiation to find a solution to a conflict.

Connotative meaning Feelings or associations we have about a word.

Contrasts Differences between two or more things.

Control In interpersonal communication, having some options and choices in life.

Costs and rewards The advantages and disadvantages of a relationship.

Credibility The believability of a speaker based on the speaker's expertise, dynamism, trustworthiness, and ethics.

Critical listening Evaluating and challenging what the speaker has said.

Deductive reasoning Reasoning from the general to the specific.

Defensive communication When one person in a communication tries to defend himself or herself against the remarks or behavior of the other.

Democratic leader A leader who lets all points of view be heard and who lets group members participate in the decision-making process.

Demographic analysis Data about characteristics of a group of people, including such things as age, sex, education, occupation, race/nationality/ethnic origin, geographic location, and group affiliation.

Denotative meaning The dictionary definition of a word.

Dialect The habitual language of a community.

Displays of feeling Facial expressions and body movements that show how we are feeling.

Dynamism In a speech, the amount of enthusiasm and energy speakers have for their topic.

Emblems Body movements that have a direct translation into words.

Emotional appeal An appeal based on listeners' needs, wants, desires, and wishes.

Empathy The ability to recognize and identify with another's feelings.

Enunciation How you pronounce and articulate words.

Ethics Conforming to acceptable standards of conduct.

Etymology The study of the origin and development of words.

Evaluative statements Statements that make a judgment.

Example Something that is used to illustrate a point.

Expertise Having the experience or knowledge of an expert.

Expressive language The language of description and feelings.

Extemporaneous speaking Speaking from notes.

Feedback The response of the senders-receivers to each other.

Follow-up questions Questions that arise out of the answers given by an interviewee.

Function How things perform or how they can be used.

Gossip Behind-the-scene talk of an intimate or personal nature.

Hierarchy of needs The physical and psychological needs of all human beings.

Hypothetical example An example that is made up to illustrate a point.

Illustrators Body movements that accent, emphasize, or reinforce words.

Impromptu speaking Speaking on the spur of the moment with very little preparation.

Inclusion In interpersonal communication, the need for involvement with others.

Indirect aggression Refusing to do something or doing it in such an inept way that it is hardly worth doing.

Inductive reasoning Reasoning from the specific to the general.

Inflection A change in pitch used to give certain words and phrases emphasis.

Informative speech A speech that concentrates on explaining how something works, what something means, or how to do something.

Instrumental language The language of orders and getting things done.

Interpersonal communication Communication on a one-to-one basis—usually in an informal, non-structured setting.

Interview A series of questions and answers, usually involving two people, which has the purpose of getting and understanding information about a particular subject or topic.

Intrapersonal communication Communication that occurs within us.

Introduction The opening remarks of a speech that aim to get attention and build interest in the subject.

Johari Window A model of self-disclosure that shows how much we do and do not disclose to others.

Kinesics The study of body movement.

Laissez-faire leader A leader who does not suggest any direction for or impose any order on a group.

Language environment A theory of language which states that language is made up of people, their purposes, the rules of communication, and the actual talk they use.

Leading questions Questions that lead the interviewee in a particular direction.

Legislative rules New rules that are created to avoid future problems.

Listening Responding intellectually and emotionally to messages we hear.

Logical appeal Using reasoning and evidence.

Main idea The central thought that runs through a message.

Maintenance roles Roles that focus on the emotional tone of a meeting.

Messages Ideas and feelings that senders-receivers share.

Metatalk The meaning behind the words we speak.

Mixed messages Contradictory messages.

Monotone Little variety in pitch in a speech.

Motivated sequence Organization of a speech that involves five steps: attention, need, satisfaction, visualization, and action.

Narratives Extended examples told in the form of brief stories.

Negative roles In groups, roles that slow down a group and keep it from functioning effectively.

Neutral questions Questions that do not show how the interviewer feels about the subject.

Noise Interference that keeps a message from being understood or accurately interpreted.

Nonstandard English Words, expressions, and grammatical structures that are not used by most speakers of English.

Nonverbal communication Any information or emotion we communicate without using words.

Nonverbal symbols Facial expressions, gestures, posture, vocal tones, appearance—all which communicate nonverbally.

Norms Expectations group members have of how the other members in the group will behave, think, and participate.

Open-ended questions Questions that permit the person being interviewed to expand on his or her answer.

Outline A way of organizing material so you can see all the parts and how they relate to the whole.

Pace How fast or slowly you speak.

Paralanguage The way we say something.

Passive listener Someone who listens without evaluation or mental questioning.

Perception How we see the world.

Periodicals The inclusive name for magazines, journals, and newspapers.

Personal inventory A look at your own knowledge,

experience, and interests in order to find a topic for a speech.

Persuasive speech   A speech where the speaker takes a particular position and tries to get the audience to accept and support that position.

Physical noise   Interference that keeps a message from being heard.

Pitch   The highness or lowness of the voice.

Polls   Surveys taken of people's attitudes, feelings, or knowledge.

Prediction   Anticipation of what is going to happen in a future communication.

Primary questions   Questions designed to cover a subject comprehensively.

Problem-solution order   Organization of a speech into two sections: one dealing with the problem and the other dealing with the solution.

Pronunciation   The ability to pronounce a word correctly.

Proxemics   The study of the distance we stay from each other and the space we keep around ourselves.

Proximity   Our physical closeness and access to others.

Psychological noise   Distractions that occur in the minds of senders-receivers which keep them from accurately hearing the message.

Psychological risks   The risks that people who feel emotionally secure are willing to take.

Psychological safety   The approval and support that we get from people we love, admire, and respect.

Public communication   Communication, usually a speech, intended for an audience.

Quality (in a voice)   The overall sound.

Questions of fact   Questions of what is true and what is false.

Questions of policy   Questions about actions that might be taken in the future.

Questions of value   Questions of whether something is good or bad, desirable or undesirable.

Quotation   The words of another person used as evidence or illustration.

Rate   The speed at which one speaks.

Reflective listening   Trying to understand what a person is feeling from his or her point of view and reflecting these feelings back.

Regulators   Body movements that indicate when you are finished speaking and when others should begin.

Remediation rules   Rules that exist but that people have to be reminded of.

Ritual language   Conventional language expected of us on particular occasions.

Roles   The parts we play and how we behave with others.

Rules   Formal and structured directions for behavior.

Scripts   The lines, or language, we are to speak that we acquire through social conditioning.

Selective attention   Focusing on what we want or need to hear.

Self-concept   How we see ourselves.

Self-disclosure   The process in which one person tells another person something he or she would not tell just anyone.

Self-esteem   The value we put on ourselves.

Self-fulfilling prophecies   Predictions that come true because we (and others) expect them to.

Senders-receivers   Persons who send and receive messages.

Setting   The place where the communication occurs.

Small group   A group made up of three to thirteen members.

Small-group communication   Communication among a small group of people who meet together to solve a problem.

Small talk   Social talk with others about unimportant or impersonal information.

Social conditioning   The messages we get from society about how we are supposed to act.

Spatial order   Organization of a speech by something's location in space (e.g., left to right, top to bottom, and so on).

Specific purpose   A statement for a speech that tells precisely what you want to accomplish.

Standard English   Conventional grammar, words, and expressions.

Statistics   Facts in numerical form.

Study   An in-depth investigation of a subject.

Style   The way we select and arrange words and sentences.

Supporting points   Material that reinforces the main idea of any communication.

Symbols   Things that stand for something else.

Synonym   A word that has the same or nearly the same meaning as another.

Task roles   Roles that help to get a job done.

Testimony   Another person's statements or actions used to give authority to what you are saying.

Time order   Organization of a speech by chronology or historical occurrence.

Topical order   Organization of a speech into subtopics.

Traditional roles   Roles that do not change from one generation to another.

Transactional communication   A theory of communication that states: people engaged in communication are sending messages continuously and simultaneously; communication events have a past, present and future; participants in communication play certain roles.

Transitions   Means of getting from one point to another smoothly in a speech.

Trustworthiness   In a speech, being perceived as reliable and dependable.

Verbal symbol   A word in the language that stands for a particular thing or idea.

Vertical file   Pamphlets and booklets written by various groups that are filed and kept by libraries.

Visual aids   Visual material that helps illustrate the points you are making in a speech or presentation.

Vocal fillers   Sounds and words we use to fill up our sentences or to cover up when we are searching for words.

Volume (of vocal sound)   How loudly we speak.

INDEX

Numbers appearing in *italics* refer to figures.